Library of
Davidson College

Mainsprings of Indian and Pakistani Foreign Policies

*The University of Minnesota Press
gratefully acknowledges the support for
its program of the Andrew W. Mellon Foundation.
This book is one of those in whose financing
the Foundation's grant played a part.*

Mainsprings
of Indian and Pakistani
Foreign Policies

S. M. BURKE

University of Minnesota Press, Minneapolis

© Copyright 1974 by the University of Minnesota.
All rights reserved. Printed in the United States of America at
the University of Minnesota Printing Department, Minneapolis.
Published in the United Kingdom and India by the Oxford
University Press, London and Delhi, and in
Canada by Burns & MacEachern Limited, Don Mills, Canada

Library of Congress Catalog Card Number: 74-78992

ISBN 0-8166-0720-6

To My Wife

Preface

This study, like my treatise on Pakistan's foreign policy (*Pakistan's Foreign Policy: An Historical Analysis,* London: Oxford University Press, 1973), is the result of several years of research and reflection for which facilities were provided by the University of Minnesota, the Hill Family Foundation, and the Ford Foundation. Part I explores the nature of India and Pakistan's heritage from their ancient past, and Part II examines their performance on the world stage since independence, under the combined effect of past influences and contemporary motives and compulsions.

I wish especially to thank my good friend Professor Hameed ud Din of Harvard University for many profitable discussions while this book was in preparation and my secretary, Mrs. Esther Schwartz, for continuous assistance in research and diligence in typing the manuscript.

S. M. Burke

University of Minnesota
February 1974

Contents

Part I. The Heritage

Important Chronology   3
1. Hinduism and Islam: The "Two Closed Systems" of the Indian Subcontinent   7
2. Origins of Indian and Pakistani Foreign Policies   22
3. Britain's "Cut and Run" Departure and Its Consequences   55
4. Jawaharlal Nehru: The Personal Factor   78

Part II. Independent India and Pakistan: The Opening Decades

5. The First Moves (1947–53): Goals of Indian and Pakistani Foreign Policies   113
6. *Panchsheel* vs. Defense Alliances (1954–58)   141
7. Warclouds over South Asia: Sino-Indian Conflict (1959–62)   159
8. Warclouds over South Asia: Indo-Pakistani Conflict (1963–February 1974)   177
9. Retrospect and Prospect   235
Appendix. The McMahon Line: Its Origin and Significance in the Sino-Indian Border Dispute   245
Notes   251
Bibliography of Sources Cited   283
Index   297

Part I
The Heritage

"A man has come into the world; his early years are spent without notice in the pleasures and activities of childhood. As he grows up, the world receives him when his manhood begins, and he enters into contact with his fellows. He is then studied for the first time, and it is imagined that the germ of the vices and the virtues of his maturer years is then formed.

"This, if I am not mistaken, is a great error. We must begin higher up; we must watch the infant in his mother's arms; we must see the first images which the external world casts upon the dark mirror of his mind, the first occurrences that he witnesses; we must hear the first words which awaken the sleeping powers of thought, and stand by his earliest efforts if we would understand the prejudices, the habits, and the passions which will rule his life. The entire man is, so to speak, to be seen in the cradle of the child.

"The growth of nations presents something analogous to this: They all bear some marks of their origin. The circumstances that accompanied their birth and contributed to their development affected the whole term of their being." (Tocqueville, Democracy in America, *volume I, chapter 2)*

Important Chronology

2500 to 1500 B.C.	The Indus civilization.
1500 to 500	The Aryan invasions.
563 to 483	Gautama Buddha.
273 to 232	Reign of Asoka.
622 A.D.	The Prophet Muhammad and his followers migrate from Mecca to Medina and set up a self-governing community combining the Church with the State. The Islamic era begins.
712	Conquest of Sind by Muhammad bin Qasim.
1526	Babar founds the Moghul Empire in India.
1556 to 1605	Reign of Akbar the Great.
1613	Emperor Jahangir permits the British East India Company to establish a trading post (factory) at Surat.
1658 to 1707	Reign of Aurangzeb after which the Moghul Empire begins to disintegrate.
1757	Clive wins the battle of Plassey and lays the foundation of the British Empire in India.
1857 to 1858	The mutiny.
1885	Founding of the Indian National Congress.
1887	Sir Syed Ahmad Khan calls Hindus and Muslims "two nations."
1905	Partition of Bengal.
1906	Founding of the Muslim League.
1909	Indian Councils Act (Morley-Minto Reforms).

The Heritage

1911	Annulment of partition of Bengal.
1914 to 1918	World War I.
1918	Montagu-Chelmsford Report.
1919	Mohandas Karamchand Gandhi assumes leadership of the Congress party.
1919 (April)	Jallianwala Bagh massacre at Amritsar and martial law atrocities in the Punjab.
1919 (December)	Government of India Act (Montagu-Chelmsford Reforms).
1919 (December)	Khilafat movement launched by Muslims of India.
1920	Noncooperation movement launched by the Congress party.
1924	Turkey abolishes institution of Khilafat.
1927	The Congress party adopts "complete National Independence" as its goal.
1928	Simon Commission.
1930 to 1932	Indian Round Table Conference (three sessions, all in London).
1930	The poet Muhammad Iqbal says the "final destiny" of the Muslims of the northwestern provinces of India is to form a consolidated "Indian Muslim State" within an all-India federation of autonomous states.
1934	Muhammad Ali Jinnah is reelected president of the Muslim League, returns from England where he had settled in 1931 to practice at the bar, and assumes the dominant role in League affairs.
1935	Government of India Act.
1937	Provincial elections: Congress wins in most provinces. It forms ministries but declines to form coalitions with the Muslim League anywhere.
1937	The Muslim League adopts "full independence" for India as its creed.
1939 to 1945	World War II.
1939 (October)	Congress ministries resign in provinces because of dissatisfaction with British war aims as applicable to India.
1940 (March)	Muslim League demands Pakistan.
1940 (August–September)	Battle of Britain.
1940 (October)	Civil disobedience movement launched by the Congress party.
1942 (February)	Fall of Singapore and increasing threat of Japanese attack on India.

Important Chronology

1942 (March–April)	Cripps mission.
1942 (August)	"Quit India" mass movement launched by the Congress party under Gandhi's leadership.
1945	Fighting on the issue of Pakistan, the Muslim League wins every Muslim seat in the Central Legislative Assembly.
1946 (25 March–29 June)	Cabinet mission.
1946 (16 August)	Muslim League observes "Direct Action Day."
1946 (16–18 August)	"Great Calcutta Killing" (Hindu-Muslim riots) and outbreak of "the war of succession."
1946 (2 September)	Interim government installed with Jawaharlal Nehru as vice-president of the governor general's Executive Council holding the portfolio of external affairs.
1947 (20 February)	Prime Minister Clement R. Attlee announces Britain will transfer power to Indian hands by a date not later than June 1948.
1947 (24 March)	Lord Mountbatten replaces Lord Wavell as viceroy.
1947 (3 June)	Partition plan is announced by the British government.
1947 (4 June)	Mountbatten announces transfer of power would take place on 15 August 1947 and not in June 1948.
1947 (15 August)	India and Pakistan become independent.

CHAPTER 1

Hinduism and Islam: The "Two Closed Systems" of the Indian Subcontinent

Prime Minister Jawaharlal Nehru averred that India's policy of nonalignment was "inherent in the whole mental outlook of India, [and] inherent in the conditioning of the Indian mind during our struggle for freedom."[1]

Liaquat Ali Khan, prime minister of the sister state of Pakistan, claimed with equal emphasis that his nation's foreign policy was a natural product of the past. But Pakistan was far from being uncommitted. Liaquat proclaimed that Pakistanis regarded the people of the Muslim countries "as our brethren" and went on to say: "Even when we were a subject people, we regarded the distress of Muslim countries as our own. Now that we are free, our attitude is the same. Even today, we are bound by those natural postulates of Islamic fraternity which were formulated for our guidance thirteen centuries ago [when Islam was founded]."[2]

Why did the two leaders view the natural sources of the foreign policies of the twin nations so differently when their peoples had been nurtured by the same motherland for centuries past?

"Divide and Rule"

At the Second Session of the Indian Round Table Conference at London, in 1931, Mahatma Gandhi asserted: "This [Hindu-Muslim] quarrel is not old; this quarrel . . . is coeval with the British advent, and immediately this relationship, the unfortunate, artificial unnatural relationship, between Great Britain and India is transformed into a natural relationship . . . you will find that Hindus, Mussalmans, Sikhs, Europeans, Anglo-Indians, Christians, Untouchables, will all live together as one man."[3]

However, several hundred years before the first Briton set foot in India, an outside Muslim scholar, having made a diligent on-the-spot study of Hindu religion and civilization, concluded that

the Hindus entirely differ from us in every respect . . . they differ from us in everything which other nations have in common . . . they totally differ from us in religion, as we believe in nothing in which they believe, and vice versa. . . . [A]ll their fanaticism is directed against those who do not belong to them — against all foreigners. They call them *mleccha,* i.e. impure, and forbid having any connection with them, be it by intermarriage or any other kind of relationship, or by sitting, eating, and drinking with them, because thereby, they think, they would be polluted. They consider as impure anything which touches the fire and the water of a foreigner; and no household can exist without these two elements. . . .

Many Hindu customs differ from those of our country and of our time to such a degree as to appear to us simply monstrous. One might almost think that they had intentionally changed them into the opposite, for *our* customs do not resemble theirs, but are the very reverse; and if ever a custom of *theirs* resembles one of *ours,* it has certainly just the opposite meaning.[4]

It was but natural that, in their irritation with British imperialism, Indian nationalists should have found it more soothing to ascribe all their misfortunes, communal, economic, and political, to the alien rulers rather than to the debilitating defects in their own society. But this does not make accurate history. R. C. Majumdar, the doyen of present-day Indian chroniclers, has frankly debunked the "rosy picture of the brotherhood and fellow-feelings of the Hindus and Musalmans" drawn by "eminent political leaders of our country in the twentieth century" and affirmed that what Alberuni had observed in the eleventh century held almost equally true at the opening of the nineteenth.[5]

Reginald Heber, lord bishop of Calcutta, who journeyed through northern India during the years 1824–25, noticed the tension between the Hindus and the Muslims, and, talking about Benares in particular, said that the two communities there were "literally armed" against each other and "the fury which actuated both was more like that of demoniacs than rational enemies": "It began by the Mussalmans breaking down a famous pillar, named Siva's walking-staff, held in high veneration by the

Hinduism and Islam

Hindoos. These last in revenge burnt and broke down a mosque, and the retort of the first aggressors was to kill a cow, and pour her blood into the sacred well. In consequence every Hindoo able to bear arms, and many who had no other fitness for the employment than rage supplied, procured weapons, and attacked their enemies with frantic fury wherever they met them."[6]

After independence, when the British no longer looked quite so black as they did while they ruled India, Prime Minister Nehru called upon his countrymen to take a more balanced view of the British connection. "The Industrial Revolution in England was helped tremendously by the original . . . loot from India," he said. "Nevertheless, if the British people went ahead, it was due to their great genius, hard work, organisation and discipline and a hundred fine qualities. We do not talk about those qualities; but we talk of the fact that because of our weaknesses they came and conquered India, controlled India and profited by their stay in India. Then we blame them for it while the blame is ours for our failures, stupidity, factions, disruptions in our country."[7] "The measure of their success in this policy [of divide and rule]," he had said on an earlier occasion, "has been also the measure of their superiority over those whom they thus exploit. We cannot complain of this or, at any rate, we ought not to be surprised at it. To ignore it and not to provide against it is in itself a mistake in one's thought."[8]

Secretary of State L. S. Amery, reviewing the unsuccessful Cripps mission to India during World War II, could truthfully state in the House of Commons that Sir Stafford Cripps "flew many thousands of miles to meet the Indian leaders in order to arrive at an agreement with them. The Indian leaders in Delhi moved not one step to meet each other, either without him or in his presence. They made no attempt to reach agreement among themselves."[9]

Though the main blame for Hindu-Muslim differences undoubtedly rests upon the shoulders of the Indian leaders themselves, the British were by no means innocent bystanders. They would have been less than human if they had failed to exploit the plain truth "that the existence side by side of these two hostile creeds is one of the strong points in our political position in India."[10] Since democracy means rule by the majority, the Muslims genuinely feared that Western representative institutions would place them under permanent Hindu raj. By making the proper satisfaction of Muslim demands a necessary condition to every step in constitutional advance, the British were able to achieve moral as well as material satisfaction. First, they were able to derive high-minded satisfaction from the largely self-induced belief that they were holding the scales of justice even between the numerically weak and the numerically strong. Secondly, the policy admirably served to prolong their hold over India. "Indeed," said Nehru, "I have always wondered at and admired the astonishing knack of the British people of making their moral standards correspond with their material interests, and of seeing virtue in everything that advances their imperial designs."[11]

Maulana Muhammad Ali, who professed to be a Mussalman first and last "where God commands" and an Indian first and last "where India's freedom is concerned," thus summed up both sides of the question: "It is the old maxim of 'divide and rule.' But there is a division of labour here. We divide and you [British] rule."[12]

The Antitheses of Hinduism and Islam

Among the universal religions there are no two more incompatible than Hinduism and Islam.

Islam is the youngest of the great religions of the world. It is also the simplest and the most explicit. The sole requirement is belief in one all-powerful God, in Muhammad as his messenger, and in the Quran as the message. Muhammad, of course, was not the first messenger of God. The first prophet was Adam, sent as soon as the world itself was created. Others followed from time to time, such as Abraham, Moses, and Christ. But Muhammad's message, being the last one in time, is the final one, taking precedence over all the others. According to the poet-philosopher Muhammad Iqbal: "The simple faith of Muhammad is based on two propositions — that God is One, and that Muhammad is the last of the line of those holy men who have appeared from time to time in all countries and in all ages to guide mankind to the right ways of living."[13]

There is no caste system in Islam. All Muslims are supposed to be equal and form a single brotherhood, under God, transcending the barriers of race and geography. The word Islam means "submission" (to the will of God) and Muslim means "one who submits." Muslims do not like to be described as Muhammadans because this might suggest they worship the prophet Muhammad, who was not a savior but just one through whom God revealed his message to the world. Belief in one

HINDUISM AND ISLAM

living God is so strong that the making of images not only is forbidden but is a cardinal sin. The Quran contains a record of Muhammad's utterances, as revealed to him by God, and collected into an authorized version after his demise.

Hinduism, on the other hand, is rooted in the ancient past and is not a religion at all in the usual sense of a faith having a prescribed dogma and scripture. Perhaps the best way of exploring its essence is to find out what it has meant to leading Hindus of our times: "Hinduism, as a faith, is vague, amorphous, many sided, all things to all men. It is hardly possible to define it, or indeed to say definitely whether it is a religion or not, in the usual sense of the word" (Nehru).[14] " 'If I were asked to define the Hindu creed, I should simply say: Search after truth through non-violent means. A man may not believe in God and still call himself a Hindu. Hinduism is a relentless pursuit after truth.' Hinduism is 'the religion of truth. Truth is God. Denial of God we have known. Denial of truth we have not known.' . . . 'I believe in the Bible as I believe in the Gita. I regard all the great faiths of the world as equally true with my own' " (Gandhi).[15] However, "many eminent and undoubted Hindus say that non-violence as Gandhi understands it, is no essential part of the Hindu creed. We thus have truth left by itself as the distinguishing mark of Hinduism. That, of course, is no definition at all" (Nehru).[16]

Jawaharlal Nehru is not the only Hindu who rejects the Gandhian proposition linking Hinduism with nonviolence. Swami Vivekananda asserts: "Our Shastras say, you are a householder; if anybody slaps you once on your face, you must return it tenfold, otherwise you will be committing a sin."[17] K. M. Panikkar thinks Indian vision has been obscured by an "un-Indian wave of pacifism" and states that India rejected the creed of *ahimsa* when she refused to follow Gautama Buddha.[18] Sarvepalli Radhakrishnan points out that Hindu society made room for Ksatriyas, a group dedicated to the use of force, and surmises that as long as human nature is what it is, the use of force will be required.[19]

Radhakrishnan directly raises the question What is the spirit of Hinduism: "The spirit of science is not dogmatic certainty but the disinterested pursuit of truth, and Hinduism is infused by the same spirit. . . . [F]ixed intellectual beliefs mark off one religion from another, but Hinduism sets itself no such limits. It is comprehensive and synthetic, seeking unity not in a common creed but in a common quest for truth. Hinduism is

THE HERITAGE

more a way of life than a form of thought. It insists not on religious conformity but on a spiritual and ethical outlook in life. It is a fellowship of all who accept the law of right and earnestly seek for the truth."[20]

Gandhi had said that in Hinduism there is "room enough" for prophets such as Jesus, Muhammad, Zoroaster, and Moses.[21] Consequently, Mrs. Vijaya Lakshmi Pandit points out, "Hinduism, Buddhism, Jainism, Islam, Sikhism, and Christianity, have all helped enrich the fabric of India's spiritual life. Hinduism cannot be described as a particular system of thought. Rather it is a commonwealth of systems; not a particular faith but a fellowship of faiths."[22] Radhakrishnan explains further:

> In the long and diversified history of man's quest for reality represented by Hinduism, the object which haunts the human soul as a presence at once all-embracing and infinite is envisaged in many different ways. The Hindus are said to adopt polytheism, monotheism, and pantheism as well as belief in demons, heroes, and ancestors. It is easy to find texts in support of each of these views. The cults of Siva and Sakti may have come down from the Indus people. Worship of trees, animals, rivers, and other cults associated with fertility ritual may have had the same origin, while the dark powers of the underworld, who are dreaded and propitiated, may be due to aboriginal sources. The Vedic Aryans contributed the higher gods comparable to the Olympians of the Greeks, like the Sky and the Earth, the Sun and the Fire. The Hindu religion deals with these different lines of thought and fuses them into a whole by means of its philosophical synthesis.[23]

> As a result of this tolerant attitude, Hinduism itself has become a mosaic of almost all the types and stages of religious aspiration and endeavour. It has adapted itself with infinite grace to every human need and it has not shrunk from the acceptance of every aspect of God conceived by man, and yet preserved its unity by interpreting the different historical forms as modes, emanations, or aspects of the Supreme.[24]

Altogether the Hindu pantheon comprises some 330 million gods. Radhakrishnan says that all the gods stand for some aspect of the Supreme.[25]

Because of its almost unlimited receptiveness, Hinduism has survived the onslaughts of other religions through the ages. Though in time it became laden with social abuses, its theory has a noble and attractive aspect. It does not crush the mind by mandatory restrictions. But its unbounded toleration also deprives it of positiveness. Its followers lack any central theme to unite them into a single-minded homogeneous unit. They are like an army with no visible flag to protect.

Hinduism and Islam
"Two Nations"

Hindu society stands internally divided not only by doctrinal disunity, which has just been discussed, but also by an equally pervasive social disunity. Nehru called Hindu society "anarchistic."[26] It subscribes to four principal castes and some three thousand subcastes. Members of one caste, however meritorious, cannot aspire to promotion to a higher rung and the fresh convert to the Hindu faith simply remains outside the pale of the caste system, an outcaste and an untouchable. "What is to be the caste of the convert?" asked B. R. Ambedkar, and answered: "According to the Hindus, for a person to belong to a caste he must be born in it. A convert is not born in a caste, therefore he belongs to no caste."[27]

It is far easier to join the brotherhood of Islam. To be converted it is sufficient to proclaim the creed, "There is no God but Allah; Muhammad is the messenger of Allah." Islam thus does not uncompromisingly slam the door in the face of nonbelievers, who can enter the fold, if they so choose, and make all of humanity one big brotherhood. The sense of equality among the members of the brotherhood is visibly emphasized on congregational occasions. At the various daily prayers and the weekly Friday prayers, worshipers occupy places of their own choice without regard to anyone's worldly status, and at the annual pilgrimage to Mecca Muslims from all over the world, rich and poor, belonging to different countries and races, wear identical flowing white robes.

However, "the notion of brotherhood of man is . . . alien to traditional Hindu practice."[28] Wilfred Cantwell Smith thinks the caste system is "the most highly organized, rigid, philosophically justified, and stubbornly persistent system of social discrimination and arrogant inequality that humanity throughout its long history of failure in fraternity has ever evolved."[29]

In his famous presidential address to the All-India Muslim League at Allahabad in 1930, Iqbal conceded that the Hindus were ahead of the Muslims in almost all respects but asserted that they had not been able to achieve the kind of homogeneity which creates a nation and which Islam had given to the Muslims of India "as a free gift." He thought the Muslims of India were the only people of that country who could be described as a nation.[30] He explained elsewhere that the purpose of the Prophet's mission was to purge the nations of the world of divisive abuses such as place, land, nation, race, and genealogy.[31] He argued:

The Heritage

The law of Islam does not recognise the apparently natural differences of race, nor the historical differences of nationality. The political ideal of Islam consists in the creation of a people born of a free fusion of all races and nationalities. Nationality, with Islam, is not the highest limit of political development; for the general principles of the law of Islam rest on human nature, not on the peculiarities of a particular people. The inner cohesion of such a nation would consist not in ethnic or geographic unity, not in the unity of language or social tradition, but in the unity of the religious and political ideal; or, in the psychological fact of "like-mindedness," as St. Paul would say. The membership of this nation, consequently, would not be determined by birth, marriage, domicile or naturalisation. It would be determined by a public declaration of "like-mindedness," and would terminate when the individual has ceased to be like-minded with others. The ideal territory for such a nation would be the whole earth.[32]

Iqbal, therefore, perceived Islam as "something more than a creed, it is also a community, a nation."[33] Nationalism, as generally practiced, was nothing short of "a subtle form of idolatry, a deification of a material object," as evidenced by the patriotic songs of various nations. Muslims could not entertain such emotions because it is their "eternal mission to protest against idolatry in all its forms."[34] He pointedly asserted: *Muslim hein hum watan hai sara jehan hamara* (we are Muslims, our motherland is the entire universe). Also: *Her mulk, mulke ma ust ke mulke Khudai ma ust* (every country is our country because it is our God's country).

As could well be expected Pakistanis have continued enthusiastically to follow the trail blazed by Iqbal. Explaining his vision of "Islamistan" at Cairo in 1949, Chaudhri Khaliquzzaman, president of the Pakistan Muslim League, declared that "nationality to Muslims is like idol worship."[35] Another Pakistani writer observes that "a Muslim is always first a Muslim — a servant or slave of Allah — and then a citizen of a state," and approvingly recalls Maulana Muhammad Ali's plain words to the Hindus that he was a Muslim first and an Indian afterwards.[36] Finally, a Pakistani, summing up the innermost feelings of his countrymen, simply reiterates that Islam itself is a nationality.[37]

Though far less restrictive than Hinduism, Islam, of course, is not without a formidable barrier of its own. It classifies mankind into two mutually exclusive categories, Muslims and non-Muslims. The spiritual bond which holds all the Muslims together serves also to segregate them from all the other peoples on the face of the earth. "The Believers are but one Brotherhood," declares the Quran.[38] Accordingly, argues Iqbal,

HINDUISM AND ISLAM

"there is only one *millat* [community] confronting the Muslim community, that of the non-Muslims taken collectively."[39] Maulana Muhammad Ali, who was Gandhi's righthand man during the civil disobedience movement of the early 1920s, had no compunction in stating publicly that "however pure Mr. Gandhi's character may be, he must appear to me from the point of view of religion inferior to any Musalman, even though he be without character."[40]

Since the dictates of Hinduism and Islam prevented their respective followers from becoming a homogeneous society, despite existence side by side for hundreds of years, Nehru aptly dubbed them "closed systems."[41] Because of a long history of conflict, Muslims and Christians still nurse a degree of antagonism toward each other but, in fact, as Arnold Toynbee points out, they both belong to the same cultural division of mankind, the other divisions being the Hindu and the Far Eastern. He adds that the differences inside the "Muslim-Christian family" are insignificant compared to those that separate it from the other two.[42]

Quaid-i-Azam Muhammad Ali Jinnah, the founder of Pakistan, was Muslim by birth but his ancestors, like those of most Indian Muslims, were converts from Hinduism. In September 1944 he and Gandhi tried to reach an understanding but gave up in despair after eighteen days of sustained effort. During this period the two leaders met personally and also exchanged letters. Gandhi, in one of his letters, raised this interesting argument: "I find no parallel in history for a body of converts and their descendants claiming to be a nation apart from the parent stock. If India was one nation before the advent of Islam, it must remain one in spite of the change of faith of a very large body of her children."[43] Jinnah replied that the Muslims were a nation by all canons of international law. They were 100 million strong with their own distinctive culture and civilization, language and literature, art and architecture, names and nomenclature, sense of value and proportion, legal laws and moral codes, customs and calendar, history and traditions, aptitudes and ambitions; in short, with their own distinctive outlook on life and of life.[44]

On an earlier occasion Jinnah had explained that as soon as a Hindu was converted to Islam his former fellow Hindus treated him as a *mleccha* (untouchable). Consequently, "it is now more than a thousand years that the bulk of the Muslims have lived in a different world, in a different society, in a different philosophy and a different faith."[45] "If religious apartheid was involved in the creation of Pakistan," declared

THE HERITAGE

Foreign Minister Zulfikar Ali Bhutto in a Security Council debate on 11 May 1964, "then the Muslims of the subcontinent were its victims and not its perpetrators."

Since conversion to Islam immediately ostracized a person from Hindu society, "Pakistan," according to Jinnah, "started the moment the first non-Muslim was converted to Islam in India long before the Muslims established their rule." Referring to the equally uncompromising attitude of Muslims, he said, in the same breath, that it was a duty imposed on the Muslims by Islam not to merge their identity and individuality in any alien society. Throughout the ages, therefore, Hindus and Muslims had not merged their entities. When asked who was the author of Pakistan, Jinnah replied, "Every Musalman."[46] Pakistan, he stated on another occasion, was not the product of the conduct or misconduct of the Hindus. It had always been there, only the people were not conscious of it. Hindus and Muslims, though living in the same towns and villages, had never blended into one nation.[47] Liaquat Ali Khan emphasized that the lives of a Hindu and of a Muslim differ in every respect from the cradle to the grave. Even after death one's body is burned and the other's buried. The concept of existence after death is also different.[48]

To understand the cultural "cleavage" between Hindus and Muslims, writes another Pakistani Muslim, it is necessary to bear in mind "the revolutionary impact" of the Islamic movement on men and peoples. Those who accept Islam have their whole personality transformed: there is a clear break with the past and a complete change of direction.[49] A noted Hindu scholar has also pointed out that Buddhism and Jainism were not unassimilable elements but Islam "split Indian society into two sections from top to bottom and what has now come to be known in the phraseology of today as two separate nations came into being from the beginning."[50]

Ambedkar allowed the Muslim claim to separate nationhood by pointing out that Hindus and Muslims have no common heritage of memories, thus lacking an essential element for coalescing into one nation. "There was no common cycle of participation for a common achievement." In fact, while the Muslims look upon the invading Muslim chiefs as their national heroes, the Hindus cherish the memory of those Hindu rulers who fought bravely against the conquerors. Spiritually, the Hindus draw their inspiration from the Ramayana and the Mahabharata, the Muslims from the Quran and the Hadith (traditions about the Prophet Muham-

Hinduism and Islam

mad). The factors that divide the two peoples are far more vital than those that unite them.[51]

During the half century preceding partition countless attempts were made to create Hindu-Muslim unity but in the prevailing circumstances no leader on either side ever had the courage to suggest a fusion of the two peoples into one by any really meaningful measures, such as intermarriage,[52] which could result in the creation of a homogeneous nation. Sultan Muhammad Shah, the Aga Khan, for many years a spokesman for Muslim causes, was aware that "the highest recognition of brotherhood and fellow-citizenship can only come by accepting intermarriage,"[53] but, knowing the conditions in his native land, he never made bold to inculcate intercommunal nuptials there.

On one occasion Gandhi was asked what was the criterion that the last trace of untouchability had been eradicated from the heart. He said, "Have you an unmarried son or daughter? If you have one, get him or her a Harijan for a bride or bridegroom, as the case may be, in the spirit of a sacrament and I shall send you a wire of congratulations at my expense."[54] Since he regarded the Harijans as a part of the Hindu family, Gandhi's support for marriages between Harijans and caste Hindus was merely an attempt to reform his own community. He was not prepared to use the same prescription for eradicating Hindu-Muslim disunity.

Hindus and Muslims do not even dine together. Communal dining among Muslims is a common sight. Several persons will eat off the same plate. Orthodox Hindus, on the other hand, will not dine with their own wives. On the question of whether Hindus and Muslims should intermarry or eat together, Gandhi said, "In my opinion the idea, that interdining and intermarrying are necessary for national growth is a superstition borrowed from the West."[55]

The introvert character of Hindu outlook is further illustrated by the fact that even after more than a hundred years of dealings with the British, Hindus considered an overseas voyage a religious offense. On the eve of his departure for England for studies, young Gandhi was summoned before a caste meeting. The verdict was that "this boy shall be treated as an outcaste from today. Whoever helps him or goes to see him off at the dock shall be punishable with a fine of one rupee four annas." When Gandhi returned home, his brother had to pacify those who had disapproved of the trip by giving Gandhi a bath in the sacred river and by giving a dinner to the members of the caste. Similar experi-

THE HERITAGE

ences befell Motilal Nehru and Bishan Narayan Dar, who later became presidents of the Congress.[56]

Hindus and Muslims emotionally seemed closest to each other during the Khilafat movement which was launched in 1919 to preserve the pre-World War I territories of the defeated sultan of Turkey, who was also the khalifa (caliph) of Islam. But as usual they were trying to build on sand. There was no real basis for a lasting unity. Certainly the British were the common target of both communities but the immediate objective of the Hindus was to redress the wrongs of the Jallianwalla massacre and the Punjab martial law excesses, while the Muslims were striving primarily to defend the status of the Turkish sultan. Gandhi naively gave out his view of the real import of the arrangement: "I claim that with us both the Khilafat is the central fact, with Maulana Mahomed Ali because it is his religion, with me because, in laying down my life for the Khilafat, I ensure safety of the cow, that is my religion, from the Musalman knife."[57] Clearly, Gandhi was not exerting himself to create a united people by merging Hindu and Muslim civilizations; rather, he was striving to create conditions which would better ensure their separate existence. "By allying himself with the Khilafatists," comments a Hindu writer, "the Mahatma apparently hoped — another instance of his infinite capacity for self-deception — to bring off a cheap solution to the Hindu-Muslim problem."[58]

In the event the feeling of Muslim nationalism roused during the Khilafat agitation increased the existing emotional gap between Hindus and Muslims and strengthened the forces which ultimately created Pakistan. The post-Khilafat period was marked by Hindu-Muslim riots on an unprecedented scale and saw the birth of blatantly communal movements such as *shuddi, sangathan, tabligh,* and *tanzim.*

In February 1912 Maulana Muhammad Ali had wisely written that "the communal sentiment and temper must change, and interests must grow identical before the Hindus and the Muslims can be welded into a united nationality. . . . Any attempt to impose artificial unity is sure to end in failure, if not in disaster." He had specially ridiculed the idea of Muslims uniting with Hindus to promote any Muslim cause abroad: "Soft-headed and some self-advertising folk have gone about proclaiming that the Muslims should join the Congress because the Government had revoked the Partition of Bengal or because Persia and Turkey are in trouble. . . . What has the Muslim situation abroad to do with the conditions of the Indian Muslims?"[59]

However, during the Khilafat movement, the Maulana, completely disregarding his own warning, joined hands with Gandhi in an attempt to bring Hindus and Muslims closer on the very basis he had so vehemently decried, and his prophecy, that any attempt to build Hindu-Muslim unity on an external Muslim cause would come to nought, was fulfilled. When the Congress, moving toward a fresh round of civil disobedience, decided to celebrate 26 January 1930 as independence day, Maulana Muhammad Ali and his brother Shaukat Ali not only stood aside but issued a press statement jointly with two other Muslim leaders asking Muslims not to participate in the demonstrations of the Congress. "Gandhi seems to have lost his grip on Hindu-Muslim relations after the collapse of the Caliphate alliance," states a biographer who knew the Mahatma well. "In 1935 he [Gandhi] wrote sadly about Hindu-Muslim unity: 'I have owned defeat on that score.' "[60]

Maulana Muhammad Ali was not the only Muslim destined to be frustrated in his quest for Hindu-Muslim unity. Sir Syed Ahmed Khan, Iqbal,[61] Jinnah, and Sheikh Muhammad Abdullah of Kashmir all started as ardent "nationalists" in their younger and idealistic years, but ultimately they were disillusioned and bowed before the reality of unbridgeable Hindu-Muslim differences.

"One Nation"

Proponents of a united India have contended that India always had a distinct personality of her own. It is true that the Himalayas do make the South Asian subcontinent a geographical unit. It is true also that among the Hindus there was a thread of cultural unity based on common religious literature and folklore, buttressed by Sanskrit as the sacred language and Brahmins as the all-India priestly class. But as Panikkar points out, "The caste system, originally a process of integration, degenerated early into a system of division and sub-division till at last the broad four castes disappeared into innumerable sub-castes, thereby rendering the development of a common Hindu feeling or a realisation of a sense of Hindu community difficult."[62] Radhakrishnan concedes that "while its [India's] culture produced individuals who had something undeniably attractive and superior, it did not develop a high civic or na-

THE HERITAGE

tional sense." Again, "while the principles were sound, Hindu India did not develop a strong organization embodying them. As a designer of national life, Hindu civilization was not a success."[63] At Allahabad Bishop Heber found that the local people there regarded Bengalis "as no less foreigners than the English and even more odious than Franks."[64] And quite outside this caste-perforated society stood millions of untouchables, living in a dark, hopeless world of their own. Finally, there were the Muslims whose religious language was Arabic, not Sanskrit, and whose guide was the Quran, not the mass of Hindu spiritual and epical literature.

The evidence of political unity before the arrival of the British is extremely fragile. Only a handful of kings in the course of the twenty-five hundred years of India's known history succeeded in bringing the major portion of India under their sway, and not a single one of them penetrated to the southern tip of the peninsula. Asoka, who ruled over the largest area of all, lived twenty-two centuries ago. That his empire should have to be persistently cited as the most shining example of political unity is itself proof of the unreality of the evidence. Moreover, these rare spans of unity were artificially imposed by the will of individual conquerors. They did not result from any voluntary expression of the people's will or from any popular indigenous movements. The British, the last overlords, wrested the country from innumerable native rulers and, in fact, refrained from annexing the territories of the remaining six hundred of them only after the uprising of 1857 had brought home to them the realization that these privileged conservative princes would be an invaluable bulwark for the alien rulers against any radical local forces that might raise their head against the established order.

Beginning with the vast Roman Empire, which endured for several centuries, Europe has had her share of empires and emperors and self-appointed apostles of unity. She has had Latin as the common classical and religious language and Christianity as the common religion. Her social inequality did not cut quite so deep as the schism of caste in India and, though Catholicism and Protestantism generated wars and conflicts, they were but branches of the same basic faith, not antithetical to each other as are Hinduism and Islam. In spite of these comparative advantages, the forces of division prevailed over those of cohesion and the conception of one Europe has remained but an elusive dream. The fact that the area in the south of Eurasia was collectively referred to as

HINDUISM AND ISLAM

Bharat is no more proof of the common nationality of its peoples than the expression Europe is proof of the common nationality of all those who inhabit the western tract of Eurasia. In his study *Advent of Independence,* A. K. Majumdar characterizes the assumption of an ancient Indian political unity and nationhood during the nationalist movement as "facile."[65]

Referring to "the great ideal of geographical political and economic unification of India," Sardar Vallabhbhai Patel, deputy prime minister of newly independent India, wistfully observed that it was "an ideal which for centuries remained a distant dream and which appeared as remote and as difficult of attainment as ever even after the advent of Indian independence."[66]

CHAPTER 2

Origins of Indian and Pakistani Foreign Policies

Centuries of dedication to such diametrically opposite systems as Islam and Hinduism could not but nurture an utterly different outlook on the outside world among their respective followers. That Pakistan has consistently sought a special relationship with other Muslim countries and, at first, elected clearly to stand with the Western countries in their confrontation with Communism, while India has uniformly professed nonalignment, is a perfectly logical consequence of each wishing to advance her national interests within the climate of her own special ideological preferences.

Islam, being an unequivocal faith, inculcates the attitude of viewing everything in sharp tones of black or white, good or bad, friendly or inimical. Hinduism, providing no clear answers and concrete guidance, makes it possible for all shades of opinion to coexist, or even to contradict one another. This extreme form of permissiveness is usually given the attractive appellation of synthesis. However, whatever the theoretical excellence of this Indian national characteristic may be, its practical consequence certainly is a lack of firm commitment to any ideology or cause.

It is conceivable that overriding considerations of security and survival will one day shake India completely out of her posture of nonalignment and that similar forces will impel Pakistan to assume an entirely uncommitted posture, but, if this should happen, it would be contrary to their basic philosophies of international life. The policy of "bilateralism" which Pakistan has been following since 1963 simply implies that she is

ORIGINS OF FOREIGN POLICIES

no longer committed to either side in the East-West struggle for world supremacy. To her greatest love — the Muslim countries — Pakistan remains as committed as ever. And India continues to affirm her customary allegiance to nonalignment, despite her August 1971 Treaty of Peace, Friendship, and Cooperation with the Soviet Union, which all others saw as a palpable deviation from such a policy.

The Injunction of Islam: Tough with Enemies and Kindly toward Friends

Though Muslim states have long accommodated themselves to the realities of the modern age by accepting coexistence with non-Muslim states, classical Islam viewed the world as divided into two parts: the *dar ul-harb* (literally the abode of strife; denoting a territory not governed by Muslim laws, i.e., not having a Muslim government) and the *dar ul-Islam* (literally the abode of peace; meaning a territory where Muslim laws prevail, i.e., having a Muslim government). Since the ultimate objective of Islam was to convert the entire world into *dar ul-Islam,* the two parts would theoretically remain in a state of war till *dar ul-harb* was reduced to nothingness. The prescribed instrument for eliminating the *dar ul-harb* was *jihad* or "exertion" which could take the form of persuasion or war. "Most of the modern books on *jihad* by Muslim writers," observes Aslam Siddiqi, "are in the nature of apologies. *Jihad,* on the contrary, is an instrument of the Islamic revolution. Its most important aspect is the concept of the just war.[1] In various *Surahs,* the *Quran* invites the Muslims to fight so that right may triumph."[2] Two injunctions in the Quran, for example, run thus:

Let those fight in God's way who sell this worldly life for the next; and whosoever fights in God's way, be he killed or victorious, we shall give him a tremendous reward. [The Chapter of Women: 75]

Verily, God hath bought from the believers their persons and their wealth in return for the paradise they will have; they shall fight in the way of God, and slay or be slain. [The Chapter of Repentance: 111]

"If neutrality is taken to mean the attitude of a state which voluntarily desires to keep out of war by not taking sides," points out a savant, "no such status is recognized in Muslim legal theory."[3]

The "attitude of being tough with the enemies and kindly to the friends distinguishes the believers in Islam from all other believers. Islam is actually not so idealistic as to ask the Muslims to turn the other cheek if they are smitten on the one."[4] The Quran says, "Muhammad is the messenger of Allah. And those with him (that is the Muslims who follow him) are firm against the unbelievers, compassionate amongst themselves (*Al-Fatah* — 29). Elaborating the same meaning, Allama Iqbal in one of his finest verses has said *'Ho Halqa-e-yaran to barisham ke tarah narm; razme haq-o-batil ho to fauled hai momin'* (if he is in the company of friends, a true believer is soft like silk; but if there is a confrontation between Truth and Falsehood then a Muslim becomes hard as steel)."[5]

In analyzing the reasons for Pakistan's alliance with the Western countries, Ian Stephens, who lived in India from 1942 to 1951 as editor of the *Statesman,* mentions Pakistan's natural affinity with the West but adds that the partnership resulted also from "a certain positive quality and simplicity, in the Muslim mind, the converse of the complexity and negativism, the neutralism, the 'no,' of the Hindu and Buddhist mind; of the non-cooperation, non-violence, non-alignment, non-attachment — concepts all really religious in origin — which infuse Indian, Burmese, and Ceylonese politics."[6] "To Pakistan," says another respected British writer who spent most of his working life in India, "a cult of non-violence, such as India advocates, appears neither practical nor possible. For one thing, the traditions of Islam harmonize pretty well with the old Puritan maxim: 'Fear God: back your friends: keep your powder dry!' — which expresses accurately Pakistan's general outlook."[7]

This natural attitude of being either friend or foe manifests itself more vigorously at the less inhibited popular level than it can at the official level where the declared policy now is one of friendship with all. When President Ayub Khan hinted in 1962 that Pakistan might be compelled to look for protection elsewhere if her allies continued to disappoint her, *Dawn* editorially said, "If we decide to take the plunge we must be prepared to go the full length in the other direction. . . . Indeed, mere non-alignment will not be enough then; we shall have to seek a different alignment — and pay the price for it. Inevitably, the capitalistic pattern of so-called free economy which we have imported — along with American dollars — will have to be scrapped and we must take the path of Socialism. The prospect is by no means frightening — except to our millionaires and billionaires — and the change is by no means impossible. If Pakistan 'looks for protection' to the other side, the alignment with that side will have to be of the closest nature."[8]

Despite occasional outbursts such as this, there is in fact no general desire among Pakistanis wholeheartedly to embrace socialism of the Communist variety. What all of them have consistently cherished above everything else is the development of the closest possible ties with other Muslim peoples. This constant dream at present finds practical, though limited, expression in the Regional Cooperation for Development (RCD).[9] Wishfully, its sweep continues to cover the entire Muslim belt from Casablanca to Djakarta.[10]

The Philosophy of Hinduism: Nonattachment

Prime Minister Nehru, as already noted, claimed that the Indian policy of nonalignment was "inherent in the past thinking of India, inherent in the whole mental outlook of India, inherent in the conditioning of the Indian mind."[11] "Now what is this coexistence?" he asked on another occasion and proceeded to explain its meaning thus: "It is a mental or spiritual attitude which . . . tries to understand and accommodate different religions, ideologies, political, social and economic systems and refuses to think in terms of conflict or military solutions."[12] Again: "Indian philosophy has always said that you can see only a bit of the truth. Let others see the other parts of the truth. Out of this synthesis may come an understanding which may help a wider appreciation of the truth. . . . We accepted religions coming there from outside. . . . India has stood for this kind of peaceful coexistence between different sets of ideas and different faiths. It is a continuation of that idea that makes us put forward the ideal of coexistence in the world today."[13]

Though nonalignment was criticized by many after the border war with China in 1962, "yet for the preceding fifteen years there were very few Indians who had questioned it; very few who did not praise it. It responded, in fact, to that non-attachment which is deeply rooted in Hindu psychology."[14] "The ideal of Indian spirituality," explains a contemporary Indian philosopher, "is sagehood which is the state of equanimity and sameness of attitude towards all beings. An oft-quoted verse of the Bhagvad Gita reads thus: 'The wise ones look with the same eye on a *Brahmana* possessed of learning and humility, a cow, an elephant, a dog, and even a dog-eater.' . . . The moral of the whole description is that the sage is not swayed by attachments and hatreds."[15]

The Heritage

As to the efficacy of this gigantic attempt at synthesis one observer remarks that "India's synthetist philosophers have always boasted of what they call unity in diversity. The unity has yet to pass a serious test; the diversity is a matter of observable fact."[16] Hinduism's "weakness," states H. N. Brailsford, who was a good friend of Gandhi's and highly sympathetic to the causes of the Indian National Congress, "is that it never denies, never rejects, never discards what is obsolete and unworthy of the noble core of its beliefs."[17] By mixing together all the imaginable shades Nehru himself visualized this final picture: "The world is neither black nor white. Neither are we. We are all rather grey, with various shades, and this simple reduction to black and white does not help in understanding a problem or in solving it. It may be that it takes away from the firm conviction which grows from faith in blackness and whiteness. Possibly it does."[18]

No wonder then that upon becoming independent India found herself unable to subscribe to either of the two ideologies represented by the United States and the Soviet Union. Radhakrishnan explained: "None of them present such flawless working ideals as India can readily accept; each of them suffers from some grievous evils with which India cannot compromise. If one is democratic, then it is also tainted with the evils of racialism and imperialism; and if the other widely provides for social justice and equality, it also at the same time suffers from regimentation and acceptance of terroristic methods in politics which to India are totally unacceptable."[19] Though this lack of commitment may keep others guessing where India is going, it affords a greater latitude to India herself. In Radhakrishnan's words, "Why look at things in terms of this or that? Why not try to have both this *and* that?"[20]

An interview Leonard Beaton of the *Manchester Guardian* had with Prime Minister Nehru on 22 October 1961 well illustrates the comfortable scope thus provided. On hearing Nehru's views on Sino-Indian relations Beaton could not help being charmed by Nehru's "strength of gentleness and the curious sense that whatever way things go he will prove to have been right."[21] A well-known Indian analyst, however, reaches a harsher conclusion. Subidjo, minister and secretary general of the National Front of Indonesia, was reported to have said that "India is in the habit of loosing doves of peace with one hand and receiving American military aid with the other." Frank Moraes of the *Indian Express* attributed this habit of double-facedness to "our passion for verbal and intellectual hair-splitting." As an illustration of this Moraes quoted an American as having said that shortly after World War II he had met many Indians at various international conferences and had been struck at first by the liveliness of their minds and their capacity for articulate speeches. Later he had been somewhat taken aback to observe that they (the Indians) could argue with equal vehemence for both sides of a case, and often did. To him it denoted a lack of basic conviction on vital matters.[22]

The Hindu and the Muslim Horizons

"Islam is an international and extrovert faith. Hinduism is a national and introvert one."[23]

While the classical Muslim legal theory of dividing the world into *dar ul-Islam* and *dar ul-harb* encompassed the entire world, the horizon of the Hindu political thinkers never moved beyond the geographical limits of the Indian subcontinent. "This was the earth, *chaturanta prthvi* which an Indian paramount king should legitimately aspire to rule. Even Kautilya never envisaged that a Hindu emperor's rule should extend beyond this."[24] Manu enjoined upon the kings of India not to meddle with the affairs of other countries.[25]

Consequently, while the Arabs within a comparatively short span of time established an empire extending from Spain to Sind and the religion of Islam permeated into all parts of the world in varying degrees, Hinduism, both as a religion and as a political force, largely has remained confined for all time within the bounds of India. There has been no Hindu imperialism and colonialism as such. The Hindu kingdoms of Southeast Asia were not ruled as colonies from India. Their founders adopted the new lands as their home and did not exploit local resources for the benefit of India.[26]

Addressing the UNESCO Seminar on Gandhian Technique at Delhi in January 1953, President Rajendra Prasad said that during his visit to Europe he had been struck by the fact that wherever he went he saw memorials to warriors, wars, and victories. "We don't see that kind of thing in this country," he pointed out. In India's long history "there has not been one instance when India sent out her invading army to another country."[27] Mrs. Pandit says that a conqueror in battles has always meant less to India than the person who conquers his appetites and emotions: "self-conquest is more important than world-conquest."[28]

The Heritage

The social taboos that compart Hindu society inevitably cramp the general outlook of its members. As Nehru once pointed out in Parliament: "Most of us in India are so situated . . . as to be normally isolated in our minds, in our social habits, in our eating, in our drinking, in our marrying, etc. We isolate ourselves in castes, this division and that division, with the result that it is a unique habit in India which does not prevail anywhere else in the world. We live in compartments, and therefore, perhaps naturally, we think in terms of isolation easily as a country too."[29] Consequently, the Hindus have no strong ties with any peoples in other lands. If India at any time leans toward this or that power, the move is purely tactical, meant to meet the exigency of the moment. Deep down in their beings the Indians are not emotionally involved to any great extent with any other people. The natural bonds of common culture and values, such as those which bind together the United States and Britain, and the United States and Western Europe, for example, do not exist between India and any other land. Chants such as *Hindi-Chini bhai bhai* (Indians and Chinese are brothers) and *Hindi-Russi bhai bhai* (Indians and Russians are brothers) which are periodically heard in contemporary India amount to no more than an exercise in time-serving slogan mongering, easily susceptible to the winds of political change.[30] "Another influence on India's posture in world affairs," states a joint Indo-American study, "has been that by and large the Indian people do not feel much hereditary or cultural attachment to other parts of the world. Although the Moslems have a lively sense of kinship with Islam in general, in cultural terms the Hindus of India have in the past been oriented inward."[31]

The Muslims of the subcontinent of India have always considered themselves as a part of the universal brotherhood of Islam and many of them, specially in the northwest, in fact carry in their veins the blood of Muslims from neighboring lands who came to India in successive waves as conquerors. Muslims of other lands are as dear to them as their own kith and kin. To some extent their feelings are comparable to European settlers overseas — in Australia, Canada, the United States, and South America — who feel a special affinity toward the countries of their origin. But this comparison is a pale one because European settlers accept territorial nationality as a determining cimcumstance while to the Muslims it is not the territorial affiliation that is paramount but the ideological link of Islam. "Personally I am an internationalist," proclaimed a member of the Pakistan National Assembly, "and I am an internationalist because I am a Mussalman. Islam itself is an international religion. It does not believe in any distinction of caste, creed, or colour."[32]

The "Foreign Policy" of Hindu India

Some writers have made much of the interest in foreign affairs which the Indian National Congress is stated to have evinced from its very inception. However, a close look at the foreign policy resolutions of the Congress in the early years will show that they mainly expressed unhappiness at British activities on the borders of India which served the interests only of imperial Britain while the resulting financial burden fell also on the shoulders of subject India. Indeed, it was pressure from the Indian Muslims that caused the Indian National Congress for the first time to take "a direct interest in a foreign event" — in 1919 the Congress passed a resolution protesting against the hostile attitude of some of the British ministers toward the Turkish and Khilafat questions and urged His Majesty's government to settle the Turkish question in accordance with the sentiments of Indian Muslims.[33] Earlier, in 1912, the Muslims of India had dispatched a medical mission to tend Turkish soldiers wounded in the Balkan Wars. "The Congress did not take any direct interest in this matter, but as a gesture of good will towards Indian Muslims its leaders did express sympathy with Turkey."[34]

In 1927 Jawaharlal Nehru, freshly returned from Europe after an extended visit lasting for more than a year and a half, assumed the role of mentor of Indian foreign policy, a position he retained till his death in 1964. In the course of his travels he had attended the International Congress against Imperialism at Brussels and had also visited the Soviet Union. He was full of zeal for socialism and a new determination to end imperialism in India. At the Madras session that year the Congress, largely under pressure from Nehru, for the first time declared complete independence as the goal of the Indian people.

There was not much hope for a weak and divided India in a straight contest with imperial Britain, then at the height of her power. At its next session (1928), the Congress, therefore, set the tune for what henceforth was to be a constant refrain in its pronouncements: "Being of opinion that the struggle of the Indian people for freedom is a part of the general world struggle against imperialism and its manifestations, [the Congress] considers it desirable that India should develop contacts

The Heritage

with other countries and peoples who also suffer under imperialism and desire to combat it. The Congress, therefore, calls upon the All India Congress Committee to develop such contacts and to open a Foreign Department in this behalf." In Nehru's own words, "India with her problems and struggles became just a part of this mighty world drama, of the great struggle of political and economic forces that was going on everywhere, nationally and internationally."[35]

Two things need to be said about this world view of the Congress. First, though the resolutions carried the label of the Congress party they were in reality the result of the efforts of just one man — Jawaharlal Nehru. Congress leadership on the whole remained apathetic to foreign affairs;[36] the Hindu masses cared even less about what was happening in the world outside. Gandhi acknowledged that it was Nehru who had "compelled India, through the Working Committee, to think not merely of her own freedom, but of the freedom of all the exploited nations of the world."[37] Secondly, the interest in the fate of other countries was indirect. It did not so much matter what happened to others; the important thing was how developments elsewhere affected the fate of India herself. The area of interest was impressive but the veneer of concern for others was thinly spread. Nehru himself summarized the extent of Congress interest in foreign affairs before independence: "In the nineteen twenties it . . . gradually developed a foreign policy which was based on the elimination of political and economic imperialism everywhere and the co-operation of free nations. This fitted in with the demand for Indian independence."[38]

Nehru often talked about the lessons taught by Buddha and Gandhi as the basis of Indian policy.[39] His sister Vijaya Lakshmi Pandit elaborated this conception in an article she contributed to *Foreign Affairs*. "Buddha," she wrote, "condemned violence in all its forms and sought through the example of his own renunciation a solution to human suffering"; and Gandhi won freedom for India by "his insistence on ethics and his creed of non-violence" thereby demonstrating their application to the world problems of today.[40]

Gandhi, like Buddha, based human happiness on a life of nonacquisitiveness. Progress and civilization for Gandhi consisted not in the multiplication of wants and higher standards of living but in the "deliberate and voluntary restriction of wants."[41] He felt that violence could not be avoided in a society which is based on a desire to extend and expand one's needs.[42] He disliked machinery and industrialization and wanted to go back to "almost a self-sufficient village."[43]

Nehru, however, made no secret of the fact that he disliked praise of poverty and suffering,[44] and he insisted that the main drive for the future would have to be toward a complete overhauling of the agrarian system and the growth of industry.[45] Indeed, "no country to-day is really independent or capable of resisting aggression unless it is industrially developed."[46] When he performed the ceremony opening the Nangal Canal, as prime minister of independent India, he confessed to feeling "a strange exhilaration" and said that, as he walked round the site of the dam at Bhakra, he thought that "the biggest temple and mosque and gurdwara is the place where man works for the good of mankind."[47] Nehru believed that ultimately foreign policy is the outcome of economic policy[48] and that a country is not really independent so long as she is economically dependent on others.[49]

Modern India's wish to build up her industrial and economic strength is, of course, in tune with the present age and no one blames her for not having followed Buddha's and Gandhi's economic philosophies; Indian spokesmen have not complicated matters by continuing to pay lip service to those principles. Very different, however, has been the case with regard to nonviolence. By insisting that Gandhi wrested freedom from British hands by applying the moral force of nonviolence and by purporting to base Indian foreign policy on that very technique, Indian spokesmen have created innumerable contradictions for themselves and confusion for others. This is not surprising.

First, the situation of an independent country, making her way on the world stage in the midst of numerous other equally sovereign states, is quite different from that of a subject people struggling for independence against an imperial power. The program which attains success in one case may have no application whatever to the other. Indeed, Gandhi's principal lieutenants have all confessed that they did not consider nonviolence as a sacrosanct principle of morality but regarded it simply as good tactics against the British government in the existing circumstances. Nehru unequivocally stated: "For us and for the National Congress as a whole the non-violent method was not, and could not be, a religion or an unchallengeable creed or dogma. It could only be a policy and a method."[50] President Rajendra Prasad, another close associate of Gandhi's, explained: "We were disarmed; we were unable to fight with arms,

The Heritage

and not a few of us saw in Gandhiji's method a way out of our difficult position."[51]

Secondly, the romantic notion that India won her freedom nonviolently ignores certain obvious realities. Indian independence, in actual fact, was accompanied by one of the greatest bloodbaths and cruelest migrations in the history of mankind. That this horrible violence was not directed against the alien rulers did in no wise convert it into "nonviolence." Though all violence is inherently bad, and must be condemned, a war of liberation against foreign rule is not without some compensation, for it rouses feelings of patriotism and fosters unity among the fighters for freedom. But the kind of violence Indians perpetrated against one another was an unmitigated curse. Mass cruelty to women, children, and the helpless aged could not but debase the character of the Hindus, the Muslims, and the Sikhs, and leave behind a legacy of bitter hatred between the twin states of India and Pakistan.

Thirdly, though Gandhi undoubtedly made the Indian masses freedom conscious, and thereby imparted momentum to the urge for freedom, this was not the deciding factor resulting in India's independence in 1947. The greatest single circumstance which brought India the boon of liberty was World War II, an occurrence of worldwide violence on an unprecedented scale, which on the one hand weakened the will and the physical capacity of India's colonial masters to hold on to their empire and on the other created a revolutionary urge among the subject races everywhere to cast off the yoke of imperialism. Lord Pethic-Lawrence, a friend and admirer of Gandhi, who, as secretary of state for India, headed the Cabinet mission to India in 1946, has written in the Mahatma's biography: "By an irony it was the Second World War, so hated by Gandhi, that finally sealed the doom of all these dominations . . . it was in the events during and arising out of the war that Asia secured her release from European domination."[52]

In fact, "these dominations" had begun to founder under the impact of the forces generated by World War I. The authors of the Montagu-Chelmsford Report had observed during the war that it was on the battlefields of France "and not in Delhi or Whitehall that the ultimate decision of India's future will be taken."[53] India's first real step toward self-government was taken under the Government of India Act of 1919. And the czardom in Russia as well as the Ottoman and the Austrian empires also collapsed in the wake of that war.

Origins of Foreign Policies

World War II had an even greater impact on the destiny of mankind. The conflict had run only half its course when Prime Minister Winston Churchill told King George VI, at one of their regular Tuesday luncheons in July 1942, that "all three parties in Parliament were quite prepared to give up India to the Indians after the war. He felt they had already been talked into giving up India."[54] During the debate following Prime Minister Clement Attlee's statement of 20 February 1947 that power would be transferred to Indian hands not later than June 1948, Sir Stafford Cripps explained in the House of Commons that "side by side with the growing demand for an acceleration of the transfer of power on the part of all parties in India, there was an obvious and inevitable weakening of the machinery of British control . . . [and] one thing that was quite obviously impossible was to decide to continue our responsibility indefinitely — and indeed, against our own wishes — into a period when we had not the power to carry it."[55]

Independent India continues to pay verbal homage to Gandhian non-violence but the fact remains that she has fought more wars with her neighbors during the first quarter century of her independence than any other major nation in the world, and has all too often been plagued by political and communal riots. As Frank Moraes has bluntly pointed out, "there is no notion more mistaken or fanciful than the widespread belief that India and the National Congress Party were at any time, in Gandhi's lifetime or after, committed to non-violence as a creed."[56] "By brandishing Gandhi on practically every occasion," complains an exasperated analyst of Indian foreign policy, "they [the Indians] have allowed a thick fog to hang over India's foreign policy. This has made it difficult for people abroad to appraise this policy correctly."[57] "Mr. Nehru knows," commented the *Round Table,* "that in this imperfect world 'moral' strength is not enough. India is doing what all others do, nothing worse, nothing better. Only persistent claims to be doing better make the affair look worse."[58]

What would India have to do if she really wished to measure up to Gandhi's conception of nonviolence? President Rajendra Prasad answered this specific question in his address to the UNESCO Seminar on Gandhian Technique, which has already been cited. India, he explained, would have to adopt "a clear-cut programme of no-war under any circumstances, defensive or offensive, and no armament of any kind." And he confessed that he was head of a state which had not renounced war or abjured violence.⁵⁹

Indeed, Gandhi's greatest contribution to the well-being of independent India does not relate to the field of foreign affairs. His most fortunate legacy to his motherland has been the Congress party, which he reorganized, turned into a grass-roots mass party, and nourished for some twenty-seven years preceding independence. It is due to this well-established political institution that India has been able to effect governmental changes more smoothly than any other Afro-Asian country.

The "Foreign Policy" of Muslim India

Many Muslims believed that India became *dar ul-harb* from the battle of Plassey (1757) when the British defeated the Muslim Nawab of Bengal and virtually became the rulers of that principality. According to them it was sufficient that the infidel rulers were now possessed of power to interfere with the religious observances of their Muslim subjects; whether they did interfere or not was immaterial. It was, therefore, incumbent upon Muslims to wage a holy war (*jihad*) against the British to reconvert the country into *dar ul-Islam*. Another school, represented by Sir Syed Ahmed Khan, while willing to concede that India could be classed as *dar ul-harb* because she no longer was under Muslim rule, declared that *jihad* against the British was unlawful for the reasons that the Muslims enjoyed peace and religious freedom under British rule and the British had a treaty relationship with a Muslim government (Turkey).

It was the former conception that provided the inspiration for the *mujahidin* movement, the first significant effort aimed at expelling the British from India.⁶⁰ The movement was inaugurated by Syed Ahmed of Rai Bareilly in the 1820s. A start was made by attacking the Sikhs from the hills near Peshawar. The grand design, evidently, was first to enlist the support of the Muslim principalities and tribes of the northwest frontier, then to liberate the predominantly Muslim territory of the Punjab from the Sikhs, and finally to confront the British in the heart of India. Syed Ahmed Barelvi died on the battlefield at Balakot in 1831 but he left behind a well-established organization and his followers stubbornly continued the fight. When the British conquered the Punjab from the Sikhs, the *mujahidin* came into direct conflict with the former.

Between 1850 and 1857 the British government was forced to send out sixteen distinct expeditions, aggregating 33,000 regular troops; and by 1863 the number rose to twenty separate expeditions, aggregating 60,000 regular troops, besides irregular auxiliaries and police. For a time the *mujahidin* "defied the whole frontier force of British India."[61]

Though there were cells of the *mujahidin* all over India, their chief spiritual center was at Patna and their chief recruiting area was East Bengal. Their success in keeping the camp on the frontier supplied with men and money across two thousand miles of enemy territory for a period of half a century is visible proof of their fanatical courage and resourcefulness.

British military operations on the frontier were supplemented by suppression of the movement at its source in India and by 1870 the situation had been brought under control. However, the danger had by no means disappeared. Writing in 1871, William Wilson Hunter, a senior member of Her Majesty's Bengal Civil Service, thus voiced British fears: "[The "Wahabi" organization] still continues the centre towards which the hopes alike of our disloyal subjects and of our enemies beyond the Frontier turn . . . and no one can predict the proportions to which this Rebel Camp, backed by the Musalman hordes from the Westward, might attain, under a leader who knew how to weld together the nations of Asia in a Crescentade."[62] Later, in 1918, the Rowlatt Report noted that the colony of *mujahidin,* "although small, has survived many vicissitudes and remains until now."[63] In fact, "there were *mujahidin* in the tribal areas, descendants of the original fighters, right up to the establishment of Pakistan."[64] In the sustained fight of the *mujahidin* to re-establish *dar ul-Islam* in India can be discerned the aspiration which, when revived by a later generation, received the name of Pakistan.[65]

The mutiny of 1857 was also fought under a Muslim flag, that of the titular Moghul emperor Bahadur Shah, though Hindus and Muslims fought together against the British. As Sir Colin Campbell surmised, "the revolt is Mahometan and not Hindoo; and therefore has little to do with Hindoo fanaticism. The fact may prove to be that the discontent of the Hindu furnished fuel, while the restlessness and ambition of the Mahometan supplied the fire."[66]

The aged Moghul emperor had no doubt lost de facto power long before but his de jure status as emperor of India was still untouched; the East India Company purported to administer the territories under its sway as the agent of the Moghul emperor and not as the representative of Queen Victoria. By extending his leadership to the insurrection the

The Heritage

emperor conferred constitutional legitimacy and an all-India complexion on a movement which otherwise might have remained qualitatively indistinguishable from numerous other outbreaks resulting from sepoy dissatisfaction at conditions of service in the British Indian army.

Far from restoring the full power of the Moghul emperor, the uprising of 1857 resulted in his banishment and in the extinction of his exalted office for all time. Obviously, the British were in India to stay, at least for the foreseeable future, and the time had come for the Muslims to adjust themselves to the existing realities, instead of clinging to dreams of their past glory. The saner elements among the Muslims realized that they must come to terms with the new masters of India and also regenerate themselves educationally and economically to catch up, and compete on equal terms, with the Hindus who, having reconciled themselves to the new order from the beginning, were already much advanced.

The British, too, for their part were now willing to reciprocate Muslim overtures. Initially, the Hindus had welcomed British rule as a more acceptable substitute for Muslim domination. The second half of the nineteenth century, however, witnessed a revival of Hinduism in the form of militant Hindu nationalism which first made its appearance in Bengal and then spread to other parts. There thus developed a community of interests between the Muslims and the British, just as there had been a community of interests between the Hindus and the British when the British first appeared in India. The British began to fear for their empire at the hands of the Hindu majority and the Muslims for their future as a backward minority should the British be forced to depart from the scene. The partition of Bengal in 1905, which gave the Muslims a Muslim majority area, and the Act of 1909, which brought them the privilege of separate electorates, were the main visible fruits of the Muslim-British conciliation of these years. With good reason, Valentine Chirol, a contemporary British expert in Indian affairs, observed in 1910, "it may be confidently asserted that never before have the Mahomedans of India as a whole identified their interests and their aspirations so closely as at the present day with the consolidation and permanence of British rule."[67]

But the political climate underwent a sudden change the very next year and opened a new phase of Muslim-British estrangement. After having repeatedly assured the Muslims in the past that the partition of Bengal was a settled fact, the British hurriedly revoked it in 1911, not on the merits but chiefly because they did not wish the violent Hindu agitation against partition to mar the resplendence of the king and queen's visit to hold a durbar in India.[68] The lesson, that the British government had given way to Hindu agitation, was not lost on the Muslims and they began to wonder whether, after all, it might not be wiser to patch up their differences with the Hindus than to rely on the British.

At about the same time events outside India added to the concern of the Indian Muslims but, in order to complete the story, let us pick up the thread from the days of the mutiny. We have already noted that the failure of the mutiny brought home to the Indian Muslims the lesson that there was no immediate prospect of reviving a Muslim empire in India. Increasingly, therefore, the eyes of the Indian Muslims turned toward Turkey which alone in the world at that time seemed capable of becoming the focus of universal Muslim regeneration. That the Ottoman sultan had also held the title of the khalifa since 1517 made him specially qualified to stand forth as the champion of Islam.

During the Russo-Turkish war of 1877 the Muslims of India for the first time demonstrated their sympathy for the Turks on a large scale. "Religious services were held in some of the mosques in Calcutta and subscriptions were raised for the relief of the Turkish sick and wounded." Many expressed a wish to fight in the ranks of their Turkish comrades. Henceforth all Turkish causes, notably the wars against Greece (1897), Italy (1911), and the Balkan League (1912), evoked agitation in India. During the Balkan War a medical mission under Dr. M. A. Ansari was sent to Turkey. "Even the poor subscribed; money came more rapidly than for any proposal for the uplift of the Indian Moslems themselves."[69] It seemed to Indian Muslims that the Christian powers were bent upon destroying the power of Islam.

The situation became still more difficult when, a few months after the outbreak of World War I in 1914, the Turks, influenced by the early successes of the Central Powers, threw in their lot with Germany and declared war against the Allies, coupling this declaration with a proclamation of *jihad* against Christendom. By promises of fair treatment of Turkey after the war, the British government was able to win over the cooperation of most Indian Muslims; and Indian troops, many of whom were Muslims, fought alongside the Allies on different fronts and significantly contributed to victories against the Turks.

After the war the Muslims of India were deeply anxious that the pre-

The Heritage

war status of the sultan of Turkey, both territorial and spiritual, should remain undisturbed. In his interview with Prime Minister Lloyd George, as the leader of an Indian Khilafat deputation, Maulana Muhammad Ali represented that, if the khalifa were to defend the faith adequately, his prewar territorial status must be restored. Asked whether he was opposed to the independence of Arabia, he replied in the affirmative. Lloyd George said that Turkey could not be treated differently from the defeated Christian powers. The principle of self-determination would be applied to all equally.[70]

Another Khilafat delegation from India led by the Aga Khan went to England in 1921 to explain the Muslim case at the invitation of the British government. Though writers of national history have generally given more prominence to the deputation led by the more colorful Muhammad Ali, the Aga Khan delegation probably carried greater weight in the British ruling circles. Since the Aga Khan had backed up the British during the war, his team was able to speak in a different vein from that of Muhammad Ali who had opposed the British government and had to be interned. The Aga Khan delegation, moreover, had an able and sober spokesman in Hasan Imam, a former judge of the Calcutta and Patna high courts. They had not come as "supplicants for favour," Hasan Imam stressed, but "as persons who have had a share in the achievement of victory" and were, therefore, entitled "to demand" the fulfillment of wartime pledges.

The delegation had two meetings with Lloyd George, on 12 March and 24 March, and also submitted a written memorandum at the British prime minister's request. Among other matters, the delegation opposed the proposal to make over Thrace to Greece on the ground that such a course would expose Constantinople to danger. "To us Constantinople means a great deal," pleaded Hasan Imam, "because our sentiments are there. For five hundred years we have been there. After we have finished our prayers towards the West, towards Mecca, we have to think of Constantinople as the center from which the influence of Islam radiates because it is the temporal capital of Islam, and we do not want to lose it." Lloyd George acknowledged India's contribution to victory — "as far as numbers are concerned, the preponderant share" — and praised "the very powerful and able advocacy" of the delegation. He promised to let them "know the further modifications which we shall press on our allies, in view of the representations you have made on behalf of the Mahome-

Origins of Foreign Policies

dans of India." On 29 April 1921 the secretary of state for India, E. S. Montagu, in a letter to the delegation said, "In the final settlement you will be able to see that, even if all your requests have not been granted, your religious sentiments have been respected, and that the undoubted claims of India to special consideration in helping to determine the peace with Turkey have been abundantly recognized in the provisions of the peace."[71]

In October 1922 the British press carried reports that the Central Khilafat Committee meeting at Delhi had passed a resolution congratulating Mustapha Kemal Pasha on his victories and resolved to present him with a sword and two airplanes.[72] "Between 1912 when the first Balkan war began and 1922 when Turkey made peace with the European powers," observes Ambedkar, "the Indian Muslims did not bother about Indian politics in the least. They were completely absorbed in the fate of Turkey and Arabia."[73]

However, the first blow to the old institution of Khilafat had already been struck in 1916 by the Arabs who, stimulated by the wartime ideas of self-determination and assisted by the British, had raised the banner of revolt against their imperial master, the sultan of Turkey, under the leadership of no less a person than Grand Sharif Husayn of Mecca, a descendant of the Prophet and guardian of the Muslim shrines. Developments inside Turkey after the war eventually resulted in the deposition and banishment of the sultan and the emergence of a national state with Mustapha Kemal Pasha as president. The institution of Khilafat, not being in tune with the mood of new Turkey, was abolished in March 1924.

Though the Indian Muslims did not succeed in saving the institution of Khilafat, their efforts on behalf of the Turks had not been in vain. In Valentine Chirol's judgment the Khilafat agitation "was one of the decisive factors"[74] at the Lausanne Conference, where Turkey was able to obtain greatly improved terms. At the time of the conference the Aga Khan was present in Lausanne holding "a watching brief" for the Muslims of India. Earlier, he had been an active participant in two events which paved the way for a more sympathetic treatment of the Turks. First, through the British editor of the *Times of India,* he had influenced the viceroy, Lord Reading, to send a dispatch to the British government urging "that the allies should evacuate Constantinople, giving back to the Sultan his former suzerainty over the Holy Places and also restore

The Heritage

Thrace and Smyrna to Turkey." Second, through Lord Beaverbrook, he had contributed to the fall of Lloyd George from premiership.[75]

However, as was often to be the experience of Pakistani Muslims later, the affection of the Indian Muslims was not fully reciprocated by its recipients. "The Turks not only abolished the Khilafat in 1924 but also, to add insult to injury, characterised certain Muslim leaders as agents of British imperialism."[76] Of course, while noticing the postwar solicitude of the Indian Muslims, the Turks could hardly have forgotten so soon that the former had contributed to the Turkish defeat by enlisting in large numbers to fight under the British flag.

With the abolition of the Khilafat, the Muslims of India lost the overseas rallying point for Muslim resurgence and increasingly began to feel that, as the most substantial body of believers in the world, it was more incumbent upon themselves than upon others to strive for the solidarity of Islam. The poet Iqbal gave voice to these thoughts in 1933: "Indian Muslims, who happen to be a more numerous people than the Muslims of all other Asiatic countries put together, ought to consider themselves the greatest asset of Islam."[77] In March 1937 he wrote to Jinnah, "We must not ignore the fact that the whole future of Islam as a moral and political force in Asia rests very largely on a complete organisation of the Indian Muslims."[78]

But it took the Muslims of India time to sort themselves out and to discover a new cause round which they could rally once more. The Muslim League had been founded in 1906 but, for many years, remained a comparatively small conservative organization, consisting mainly of upper-class professional and landed Muslims. From 1919 till 1924 the League had been almost totally eclipsed by the revolutionary Khilafat movement. In 1924 the League met again under the presidentship of Jinnah but Muslim politics did not appreciably stir till the middle of the 1930s when the League decided to contest the elections under the newly passed Government of India Act of 1935. Assisted by some major Congress blunders and Jinnah's skillful leadership, it soon became a mass party. In 1940 the League declared the setting up of a separate Muslim homeland to be its objective, once more giving the Indian Muslims a concrete goal to fight for. During the succeeding seven years the attention and the energy of the Muslims were almost wholly occupied with the seemingly impossible task of wresting Pakistan from the unwilling hands of the Hindus and the British. Remarkably enough, however, throughout this period the League never flagged in its concern for developments in other Islamic lands.

In 1925, suspecting that Iraq was about to be handed over to Britain as a mandatory power, the League passed a resolution declaring that Iraq was a part of Jaziral-ul-Arab and as such should not be left under the non-Muslim control of the British as the mandatory power.[79] At the Delhi session in November 1933 the League placed on record its "emphatic protest" against the policy of the British government in trying to make Palestine the national home of the Jews. Four years later, in 1937, the League demanded the annulment of the British mandate in Palestine and warned the British government that if it failed to alter its present pro-Jewish policy in Palestine "the Mussalmans of India in consonance with the rest of the Islamic world will look upon the British as the enemy of Islam and shall be forced to adopt all necessary measures according to the dictates of their faith." In the same year Iqbal stated that "the impression given to the unprejudiced reader is that Zionism as a movement was deliberately created not for the purpose [of] giving a National home [to] the Jews but mainly for the purpose of giving a home to British imperialism on the Mediterranean littoral."[80] Again, commenting on the report recommending the partition of Palestine, he said that the idea of a national home for the Jews in Palestine was only a device. In fact British imperialism sought a foothold for itself in the form of a permanent mandate in the religious center of the Muslims.[81] The next year the League called for the observance of "Palestine Day," for the holding of protest meetings, and for the offering of prayers. A deputation consisting of four leaders was sent abroad to promote the Arab cause. It remained overseas for nine months visiting Cairo, London, Geneva, Rome, and Beirut.

In December 1938 the Muslim League resolved that "the unjust Balfour Declaration, and the subsequent policy of repression adopted by the British Government in Palestine, aim at making their sympathy for the Jews a pretext for incorporating that country into the British empire with a view to strengthen British imperialism and to frustrate the idea of a federation of Arab states and its possible union with other Muslim states. . . . This session of the League warns the British Government that if they persist in trying to give a practical shape to the idea prevalent among certain sections of the British and Americans that Palestine be made the national home of the Jews, it will lead to a state of per-

THE HERITAGE

petual unrest and conflict." In the following year a Palestine Fund was opened.

After the outbreak of World War II, in September of the same year, the League Council "resolved that in view of the repeated reports that have reached India recently that there is a probability of war flames spreading and of aggression by foreign powers against the independence and sovereignty of the Muslim countries such as Egypt, Palestine, Syria and Turkey, the President is hereby authorized to fix a day for the purpose of expressing and demonstrating deep sympathy and concern of Muslim India with Muslim countries and also conveying to those who have any such design that in the event of any attack upon Muslim countries, Muslim India will be forced to stand by them and give all the support it can." The League also decided to organize a Red Crescent branch of the Muslim National Guard so that it could dispatch medical missions to Islamic countries should the ravages of war spread to them.

In 1941, fearing that Britain might abolish the mandates and take over direct possession of the mandated territories, the Working Committee of the League stated that the Muslims of India were greatly perturbed, and viewed with alarm the military occupation of certain Muslim states in the Near East by Great Britain and her allies. It urged the British government and its allies to declare unequivocally that the sovereignty and independence of those Muslim states would be restored as soon as circumstances permitted and that the pernicious system of mandates and the creation of zones of influence for European powers over these countries would not be resorted to.

From 1942 to 1946 the League continued to express increasing anxiety about the Palestine question. It regretted that Britain was "trying to force Jewish domination over the Arabs against their will, in direct violation of the pledges made in the last war, and the principle it claims to follow for winning the present war" and assured "its Arab brothers in Palestine that Muslim India will stand by them in their fight for their rights against the domination of international Jewry" (1942); it "viewed with concern and alarm the new Zionist propaganda and move in the U.S.A. Government for exercising its influence with the British Government firstly to remove all present restrictions on Jewish immigration in Palestine and secondly to adopt the policy of converting Palestine into a Jewish state" (1943); it "noted with apprehension and dismay that forecasts from authoritative sources credit the Javit Anglo-American

Commission of Inquiry into Palestine . . . with the intention of recommending inter-alia the immediate admission of 100,000 Jews into Palestine and the Partition of Palestine for the purpose of establishing a so-called Jewish National home" (1946).

In the course of his presidential address at the historic Lahore session of the League in March 1940, during which the resolution demanding a complete separation of Muslim majority areas from the rest of India was passed, Jinnah said that the Muslims wanted "that the British Government should in fact and actually meet the demands of the Arabs in Palestine."[82] Addressing the students of the Aligarh Muslim University in March 1944 he warned that if President Roosevelt, under the pressure of the powerful world Jewry, committed the blunder of forcing the British government to do injustice to the Arabs in Palestine, this would set the whole Muslim world ablaze from one end to another.[83] The next year the League president telegraphed to Prime Minister Attlee: "President Truman's reported Palestine immigration proposal is unwarranted, encroaching upon another country, monstrous and highly unjust. . . . [A]ny surrender to appease Jewry at the sacrifice of Arabs would be deeply resented and vehemently resisted by Muslim world and Muslim India and its consequences will be most disastrous."[84] At Quetta, in October 1946, Jinnah stated that over half a million Jews had already been accommodated in Jerusalem against the wishes of the people. "May I know," he asked, "which other country has accommodated them?"[85]

Muslim causes other than the Palestine question equally evoked the League's solicitude.

The Muslim League characterized the wartime occupation of Iran by British and Soviet troops as "unprovoked aggression" which would "alienate the sympathies of the Muslims of India and create bitterness in their hearts" resulting "in the withdrawal of every help by them to the allied cause" (1941).

In December 1943, the League urged Britain and the Allied powers not to hand back to the Italian government the territories recently released from the control of Italy, namely Cyrenaica, Libya, and Tripoli, but to constitute them as independent sovereign states. At the same time the League demanded the abolition of the "vicious system of mandates" and the restoration of Palestine, Syria, and Lebanon to the peoples of those countries to enable them to set up their own sovereign governments. Finally, referring to the oft-repeated declarations by the Allies

THE HERITAGE

that they sought to liberate subject nationalities, the League, in the same resolution, demanded that the Allied Powers press France to liberate Morocco, Algeria, and Tunis.

When the Netherlands landed fresh troops in Indonesia, the League, in an April 1946 resolution, noted with regret that the right of the Indonesian people to independence had not yet been recognized, condemned the delay in the withdrawal of British troops from Indonesia, and sent a message of greetings and congratulations to the Indonesian people for their struggle for freedom against heavy odds and assured them "of the sincerest sympathy and support of the Muslim nation of India for their just and patriotic causes." A few days later in the course of a press statement, Jinnah also condemned the Dutch imperialist hold on Indonesia and said that Britain had not played an honorable part in the situation.[86]

"It is difficult for any non-Indian Moslem to realise," lamented Dr. M. A. Ansari, who had led the Muslim medical mission during the Balkan War, "what Pan-Islamism means to Indian Moslems. . . . Pan-Islamic sentiment has been one of the Indian Moslem's most sacred and exalted passions."[87] Perhaps the following examples will give the reader some idea of the intensity of emotions that convulsed the Muslims.

1. No other single incident in modern Indian history so graphically depicts the desperate identification of Indian Muslim masses with the threatened existence of the Turkish caliph of Islam as does the tragic *hijrat* movement which reached its highest pitch in the summer of 1920.[88] Its raison d'être was the Islamic doctrine that "if a Muslim finds himself helpless against iniquity and cannot resist it, he should migrate to a place where he is not faced with the same problem."[89] Some half a million men, women, and children, principally from Sind and the northwestern areas, loaded their meager belongings on camels and bullock carts and trekked to the nearest Muslim kingdom of Afghanistan. But the expected haven was denied to them by their fellow Muslims in that country. Many of the pilgrims perished on the wayside. Others returned broken and destitute.

2. "My feelings during the disastrous war in the Balkans," relates Maulana Muhammad Ali, "were at one time so overpowering that I must confess I even contemplated suicide. . . . The latest message of Reuter that had reached me was that the Bulgarians were only twenty-five miles from the walls of Constantinople — from Constantinople, a name that

had for five centuries been sacred to every Muslim as the center of his highest hopes."[90]

3. When the Ansari medical mission returned from Turkey, among those who went to receive it at the railway station was Maulana Shibli, an eminent scholar who, for some years, was a member of the faculty of the Aligarh Muslim University. Shibli was so overcome with emotion that he bent down, kissed Ansari's feet, and wept for the Turks who were struggling for their existence.[91]

4. "All her long life my mother had been animated by one simple, sincere desire," recounts the late Aga Khan, "that when the time came, she should . . . be buried on Muslim soil, by which she meant a land ruled by a free, independent and sovereign Muslim government." She was, accordingly, taken to Iraq during her fatal illness, died there, and was buried near her husband at Nejef, near Karbala.[92]

5. The Muslims of Pakistan in their hearts remain as closely attached to fellow Muslims in other lands as were their ancestors in pre-independence India. A member of the National Assembly of Pakistan, Major Muhammad Afsaruddin, for instance, told his legislative colleagues that when he "had the great honour and pride" of visiting the battlefield of Acre in Palestine, where Salahuddin had defeated the Christian crusaders, he lay down and "kissed the ground because Muslims laid their lives in the battle of the Crusade."[93]

"After the creation of Pakistan," observes a Pakistani writer, "the feelings of brotherhood and sympathy with the cause of the Arab world became all the more crystallised and found an unambiguous expression in the country's foreign policy which is in fact a carry over policy pursued by Muslims of the subcontinent during the last one century."[94]

The deep sympathy which the Muslim masses in India had always felt for fellow Muslims elsewhere, however, was not fully requited by the latter. There were good reasons for this. Since the death of the Emperor Aurangzeb, two centuries ago, Muslim India had been in a state of decline and confusion. And during British rule the Muslim aristocracy, professional classes, and members of the services had, by and large, cooperated with the colonial power, because such a course protected their own vested interests and also because many of them genuinely believed that it was the only way in which the Muslims could avoid being overwhelmed by the Hindus. If there were expressions of sympathy for Turkey at the popular level in the second half of the nineteenth century,

THE HERITAGE

there was also Sir Syed Ahmed Khan's statement to his compatriots that "we are devoted and loyal subjects of the British Government. . . . We are not the subjects of Sultan Abdul Hamid II. . . . He neither had, nor can have any spiritual jurisdiction over us as *Khalifa*. His title of *Khalifa* is effective only in his own land and only over the Muslims under his sway."[95]

During World War II, when the sultan of Turkey proclaimed *jihad* against Christendom, the Aga Khan "joined with other Muslim leaders in an earnest appeal to the whole Islamic world to disregard the so-called *jehad*."[96] After the war the Aga Khan and other Muslims strenuously pleaded for leniency toward Turkey and, as already related, met with a degree of success in their efforts, but the Turks could not quite forget that, not long before, many Muslims from India had also faced them on the battlefield under the British flag. Some years later the Muslim League leader Chaudhuri Khaliquzzaman asked the Turkish ambassador in London why the Turks had thrown away the institution of Khilafat, which had given them a unique status in the world. The envoy bluntly reminded him that the war, in which the Indian army including many Muslims had fought against the Turks, had resulted in the diminution of Turkey's empire and resources with the result that she could no longer meet the obligations which went with the institution of Khilafat.[97]

But the main reason why the Muslims in other lands were not as Islam-conscious as the Muslims of India was that the former took their religion for granted. Their faith was in no danger of being overwhelmed by an alien philosophy. Their nationalism, therefore, took the familiar direction of a straight fight against Western control. The task before the Indian Muslims, however, was quite different. It was not enough for them that the Indo-Pakistani subcontinent wrested its freedom from Britain. They had also to guard against falling from the frying pan of British imperialism into the fire of perpetual Hindu domination. Their sole hope was that Islam, which had for so long enabled them to maintain their distinct identity in India, would also win them a separate homeland of their own.

Thus, while the Indian Muslims were harking back to the greater Islam of pristine days, the Muslims in other lands were infused with the urge to catch up with the movement for territorial nationalism of the current age. Indonesia still had to shake off Dutch control, Iran still had to settle the oil question with Britain, Egypt still had to have British bases vacated from her soil, the Arabs still were anxious about the future of Palestine, and the North African Muslim principalities still were struggling to be free. Not surprisingly they all felt themselves more in tune with Gandhi and Nehru, who too were battling with similar outside forces, than with the Muslim League, which seemed to be acting as the stooge of imperialism.

Chaudhuri Khaliquzzaman has disclosed that during a visit to Egypt in 1938 he met Nahas Pasha, the leader of the Wafd party, and requested him not to send any delegation to India to support the Indian National Congress. The Pasha said, "In our country Zaghlul Pasha settled the minority problem and now we are a nation. Why cannot you settle your problem?" Khaliquzzaman pointed out that the minority problem in Egypt concerned a very much smaller group than in India, where the Muslims numbered a hundred million. The Pasha, nevertheless, sent a delegation consisting of Mohammed Baswamy, the speaker of the Egyptian Parliament, Mahmud Abul Fath, the editor of *Almisri,* and Ahmed Hamza, a former minister, to advise the Muslims to cooperate with the Congress.[98]

On 24 May 1948, Begum Shah Nawaz described in the Constituent Assembly of Pakistan a similar disappointment relating to the period when the first Indian delegation to the United Nations General Assembly was making a glamorous debut under the leadership of Mrs. Pandit. All that Jinnah could do at the time was to dispatch a party of two — M. A. H. Ispahani and Begum Shah Nawaz — to participate in a debate on India in the *New York Herald Tribune* Forum. These unofficial emissaries used the opportunity provided by the trip to place the case for an independent Muslim state before such other circles in the United States as would lend them an ear. Speaking of leaders of delegations to the United Nations the Begum recounted, "I do not like to divulge the name, but even a Muslim country, when we approached the Secretariat of that Delegation, we were told that the head of the delegation may not be able to see us as the lady heading the Indian delegation, Mrs. Vijaya Lakshmi Pandit, would not like his meeting us."[99]

Hindu and Muslim Attitudes toward the Western Countries and Communism

Historical and ideological reasons made it easier for Muslim Pakistan than for Hindu India to join hands with the Western countries after

The Heritage

independence. In the first place, the Hindus had been a subject race for several hundred years thereby developing a strong inferiority complex toward the Western countries, who had been the latest embodiment of dominance and one of whom had directly held India in a painful grip. The Muslims had felt the effect of British rule in India no less but their anguish was tempered by memories of a glorious imperialism of their own, far longer in fact, than that of Britain in India. Secondly, none of the Muslim League leaders had ever seen the inside of a British jail whereas all the top Congress leaders had languished in prison for years. During the last phase of the British rule in India, the relations between the followers of the Congress and the British government had been specially bitter. The Congress launched a rebellion in India under the slogan "quit India" just when things were at their blackest for Britain during World War II. The relations between the Muslim League and senior British officials on the other hand were so cordial that Nehru referred to a "mental alliance" between the two of them.[100] Thirdly, while the Hindus could never forgive the British for acceding to the demand for Pakistan, the Muslims could hardly overlook the fact that without British support their cherished dream might never have become a reality.[101]

Certainly, at the time of independence, as on all important political occasions, there was the usual polite exchange of compliments between the Indians and the British for the so-called peaceful transfer of power, made possible by the fundamental nobility of spirit on both sides, but old internal wounds are not so quickly healed by a sudden shower of sweet words. There remained a powerful urge in India to get even with the Western Powers and to demonstrate the superiority of ancient Asian spiritual wisdom, represented by India and China, over the newly acquired material strength of the immature West, and this took the form of an aggressive display of disagreement with the positions adopted by the Western countries in the post-independence period. Chester Bowles recounts that when Prime Minister Jawaharlal Nehru touched upon an ancient Asian wound, like colonialism or racial discrimination, his voice sometimes would become tense with emotion.[102]

During the Korean War, Robert Trumbull wrote in an article from New Delhi: "A resurgent Asianism also influences Indian thinking. Having thrown off Western bondage themselves, after experiencing color bars and other humiliating treatment at the hands of white strangers, they naturally feel a strong bond with other peoples who are trying to do

Origins of Foreign Policies

exactly the same thing. This is, in fact, nearly all that the Indians have in common with the Chinese. When Asians hand the white race a licking as the Chinese-North Korean army did to the U.N. forces before Inchon, a thrill runs through all other Asians that they cannot keep entirely secret."[103] Krishna Menon, till 1962 Nehru's principal adviser on foreign affairs, says, *"We were not frightened of American strength at the U.N. Nehru allowed me — in effect, he put me on — to draw their fire."*[104]

According to Prime Minister Indira Gandhi the roots of nonalignment are deep in those nations which fought valiantly for their independence from imperial rule. She feels sure that the strong sense of national self-respect, independence, and "refusal to be lorded over" will continue to motivate them in the 1970s.[105]

It is not without significance that no Western statesman has ever been honored in India with the chorus of *bhai bhai* (we are brothers) with which massive Indian crowds exuberantly regaled the Communist leaders Chou En-lai and Bulganin and Khrushchev. The blatant display of greater affection for the Chinese and the Russians, with whom Indian intercourse historically had been insignificant, was not meant only to please the visiting dignitaries. The outpouring was also a form of self-therapy for soothing the rankling resentment Indians still felt against the domineering peoples of the Western world.

Pakistan, however, was not impelled by any comparable compulsion to bait the Western countries. Indeed, there was a degree of mutual respect for each other between the British and the Muslims as the successive overlords of India. When the famous Muslim delegation of 1906, led by the Aga Khan, pleaded for electoral concessions for their community because of "the position [of rulers] which they [had] occupied in India a little more than a hundred years ago," the viceroy, Lord Minto, endorsed the claim, echoing the Muslim assertion that they were "the descendants of a conquering and ruling race." At a personal level, the Indian Muslim and the Briton had got on rather well. As Leonard Mosley noted, "A British official could visit a Muslim in his home and take a meal without feeling, as in the case of a Hindu, that afterwards a whole ritual of 'purification' would have to be gone through because the house had been sullied by the presence of a foreigner."[106]

Moreover, because of Hinduism's tolerance and receptiveness, India feels no real abhorrence for Communism, but Muslim Pakistan, at least for a decade and a half, regarded Godless Communism as a real menace

THE HERITAGE

to her ideology and security, and fully agreed with Christendom that a concerted effort by all God-fearing nations was necessary to prevent it from spreading. "So far as we are concerned, I mean most people in India," said Nehru, "we are not opposed to Communism as an ideal in society. Or to Socialism; they are all the same as an ideal. It is the Communist technique of action that one rebels against."[107]

In order to create the impression in the mind of Pakistan's Western allies that Pakistan was an unreliable ally, Indians had, of course, always contended that Pakistan's alliance with the West had not resulted from any desire to fight Communism but was solely a device to strengthen Pakistan against India. Now that Pakistan aspires to good relations with Russia and China, it also suits Pakistanis to forget the tensions of the past and play down the anti-Communist phase of Pakistan's foreign policy. But the record on the subject is unambiguous.

As a matter of fact, Pakistan felt threatened by two dangers, India and Communism, and joined the Western system of defense as an insurance against both of them. No Muslim League leader had ever visited Russia or China and none had made any deep study of Communism or the socioeconomic problems of the day. Muslim politicians as well as the Western-oriented members of the services who shared power with them unquestioningly accepted the contemporary British capitalist upper-class view that Communism was an unmitigated evil. Pakistan treated the danger from India as the more imminent and serious of the two because India regarded Pakistan as a part of greater India and would have liked to end Pakistan's separate existence for all time. Pakistanis felt that no one would have come to Pakistan's aid because, not having a correct appreciation of the reasons for the partition of India, other countries would have treated the Indo-Pakistani conflict as simply a civil war.[108] However, if Russia or China had invaded Pakistan, the Western countries in their anxiety to curb the spread of Communism would have automatically come to Pakistan's assistance.

Since Pakistan's original abhorrence of Communism is becoming obscured by latter-day developments, it is necessary to describe the actual position in some detail.

The philosopher-poet Muhammad Iqbal, from whom Pakistanis draw their inspiration, in a letter published in the Urdu daily *Zamindar* of Lahore in 1923, had declared that to hold Communist views was "to place oneself outside the pale of Islam."[109] Prime Minister Liaquat Ali

50

Origins of Foreign Policies

Khan in 1950 invited the United States to encourage the idea of territorial guarantees to Pakistan and India so that they could use their resources for economic betterment in order to "keep out the potential menace of Communism."[110] During the debate on foreign policy in the National Assembly of Pakistan in March 1952, Syed Khalilur Rahman, who afterwards became a member of the Pakistani Cabinet and an ambassador of Pakistan, said that, if the government of Pakistan wanted to combat Communism, it could have no better allies than Pakistani Muslims because they were God-fearing people and had established Pakistan "to serve as a laboratory for our Islamic ideology."[111] In 1954 *Dawn* editorialized that, since the "Kremlin Bosses" did not believe in God, they could not have any morals "because 'religion' . . . is the basis of all moral codes."[112] In his famous foreign policy address to the students at Salimullah Muslim Hall, Dacca, on 9 December 1956, Prime Minister Huseyn Shaheed Suhrawardy told the audience that the cold war had resulted from international Communism's efforts to impose its ideology upon the whole world. He warned that, though Pakistan had succeeded in winning independence from Britain, she would never be able to shake off Russia's hold if she once became her satellite, and in this connection he cited the examples of East Germany, Poland, and Hungary. Lecturing in 1958 at the Pakistan Society, London, on the strategic problems of the Middle East, the commander in chief of the Pakistani army, General Muhammad Ayub Khan, observed that, though Communist Russia was talking of equal social status for everybody, her policy was in fact imperialist. She desired to expand and occupy territory to increase her influence and domain. Heaven forbid! If Communism were to come to South Asia, India might survive because of her size but Pakistan would become a mere satellite and would be just "grinded away"; this is a point which "we must all realize and a thing we must all avoid with all the power at our disposal."[113] Analyzing Pakistani foreign policy on the American Broadcasting Company's television network on 6 January 1963, Ayub said that Pakistan had joined CENTO (previously the Baghdad Pact) and SEATO to seek security from Communist countries as well as from India.

In direct contrast to their dismal view of Communism, Pakistanis looked on Christianity with considerable benignancy, making Pakistan and the West natural friends. Iqbal said the world of Islam was spiritually moving toward the West with "enormous" rapidity because "Euro-

THE HERITAGE

pean culture on its intellectual side is only a further development of some of the most important phases of the culture of Islam."[114] Ambassador Muhammad Ali Bogra, on the eve of his appointment as prime minister in 1952, stated at Washington, D.C., that Islam, Judaism, and Christianity, which believed in God, should together meet the challenge of Communism which was "raising its head like a hydra-headed monster."[115] Calling Communism a "prowling monster," *Dawn* in 1953 stressed that the core of both the Muslim and the Christian democratic societies was the pursuit of a righteous life "in the ever present consciousness of the Eternal."[116]

Undoubtedly, there are some outward similarities between orthodox Communism and Islam. Each claims to provide a complete answer to the problems of life, each divides humanity into two classes, each aims at converting all of humanity to its own way of life, and each advocates an equitable distribution of worldly goods. But the similarities are more apparent than real.

Most of all the Islamic belief in an all-powerful God makes the two systems totally irreconcilable. "Islam expects man to place his duty towards his Creator before every other consideration," says a Muslim writer, "whereas Communism denies the Creator and substitutes the State."[117] While Communism interprets human history and existence dialectically in terms of material and economic principles, observes another savant, "Islam, as a theistic religion, inculcates belief in revelation which means that it acknowledges supra-sensible and supra-rational sources of knowledge. These sources of knowledge may reveal realities which are other than those to which the senses and reason have access."[118] As a consequence, while Communism is entirely material and this worldly, Islam is deeply concerned with the more important life that lies beyond mortal existence and warns that man's status there will be determined, not by the amount of material success achieved during his sojourn on this planet, but by the degree of ethical success in preferring good over evil. According to a Pakistani writer there is also little in common between the brotherhood concepts of Islam and Communism because "under the Soviet system Man is loyal only to the totalitarian State, not to any person or any group."[119]

Islamic socialism, too, has little in common with Communist socialism. Though Iqbal once said that "Bolshevism plus God is almost identical with Islam,"[120] his considered view, as expressed in "Islam and

ORIGINS OF FOREIGN POLICIES

Bolshevism," was that Islam does not abolish capitalism, as Communism does, but prescribes laws of inheritance and *zakat* to temper the excesses of capitalism. A member of the Pakistani National Assembly, during his election campaign, averred that Islam is a "capitalistic" religion and does not bar the accumulation of wealth. His personal opinion was that religion only regulates the distribution of wealth through *zakat* and *fitra*. The third caliph, Hazrat Usman, was a wealthy man and the wife of the Prophet was herself a capitalist.[121] President Ayub Khan said that "what is basic to the establishment of Islamic Socialism is the creation of equal opportunities for all rather than equal distribution of wealth."[122]

The Pakistani author of *Islam and Communism* has portrayed Islam as the creed of the middle path between Communism and capitalism but Husein Rofe appears to be nearer the mark in his assessment that, "in questions of family ties, property and inheritance, Islam also has more in common with capitalist powers."[123] With world forces pushing for welfare states and greater socialism, it is possible, indeed probable, that Pakistan and other Muslim states ultimately will be compelled to move closer to the Communist variety of socialism. Self-justifiers then, no doubt, will plead that Islamic socialism and Communist socialism basically are alike, but this would not be true.

Be that as it may, it cannot be gainsaid that Pakistanis formulated their policy in the early years on the basis that Communism in all its aspects is incompatible with Islam. Until and including the first years of Ayub Khan's martial-law rule, recalls former Ambassador Ispahani, Pakistanis "were more anti-Communist than the United States itself. Our Foreign Ministers and other representatives . . . spoke against Communism in a language and with a vehemence which would have done credit to John Foster Dulles himself."[124]

It was only after Pakistan's alliance with the West had eroded, and Pakistan had to look around for friends wherever she could find them, that Pakistani spokesmen began to talk less of ideology and more of equal friendship with all countries. But the basic dislike for Communism has not altogether disappeared. Even after "normalizing" relations with Russia and China, President Ayub Khan referred to Communism as "a panacea for an acutely diseased society."[125] In the aftermath of President Richard Nixon's visit to Pakistan early in August 1969 and his enthusiastic reception there, the representative of the *New York Times*

The Heritage

reported in his analysis from Karachi that a factor which makes ties with the United States attractive to Pakistanis as a counterpoise to the Soviet Union and China is that "Pakistan's Islamic outlook is incompatible with the ideology of the two big Communist powers and limits her closeness to them."[126]

CHAPTER 3

Britain's "Cut and Run" Departure and Its Consequences

If the bitterness of the past could have been forgotten and a new chapter had opened with the partition of the British Indian empire into the Union of India and Pakistan, the story of Indo-Pakistani relations would have been different from what it has turned out to be. The balance-of-power situation on mainland Asia too would have been healthier. Acting together India and Pakistan could have provided that massive regional counterpoise to China which at present is lacking. Unfortunately, however, the attitude of India and Pakistan toward each other simply has been a continuation of the Hindu-Muslim tension of pre-independence days.

This tension had become specially marked in the 1920s, after the Congress party abandoned its stand of loyalty to Britain and increasingly pressed for autonomy. For their part, the Muslims anxiously pondered the question of their own place in new India where they would be a permanent minority among Hindus, with no British to redress the balance of power. "When the Indian National Congress stepped up its campaign for freedom," recalls President Ayub Khan, "we Muslims began to wonder what would happen to us. Freedom, as far as we were concerned, meant freedom from both the British and the Hindus."[1] "So long as authority was firmly established in British hands," commented the Indian Statutory Commission in its report, "and self-government was not thought of, Hindu-Moslem rivalry was confined within a narrower field. This was not merely because the presence of a neutral

THE HERITAGE

bureaucracy discouraged strife. A further reason was that there was little for members of one community to fear from the predominance of the other. . . . But the coming of the Reforms and the anticipation of what may follow them have given new point to Hindu-Moslem competition."[2] After reviewing the harrowing record of Hindu-Muslim riots during the period 1920 to 1940, Ambedkar concluded: "Placed side by side with the frantic efforts made by Mr. Gandhi to bring about Hindu-Muslim unity, the record makes most painful and heart-rending reading. It would not be much exaggeration to say that it is a record of twenty years of civil war between the Hindus and the Muslims in India, interrupted by brief intervals of armed peace."[3]

As the date of the transfer of power approached, "the war of succession" reached an unbelievable tempo and spilled over into the era of independence, resulting in one of history's biggest mass migrations and killings. The embers of hostility have remained alive and on numerous occasions they have burst into flames of rioting and on four occasions into the conflagration of war. The legacy of this bitterness is deep and difficult to eradicate but unless a cure is found it will continue to sap the vitals of both India and Pakistan, making it increasingly difficult for them to preserve the values they so staunchly profess to hold dear.

Though neither side is free from blame, there was one vital difference in their respective attitudes at the time of partition. While the Pakistanis had a comforting sense of fulfillment at having achieved Pakistan, the Indians had a needling sense of frustration at having lost what they considered a natural part of mother India. The Pakistanis, therefore, were mentally better conditioned to let bygones be bygones than the Indians who found it harder to disregard what they considered a grievous and continuing wrong within their natural portals. Rajendra Prasad, afterwards president of free India, had presciently written that partition "is bound to leave behind a bitter legacy. Its enforcement is bound to be followed by ebullient, joyous exuberance on one side and sullen, smoldering resentment on the other. It is of such stuff that fratricidal feuds and world-wide wars are made."[4] Typical of the Muslim sense of joy was Jinnah's remark as he ascended the steps of the governor general's house on 7 August 1947: "Do you know, I never expected to see Pakistan in my lifetime. We have to be very grateful to God for what we have achieved."[5]

The Congress leaders had passionately opposed the demand for Pak-

BRITAIN'S "CUT AND RUN" DEPARTURE

istan. On 5 April 1946, Nehru declared, "Congress is not going to agree to the Muslim League's demand for Pakistan under any circumstances whatsoever, even if the British Government agrees to it. Nothing on earth, not even UNO [United Nations Organization] is going to bring about Pakistan which Jinnah wants."[6] Similarly Gandhi said on 31 March 1947, "If the Congress wishes to accept partition, it will be over my dead body. So long as I am alive, I will never agree to the partition of India. Nor will I, if I can help it, allow Congress to accept it."[7]

The question naturally arises: Why did the Congress party eventually agree to partition, when its leaders had previously expressed the contrary view in such strong language? There is a twofold answer to this interesting and important query. The first is that acceptance of the proposed territorial division seemed to them, at the time, the only sure way of speedily getting the British out of the country. "Nehru and Menon told me in India in 1946," relates Louis Fischer in his introduction to Azad's book *India Wins Freedom,* that "when Mountbatten made it clear that, given partition, Britain would indeed leave, Nehru and others eagerly seized the offer lest (who knows?) it be withdrawn." Both Nehru and Menon subsequently reaffirmed this. Speaking at a luncheon in his honor at San Francisco during his tour of the United States in 1949, Nehru explained that Indian leadership had accepted partition in order not to delay freedom.[8] At Manchester, England, High Commissioner Krishna Menon also declared that India had paid the price of partition to get rid of the empire.[9]

But the wish to free themselves from British domination was not the only factor that weighed in the calculations of the Congress leading to the acceptance of Mountbatten's partition plan. Another was that "the acceptance of Pakistan would teach the Moslem League a bitter lesson. Pakistan would collapse in a short time and the provinces which had seceded from India would have to face untold difficulty and hardship."[10]

The very wording of the resolution of the All-India Congress Committee accepting partition shows that the Congress regarded the division as a transitory situation. "The picture of India we have learnt to cherish," it ran, "will remain in our minds and hearts. The All-India Congress Committee earnestly trusts that, when present passions have subsided, India's problems will be viewed in their proper perspective and the false doctrine of two nations in India will be discredited and discarded by all."[11] As could well be expected, the resolution of the Hindu Mahasabha

The Heritage

put the same thought in more militant words, "India is one and indivisible and there will never be peace unless and until the separated areas are brought back into the Indian Union and made integral parts thereof."[12]

When leaving Delhi for Karachi on 7 August 1947, to take over as governor general of Pakistan, Jinnah wished India prosperity and peace and appealed that the past be buried. "Let us start afresh as two independent sovereign states of Hindustan and Pakistan," he said. Meanwhile, Gandhi announced in Lahore that he would spend the rest of his life in Pakistan. The well-informed Indian newspaper *Amrita Bazar Patrika* reported that he would retire from public life on 15 August and had decided to settle down in Noakhali to carry on "constructive work" among Muslims in Pakistan to bring them into the Union of India and to restore Indian unity.[13]

This reluctance on the part of the Indian leadership to forget the past, accept Pakistan as a permanent fact, and base their policies on that reality, has been a serious psychological hindrance to the reconciliation of the two sister countries.

Six weeks after partition, the supreme commander, Field Marshal Claude Auchinleck, reported "his considered opinion of the situation" in India to Prime Minister Attlee in these terms: "The present India Cabinet are implacably determined to do all in their power to prevent the establishment of the Dominion of Pakistan on a firm basis. . . . The attitude of Pakistan, on the other hand, has been reasonable and cooperative throughout. This is natural in the circumstances, as Pakistan has practically nothing of her own and must obtain most of what she wants from the reserves of stores, etc., now lying in India."[14] Early the next year an American writer, as a result of an on-the-spot observation, reported: "I do not take all Pakistan statements for gospel by any means. But all the facts adduced, taken together, do seem to support the general case, which is that India wishes to destroy Pakistan as rapidly as possible so as to restore it to the dominions of Delhi."[15]

At least five Indian dailies in August 1953 reported meetings held on Akhand Bharat Day (United India Day) at which the reunification of the subcontinent had been presented as the goal of the patriots. An editorial in one of the papers, *Parbhat,* stated that "Pakistani leaders are well aware of the fact that the majority of the Indian people does not accept the partition of 1947 and will come out in the open to do away with it at the first opportunity."[16]

Britain's "Cut and Run" Departure

Eustace Seligman, chairman of the board of the American Foreign Policy Association, after a fact-finding visit to India in the summer of 1955, concluded that the real reason why India objected to the grant of military aid to Pakistan and to a plebiscite in Kashmir, which she knew would favor accession to Pakistan, was that they would both "create further obstacles to the ultimate unification of Moslem and Hindu India. . . . If one accepts the Indian point of view that partition was a mistake, which sooner or later must be corrected by the inevitable forces of history, it follows logically that everything done to strengthen Pakistan is moving backward against the stream of progress."[17]

The *Times* commented much on the same lines in two June 1956 editorials: "Indian attitude to Pakistan is still determined by the circumstances and the lasting emotions of the partition of 1947. To many Indians this was a dismemberment, which they still look back on as a tragedy. . . . It is this basic emotion which clouds Indian logic. Relations with Pakistan are not properly part of Indian foreign policy at all, for the issues that divide the two have never been seen as foreign issues." Again: "Indeed, the view is unfortunately growing that India's basic motive for refusing to risk the possible transfer of Kashmir to Pakistan is that she believes that the continued existence of the latter as an independent state is contingent upon such a transfer, and that she would prefer to see Pakistan disintegrate."[18]

Giving Indian and Pakistani views of each other, the *Round Table* perceptively stated that "to the Indian mind, with its characteristic tenacity of purpose and occasional inability to let bygones be bygones, the emergence of Pakistan is still something which ought not to have happened. . . . Broadly speaking, the average Pakistani, although he may resent what he considers the injustice of some of India's actions, displays no animosity against the fact of her existence. . . . The complaints which are made against India are directed, not against her superior wealth and power, but against her behaviour towards Pakistan over particular issues."[19]

A close observer of Indo-Pakistani affairs, Kingsley Martin, declared in 1963 that "Hindus . . . have not forgiven the Muslim League for destroying the unity of the subcontinent when the British agreed to independence." "It was deeply exasperating to most Hindus," observes another well-known writer, "that a Moslem state should be created in part of the motherland envisaged in the ancient Hindu scriptures. . . .

THE HERITAGE

India appears emotionally incapable of assuming the benign posture which might be expected of her as the overwhelmingly larger of the two neighbors." "The argument between the 'one-nation' and 'two-nation' theories," penetratingly remarks Alastair Lamb, "is really concerned with the problem whether Pakistan has a right to exist at all. . . . The 'one-nation' theory did not prevent Pakistan from coming into being — it did, however, guarantee that the relations between Pakistan and India would be subject to constant stress and strain."[20]

Mutual suspicion and stubborn ill will between the two neighbors was not the only evil legacy left behind by partition. The inordinate haste with which this stupendous task was accomplished added innumerable special problems to those which in any case would have resulted from a gigantic bisection of this nature. If the task facing India was staggering, that confronting Pakistan was crushing. Indeed, the survival of Pakistan in the face of such overwhelming odds is one of the miracles of modern times.

Most of the concrete disputes that have plagued Indo-Pakistani relations are directly traceable to the loose ends left behind by Britain's over-hasty departure from the scene. Cases in point are the disposition of the property left behind by the evacuees in either country; the equitable division of financial, military, and other assets; the innumerable boundary disputes; the Indus waters dispute; and the unsettled future of the princely states of which two — Hyderabad and Junagadh — generated much bitterness between India and Pakistan, and one — Kashmir — has already caused two wars and could lead to further conflict. In retrospect it seems amazing that no one thought of making an Indo-Pakistani treaty of friendship as a necessary part of the partition arrangements. Such a treaty could have renounced war and set up self-executing machinery for the settlement of disputes which everyone knew were bound to arise between the twin states. "Its [the Kashmir dispute's] origin," writes Ian Stephens, "can plainly be traced — like those of the Sikhs' 'war of revenge,' and of the Boundary Force's failure to cope with it — to the impetuous and (some might reckon) unprincipled haste with which the British, under Lord Mountbatten's lead, extricated themselves in August 1947 from their governing responsibilities."[21]

V. P. Menon, one of the main architects of the partition plan, was himself awed by the incongruity between the immensity of the task and the shortness of the time allowed for its completion: "Here was a task

Britain's "Cut and Run" Departure

which normally should have taken years to accomplish but which had to be compressed into the short space of a few weeks! It was a task before which anybody would have quailed, for it was one which seemed verily to tempt the Gods."[22]

Each substantial constitutional step previously had, in fact, taken the British government several years to conceive and complete. The uniformly stated reason for the slowness of the process was that the Indian problem was an inordinately complicated one and any hasty action would jeopardize the welfare of millions of people. Excluding the indeterminable length of time consumed by the behind-the-scenes preliminaries, the Government of India Act of 1935, for example, was the result of some eight years of labor — the Simon Commission was formally appointed in November 1927 and the Act received royal assent in August 1935.

Admittedly, the urgency of the situation on the eve of independence called for a quicker pace than had been followed at the time of shaping previous constitutional changes but surely the British departure could have been executed at a comparatively more reasonable speed and with much greater regard for the consequences. Mountbatten announced his plan for the transfer of power on 3 June 1947 and only seventy-two days more were allowed for winding up the extensive empire and dividing it between the two successor states.

An official with considerable experience and knowledge of Indian conditions has described the sudden decision to advance the date of transfer of power from June 1948 to August 1947 as "an utterly panic measure." The one idea of the government at home was to off-load this nasty problem before it "blew up."[23] Viscount Templewood, a former secretary of state for India, said, "I blame the British, not the two Indian Governments, for this excessive haste. . . . I shall always regard the final chapter as one of the most discreditable in the long history of our Indian connection."[24]

The present author would not go as far as Viscount Templewood and place the entire blame for the evil happenings of those shameful days on Britain because the British did not kill the Indians. The Indians themselves were at one another's throats and, therefore, must primarily carry the guilt. The fact, nevertheless, remains that constitutional responsibility, and final authority, still rested with Britain and she could very well have played a more courageous and positive role in the sorry business instead of the largely negative one of letting her warring subjects sort out things for themselves. "In defense of themselves and their own Raj," comments Penderel Moon, "the British had used unlimited force, but in defense of one Indian community against another they had appeared content to stand aside and do nothing."[25]

The sole notable effort to maintain peace in the explosive border areas between the two new Punjabs was the setting up, from 1 August 1947, of a Boundary Force. Though its commander was a British officer, the personnel was communally mixed, containing Hindus, Muslims, and Sikhs. Such a force "could not in any circumstances have controlled the riots . . . for the reason that it was composed of members of all the three communities which were trying to extricate themselves and divide themselves into separate bodies."[26] The only effective answer to the problem would have been deployment of British troops, who alone were free from the contagion of the prevailing communal virus. As a matter of fact, Mountbatten had stated at a meeting of the Defense Committee on 25 April 1947, "I bear personal responsibility for law and order. I must carry this until such time as I can hand it over to one or more responsible authorities. While I bear that responsibility I have, in the last resort, the use of British troops to fall back on."[27]

At the crucial time, however, the British troops were held back because the British government "would have incurred tremendous odium on both sides . . . the possibility of British troops undertaking the risk of incurring that odium was something which no Government could have accepted."[28] Not surprisingly, the commander of the Boundary Force reported on 25 August that "the atmosphere within his Force had become very explosive, and any small incident might provoke fighting."[29] A week later, while the holocaust was still raging at its fiercest, the Boundary Force was perforce dissolved.

Another circumstance that added to the prevailing confusion was that Radcliffe's Boundary Award,[30] though ready on 13 August, was not announced till 17 August. Even 13 August was too near the day on which power was to be transferred but the date of 17 August was far worse because at the actual time of assuming sovereignty, on 15 August, the authorities of neither dominion knew where exactly their boundaries ran. No proper arrangements for the administration of border areas could, therefore, be made in time and, when the declaration did come, millions of refugees found themselves on the wrong side of the line.

Alan Campbell-Johnson has explained why the decision was not an-

Britain's "Cut and Run" Departure

nounced immediately. "Mountbatten said that if he could exercise some discretion in the matter he would much prefer to postpone its appearance until after the Independence Day celebrations, feeling that the problem of its timing was really one of psychology, and that the controversy and grief that it was bound to arouse on both sides should not be allowed to mar Independence Day itself."[31] This greater concern for British reputation and unmarred enjoyment of Independence Day celebrations than for the countless Indian lives that were being cruelly lost is understandable as the conduct of ordinary mortals treading the path of self-interest but it scarcely justifies the noble claim, endlessly reiterated, that Britain did her utmost to transfer power in India as smoothly as the prevailing conditions permitted.[32]

In December 1946 Lord Wavell had urged the British government to formulate a definite program of withdrawal and annouce a date, not later than March 1948, by which, in the absence of agreement between the Indian parties, British power would be transferred to successor authorities. He recommended "a withdrawal by stages beginning with the Congress-controlled provinces of peninsular India and allowing for a concentration in Northern India of British administrative and military forces." Attlee, however, told the king that Wavell's plan for leaving India savored too much of a military retreat and that Wavell did not realize it was a political problem and not a military one.[33]

In the end what Attlee himself decided resembled the Wavell plan at least in one important respect, i.e., the announcement of a definite date by which power would be delivered to Indians. He and Mountbatten would have done well to have also heeded Wavell's plan for the evacuation of British power. Wavell had wisely recommended an orderly withdrawal, beginning with the comparatively peaceful south, and ending with, and paying special attention to, the highly flammable north. In his letter to the king explaining his policy, Wavell stated that he had put his plan for withdrawal to a civil and military committee "and they had been unable to recommend to me any better plan."[34] John Connell rightly points out that Wavell's plan "was an admission of the implacable facts."[35] Mosely also holds that Wavell's plan "might not only have worked, but might have saved hundreds of thousands of lives."[36] Attlee was not right in holding the view that the problem of handing over power was merely political and not military. In fact the problem was political as well as military. If Wavell's plan was simply military, Mountbatten's was only

The Heritage

political. Each was insufficient by itself. What the situation demanded was a combination of the two. Attlee also told the king that, though Wavell had done very good work till then, he (Attlee) doubted whether Wavell had "the finesse to negotiate the next steps when we must keep the two Indian parties friendly to us all the time." The same preoccupation with avoiding unpopularity for Britain, rather than with saving Indian lives, which we have already noticed, seems also to have influenced Prime Minister Attlee's judgment.

At least half a million persons were slaughtered in the carnage attending the chaotic partition and no fewer than fourteen million moved across the new international borders, leaving behind most of their belongings. Many of those who left their homelands carried harrowing memories of organized attacks by armed gangs on the wayside and of the slaughter of many of their dear ones before their very eyes. The presence of such a large number of destitute refugees in both the new dominions was bound to add to the duration and depth of bitterness already existing between their peoples. Pakistan's refugee problem was proportionately a much heavier burden than India's. The biggest migration took place across the borders of the newly divided province of the Punjab.[37] In this exchange Pakistan received some 1.7 million more persons than she sent out.[38] This meant that one person in every four or five in West Pakistan was a homeless refugee. For smaller Pakistan this created a far greater problem than the lesser number posed for the much larger India.

Moreover, India administratively was in a far better shape to face the difficult situation than Pakistan. The capital of New Delhi, with its well-organized secretariat and other buildings, and all the records remained in India's possession while Pakistan had to begin everything from scratch. At first Pakistan did not even have her own currency or postage stamps. India was further fortunate in having a better established and older political party with a large number of prestigious and experienced leaders. She was much better off, too, in regard to the number of civil servants of all ranks, doctors, lawyers, bankers, industrialists, and white-collar workers of all types. The main industrial centers of the subcontinent fell within India. Pakistan grew raw jute and cotton but the mills processing these commodities were concentrated in the Calcutta and Bombay areas; and there were no known resources of coal, oil, or iron with which Pakistan could build up her industrial strength. Mountbatten "appreciated

Britain's "Cut and Run" Departure

the many administrative difficulties, particularly those facing Pakistan, but these were inherent in the situation anyhow. 'What are we doing?' he asked. 'Administratively it is the difference between putting up a permanent building, a nissen hut or a tent. As far as Pakistan is concerned we are putting up a tent. We can do no more.' "[39]

Another serious handicap for Pakistan was her military weakness. Though Muslims traditionally had formed the backbone of the celebrated British Indian army, the organization of that army had been such that it created special problems for Pakistan when the armed forces were split into two. Muslim intransigence toward British rule in the early period, specially the role of the Muslims in the great mutiny of 1857, had left a lasting impression on the British mind. Consequently, while there were several purely Hindu, Sikh, and Gurkha regiments in the pre-partition Indian army, the British never set up any combatant all-Muslim unit. The Pakistani army had, therefore, to be formed out of "bits and pieces like a gigantic jig-saw puzzle with some of the bits missing." The men "came from different units and different areas and they had all to be welded into fighting and ancillary units, divisions, and corps."[40]

The main ports of the subcontinent, as well as the bases set up during the war for military operations against Japanese-occupied Southeast Asia, went to India. Most of the military stores, having been concentrated there, fell into Indian hands and Pakistan received only a fraction of the share allotted to her. "The position was so bad," recalled Ayub Khan, "that for the first few years we could only allow five rounds of practice ammunition to each man a year."[41] Out of forty ordnance depots, only five small retail depots were located within Pakistan; all the seventeen ordnance factories were situated in Indian territory. Pakistan "had no procurement machinery: training establishments were non-existent. In fact it seemed that only a miracle could save the Pakistan army from the fate which the enemies of the young nation were only too ready to forecast for it."[42]

While the means at the disposal of the defenders of Pakistan were almost nonexistent — making them little better than "tin soldiers," to borrow Prime Minister Liaquat Ali Khan's expression — the area to be shielded was specially difficult to protect. One of the main reasons given by the Cabinet mission in its statement of 16 May 1946 for rejecting the demand for Pakistan was that "the two sections of the suggested Pakistan contain the two most vulnerable frontiers in India and for a successful

THE HERITAGE

defense in depth the area of Pakistan would be insufficient." In a note to the viceroy, giving his opinion on the strategic implications of the setting up of an independent Pakistan, Field Marshal Auchinleck wrote that "the provision of adequate insurance in the shape of reasonably good defensive arrangements for Pakistan would be a most difficult and expensive business, and that no guarantee of success could be given."[43]

When making these appraisals, the Cabinet mission and Auchinleck were probably thinking in terms of a threat from outside the natural frontiers of the Indian subcontinent — to talk about the possibility of war between two members of the Commonwealth is something which was "not done" in the best British circles — but, since the lines dividing India and Pakistan do not contain any geographical barriers at all, the vulnerability of Pakistan to an Indian onslaught would be even greater than it would be to an attack by an outside power. East Pakistan, surrounded as she was by India on three sides, was specially hard to defend. As Mountbatten put it during the Indo-Pakistani tension over the accession of Junagadh, war between India and Pakistan "might be the end of Pakistan altogether."[44] He could very well have expanded the context and stated that war between India and Pakistan over any issue might have been the end of Pakistan. This utter disparity in physical power between Pakistan and India in the opening phase of their separation gave the latter a decisive advantage over her weaker neighbor in all their disputes.

It has been asserted in some quarters that all three principal parties concerned, the British, the Indians, and the would-be Pakistanis, were equally in favor of advancing the time of transfer of power from the original date of June 1948 to 15 August 1947.[45] However, the weight of available evidence suggests that the date was accelerated by Mountbatten under pressure from Congress leaders and that the Muslim League was for adhering to the original timetable.

The Indian nationalists wanted to get rid of the British as soon as possible not only because it would bring the desired goal of independence nearer but also because the more hurriedly Pakistan was set up the more unstable she would be and the quicker would be her predicted collapse and expected return to the waiting arms of India. A quick departure was not unwelcome to the British authorities either. Once they had decided to renounce their possession, they had no special wish to risk burning their fingers by meddling in the flaming conflict that was raging between the major communities in India. Pakistanis alone, hoping a more delib-

BRITAIN'S "CUT AND RUN" DEPARTURE

erate departure by the British would improve their chances of getting their due share of joint assets, had a vested interest in a slower transition.

Even before Mountbatten had arrived in India to take charge as viceroy, V. P. Menon had tried to sell to Patel the idea that it would be better to accept division than to gravitate toward civil war. Menon had also pointed out the advantages of accepting dominion status to start with. Patel assured him "that if power could be transferred at once on the basis of Dominion Status, he for one would use his influence to see that Congress accepted it."[46] When Menon's scheme was adopted by Mountbatten and presented by the latter to Nehru, before finalizing it, Nehru too "said that it was very desirable that there should be a transfer of power as soon as possible on a Dominion Status basis."[47] Sardar Patel, personally, also revealed in the Constituent Assembly later that when agreeing to the partition of the country one of the conditions he had laid down was that power should be transferred "in two months time."[48]

Such indications as are available from Pakistani sources, on the other hand, all point to the conclusion that the Muslim League leaders would have preferred adherence to June 1948 as the date of British departure from India. After independence Prime Minister Liaquat Ali Khan related the League's unsuccessful effort to slow up the process of partition: "We urged that it was impossible, within a short span of two months, to establish, in a country so vast and with a population so large, a Government which had neither any staff nor office, nor even paper and pencil. We were told there was no other alternative. . . . Even if the British Government were told to quit London and establish a new Government somewhere else in two months, they could not, I am sure, have succeeded even in time of peace."[49]

A close associate of Jinnah, M. A. H. Ispahani, has also written that Pakistani representatives, including Jinnah, pressed to have the date of transfer of power delayed but their efforts were of no avail.[50] Mountbatten parried Jinnah's importunities with the advice that it was in the League's interest to speed up the process and clinch the matter lest the Congress leaders, many of whom including Gandhi were opposed to partition, revoked their acceptance of Pakistan.[51]

An important question involved in the partition settlement was whether the two newly established dominions should have a common governor general or two separate governors general. Mountbatten and the British government initially assumed that Mountbatten would be accepted as

The Heritage

governor general by both India and Pakistan, but on 2 July 1947, Jinnah informed Mountbatten that he, Jinnah, would himself be the first governor general of independent Pakistan. At India's request Mountbatten, however, continued as governor general of that dominion till June 1948. Jinnah's refusal to accept Mountbatten as the joint governor general of India and Pakistan has given rise to a great deal of controversy but it is no easier to find conclusive answers in this case than it is to do so in the case of the innumerable other might-have-beens of history. The matter has been complicated further by fulsome praise showered on Mountbatten in India and intemperate criticism leveled at him in Pakistan.

Mountbatten's warm friendship with Nehru and cold relationship with Jinnah was an open secret from the very beginning. Nehru and Mountbatten first met in Singapore in March 1946, when the former went to visit the large Indian community there in his capacity as president of the Indian National Congress. Mountbatten was in Singapore as Allied supreme commander for Southeast Asia. The British military authorities in Singapore viewed Nehru's visit with disfavor because not long before he had been concerned with sabotaging the war effort under Gandhi's "quit India" movement. Also, during the war Singapore had been the main center of the Indian National Army, consisting of war prisoners of the British Indian army who had obtained their release by declaring that they would fight by the side of the Japanese to obtain India's freedom. To the British these men had been traitors; to the Congress party they were heroes. It was the intention of the local British authorities, therefore, to ignore Nehru's visit except for precautions to prevent disorder.

Mountbatten, however, took the line that Nehru's standing entitled him to be treated with appropriate respect. On arrival Mountbatten entertained him for lunch at Government House, and drove with him in an open car through lines of cheering Indians. When Nehru reached the Red Cross Indian Recreation Center he found Lady Mountbatten waiting to welcome him. Mountbatten's acumen paid off: "Nehru had been so surprised and delighted by the considerate and gentlemanly way in which he had been received that he decided to respond in kind. At Mountbatten's request he readily abandoned a plan to place a wreath on the Indian National Army monument."[52] When Mountbatten was appointed viceroy, Lord Ismay "felt there was a danger of an issue being made of Mountbatten's selection as a pro-Hindu and anti-Moslem League appointment."[53]

Britain's "Cut and Run" Departure

While Nehru and Mountbatten hit it off well, the reverse was the case with Jinnah and Mountbatten. After the first Jinnah-Mountbatten encounter, Mountbatten's reaction was, "My God, he was cold. It took most of the interview to unfreeze him."[54] And of course matters could not have improved by Mountbatten's strong personal preference for a united India.

Though Mountbatten's special relationship with the Congress leadership, especially with Nehru, is undeniable, it is relevant also to refer to some other facts and circumstances which Pakistanis are apt to forget. It is interesting to ponder, first, whether this close friendship with the Congress leaders was not one of the factors which enabled Mountbatten to sell the idea of Pakistan to the Indians who had been totally opposed to it till then. There seems justification for Mosley's lively assessment that "the Viceroy, in persuading Nehru [to accept partition], had performed the confidence trick of the century."[55] It follows that Pakistanis have at least one very good reason to be thankful to Mountbatten. The Indians may have had mental reservations regarding the future of Pakistan but that Mountbatten did succeed in making them accept Pakistan, at least for the time being, was in itself a fact of far-reaching importance.

There are indications, moreover, that Mountbatten was not averse, at first, to Kashmir going to Pakistan. It has been suggested by some Indian and Soviet writers that, on account of its strategic location, Britain and the United States wanted to turn Kashmir into an "imperialist" base and that it would have facilitated their designs if Kashmir had gone to Pakistan which was more likely to toe the Western line.

Giving his reasons for the alleged British and American partiality toward Pakistan, in the opening phase of the Kashmir debate in the Security Council, a former Indian Foreign Office official, who had been closely connected with the Kashmir question, stated that "the U.K., whose lead was generally accepted by most members, considered Kashmir of vital interest to the Western world. . . . Such an important listening post so close to the soft belly of the Soviet Union would be lost if the Indian case was accepted; for India talked about keeping away from military blocs and pursuing a policy of nonalignment. Kashmir, if included in Pakistan, would be a different matter, for a large number of British civil and military officers had already opted for Pakistan which still offered a willing and valuable base for protecting British oil and other interests in West Asia."[56] A joint study by several Russian specialists on South Asia expresses an identical view: "British imperialists attached exceptional importance to this State [Kashmir] as a strategic base near the frontiers of the Soviet Union and China, and gave their backing to Pakistan's claims to Kashmir, as Pakistan was more dependent upon them."[57]

During a visit to Kashmir in June 1947, Mountbatten urged the maharaja and his prime minister not to make any declaration of independence, but to ascertain the will of the people of Kashmir as soon as possible, and announce their intention by 14 August to join India or Pakistan. He told them that the Indian States Department was prepared to give an assurance that if Kashmir went to Pakistan this would not be regarded as an unfriendly act by India. This advice was given privately during various car drives and it was Mountbatten's intention to repeat it at a formal meeting with others present when minutes could be kept. The maharaja artfully suggested that such a meeting should take place on the last day of Mountbatten's visit since this would allow him the maximum time for making up his mind, but when the moment arrived the maharaja excused himself with the message that he was in bed with colic.[58] According to the Soviet scholars mentioned above, Mountbatten's advice to the maharaja, to ascertain the will of his people, "was tantamount to a direct demand to join Pakistan, since three-quarters of the population of Kashmir were Muslims, who, in Mountbatten's view, could want nothing more than to live in a Muslim state."

A few days after independence, but before the Kashmir dispute erupted openly, when Lord Ismay visited Kashmir to convalesce after an illness, Mountbatten asked him to take the opportunity of seeing the maharaja and advising him to hold a referendum at once on the question whether his people wished to accede to India or to Pakistan. "His Highness himself was a Hindu, but ninety per cent of his subjects were Moslems," comments Ismay, "and there was little doubt as to which way the referendum would go." Having foiled Mountbatten not long before, the maharaja was not likely to be pinned down by a lesser personality. Whenever Ismay tried to talk serious business, the maharaja abruptly left him for one of his other guests. "You may take a horse to the water," ruefully concluded Ismay, "but you cannot make him drink."[59] Another source, on the authority of Wilfred Webb, who was the British resident in Kashmir at the time of the Mountbatten visit, goes further than Campbell-Johnson and Ismay and reveals that the viceroy "had advised the Maharaja in no uncertain terms that in his own interests and that of the State

Britain's "Cut and Run" Departure

he should lose no time after August 15th in acceding to Pakistan."[60] Mehr Chand Mahajan, who was temporarily released from the office of judge of the East Punjab High Court to serve as chief minister of Kashmir during the crucial period 15 October 1947 to 5 March 1948, for "strategic and tactical reasons" called on Mountbatten before proceeding to Srinagar and from an hour's talk with him inferred that Mountbatten "felt that there was no option for the Maharaja but to accede to Pakistan in view of the geographical position of the State."[61] If there is any truth in all these assertions, it follows that Pakistan did not improve her chances of getting Kashmir by not agreeing to have Mountbatten as her governor general.

The same considerations would apply to the division of assets and the settlement of other disputes.[62] When Mountbatten asked Jinnah what his decision to become governor general would cost the new state of his creation, the latter replied it might cost several crores of rupees in assets. Mountbatten said, "It may well cost you the whole of your assets and the future of Pakistan."[63]

In fairness to Mountbatten, it must be pointed out that he opposed Nehru and Patel when they decided to withhold fifty-five crores of rupees still due to Pakistan out of the cash balances of the government of India at the time of partition. The stated reason was that the "money might be utilized for warlike operations against India." India, ultimately, handed over the amount under the pressure of Gandhi's fast "to remove ill will, prejudice, and passion which poisoned the relations between India and Pakistan."[64] Before commencing the fast Gandhi had seen Mountbatten and asked "for a frank opinion about India's refusal to pay to Pakistan the fifty-five crores from the cash balances, which Mountbatten did not hesitate to give him, saying that he considered the step to be most unstatesmanlike and unwise."[65]

Mountbatten was also decidedly unhappy at the prospect of a war between India and Pakistan. When Patel called for a "show of strength" in respect of Junagadh, Mountbatten urged that the question be referred to the United Nations but Patel and Nehru did not agree. He also emphasized that though a war between India and Pakistan might be the end of Pakistan altogether, "it would also be the end of India for at least a generation to come. He was anxious that India should not lose her great international position by taking incorrect action."[66] When open war between India and Pakistan over Kashmir seemed imminent Mountbatten

THE HERITAGE

again proposed that the dispute be taken to the United Nations. This time he was more successful: "Nehru ultimately accepted the suggestion, though some of his colleagues had misgivings about the wisdom of the step."[67] It is possible that Mountbatten's primary concern in preventing war was to protect not Pakistan but the good name of the family of nations, the British Commonwealth, of which India and Pakistan were members and Britain the proud founder. But the fact remains that his influence may well have saved Pakistan from possible disaster.

Yet another occasion on which Mountbatten intervened to alleviate Pakistan's immediate suffering was in May 1948, when India cut off the vital supply of canal waters which were the lifeblood of West Pakistan. Finance Minister Ghulam Muhammad, who had come to Delhi as the head of the Pakistani delegation, appealed to Mountbatten "who immediately telephoned Pandit Nehru, and expressed his disgust that miserable peasants and refugees were being made to suffer while such a matter was under negotiation."[68] The water supply was released under an interim arrangement.

In the light of the considerations mentioned above Jinnah's decision to reject Mountbatten as governor general of Pakistan is indefensible in terms purely of Kashmir, the division of assets, and other disputes with India. But on a broader and long-term view its wisdom cannot possibly be questioned. We must bear in mind that Mountbatten, Prime Minister Attlee, and all the other British statesmen were extremely unhappy that the unity of India, which they regarded as the proudest product of their glorious regime, had been destroyed by the creation of Pakistan. In his directive to Mountbatten Attlee had said, "It is the definite objective of His Majesty's Government to obtain a unitary Government for British India and the Indian States . . . and you should do the utmost in your power to persuade all Parties to work together to this end."[69] Mountbatten personally also favored united India. He made no secret of this preference, and did his utmost to achieve it.[70] Though under pressure from the Muslim League he reluctantly agreed to the division of India to avoid prolonged civil war, he never changed his opinion on the subject. In his broadcast on 3 June 1947 announcing the partition plan he reiterated, "Nothing I have seen or heard in the past few weeks has shaken my firm opinion that with a reasonable measure of goodwill between the communities a unified India would be by far the best solution of the problem." After his retirement from India he said in an address

Britain's "Cut and Run" Departure

to the East India Association at London that his opinion had not changed that the right answer to the problem of India would have been to have kept a united India.

During the Indian Independence Bill debate in the House of Commons Attlee had declared, "For myself, I earnestly hope that this severance may not endure and that the two new Dominions which we now propose to set up may, in course of time, come together again to form one great member State of the British Commonwealth of Nations."[71] Opposition leader Harold Macmillan echoed these sentiments: "We must hope with the Prime Minister that in this partition are also the seeds of some form of future unity."[72] In the Upper House, the secretary of state for India, Lord Listowel, similarly said, "It is greatly to be hoped that, when the disadvantages of separation have become apparent in the light of experience, the two Dominions will freely decide to reunite in a single Indian Dominion, which might achieve that position among the nations of the world to which its territories and resources would entitle it."[73]

With British political leaders openly talking about the desirability of the reunion of India and Pakistan, and the Indians doing everything in their power to bring this about, the uppermost thought in the mind of the Muslim League leaders naturally was how to give their new country a separate identity. They could not very well be expected to think about Kashmir, and their share of assets, when their very existence seemed threatened by a combination of such formidable forces. Under a joint governor general Pakistan would have been a mere appendage to India and, who knows, the weight of problems, the death — a year later — of the already ailing Jinnah, and other unforeseen troubles and insidious pressures might have proved too much for the fragile state. Mountbatten may have been averse to the spectacle of open war between the two new members of the Commonwealth, but there was no reason why he should have hesitated to use his position and powers of persuasion to undo partition, which the British government of the day openly declared was a mistake and frankly hoped would be rectified by the pressure of its own disastrous consequences.

As a matter of fact in a book based on the Mountbatten papers, it has been subsequently revealed that his mind was working toward precisely such an objective. He did not accept partition as the final word and secretly hoped to recapture the lost ground after passions had cooled down. His instruments for achieving the desired result were to be a common

THE HERITAGE

governor generalship for the initial period and the extension of the life of the Joint Defense Council for at least one year beyond the originally fixed date of 1 April 1948. Jinnah prevented the first of these from coming into being and both dominions refused the continuation of the latter. "It was in my mind," wrote Mountbatten to the king about the Joint Defense Council, "that its scope might indeed expand, to cover financial and economic matters also, and eventually External Affairs and Communications, which would mean a 'virtual accession' of the two Dominions to one another, on the same basis as the States."[74]

It needs little imagination to realize that such an "accession" by unequals to each other would have spelled the end of Pakistan as a sovereign state and assured her absorption by India. Precisely this became the fate of all the princely states which had been initially persuaded to surrender to the government of India only the three specified subjects of defense, external affairs, and communications, with unequivocal assurances that the terms of the instrument of accession would not be varied without a ruler's consent and his sovereignty in all other matters would continue intact.[75] A completely separate existence from the very beginning, and a successful fight against the dreadful forces threatening to destroy their newly found independence, undoubtedly added to the feeling of confidence and self-reliance among the people of Pakistan and cannot but have strengthened their will and capacity to survive as a sovereign nation.

Such, then, was the manner in which the partition of the great Indo-Pakistan subcontinent was executed. It was, in the words of the *Manchester Guardian* a "cut and run" operation on the part of the British government. Considering the record of bitter animosity between Hindus and Muslims, the relations between India and Pakistan would have got off to a poor start in any case. The manner in which they were separated made the situation many times worse, with far-reaching consequences not only for the two countries themselves but also for the world beyond. Not surprisingly, the disorderly division left behind innumerable unsettled questions, some of which took on the proportions of major international disputes, providing an almost interminable supply of fuel to keep the fires of hate burning.

Having been born frail, India and Pakistan have both remained weak. They have expended on destructive implements of war treasure badly needed for relieving the miserable plight of their teeming millions. They

Britain's "Cut and Run" Departure

have subjected their own peoples to an unceasing threat of war, and four actual wars. Beyond their own borders they have failed to achieve the prestige to which they are rightfully entitled as the largest newly independent countries in the world, boasting a highly civilized past. Their mutual confrontations have also more than once threatened world peace by involving the great powers in Indo-Pakistani disputes.

Pakistan's extreme preoccupation with the problems of sheer survival was sufficient by itself to have greatly impaired her capacity to project herself in the world outside. But the struggle to keep alive was not the only disabling factor. There were other handicaps too.

Jawaharlal Nehru, since the inauguration of the interim government in September 1946, had held the portfolio of external affairs and had begun to advance the interests of India long before it was even decided whether there would ever be such a country as Pakistan. Constitutionally India became a sovereign state on 15 August 1947 but Nehru had been permitted by the British government to function as if he were the foreign minister of an independent country from the day he became head of the interim government. "We shall take full part in international conferences," he had said, "as a free nation with our own policy and not merely as a satellite of another nation."[76] British India had been an original signatory to the Charter of the United Nations at San Francisco and new India was allowed to continue this membership while Pakistan had to apply for membership as a new entrant to the world organization. Nehru sent an Indian delegation to the fall 1946 session of the General Assembly under the leadership of his sister, Vijaya Lakshmi Pandit. Pakistan could not show up in the United Nations arena till a year afterwards. Membership in all other international organizations also automatically devolved on India; Pakistan had to apply for membership everywhere.

Indian ambassadors to the more important countries were accredited even before India legally became independent. The Indian high commissioner in the United Kingdom, hitherto principally concerned with trade and administrative matters, assumed full diplomatic functions in September 1946. Asaf Ali presented his letter of credence to Truman in Washington on 1 March 1947, and Mrs. Pandit to Shvernik in Moscow on 13 August 1947. For Pakistan Habib Rahimtoola did not arrive in London as high commissioner till the middle of August 1947; M. A. H. Ispahani presented his credentials in Washington on 8 October 1947, Shoib

The Heritage

Qureshi in Moscow on 31 December 1949, and General Raza in Peking on 12 November 1951.

When the date of the constitutional independence of India and Pakistan (15 August 1947) arrived the Indian Ministry for External Affairs simply continued to function as it had already done for a year. Nehru literally kept sitting in the same chair as foreign minister which he had occupied as vice-president of the viceroy's Council and all the existing diplomatic representatives, who had been formally selected by the then united India but in fact by Nehru for the new Indian Union, continued to function for India. All the premises of the diplomatic and trade missions abroad were also taken over by India as running concerns. Pakistan had to buy or build new embassies and offices everywhere and to recruit personnel in a hurry to man them as best as she could. Among other advantages this substantial head start enabled India further to exploit the already existing conception of herself as one of the world's new leading powers and that of Pakistan as an unnatural temporary growth in the international field.

Also, it was during the period, when it was still to be decided whether there ever would be a country called Pakistan, that India convened an Asian Relations Conference in which twenty-five Asian countries participated.[77] Though nominally the gathering was unofficial, both delegates and observers included a high proportion of ministers or persons holding responsible positions in their respective governments.[78]

It was not till August 1947 that the Pakistani Foreign Office at Karachi was set up amid utter turmoil with practically no available resources in men and material. "I shall never forget," recalls Vincent Sheean, "that when I first visited the new establishment . . . there was only one typewriter in the whole Foreign Office."[79] Pakistan did not have a foreign minister till December 1947. Till then Prime Minister Liaquat Ali Khan had carried the responsibility for external affairs, in addition to his burdens as prime minister and minister for defense. The Foreign Office itself began with a handful of officers collected in haste from heterogeneous sources. The first batch of young recruits to the Foreign Service was selected by competitive examination in 1948 but these young entrants, numbering thirteen, required training and after that they could join only as third secretaries. Several years of experience were necessary before they could be expected to fill senior positions. It was therefore decided to recruit eighty-five members for the new Foreign Service from

Britain's "Cut and Run" Departure

different age groups on an ad hoc basis but the vacancies were not advertised till November 1948 and it took considerable time to complete the recruitment and basic training before the candidates could be effectively used. Also, owing to the general shortage of qualified persons in the country those selected were of uneven quality.

While the wherewithal was woefully insufficient, the task to be performed by Pakistan was uniquely formidable. The country was born in a completely unsympathetic world. Gandhi and Nehru were world figures, admired and respected for their stout and prolonged fight against British imperialism. The deep differences between Hindus and Muslims being a phenomenon peculiar to India, its significance was not fully appreciated by others. As we have already noticed, even the British, who knew the conditions firsthand, and fellow Muslims of other lands, who the Indian Muslims had hoped would be sympathetic toward the struggle for Pakistan, did not accept the rationale for setting up a separate Muslim homeland in the South Asian subcontinent. Not surprisingly, "in the first appraisal of her position among the community of self-governing nations, Pakistan could find no single country which could be counted as an unfailing friend and ally willing to lend aid and comfort in time of need."[80]

CHAPTER 4

Jawaharlal Nehru: The Personal Factor

Jawaharlal Nehru claimed that India's policy of nonalignment mirrored India's thought and would have been basically the same if some group other than the Congress party had come into power.[1] It is true that Hinduism's tradition of accepting different cultures, religions, and systems of thought within its ample folds makes India averse to taking a hard line on any controversial issue and that an uncommitted foreign policy would, therefore, seem to be her logical preference. Nevertheless, an individual's translation of this broad concept into practice would necessarily be influenced by his own reading of the world situation and his personal predilections, specially if that individual happened to be Jawaharlal Nehru, a person given to intense emotional commitment to causes nearest his heart,[2] and able to impose his will on his countrymen. Referring to Nehru's domination in the field of Indian foreign policy his biographer, Michael Brecher, says: "So overwhelming is his influence that India's policy has come to mean in the minds of people everywhere the personal policy of Pandit Nehru. . . . [H]e has impressed his personality and his views with such overpowering effect that foreign policy may properly be termed a private monopoly."[3]

In this connection it is interesting to ponder the hypothetical question: What direction would Indian foreign policy have taken if, instead of Nehru, it had been determined by either of his two most senior colleagues, Deputy Prime Minister Sardar Patel or Governor General Rajagopalachari? It would seem that the Indian approach to at least three extremely important problems could very well have been different, with far-reaching effects on the political kaleidoscope of Asia and the world. These questions, which will be considered shortly, were Indo-Pakistani relations in general, the Kashmir dispute in particular, and India's stance in the East-West cold war.

Be that as it may, the stars had decreed that for seventeen years after India and Pakistan became independent Jawaharlal Nehru should direct India's external affairs as he thought best. And the basic philosophy of India's relations with other countries today, by and large, remains the same as he left it upon his death. His daughter and close collaborator, Prime Minister Indira Gandhi, has unequivocally declared that India's "consistent and steadfast" adherence to the policy of nonalignment is "absolutely non-negotiable" and India would continue to follow that policy as long as she (Mrs. Gandhi) has anything to do with the government of the country.[4] If Nehru was indeed the personification of Indian foreign policy, an examination of the important facets of his prejudices, philosophy, and personality becomes an essential prerequisite for a proper comprehension of that policy.

There can be no doubt that Nehru is assured of a permanent place in history, for he was an outstanding figure who left his mark on his time. His contribution to India's freedom was next only to Gandhi's. What Gandhi was to the masses, Nehru was to the intelligentsia of India. His renunciation of a life of luxury to which he was born and his internment in British prisons for some nine years are ample proof of his sincerity of purpose and devotion to his motherland. His writings are expressions of an attractive, sensitive, and highly cultivated mind, often at odds with the coarser realities of life that surrounded him. His devotion to peace and abhorrence of bigotry were undoubtedly genuine. But his temperament was more that of a thinker and a writer than that of a man of action. His analysis of problems was persuasive and his aims impressive but, despite his almost complete control over the government and people of his country, he carried few of his schemes to meaningful completion.[5] As Louis Fischer has said, "The fight for freedom, under moral leadership, breeds giants. The task of governing, through compromise, cuts them down to normal size."[6]

Nehru called idealism the realism of tomorrow and ridiculed the "practical person, the realist" because such a person "looks at the tip of his nose and sees little beyond; the result is that he is stumbling all the

THE HERITAGE

time."[7] The Indian leader seemed to overlook the simple fact that unless idealism is coupled with realism it remains a barren dream.

The "supreme question" of the day, in Nehru's view, was how to avoid war.[8] Since fear was the basic cause of wars, the problem became one of lessening, and ultimately putting an end to, fear.[9] But the only means conjured up by him for eradicating fear was the creation of the right psychological climate. As will be explained in a later chapter, *panchsheel*, which Nehru regarded as India's special contribution toward creating the desired atmosphere, demanded nothing from its converts beyond a verbal affirmation of five well-worn clichés.

His invitation to Pakistan, in November 1949, to subscribe to a nowar declaration jointly with India is another case in point. Liaquat Ali Khan welcomed the suggestion but argued that "it is essential that there should be tangible action to match the spirit of the declaration, since peoples and Governments are judged by their actions rather than by their words." This action, Liaquat thought, should take the form of an agreed procedure and timetable for the peaceful settlement of Indo-Pakistani disputes.[10] He pointed out that India's and Pakistan's membership in the United Nations itself constituted a declaration that they had renounced force as a method of settling disputes, and a bare no-war declaration would add nothing to that commitment. After a lengthy correspondence the idea fell through because Liaquat's proposal, that a self-executing machinery for the settlement of disputes should form a part of the proposed agreement, was not acceptable to Nehru.[11] The Indian prime minister contended that a simple declaration such as that proposed by him would "itself be a great service to our two countries and the world, because it will remove the fear of war from the minds of our peoples."

Nehru, in fact, had a curious aversion to committing himself to tangible action of any kind that would put into practice the broad principles he so passionately preached. At both the international conferences he called at New Delhi in the early years of his assumption of office, he recognized the desirability of setting up a secretariat to facilitate continued consultation. In the course of his inaugural address at the Asian Relations Conference (23 March 1947) he expressed the hope that a permanent Asian Institute would be set up for the study of Asian problems; also, a school of Asian Studies. At the Conference on Indonesia (20 January 1949) he stated that one of the tasks before the meeting was to devise machinery by which governments represented at the meeting could keep in touch with one another. No standing structural arrangement, however, emerged from either gathering.

In the middle of the 1950s, when Nehru was offering "collective peace," Peking suggested the making of a "collective peace pact" but Nehru shied away from any such tie.[12] The upshot was, as one critic said at the time, that India "is not even committed to those States which are equally uncommitted."[13] At the Asian-African Conference at Bandung (April 1955) he berated countries which had joined stronger powers in arrangements for collective defense. Representatives of some of those countries pleaded that their countries being small could not stand alone. One of them pointedly asked whether India would collect them under her wing, and give them protection, but the Indian leader declined to extend any such hope.[14] His concern impressively encompassed all the main problems currently facing the family of man but he failed to chalk out any effective plan for mounting a cooperative effort to tackle any of those problems. His diplomatic methodology seems to have been guided by his own enigmatic maxim that "the most intimate ties are ties which are no ties."[15] As concluded by the author of *Jawaharlal Nehru's World View,* "a major weakness of Nehru's theory is that it does not provide us with sufficient guidance as to how we should go about bringing into being the attitudes, institutions, and methods he advocates."[16]

More than any other man in India Nehru had the power to soften the hatred between Pakistan and India, for among the peoples of the two sister countries, who had lived in the same villages and towns for centuries, the relationship is not one of pure hatred but one of love-hate and it should have been the task of statesmanship to strive to dispel the causes that generate bitterness and encourage the forces that would bring the latent feelings of affection to the surface. Though compelled at times by considerations of public opinion and national interest to resort to armed action, Nehru by temperament was opposed to violence and war. His refusal to go over the brink in the Indo-Pakistani crises of 1950 and 1951, and his acceptance of Mountbatten's advice in 1948 to take the Kashmir dispute to the United Nations, instead of resorting to an all-out war over it with Pakistan, may very well have saved Pakistan from an early collapse. But if his pacifism prevented him from resorting to war as a means of uniting India and Pakistan, another equally strong trait in his character rendered him incapable of accepting Pakistan as a settled fact and putting Indo-Pakistani relations on a neighborly footing on that

The Heritage

basis. This other trait was his complete attachment to the principle of secularism in affairs of state which made it impossible for him ever to become reconciled to a political division based on religion.

Other Nehru predilections were belief in his own infallibility, making it hard for anyone to negotiate any concrete dispute with him on a give-and-take basis;[17] his emotional attachment to Kashmir, and to China, which was responsible for his two biggest mistakes; and his burning conviction that capitalism is the mother of imperialism, which made him wary of Western overtures and inevitably tilted him toward Communism, the sworn enemy of capitalism, and toward the Soviet Union, the first major champion of that system. Since Pakistan was openly anti-Communist, at least till the early 1960s, she was drawn into the Western system of defense alliances while India in unison with the Soviet Union and China proclaimed the five principles of *panchsheel* as the real path to universal peace. With China, in particular, Nehru strove to build up a special relationship, symbolized by the Indian chant of *Hindi-Chini bhai, bhai* (Indians and Chinese are brothers), till the shock of the Sino-Indian border clash of October 1962 shattered the existing pattern and led to new power alignments.

Nehru's Secularism

"Several times Nehru told me," relates Chester Bowles, "that if he were to die today this [creation of a secular state] would be his most enduring accomplishment."[18] Though the India Nehru left behind is more secular in theory than in fact,[19] his remark to Bowles does show that personally he rated the setting up of a secular state in India as his greatest achievement. By the same token, he could not but regard the establishment of an openly religious state next door as the biggest tragedy, more specially as he felt that the territory it comprised was a natural part of the secular India of his conception.

Nehru was quite frankly an agnostic. "Religion, as I saw it practiced, and accepted even by thinking minds," he wrote, "whether it was Hinduism or Islam or Buddhism or Christianity, did not attract me. It seemed to be closely associated with superstitious practices and dogmatic beliefs, and, behind it lay a method of approach to life's problems which was certainly not that of science."[20] Again: "The final mysteries still remain far beyond the reach of the human mind and are likely to continue to remain so. . . . It is therefore with the temper and approach of science, allied to philosophy, and with reverence for all that lies beyond, that we must face life."[21] "To talk of a 'Muslim nation,' therefore, means . . . just nothing at all except an emotional state of mind and a conscious or unconscious desire not to face realities, especially economic realities."[22] Consequently, even if "some division of India is enforced with some tenuous bond joining the divided parts . . . I am convinced that the basic feeling of unity and world developments will later bring the divided parts nearer to each other and result in a real unity."[23]

Though Nehru was as critical of Hindu nationalism as he was of Muslim nationalism, it must be pointed out that his own make-up was fundamentally Hindu. Hinduism permits her children to think as freely as they wish and Nehru's agnosticism by no means took him outside the pale of the religion into which he had been born. He himself has explained this in his autobiography: "One may even be a professing atheist — as the old Hindu philosopher, Charvaka, was — and yet no one dare say that he has ceased to be a Hindu. Hinduism clings on to its children, almost despite them. A Brahman I was born, and a Brahman I seem to remain whatever I might say or do in regard to religion or social custom."[24]

In a long passage in his autobiography glorifying India's past culture,[25] Nehru does not spare one word for the more than a thousand years of Muslim connection with India. "Throughout her long journey," he writes, "she [India] had clung to her immemorial culture, drawn strength and vitality from it, and shared it with others lands. . . . [S]he had never wholly forgotten the inspiration that some of the wisest of her children, at the dawn of history, had given her in the Upanishads." Even "the principles of socialism, of co-operation, and service to the community for the common good . . . [are] not so unlike the old Brahman ideal of service."

"There are some inherent contradictions in Nehru's vision of national unity," comments Dietnam Rothermund. "He has not based his definition of this unity on purely economic terms, and he often referred to cultural values which are capable of arousing communal feelings."[26] "Behind me lie, somewhere in the subconscious," confessed Nehru, "racial memories of a hundred, or whatever the number may be, generations of Brahmans."[27]

If everyone in India had shared Nehru's views on the separation of politics from religion all might have been well. By far the greater ma-

The Heritage

jority of Indians, however, do believe in organized religion and frankly base their politics on the faith to which they subscribe. The feelings of the Indian Muslims on the subject have already been described. Their Hindu compatriots were no different.

Gandhi, Nehru's own mentor, vehemently averred, "I can say without the slightest hesitation and yet in all humility that those who say that religion has nothing to do with politics do not know what religion means. . . . Thus it will be seen that for me there are no politics devoid of religion. They subserve religion. Politics bereft of religion are a death-adder because they kill the soul."[28] Also, "the politician in me has never dominated a single decision of mine, and if I take part in politics, it is only because politics encircle us today like the coils of a snake, from which one cannot go out, no matter how much one tries. In order to wrestle with this snake, I have been experimenting with myself and my friends in politics by introducing religion into politics."[29] And he declared, "Every fibre of my being is Hindu."[30]

As a matter of fact the secret of Gandhi's hold over the masses, and therefore the main reason for his success as a political leader, was his religious appeal. "When the Mahatma speaks," wrote Subhas Bose, "he does so in a language that they [the people] comprehend, not in the language of Herbert Spencer and Edmund Burke . . . but in that of the *Bhagavad-Gita* and the *Ramayana*. When he talks to them about Swaraj, he does not dilate on the virtues of provincial autonomy or federation, he reminds them of the glories of *Rama-rajya* (the kingdom of King Rama of old) and they understand."[31] Nehru, similarly, said, "I used to be troubled sometimes at the growth of this religious element in our politics, both on the Hindu and the Muslim side. . . . Even some of Gandhiji's phrases sometimes jarred upon me — thus his frequent reference to *Rama Raj* as a golden age which was to return. . . . Gandhiji used the words because they were well known and understood by the masses. He had an amazing knack of reaching the heart of the people."[32]

Orthodox Hindus, themselves devoted to their own particular faith, were psychologically more conditioned to accept the concept of religious nationalism than was the agnostic Nehru. The *National Paper*, organ of the Hindu Mela, which met fourteen times from 1867 to 1880, asserted that "Hindus . . . certainly form a nation by themselves."[33] In 1924, Lala Lajpat Rai, a highly respected Hindu leader and one-time president of the Indian National Congress, despairing of Hindu-Muslim unity, proposed a division of India on religious lines. "Under my scheme," he said, "the Muslims will have four Muslim states: (1) The Pathan province or the North-West Frontier; (2) Western Punjab; (3) Sind; and (4) Eastern Bengal. . . . It means a clear partition of India into a Muslim India and a non-Muslim India."[34] V. D. Savarkar, president of the Hindu Maha Sabha, stated that "the Hindu Maha Sabha is not a Hindu Mission . . . but a Hindu-National Maha Sabha . . . pledged to protect and promote all that contributes to the freedom, strength and glory of the Hindu Nation."[35] From the belief that the Hindus formed a nation, it was a logical step to concede that the Muslims formed another nation. "It is safer," said Savarkar, "to diagnose and treat deep-seated disease than to ignore it. Let us bravely face unpleasant facts as they are. India cannot be assumed today to be a unitarian and homogeneous nation, but on the contrary these are two nations in the main, the Hindus and the Muslims in India."[36]

Significantly enough, the first to accept the idea of Pakistan, even among the ranks of the Congress leaders, were the more orthodox Hindus. Soon after the failure of the Cripps mission, Rajagopalachari openly began to say that if the Congress would accept the demand of the Muslim League, the main obstacle to India's independence would be removed. In April 1942, he got a resolution passed by the Madras Legislature Congress party that "to sacrifice the chances of the formation of a National Government at this grave crisis for the doubtful advantage of maintaining a controversy over the unity of India is a most unwise policy and that it has become necessary to choose the lesser evil and acknowledge the Muslim League's claim for separation."[37] When reprimanded for sponsoring a resolution contrary to the declared policy of the Congress party without consulting his colleagues, Rajagopalachari refused to withdraw the resolution and resigned from the Working Committee of the Congress.

Under Rajagopalachari's persuasion, Gandhi in September 1944 invited Jinnah to discuss the question of a political settlement on the basis of certain proposals drafted by Rajagopalachari and known as the "Rajaji Formula." This formula envisaged the formation of a provisional interim government with the promise of a separate Muslim state after the war, should the inhabitants of contiguous Muslim majority areas in the northwest and east of India favor it in a plebiscite. The Gandhi-Jinnah talks failed principally because Gandhi insisted that the separate Muslim state should come into existence after India had won freedom while Jinnah wanted this issue decided immediately, and also because Gandhi wished that a treaty of separation should provide for a common administration of foreign affairs, defense, internal communications, customs, commerce, and the like, which to Jinnah did not appear to be independence but merely a form of provincial autonomy.

Nearer the time of transfer of power the first front rank leader to accept Pakistan was Sardar Patel, another staunch Hindu. Menon has revealed that he obtained Patel's consent to a division of British India in December 1946 or January 1947.[38] Azad has also written, "It must be placed on record that the man in India who first fell for Lord Mountbatten's idea [of partition] was Sardar Patel."[39] Patel said that, like it or not, there were two nations in India.[40] Azad suggests that Patel also influenced Gandhi to accept Pakistan.[41] In a conversation with Mosley in 1960 Nehru said if Gandhi had told them not to accept partition, "we would have gone on fighting, and waiting. . . . We expected that partition would be temporary, that Pakistan was bound to come back to us."[42]

Thus while Gandhi,[43] Rajaji, and other Hindu leaders showed an inclination to solve the Hindu-Muslim problem by accepting Muslim nationalism as a fact of Indian political life, Nehru never budged from his strong belief in the separation of nationalism from religion.[44] On two crucial occasions he definitely frustrated opportunities for Hindu-Muslim conciliation which involved concessions to Muslim susceptibilities. These were his successful opposition to a Congress-League coalition in forming provincial governments following the 1937 elections, and his sabotage of the Cabinet mission proposals.

The Muslim League Manifesto for the 1937 elections and Jinnah's campaign speeches clearly expressed a willingness to cooperate with the Congress. "Ours is not a hostile movement," declared Jinnah. "Ours is a movement which carries the olive branch to every sister community. We are willing to co-operate, we are willing to coalesce with any group or groups, provided their ideals, their objects are approximately the same as ours."[45] Also, "there is no difference between the ideals of the Moslem League and of the Congress, the idea being complete freedom for India."[46]

After the election the question of a Congress-League coalition in the United Provinces was specially crucial, for it was there that the League had scored its best success in the elections. The local League leaders were willing to cooperate with the Congress and one of them, Chaudhuri Khaliquzzaman, went to see Jawaharlal Nehru to impress upon him the necessity for cooperation between the Congress and the Muslim League in the Legislative Assembly, which, in Khaliquzzaman's opinion would have once and for all put an end to British interference in Indian affairs and paved the way for the complete independence of the country. However, relates the Muslim League leader, Nehru "ridiculed the idea of Muslims having any separate organization carried on within the precincts of the Legislature. . . . We could not agree and I had to leave disappointed."[47]

The Muslim League was told that its members could join the Congress in forming the Ministry on the understanding that "the Moslem League group in the United Provinces Legislature shall cease to function as a separate group. . . . The Moslem League Parliamentary Board in the United Provinces will be dissolved, and no candidates will thereafter be set up by the said Board at any by-election."[48] Since this was tantamount to asking the League to sign its own death warrant as a separate political party, the terms were naturally rejected and the proposal for a coalition government fell through. "This was a most unfortunate development," comments Azad. "If the U.P. League's offer of cooperation had been accepted, the Moslem League Party would for all practical purposes have merged in the Congress. . . . Mr. Jinnah took full advantage of the situation and started an offensive which ultimately led to Pakistan."[49] "In historical perspective," according to Brecher, "Nehru's attitude to the League in 1937 was a grave error of judgment."[50]

Some other observations made by Nehru shed further light on his view of the Hindu-Muslim problem at the time. A year earlier in his presidential address at the Lucknow Congress, Nehru had stated, "I am afraid I cannot get excited over this communal issue, important as it is temporarily. It is after all a side issue, and it can have no real importance in the larger scheme of things." In March 1937 Nehru had haughtily remarked, "There are only two forces in India today, British imperialism, and Indian nationalism as represented by the Congress." Jinnah retorted, "No, there is a third party, the Mussulmans." History was to bear him out.[51]

Nehru's second disastrous intervention took place in 1946, when the Cabinet mission came to India with the declared object of helping India

THE HERITAGE

obtain her freedom as speedily as possible. This was the last occasion on which the conception of a united India could have been salvaged from the continuing political storm. After the perennial lack of agreement between the Indians themselves had once more manifested itself, the Cabinet mission put forward its own proposals. The idea of Pakistan was rejected in unmistakable terms on the grounds that such a course would not provide an acceptable solution of the communal problem and would be open to serious administrative, economic, military, and geographical objections. There would be a Union of India to start with but, to allay Muslim fears, provision was made for a province to come out of any of the three sections in which it was initially grouped and also for reconsideration of the terms of the constitution after an initial period of ten years and at ten yearly intervals thereafter.

Both the Congress and the Muslim League at first accepted the Cabinet mission plan. However, the opportunity, once again, was decisively torpedoed by Jawaharlal Nehru. In a press statement issued on 10 July at Bombay he asserted that the Congress would be entirely and absolutely free to determine what it did in the Constitution Assembly. "We have committed ourselves on no single matter to anybody."[52]

"It was a compromise plan which obviously could not afterwards be altered in favour of one side or another," comments Mosley. "In the circumstances, Nehru's remarks were a direct act of sabotage."[53] Louis Fischer, who attended the fateful press conference, said to Nehru when it ended, "You have changed the entire basis of the agreement with England." He smiled and replied, "I am fully aware of that."[54]

With this long background of stubbornly held convictions it was not easy for Nehru suddenly to change his attitude toward Pakistan after independence. In December 1947 he said, "I have little doubt that India and Pakistan will sometime or other come closer to each other because nothing can overcome the basic urges, historical, cultural and economic, that tend to bring us nearer to each other. . . . Even though Pakistan is a separate and independent country and we must treat it as such, I find it a little difficult to think of it as alien to India and of its people as anything but Indians."[55] In 1948 he told a member of the United Nations Commission for India and Pakistan, Josef Korbel, "One day integration [of India and Pakistan] will inevitably come. If it will be in four, five, ten years — I do not know."[56] Similarly, he said to C. L. Sulzberger of the *New York Times*, "Twenty years ago I would have said that certainly we should have some kind of confederation, not federation — independent states with common defense and economic policies. . . . The difficulty now is that if we talk about it. This upsets our neighbours because we are so much bigger. Nevertheless, of course, this remains the logical future path, confederation with each member nation maintaining its independence intact therein."[57]

It is true that Nehru is also on the record for having said that he would not favor the undoing of partition. In the course of his convocation address to the Muslim University of Aligarh on 24 January 1948 he declared: "If today by any chance I were offered the reunion of India and Pakistan, I would decline it for obvious reasons. I do not want to carry the burden of Pakistan's great problems. I have enough of my own." However, his very next sentence shows that he did not rule out the possibility of an eventual confederation of states which would include India and Pakistan, provided such a union was based on mutual consent. "Any closer association," he said, "must come out of a normal process and in a friendly way which does not end Pakistan as a State, but makes it an equal part of a larger union in which several countries might be associated."[58]

On another occasion he made a similar disclaimer when Prime Minister Suhrawardy alleged that India had not accepted Pakistan's existence and there was a possibility of a future leadership arising in India which might undo partition. Nehru retorted that he could not imagine anything more remote from reality than Suhrawardy's statement and added that the people of India had completely accepted Pakistan not only because Pakistan had come into existence with India's consent but also because all that had happened had made it perfectly clear "that any kind of the slightest reversal of partition would be highly injurious certainly to India."[59]

But his well-considered view was that the best long-term solution of the problems facing both India and Pakistan was for them to join together in a confederation. Besides the instances already quoted, he put forward the idea of a confederation on two occasions when he seemed to be genuinely searching for a cure for the continual differences between the two neighboring countries. The first of these was in December 1962. India then had recently suffered a humiliating defeat at the hands of the Chinese in the Himalayas and the United States and the United Kingdom were strongly urging Nehru to arrive at a settlement with Pak-

The Heritage

istan. Nehru believed that the threat from China would continue for a long time to come. The pressure of events for a conciliation with Pakistan had, thus, seldom been greater. In an interview with the correspondent of the *Washington Post* at the time Nehru said, "Confederation remains our ultimate goal, though if we say it, they are alarmed and say we want to swallow them up. Look at Europe, at the Common Market, the urge everywhere is for that and there are no two peoples anywhere who are nearer than the people of India and Pakistan. But please give us time."[60] The second occasion was in April 1964, a few weeks before his death, when he was believed to be truly anxious to seek a way out of the debilitating Kashmir impasse before departing from the political stage forever. He released Sheikh Abdullah from prison and sent him to Pakistan to talk with President Ayub Khan. The proposal carried by Abdullah was that India, Pakistan, and Kashmir should together form a confederation.[61] Nehru also gave vent to the wish in the course of a speech in the Lok Sabha on 13 April 1964: "I would have hoped that India and Pakistan would be able to come together much closer, even constitutionally closer. I do not say so because this annoys Pakistan that we are trying to upset them; I wish them well, but there is no other way for India and Pakistan to live except to live at peace. It may take years to achieve that; that is a different matter." Pakistan's reaction to the suggestion was aptly summed up by Ayub when he referred to Abdullah's mission at a Muslim League gathering at a later date. "The objective of our struggle for Kashmir," said the Pakistani president, "is to liberate Kashmir and not to undo Pakistan."[62]

This perpetual hankering after a reunion of India and Pakistan in the post-independence period, instead of accepting India and Pakistan as two quite separate countries, caused the same kind of difficulty for the establishment of a normal relationship between the two neighbors as had been caused earlier by Nehru's failure to put Hindu-Muslim relations on a realistic basis by first accepting the deep differences that in fact divided them. As the *Round Table* put it, Nehru was tough with Pakistan because he did not treat her as a foreign country.[63]

Nehru was himself fully conscious of the fact that his way of thinking was not typical of his countrymen. In the chapter "What Is Religion?" in his *Autobiography* he sadly referred to the gulf which separated him from the great majority of his compatriots: "I felt lonely and homeless, and India, to whom I had given my love and for whom I had laboured, seemed a strange and bewildering land to me. Was it my fault that I could not enter into the spirit and ways of thinking of my countrymen?"

One cannot help thinking that perhaps a conforming Hindu leader would have, in time, found it easier to live with Pakistan on a normal footing than did Jawaharlal Nehru, the exceptional Hindu. The very qualities that distinguished him from his countrymen appeared to render Nehru the least capable among them of ever accepting Pakistan as an established fact. An entry of 1 December 1947 in Campbell-Johnson's diary about Kashmir provides a further illustration of this seemingly paradoxical thesis. Nehru desired Kashmir because of his special love for her as a Kashmiri Brahman but also, he said, because it could be a showpiece for proving that Hindus and Muslims could live together in peace in secular India. Pakistanis and Kashmiris have disputed the Indian claim to the predominantly Muslim Kashmir and the issue has been the chief bone of contention between India and Pakistan. It would seem that, if the orthodox Hindus had their way, this dispute might never have arisen. "Those in the Congress," wrote Campbell-Johnson, "who want a Hindu state do not want Kashmir, but the Government's action in Kashmir has temporarily silenced them."[64]

His Superiority Complex

In a two-hour talk with a Ceylonese parliamentary delegation, some months after the death of Prime Minister Jawaharlal Nehru, the Chinese prime minister, Chou En-lai, called Nehru the most arrogant man he had ever met. "I have met Chiang Kai-shek, I have met American generals," he said, "but I have never met a more arrogant man than Mr. Nehru. I am sorry but this is true." According to one of the delegates Chou En-lai complained that Nehru was "almost implacable."[65] In a speech to the National Assembly on 13 July 1965, Pakistani Foreign Minister Zulfikar Ali Bhutto also alleged that Nehru's arrogance was the main cause of continuing Indo-Pakistani differences, indeed the reason for India's troubles with all her neighbors. It would be easy to dismiss these two views for the reason that they originate with persons who were prejudiced against the Indian statesman because of irreconciled differences with him. But they were not the only observers to note the superior opinion Nehru entertained of himself.

In a letter to Nehru, written on 15 July 1936, Gandhi had stated that Nehru's colleagues "dreaded you because of your irritability and impatience of them. They have chafed under your rebukes and magisterial manner and above all your arrogation of what has appeared to them your infallibility and superior knowledge."[66] Giving thumbnail sketches of world figures he had dealt with as president, Dwight D. Eisenhower called Nehru "a very complex man" who "thinks everybody's wrong except his own solution," adding politely, "but that's what a self-confident man does."[67]

Nehru himself was not unaware that he was a difficult person to negotiate with. "I am afraid I am a bad bargainer," he said in the Constituent Assembly once. "I am not used to the ways of the market place. I hope I am a good fighter and I hope I am a good friend. I am not anything in between and so when you have to bargain hard for anything, do not send me."[68]

Since flexibility is the sine qua non of any negotiations if they are to be fruitful, Nehru's implacability negated in practice his desire for a peaceful settlement of disputes which he professed so often. He drew a distinction between talking and negotiating. The purpose of talking which "must always be encouraged" was to probe each other's mind; "it may not yield any [concrete] result."[69] Negotiation, however, was a different matter and, as practiced by him, meant "persuading the other side of the validity of the Indian position."[70] No wonder his talks with both China and Pakistan failed and left war as the sole alternative. Unfortunately, the example set by Nehru "has since become a staple device of Indian foreign policy articulation, understood and accepted in India."[71] On 1 October 1970, Foreign Minister Swaran Singh said in the General Assembly of the United Nations that India was "always willing" to enter into negotiations with Pakistan on Kashmir "and on all other Indo-Pakistan differences without any preconditions" but added in the same breath that Kashmir had been an integral part of India from the time of her accession to India and that "that position cannot be changed." Not surprisingly, a baffled Agha Shahi exclaimed: "They say that Kashmir is an integral part of India and simultaneously offer to open negotiations on Kashmir. We do not understand this."[72] In the following year Ambassador Sen asserted before the same assembly that India had "repeatedly stated" that as regards Kashmir "the only problem" was the question of withdrawal by Pakistan from the occupied part of Kashmir and India was "always ready to enter into negotiations with Pakistan to bring this about."[73]

JAWAHARLAL NEHRU

Independent India, purporting to follow in Gandhi's footsteps, thus seems completely to have overlooked an important Gandhian principle: compromise. "The very insistence on truth," Gandhi wrote in his autobiography, "has taught me to appreciate the beauty of compromise. I saw in later life that this spirit was an essential part of *Satyagraha*."[74]

It was not surprising that Nehru's assumption of his own superiority should have been reflected in his exaggerated estimate of India's importance and greatness in the world and in the manner he conducted India's foreign policy. Before independence, in his *Discovery of India*, he had given an indication of things to come. "India constituted as she is," he had written, "cannot play a secondary part in the world. She will either count for a great deal or not count at all. No middle position attracted me. Nor did I think any intermediate position feasible."[75] Also, "The Pacific is likely to take the place of the Atlantic in the future as a nerve centre of the world. Though not directly a Pacific state, India will inevitably exercise an important influence there. India will also develop as the centre of economic and political activity in the Indian Ocean area, in south-east Asia and right up to the Middle East."[76]

After India became the mistress of her own affairs, Jawaharlal Nehru as prime minister continued the theme: "And may I point out to this House that the political unit that is India today is, in terms of population, the largest political unit in the world? But population and numbers do not count, it is quality that counts. I would say further that from the point of view of our potential resources and our capacity to use those potential resources, we are also potentially the biggest unit in the world."[77]

With great respect to commentators who have likened India's policy of nonalignment to the isolationist attitude of early America, it must be pointed out that those who hold such a view have failed to grasp the rudiments of Nehru's foreign policy. In his farewell address Washington had stated, "Our detached and distant situation invites and enables us to pursue a different course" from Europe which perforce must engage in frequent controversies. "Physical separation from Europe and Asia," explains the historian Thomas Bailey, "enabled the United States to pursue, notably in the 19th Century, an isolationist course. The two oceans have been referred to as America's greatest 'liquid assets.' "[78] Jules Jusserand, ambassador of France to the United States from 1902 to 1925, "once quipped that America was blessed among the nations. On the north, she had a weak neighbour; on the south, another weak neighbour, on the

THE HERITAGE

east, fish; on the west, fish."[79]

About India, on the contrary, a typical Nehru pronouncement ran, "Look at the map. If you have to consider any question affecting the Middle East, India inevitably comes into the picture. If you have to consider any question concerning South-East Asia, you cannot do so without India. So also with the Far East. While the Middle East may not be directly connected with South-East Asia, both are connected with India. Even if you think in terms of regional organizations in Asia, you have to keep in touch with the other regions. And whatever regions you may have in mind, the importance of India cannot be ignored."[80] Moreover, "in the world of today, neither you nor we can afford to be purely national or even continental in our outlook; the world has become too small for that. If we do not all cooperate and live at peace with each other, we stumble on one another and clutch at one another's throats."[81]

Another strong element in the formulation of early American policy was the genuine feeling that America had no direct stake in European developments: "Europe has a set of primary interests, which to us have none, or a very remote relation. Hence she must be engaged in frequent controversies, the causes of which are essentially foreign to our concerns. Hence, therefore, it must be unwise in us to implicate ourselves, by artificial ties, in the ordinary vicissitudes of her politics, or the ordinary combinations and collisions of her friendships, or enmities."[82] But Nehru declared quite emphatically, "We do not wish to be isolated. We wish to have the closest contacts, because we do from the beginning firmly believe in the world coming closer together and ultimately realizing the ideal of what is now being called One World."[83]

Indeed, considering the impressive role her prime minister had cut out for India in world affairs, any thought of noninvolvement was wholly beside the point. Nehru reiterated, time and again, that India was interested in all the major issues of the time — peace and war, end of imperialism and colonialism, eradication of racial discrimination, and improvement in the hard lot of the poor peoples of the world. The very purpose of remaining outside power rivalries was to be able to intervene more effectively in the crucial questions, not to stand idly aside. "Some people," he complained, "use the word 'neutral' in regard to India's policy. I do not like that word at all, having myself been in the past, perhaps even now to some extent, not exactly a negative individual but a positive individual working for positive causes . . . and having, if I may say so with all respect, a certain contempt for a neutral person who has no views at all."[84]

The supreme question in the world was how to avoid a world war and in that "India can play a big part, and perhaps an effective part. . . . Therefore, it becomes all the more necessary that India should not be lined up with any group of powers which for various reasons are full of fear of war and prepare for war."[85] By joining one power group India would do harm to the interests of peace because she would "lose that tremendous vantage ground that we have of using such influence as we possess (and that influence is going to grow from year to year) in the cause of world peace."[86]

Nehru's replies to the direct question of whether there was a similarity between the foreign policies of America in her early years and India make the position abundantly clear. "The parallel is not exact, nevertheless there is much in it. Whether we want to or not, in India we have to play an important role. It is not to our liking, because we have enough burdens of our own and we do not wish to add to them. But, as I said, we just can't choose in the matter."[87] In fact he thought the parallel was closer to present-day America, which has been compelled by circumstances to assume a global role, than to early America, which was unconcerned with the rest of the world. "Just as the United States," he explained, "almost against her wishes or desires has been thrust into a position of extreme importance in world affairs, and, whether she wishes it or not, has to assume leadership in world affairs, so in a different, entirely different context, India is inevitably drawn into the vortex of Asian and world affairs."[88]

India potentially might be a great power but her physical power, at least for the time being, was limited. So what, in Nehru's view, were her special qualifications for a world role? "In the family of nations she was a newcomer and could not influence them greatly to begin with," Nehru conceded, but, he went on, "she had a certain advantage. She had great potential resources that no doubt would increase her power and influence. A greater advantage lay in the fact that she was not fettered by the past, by old enmities or old ties, by historic claims or traditional rivalries. Even against her former rulers there was no bitterness left. Thus, India came into the family of nations with no prejudices or enmities, ready to welcome and be welcomed. Inevitably she had to consider her foreign policy in terms of enlightened self-interest, but at the same time she brought to it a touch of her idealism."[89] A country's capacity to influence events is determined by various factors. India is lacking in most of those factors but "if we have been successful in some measure, the success has been due not obviously to any kind of military strength or financial power, but because we took a correct view of events. If I may say so in all modesty, we understood them more correctly than others, because we were more in tune with the spirit of the age."[90]

Why was India's weight increasing in the unofficial councils outside the United Nations? "Because, progressively, people see that within the United Nations things are done far from the idealistic, moral way, or in terms of the underdog, the smaller nations, or the Asian nations. Therefore, more and more of these people try to find someone else and in their search for someone else who might perhaps give a lead in these matters, almost automatically their eyes turn towards India."[91]

His Love for Kashmir

Nehru's deep sentimental attachment to his beautiful ancestral homeland, Kashmir, is well known and, indeed, no one has expressed this love in more lyrical terms than Nehru himself. Writing of a visit he made there in 1940, he said that he had been repeatedly invited to go there by Sheikh Abdullah and other friends "and everyone who was of Kashmir reminded me that I, too, was a son of this noble land and owed a duty to it. I smiled at their insistence, for the urge within was far greater than any that they could have placed before me." And on getting there "my mind was filled with the excitement of my return, and it pleased me to be welcomed everywhere as a brother and a comrade, who, in spite of long absence, was still of Kashmir, and was coming back to his old homeland. . . . Wherever I went these women of Kashmir came to welcome me and treat me as a brother or a son. It was a joy to meet them and see the affection in their eyes. At Mutton, old Kashmiri ladies came to bless me and kiss me on the forehead, as a mother does to her son." Kashmir herself was "like some supremely beautiful woman, whose beauty is almost impersonal and above human desire. . . . As I gazed at it, it seemed to me dream-like and unreal, like the hopes and desires that fill us and so seldom find fulfilment. It was like the face of the beloved that one sees in a dream and that fades away on awakening." The visit was over, "but Kashmir calls back, its pull is stronger than ever, it whispers its fairy magic to the ears, and its memory disturbs the mind. How can they who have fallen under its spell release themselves from this enchantment?"[92] With a remarkable premonition of what happened after independence, he wrote at another time, "My partiality for it [Kashmir] occasionally leads me astray."[93]

On the eve of the transfer of power, when Lord Mountbatten tried to dissuade Nehru from making a visit to Kashmir because the Kashmir government was against a political visit at that time and because Mountbatten also did not "know how the future Prime Minister can be spared from Delhi with only 18 days left for him to take over," Nehru replied, "As between visiting Kashmir when my people need me there and being Prime Minister, I prefer the former."[94] To a British officer Nehru is reported to have said, "In the same way that Calais was written on Mary's heart, Kashmir is written on mine."[95] "May I take the House into my confidence?" he said, in a speech to the Constituent Assembly on 7 September 1948. "In the early stages, towards the end of October and in November, and indeed subsequently, I was so exercised over Kashmir and if anything had happened or was likely to have happened to Kashmir, which, according to me, might have been disastrous for Kashmir, I would have been heartbroken. I was intensely interested, apart from the larger reasons which the Government have, for emotional personal reasons; I do not want to hide this: I am interested in Kashmir."[96] Four years later he complained that people in other countries thought of Kashmir merely as a geographical unit and added that "our history and our circumstances had made Kashmir so closely associated with our feelings, our emotions, thoughts and passions that it was a part of our beings."[97]

That other Indians do not necessarily share the intense personal attachment that Nehru had felt for the land of his forefathers was noticed by Josef Korbel, who visited Kashmir as a member of the United Nations Commission in September 1948, while the first Indo-Pakistani war in Kashmir was raging. "At Srinagar and elsewhere," he narrates, "we spoke with Indian [military] officers. . . . Some of them, whose darker skins indicated that they came from South India, showed complete disinterest in the Kashmir conflict, saying they never had any sentimental attachment to the country or any political understanding of why Kashmir should be part of India."[98]

Though Sardar Patel initially desired the accession of Kashmir to India as much as any other Indian, and in the first part of October 1947 temporarily released Mehr Chand Mahajan, a judge of the East Punjab High Court, to be prime minister of Kashmir so that he could influence

THE HERITAGE

the maharaja to join India, he was realistic enough, when the fate of both Hyderabad and Kashmir hung in the balance, to face the fact that Hyderabad logically belonged to India and Kashmir to Pakistan. As Chaudhri Muhammad Ali has stated on the basis of his direct knowledge of the negotiations, Patel and Mountbatten, in November 1947, were agreeable that Indo-Pakistani differences be resolved on the basis of Hyderabad acceding to India and Kashmir to Pakistan but the proposal fell through on account of Nehru's opposition to it. "Patel's view at this time and even later," writes Chaudhri Muhammad Ali, "was that India's effort to retain Muslim majority areas against the will of the people was a source not of strength but of weakness to India."[99]

Ambassador Bowles has written that Nehru always talked freely and fully but "there was one exception to this, Kashmir. . . . On its beauty and history he had much to say, but on the present conflict with Pakistan, he was always reluctant to talk." Prime Minister Atlee, on the whole a long-time admirer of Nehru, considered Kashmir "the blind spot of a great statesman."[100]

His Other Biases

Jawaharlal Nehru was never a professing Communist. The pacifist in him could never condone the violent methods practiced by the Communists, and the nationalist in him was vexed at the extraterritorial loyalty Communists in their lands showed originally toward Moscow and later either toward Moscow or Peking. Moreover, he was too much of an individualist ever to give his entire allegiance to any single system, especially since he believed India had the unique capacity to pick out the best from every line of thought and synthesize it with her own basic philosophy. What he said during World War II seems very nearly to sum up his political philosophy: "In regard to individual and political rights and civil liberties we were influenced by the ideas of the French and American revolutions as also by the constitutional history of the British Parliament. Socialistic ideas, and the influence of the Soviet revolution came in later to give a powerful economic turn to our thoughts."[101]

Though he often referred to Buddha and Gandhi as his preceptors, he was in fact a faithful product of his own era and upbringing: a pacifist intellectual, attracted by the historical analyses and economic theories of Marx and Lenin, but repelled by the violent methods and extreme dogmatism of the Communists and preferring the freedom of the Western political institutions. Two well-known personalities, typical of this cult so fashionable in British universities during Nehru's impressionable years, were Harold Laski and Stafford Cripps. Nehru's reference to Soviet Communism as a "new civilization," in his presidential address to the Lucknow session of the Congress in April 1936, was directly borrowed from the title of Sidney and Beatrice Webb's apology, *Soviet Communism: A New Civilization*, published only five months earlier.

His hatred of capitalism and what he considered to be its ill-begotten child, imperialism, drove him, during the independence movement, very close to Communism and its then visible embodiment, the Soviet Union, which had vowed to put an end to both these scourges. After independence he regarded Russia and China as necessary antidotes to the tensions caused by the continued ambition of the Western powers to preside over the destiny of Asian lands under new pretexts. A partnership between India and China, in particular, seemed to him to hold out the promise of emancipation from the control of the West, under which he had chafed so long, and of a shift of power in favor of Asia, which he felt was long overdue.

Nehru has written that the Indian National Congress began to develop its foreign policy in 1927.[102] The significance of the date lies in the fact that Nehru that year returned after a prolonged stay in Europe, and assumed the role of the Congress spokesman on questions of foreign policy. He had attended the International Congress against Imperialism at Brussels, and had made his first direct contact with the Soviet Union by visiting Moscow, accompanied by his wife, sister, and father, to attend the tenth anniversary celebrations of the Russian Revolution. The impressions gained during the trip shaped much of Nehru's future outlook on world affairs.

In his report to the All India Congress Committee on the Brussels Congress, Nehru called it "an event of first class importance" which was "the outward symbol of the intense desire for mutual co-operation which had taken possession of the oppressed and the exploited all over the world."[103] By meeting the South American delegates he realized for the first time "how the rising imperialism of the United States, with its tremendous resources and its immunity from outside attack, is gradually taking a strangle-hold of Central and South America," and concluded that "the great problem of the near future will be American imperialism, even more than British imperialism, which appears to have had its day and is

THE HERITAGE

crumbling fast. Or, it may be, that the two will unite together in an endeavour to create a powerful Anglo-Saxon bloc to dominate the world."

The strongest delegation at the International Congress was that of China and the problem of China dominated the proceedings, with India's problem coming next. One of the resolutions of the Congress took the form of a joint declaration by Indian and Chinese delegates. This pronouncement saw the birth of the romantic myth, often to be repeated by independent India and China, and readily picked up later by Pakistan and China, that "for more than three thousand years the people of India and China were united by the most intimate cultural ties. From the days of Buddha to the end of the Mughal period and the beginning of British domination in India this friendly intercourse continued uninterrupted." The declaration also hoped that the leaders of India would coordinate their struggle with that of China "so that by simultaneously engaging British Imperialism on two of its most vital fronts, China may receive active support in her present struggle and the final victory of both peoples may be secured."

From Russia Nehru brought back great admiration and enthusiasm for Soviet Communism. "Great Britain," writes K. P. S. Menon, a former ambassador of India to the U.S.S.R., "took care to see that no literature or news came to India unfiltered from Russia. . . . It was Nehru's letters from Russia which opened the eyes of the Indian people to the tremendous happenings in that country."[104] After his return to India from Russia, he extensively lectured on Soviet Russia and also wrote numerous articles. The latter were eventually published in the form of a book.[105] In one of the articles, "Russia and India," he wrote that the danger of war was real but it was not Russia that was seeking war but Great Britain the whole basis of whose policy "has been to encircle Russia by pacts and alliances, ultimately to crush her." He saw no reason why India should inherit the age-long rivalry between England and Russia because it was "based on the greed and covetousness of British imperialism, and our interests surely lie in ending this imperialism and not in supporting and strengthening it."

Here is a sampling of some further Nehru views expressed during the years that followed:

Russia stands today as the greatest opponent of imperialism and her record with the nations of the East has been just and generous.[106]

I am convinced that the only key to the solution of the world's problems and of India's problems lies in Socialism. . . . Some glimpse we can have of this new civilization in the territories of the U.S.S.R. Much has happened there which has pained me greatly and with which I disagree, but I look upon that great and fascinating unfolding of a new order and a new civilization as the most promising feature of our dismal age. If the future is full of hope it is largely because of Soviet Russia and what it has done, and I am convinced that, if some world catastrophe does not intervene, this new civilization will spread to other lands and put an end to the wars and conflicts which capitalism feeds. . . . Socialism is thus for me not merely an economic doctrine which I favour; it is a vital creed which I hold with all my head and heart.[107]

The Soviet Union stood as the one real and effective bulwark against Fascism in Europe and Asia. Without her Fascist reaction would triumph everywhere and democracy and freedom would become dreams of a past age.[108]

Thus we see the world divided into two vast groups today — the imperialist and fascist on one side, the socialist and nationalist on the other. . . . Inevitably we take our stand with the progressive forces of the world which are ranged against fascism and imperialism.[109]

Modern imperialism is an outgrowth of capitalism and cannot be separated from it.[110]

Fascism is a development, and more dangerous form of imperialism.[111]

Russia is not supposed to be a democratic country after the Western pattern, and yet we find the essentials of democracy present in far greater degree amongst the masses there than anywhere else.[112]

For my part, I would like to have a socialist economy all over India, and I think that the Soviet form of government, with certain variations and adaptations suited to India may well fit in here.[113]

Soviet expansion did not pass unnoticed by Nehru but he held to the view that imperialism was peculiarly the child of capitalism. A socialist economy can be made self-sufficient and has no need for expansion. Soviet expansion was a defensive measure against encirclement by Western powers.[114]

But Nehru's views were too revolutionary to be entirely palatable to his colleagues in the Congress leadership. His radical views in the presidential address at Lucknow in 1936 specially alarmed them, resulting in the resignation from the Working Committee of six members including such stalwarts as Prasad, Patel, and Rajagopalachari on the ground "that

THE HERITAGE

the preaching and emphasizing of socialism particularly at this stage by the President and other socialist members of the Working Committee while the Congress has not adopted it is prejudicial to the best interests of the country and to the success of the national struggle for freedom which we all hold to be the first and paramount concern of the country." At Gandhi's intervention the resignations were withdrawn, but not the charges against Nehru.[115]

In mellower years Nehru's original infatuation with Soviet Communism, naturally, lost much of its intensity. "Nevertheless, the emotional hangover" remained "and with it the belief that Soviet achievements can be reproduced in India without its repulsive methods." Asked by Tibor Mende, during his "conversations" in January 1956, to comment on the relatively slow progress under the Indian democratic process as compared to what had reportedly deeply impressed him (Nehru) during his recent visits to Russia and China, the prime minister replied, "Considering the influence of this large organization: of the Congress; and considering the influence I have, I would say that there is very little that we cannot get through here through the democratic process." His basic admiration for Communist economic philosophy, however, remained undimmed because "the Communist ideal and, I suppose, the Socialist ideal do not differ very much."[116]

After the International Congress against Imperialism at Brussels, Nehru's love for China and his desire for a specially close Sino-Indian relationship continued to grow, and was reflected in the India National Congress policy toward China and in Nehru's own writings. In May 1927 the All India Congress Committee declared its sympathy for the Chinese people and demanded that Indian troops be withdrawn from China and in December of that year the Congress described the Chinese as comrades of the Indian people in their struggle against imperialism. When Japan invaded China in 1937, the Congress expressed strong sympathy with China. Meetings and demonstrations were held; a boycott of Japanese goods was called for; 12 June 1938 was proclaimed China day and the Congress and Chinese flags were flown side by side; and an ambulance unit was dispatched to China.[117] Nehru's first visit to China was made in August 1939 but he had to rush back to India after two weeks because war had broken out in Europe and he was needed at home for meeting the developing crisis there between the British government and the Congress party. However, he was able to meet Chiang Kai-shek and his wife several times and would have been stranded in China but for the fact that the Chinese government placed a plane at his disposal to fly back. He called the two weeks spent in China "memorable ones" for him personally as well as for the future relations of India and China. Describing his feelings as he flew to China, he wrote that his "mind went back to the long line of illustrious pilgrims and travellers who had journeyed between India and China for thousands of years" and had forged the "imperishable links" which bound India and China together. And he imagined himself "as one of a long line, yet another link joining together these two Ancients in history and civilization, who had found rebirth and youthful vitality again, and were facing the future with hope and confidence."[118]

When the Japanese advance westwards attained menacing proportions in early 1942, Chiang Kai-shek decided to visit India to rally Indian opinion against Japan and arrived in Delhi on 9 February 1942, accompanied by his wife. Though Prime Minister Churchill had asked Chiang Kai-shek not to press his wish to see Gandhi "contrary to the wishes of the Viceroy or the King-Emperor," the visiting Chinese leader "made it clear that he had come to India to discuss the war situation, not only with the Viceroy and the Commander-in-Chief, but with the Congress leaders."[119] Accordingly, Chiang Kai-shek called on Gandhi and was closeted with him for two hours. The government of India had made official arrangements for the distinguished visitors to see the Taj Mahal but at Madame Chiang Kai-shek's insistence Jawaharlal Nehru had to be included in the party. On the eve of his departure the generalissimo made a strong appeal to the British government to give real political power to Indians as speedily as possible. When the Congress leaders were arrested in the "quit India" movement (August 1942) Chiang Kai-shek protested to Roosevelt who forwarded the representation to Churchill.

Nehru's strong personal feelings toward China were eloquently reflected in his own words from time to time. "What a long past that has been of friendly contacts and mutual influences, untroubled by political conflict and aggression!" he wrote. Also, "China and India, sister nations from the dawn of history, with their long tradition of culture and peaceful development of ideas, have to play a leading part in this world drama, in which they themselves are so deeply involved."[120]

At a meeting in Paris in July 1938 convened to protest the bombardment of open towns in Spain and China, he said that the spirit of India,

THE HERITAGE

like that of her great sister nation of China, had been a spirit of peace. To the people of China, knit to the people of India by a thousand bonds since the dawn of history, he offered respectful homage and stretched out hands in comradeship on behalf of the people of India, adding that "their perils are ours, their suffering hurts us, and we shall hold together whatever good or ill fortune may befall us."[121] In his view

China and India will have a powerful effect on the shape of things to come, whatever that ultimate shape might be. This is not only because of the vast numbers of human beings that live in these two countries — between 800 and 900 millions; not only because of their rich and tremendous past heritage; but because of their enormous resources and potential political and economic strength. There is much talk of a new order and of world co-operation. There can be no stable order or effective co-operation in the world if China and India are ignored, and relatively weak though they might be today, they are not so weak as to submit to any such treatment.[122]

In a letter to Chiang Kai-shek, explaining that the "quit India" movement against Britain was not meant in any way to embarrass China in her struggle against Japan, Gandhi stated that Nehru's "love of China is only excelled, if at all, by his love of his own country." Nehru expressed the belief that India and China had both shown tremendous staying power for ages past "because of their sense of moral values." On another occasion he wrote, "The future of which I dream is inextricably interwoven with close friendship and something almost approaching union with China."[123]

What was the reality of this so-called three thousand years of peaceful intercourse and cooperation between the Indian and Chinese peoples of which Nehru had so strongly convinced himself?

Before the age of modern transport and technology the high Himalayas presented an almost insuperable barrier and a voyage across the seas posed its own special perils. Any meaningful political relations or sizable exchange of visits between India and China in the old days was, therefore, simply out of the question. When Buddhism spread from India to China, in the opening centuries of the Christian era, a religious and cultural link was created between the two countries and led to some mutual traffic of pilgrims, scholars, monks, and traders but the trickle perforce remained thin. For example, it took one Janaogupta three years to reach the province of Kasnu in northwest China from West Punjab.[124] In the reverse direction, "Fa Hsien and his five companions took one month to cross the Pamirs. There they encountered numerous dangerous precipices. The crags rose sheer to a formidable height. 'If a man looks down he becomes dizzy, and if he wishes to go forward he can find no foothold.' In such a place, the ancients hewed a path out of the rocks, like a stairway, with seven hundred steps. After passing this stairway, these Chinese travellers crossed the Indus by a rope suspension bridge. They wrote that the banks of the river were eighty paces apart."[125] From about the eleventh century, with the Muslim conquest of northwest India and the decline of Buddhism in India, even this tenuous connection was severed.

In the twentieth century the Chinese and Indian leaders became interested in each other's problems because of their common desire to shake off Western domination from their respective lands but direct contacts and knowledge were still of the flimsiest kind. When Panikkar took up his duties as ambassador to the People's Republic of China at Peking in May 1950 he noticed that "their knowledge, as of ours in India, was more of western countries than of their eastern neighbours. . . . [A]s communists they could only think of India as a capitalist country, and by all textbook maxims it seemed clear that India must be reactionary and must belong to the opposite camp."[126]

Noting that Nehru had set before his countrymen the ideal of a close oriental partnership between themselves and the Chinese, Guy Wint, with many years of direct knowledge of China and India, wrote perceptively in 1941 that China's experience could be turned into account by India only if it was properly interpreted. "Otherwise," he warned, "the similarity of their present state may be superficial, and if allowed to influence actual aims and policy may be actually misleading."[127]

As an Indian scholar pointed out in a study of Indian foreign policy made in the middle 1950s, it was possible to talk of thousands of years of peaceful relations between India and China because "Indian expansion northward was limited by high mountain barriers, and hence India never came into a headlong clash with the Celestial Empire of China."[128] India's romanticized affinity with China, says an American writer, "can be traced in large part to the relative isolation of India and China from one another for many centuries."[129]

Romanticizing the hoary past might have remained harmless by itself but it led to dangerous consequences because the emotions thus generated made Nehru and his immediate advisers blind to the fundamental

THE HERITAGE

differences between modern India and modern China with the result that Indian policy toward China was formulated more on the basis of the myth of an ancient friendship and less on the reality of current basic differences. It was inevitable that, after a period of artificially created cordiality, the followers of Mohandas K. Gandhi, the apostle of nonviolence, should have fallen out with the followers of Mao Tse-tung, who frankly proclaims that political power grows out of the barrel of a gun.

As often is the case, Nehru's own statements provide the most interesting postmortem observations after the much publicized Sino-Indian friendship had collapsed in the heat of altercation following the Dalai Lama's escape into India in the spring of 1959 and turned into positive hostility because of the border clash of 1962:

I doubt if there is any country in the world which cares less for peace than China today.[130]

Nothing in my long political career has hurt and grieved me more than the fact that the hopes and aspirations for peaceful and friendly neighbourly relations which we entertained, and to promote which my colleagues in the Government of India and myself worked so hard, ever since the establishment of the People's Republic of China, should have been shattered by the hostile and unfriendly twist given in India-China relations during the past few years.[131]

It is sad to think that we in India, who have pleaded for peace all over the world, sought the friendship of China, and treated them with courtesy and consideration and pleaded their cause in the councils of the world, should now ourselves be victims of a new imperialism and expansionism by a country which says that it is against all imperialism.[132]

In a television interview in the United States, in November 1961, Nehru told Adlai Stevenson that "the Chinese go on saying that they stand for coexistence, but it seems to me evident that the meaning which they attach to it is somewhat different from mine." He illustrated this by recalling what had taken place when Chou En-lai came to India for the first time and asked him to draft a joint statement for the press. Looking at the English version, the Chinese premier said that it seemed all right to him but he would like to see the Chinese translation of it. When it came he protested that it sounded funny in Chinese. After hours of argument a version was agreed to in the small hours of the morning. "That experience made me think how different was the genius of the Chinese language from not only English but all the other languages, including the Indian languages, because we are all one family of languages."[133] About a month later, Nehru told an Asian History Congress at New Delhi that India was nearer the European "way of thinking" than the Chinese way. Even Indian languages were closer to European than to Chinese.[134] At last he seemed to be tacitly admitting the truth that geography had compelled traffic to, and from, India throughout the ages to follow an East-West rather than a North-South course. In the meantime, however, Nehru's emotional bias in favor of China and against Pakistan had resulted in the unfortunate Indian policy of treating China as India's best friend and Pakistan as India's enemy number one. "Within India," comments a Dutch diplomatist, who served at New Delhi in the late 1950s, "it led to underemphasizing the threat from China as compared with Pakistan and, despite the existence of a considerable military budget, a wrong deployment of the forces available."[135]

Not surprisingly, the net result of all this detachment from the real facts of international life was that Nehru's India, which had set out to lead all the other countries of the world toward the shining goal of universal peace and goodwill, ended up with the bitter enmity of her own important neighbors, China and Pakistan.

India's China policy being almost entirely a Nehru creation, one is left wondering once more what course South Asian politics might have followed if a person other than Nehru had been guiding his country's fortune. The deputy prime minister, Sardar Vallabhbhai Patel, and India's first native born governor general, Rajagopalachari, for instance, would almost certainly have acted differently from Jawaharlal Nehru if they could have had their way. It has already been mentioned that Rajagopalachari was essentially a right-winger, keen to win Muslim friendship by conceding the demand for Pakistan. After partition he continued to plead for reconciliation with Pakistan and alignment with the Western countries. In the tense days in India, following her military defeat by China in 1962, Rajagopalachari pleaded for a settlement with Pakistan and an alliance with the United States and Britain to redress the balance of power upset by the emergence of the Chinese menace.[136] Patel also "very often warned the people of the danger of developments within the country similar to those in China."[137] In a broadcast on the first anniversary of Indian independence he said, "China, which at one time was expected to be the leading nation of Asia, had serious domestic troubles. . . . The conditions in Malaya, Indo-China and Burma were disturbing. . . . If the undesirable elements in the country were not put down with a firm hand immediately, they were sure to create the same chaos as they found existing in some other Asiatic countries."[138] According to the Communist writer R. Palme Dutt, Patel's broadcast showed that "the right-wing leadership of Indian bourgeois nationalism was blossoming into Indian neo-imperialism seeking to act as the junior partner of Anglo-American imperialism."[139] In May 1950 Patel, warning Indian communists not to resort to Chinese-style methods, said, "Certain young men believed that a few bombs thrown on our own people, a few murders committed and a few dacoities will convert this land into the heaven which they think has come to China and will come to us. It will take a long time for China to build its own country. Mutual slaughter will do no good to any country. It will never do good to India."[140] On 7 November 1950, not long after the Chinese invasion of Tibet, Patel warned Nehru in a letter that the Chinese government had tried to delude India by professions of peaceful intentions and urged that "a military and intelligence appreciation of the Chinese threat to India, both on the frontier and to internal security," be undertaken.[141] Two days later he publicly condemned China for using the sword against the peace-loving Tibetans and declared: "It is possible that when a country gets drunk with its own military strength and power, it does not think calmly over all issues. . . . [I]f anybody resorts to force against us, we shall meet it with force."[142] Sardar Patel "would like a more definite alignment with the Anglo-American bloc," noted the *Economist*.[143]

It is not unlikely that, had Patel or Rajagopalachari presided over India's destiny, the shape not only of Indo-Pakistani relations but also of world politics would have been different from what it is today. The foreign policies of India and Pakistan would not have been dissimilar and naturally it would have been easier for them to cooperate. In 1959, when President Ayub Khan suggested that India and Pakistan agree to defend the subcontinent jointly against all outsiders, one of the main objections Nehru put forward was that the two countries followed diverse foreign policies and this made it impracticable for them to join together in any defense arrangements. An Indo-Pakistani agreement for cooperation in defense would have greatly benefited the peoples of both the countries and would have, at the same time, provided a corrective to the unhealthy balance of power in favor of China in Asia. Further, India's preference for the West would have importantly affected the attitude of the remaining Afro-Asian countries. A pro-Western stance, thus, could very well have become more prevalent among the newly independent countries than a policy of leftist nonalignment.

Part II
Independent India and Pakistan: The Opening Decades

"Their geographical position being what it is, India and Pakistan cannot help playing an important role in Asia. . . . If India and Pakistan follow a contrary policy and are opposed to each other, they will obviously be neutralizing each other and cannot play that role. . . . Because of our very close contacts we cannot be indifferent to each other. We can either be more than friends or become more than enemies. . . . This conflict and wasteful effort will wipe us out from the face of the earth." (Jawaharlal Nehru, Speeches, *volume II, p. 446)*

CHAPTER 5

The First Moves (1947-53): Goals of Indian and Pakistani Foreign Policies

As noted in the preceding chapters, the strongest proclivities India and Pakistan have inherited from their past are, respectively, a deep-seated penchant for nonalignment and an ardent desire to forge a brotherhood of Muslim countries. Of course, by the time India and Pakistan were reborn as independent states in the middle of the twentieth century, sudden breakthroughs in the science of communications had made all the countries of the world neighbors of one another. Nations were being affected by the conduct of others more than ever before, especially by that of the big powers, whose interests spill out far beyond the confines of their own shores. Both countries, moreover, have been influenced by considerations of physical security, self-interest, and geographical location as much as all the other countries who share the planet earth with them. But, just as the magnetic needle invariably resumes its fixed course after each fluctuation caused by extraneous pulls, India and Pakistan have always faithfully returned to their own standing themes of nonalliance and Islamic solidarity following every reluctant deviation from them by the force of circumstances.

Everybody knows that in 1971 India had a walkover in the Indo-Pakistani war thanks to the protective umbrella of her August 1971 treaty with the Soviet Union which ensured that China would not enter the fray on the side of Pakistan. Nevertheless Indians vehemently continued to insist that their sacred mantle of nonalignment had emerged from the crisis as spotless as ever. Pakistanis admit that it was pressure from the United

INDEPENDENT INDIA AND PAKISTAN

States and China that saved West Pakistan and Azad Kashmir from a full-scale Indian onslaught after the Indian forces had conquered East Pakistan in December 1971. Nevertheless, it was to the Muslim countries that President Bhutto hastened on his first trip of thanksgiving in January 1972; he called it a "journey among brothers." And he has affirmed, echoing Liaquat's words, that Pakistan was created not only to serve the Muslims of the subcontinent but "to be at the service and command of the world of Islam."[1]

The only other running thread in Indian and Pakistani policies, at least until Pakistan's defeat in the Indo-Pakistani war of 1971 and the consequent dismemberment of East Pakistan from West Pakistan, has unfortunately been confrontation with each other, resulting in four useless wars and the wastage of their all too scarce resources in building up implements of mutual destruction instead of employing them for the beneficial purpose of relieving the grinding poverty of their long-suffering peoples.

A brief review of India's and Pakistan's performance in the world arena during the opening decades of self-government will indicate the combined effect on their behavior of past influences and contemporary compulsions.

Perhaps the best exposition of the guidelines of Indian foreign policy can be found in three pronouncements of its acknowledged architect, Jawaharlal Nehru: his broadcast from the All-India Radio, New Delhi, on 7 September 1946, six days after assuming the portfolio of external affairs in the viceroy's Executive Council; his speech at the Paris session of the General Assembly of the United Nations on 3 November 1948, when he appeared before that body for the first time; and his address at Columbia University, New York, on 17 October 1949, during his first visit to the world's leading power.[2]

In his broadcast Nehru, now in the seat of power, reiterated what he previously had so often said as the foreign policy theoretician of the opposition Congress party, namely, that India proposed to play an influential role in world affairs, as behooved a potentially great country. "Too long have we been passive spectators of events, the playthings of others," he said. But "the initiative comes to our people now and we shall make the history of our choice." He spoke of friendly relations with the British Commonwealth and the United States, and with the Soviet Union, "our neighbours in Asia," and China, "that mighty country with a mighty past,

THE FIRST MOVES (1947–53)

our neighbour, [which] has been our friend through the ages and that friendship will endure and grow." Among international issues he singled out "emancipation of colonial and dependent peoples" and elimination of "the Nazi doctrine of racialism" as special targets for Indian attention. However, he emphasized that India's efforts would be made within the framework of nonalignment because "power politics of groups aligned against one another" had led in the past to world wars and might again lead to disasters on an even vaster scale.

At the General Assembly the Indian prime minister added to colonialism and racism the problem of hunger and want in many parts of the world as a world issue of Indian concern. He deprecated the fear of war and other forms of fear which were gripping the world and proceeded to discuss the "psychology of fear." Fear, he argued, is not a good companion because it leads to evil consequences. "I have no fear in my mind," he claimed, "even though India, from a military point of view, is of no consequence." He was not afraid of the armies, fleets, and atom bombs of the great powers because "that is the lesson which my Master [Gandhi] taught me. We stood as an unarmed people against a great country and a powerful empire." India weathered that ordeal successfully because she "decided not to submit to evil"; and he commended this example to the rest of the world.

Nehru adopted "Ends and Means" as the caption of his address at Columbia University. He said lack of wisdom on man's part in his own generation had resulted in two world wars and the tragedy was that even that terrible price had not purchased real peace. He believed "that there is always a close and intimate relationship between the end we aim at and the means adopted to attain it. Even if the end is right but the means are wrong, it will vitiate the end or divert us in a wrong direction. Means and ends are thus intimately and inextricably connected and cannot be separated. . . . The great leader of my country, Mahatma Gandhi, under whose inspirational and sheltering care I grew up, always laid stress on moral values and warned us never to subordinate means to ends."[3] Since India had won her freedom in "a peaceful way," there was no bitterness on either side and India had, therefore, decided of her own free will to continue cooperation with her erstwhile rulers. He suggested that the lesson of India's "peaceful revolution" be applied to the larger problems before the world. That lesson was that "physical force need not necessarily be the arbiter of man's destiny and that the method of waging a struggle and the way of its termination are of paramount importance." Specifically, India's foreign policy objectives were "the pursuit of peace, not through alignment with any major power or group of powers but through an independent approach to each controversial or disputed issue, the liberation of subject peoples, the maintenance of freedom, both national and individual, the elimination of racial discrimination and the elimination of want, disease and ignorance which afflict the greater part of the world's population." India did not align herself with any group, he explained, because "the very process of marshalling the world into two hostile camps precipitates the conflict which it has sought to avoid." He reverted to the theme that there was nothing so dangerous in life as fear and "our problem, therefore, becomes one of lessening and ultimately putting an end to this fear." Fear would not be abolished, he warned, if all the world takes sides and talks of war, because "war almost becomes certain then."

Pakistan had no spokesman on external affairs as glamorous or as voluminous as Nehru but a typical formulation of her aspirations was placed before the Motamar-e-Alam-e-Islami (World Muslim Conference) at Karachi by Prime Minister Liaquat Ali Khan on 9 February 1951:

> To us in Pakistan nothing is dearer than the prospect of the strengthening of the world-wide Muslim brotherhood. Any endeavour, from whatever direction it is made, to bring the Muslims of far-flung countries together and to stimulate in them brotherly feelings of mutual affection, understanding and co-operation readily finds an echo in the hearts of the Muslims of Pakistan. . . . The underlying idea of the movement for the achievement of Pakistan was not just to add one more country to the conglomeration of countries in the world or to add one more patch of colour to the multi-coloured global map. Pakistan came into being as a result of the urge felt by the Muslims of this sub-continent to secure a territory, however limited, where the Islamic ideology and way of life could be practised and demonstrated to the world. A cardinal feature of this ideology is to make Muslim brotherhood a living reality. It is, therefore, part of the mission which Pakistan has set before itself to do everything in its power to promote closer fellowship and co-operation between Muslim countries.[4]

A few months later he argued, "If the Western democracies can enter into pacts to protect their way of life and if the Communist countries can form a bloc on the basis that they have an ideology, why cannot the Muslim peoples get together to protect themselves and show to the world

THE FIRST MOVES (1947–53)

that they have an ideology and a way of life which ensures peace and harmony in the world?"[5]

Internal Conditions in India and Pakistan

Both India and Pakistan were faced with tremendous problems when they became mistresses of their own destiny in August 1947. Each had to rehabilitate millions of destitute refugees, tone up a governmental machinery shaken by the departure of hundreds of British officials in key positions, frame a new constitution, and reconstruct an economy dislocated by a division which had placed the areas growing the main raw materials in Pakistan and the factories processing them in India. India, as already explained, had been comparatively less scathed than Pakistan in the holocaust of partition. She also commanded greater resources and a far better organized political party, and would have Jawaharlal Nehru's unbroken leadership for no less than seventeen years. By the time she launched her new constitution, on 26 January 1950, her worst period was over and she seemed poised for a leap forward toward great-power status, which was generally believed to be her natural due. Pakistan, on the other hand, not only came out in a far worse shape from the ravages of partition but had the further misfortune of losing Jinnah by illness in September 1948 and Liaquat Ali Khan to an assassin's bullet in October 1951. The Muslim League, structurally never as sound as the Congress party and now lacking any outstanding leader to give it firm direction, fragmentized into factions grouped around persons with local or regional outlook and influence. That the League was no longer a cohesive national force was demonstrated by the frequent administrative changes in the central government as well as in the governments of the various provinces of West Pakistan[6] and even more dramatically by events in East Pakistan.

Trouble in East Pakistan first erupted when the central government tried to impose Urdu as the sole state language in both wings of Pakistan, while most East Pakistanis desired that Bengali too should enjoy official status. Prime Minister Liaquat Ali Khan said in the Constituent Assembly of Pakistan on 25 February 1948 that "Pakistan is a Muslim state and it must have, as its *lingua franca*, the language of the Muslim nation. . . . It is necessary for a nation to have one language and that language can only be Urdu and no other language." When Jinnah declared at both the meetings he addressed at Dacca in March 1948 that Urdu must be

INDEPENDENT INDIA AND PAKISTAN

the only state language of Pakistan, the audiences demonstrated to show their resentment. The climax of the agitation over language was reached on 21 February 1952 when two students were killed in riots in Dacca and became the first martyrs in the fight of East Bengalis against West Pakistani domination.

East Pakistani pride was sharply pricked when Governor General Ghulam Muhammad unceremoniously dismissed his Bengali prime minister, Khwaja Nazimuddin, in April 1953, and installed in his place another Bengali, Muhammad Ali Bogra, who had been a successful ambassador but had no popular following in his own homeland. The politicians of the Eastern Wing gave vent to their accumulated wrath by joining hands in a United Front, standing for provincial autonomy,[7] and trouncing the ruling Muslim League in the provincial elections of March 1954 by an overwhelming majority of 233 to 10.

Soon after taking over the premiership of East Pakistan as the nominee of the victorious Front, Fazlul Haq, who while moving the Lahore resolution in 1940 had claimed he was a Muslim first and a Bengali afterwards, declared that East Pakistan wished to become independent. He said the central government undoubtedly would resist such a movement, "but when a man wants freedom, he wants it."[8] During his speech in the national parliament, on 6 and 7 September 1955, an East Pakistani member, Ataur Rahman Khan, complained that West Pakistanis fancied themselves as a race of conquerors and looked down upon East Pakistanis as a subject race. He also quoted some "leaders of the central government" as saying that "money sent to East Bengal will be thrown into gutters because East Bengal is not going to stay with us."

Indo-Pakistani Tension

The period immediately following the sanguinary partition naturally was the tensest between India and Pakistan. Of the numerous disputes which kept adding fuel to the fierce fires of hatred on both sides, the two most serious related to the Indus Waters and Kashmir. Luckily for weaker Pakistan, India accepted the good offices of the International Bank for Reconstruction and Development for a peaceful settlement of the waters question before it could escalate to armed hostilities. The problem of Kashmir, however, has spawned endless tension, caused two wars, and remains unresolved till this day. It also provided an early indication that India was not prepared to apply to issues in which her own national in-

THE FIRST MOVES (1947–53)

terest was involved the high standards she commended to others for settling their differences.

Had Kashmir not been a princedom she would have, by virtue of her 78 percent Muslim population, automatically formed a part of West Pakistan under the partition scheme. However, according to the Indian Independence Act, the suzerainty of the British government over the Indian princely states lapsed which meant that, constitutionally, each of them became independent and could remain so or join either dominion; and the Hindu maharaja of Kashmir signed a deed of accession in favor of India. But in the cases of Jodhpur, whose maharaja wished to join Pakistan, Junagadh, whose nawab acceded to Pakistan, and Hyderabad, which wished to remain independent or join Pakistan, India contended that, though it was the hand of the ruler which formally signed the document of accession, it was the religious complexion of the majority of subjects, or their expressed wishes, which in fact determined the question of accession. Indeed, in the case of Kashmir too, the governor general of India accepted accession only provisionally. "In consistence with their policy," he wrote to the maharaja, "that in the case of any State where the issue of accession has been the subject of dispute, the question of accession should be decided in accordance with the wishes of the people of the State, it is my Government's wish that, as soon as law and order have been restored in Kashmir and its soil cleared of the invader [the tribesmen], the question of the State's accession should be settled by a reference to the people."[9] Though Indian spokesmen now aver that the maharaja's signature on the Instrument of Accession completed the transaction, Nehru at the time clearly acknowledged that the governor general's covering letter was meant to be "a proviso to the Instrument of Accession."[10]

The same disregard for consistency on the part of India has been apparent in other aspects of this malignant dispute which has cost both sides so dearly. During the Korean war India, as a third party, assumed a vigorous role as a mediator between the combatants. When the United States opposed her inclusion in the proposed Political Conference on Korea, Nehru resented the American action on the ground that countries which are neutral in a dispute "can sometimes help in toning down differences and easing a tense situation."[11] However, India has consistently resented third-party efforts to mediate the Kashmir dispute. Again, during the Korean war as well as the crisis in Hungary in 1956, India criti-

INDEPENDENT INDIA AND PAKISTAN

cized the condemnatory resolutions sponsored by the Western powers on the grounds that calling China an aggressor in Korea could not lead to peace but only "to an intensification of the conflict and might, perhaps, close the door to further negotiations" and condemning Russia for her role in Hungary would not assist in a solution.[12] But in the case of Kashmir a standing Indian grievance against the United Nations is that it has not yielded to the persistent Indian demand that Pakistan be declared an aggressor.

It is difficult to overestimate the evil effects of the tragic Kashmir imbroglio. Not only have the people of Kashmir suffered from the continuing uncertainty and strife but this dispute, more than anything else, has also kept alive the mutually destructive bitterness between India and Pakistan. India's known intransigence on Kashmir, moreover, has often made otherwise sensible and constructive Indian positions in international affairs look hypocritical because of the glaring gap between her precept and her practice. And Kashmir has not only deprived both of the South Asian countries from playing the positive and stabilizing role in world affairs which rightfully belongs to them by virtue of their size and the intelligence of their peoples but, by creating openings for the great powers, has made the subcontinent a cockpit of their rivalries. The Indian contention that Kashmir is a symbol of Indian secularism would have had force if the Kashmiri Muslims were living happily within the Hindu majority state of India. But the fact is that they have throughout been manifestly rebellious under the Indian yoke.

India and Pakistan fought an undeclared war inside Kashmir from May 1948 till January 1949, and twice during the period under review, in the spring of 1950 and the summer of 1951, all-out war nearly broke out between them. Pakistan was in no shape, at that time, to fight against her more powerful neighbor. At the independence parade on 14 August 1947, the authorities could muster only four aircraft from all over the country to participate in the celebrations, and East Pakistan, almost an island within India, was defended by an insignificant garrison of two infantry battalions which "had virtually nothing at all; not even any maps of East Pakistan." At the time of the 1951 crisis Pakistan's heaviest armor totaled thirteen tanks with less than fifty hours' engine life left in the best of them.[13] The crisis of 1951 finally convinced Pakistani leadership that, if Pakistan hoped to survive as an independent nation, she must procure arms for herself and look for powerful friends to back her

The First Moves (1947–53)

up. Her early hopes in the Commonwealth, and initial moves to forge a Muslim bloc, had not brought the desired results. Close links with Russia and China at this stage were ideologically unattractive and, in any case, would have been of little help materially because neither of these Communist giants was yet in a position to assist others substantially.

So it was to America that Pakistanis turned in right earnest for badly needed succor. For her part the United States, too, at about this time, had begun to despair of her efforts to enlist India on her side in the cold war, and to turn toward Pakistan as the obvious alternative in the region. Though formal ties were not forged till 1954, State Department officials conceded in November 1953 that informal discussions concerning Pakistan's role in the defense of the Middle East had in fact been going on "for the last year or two."[14] In November 1952 Admiral Arthur W. Radford, the United States commander in chief of all the armed forces in the Pacific, paid an official visit to Pakistan, stayed as an honored guest of the governor general, toured the strategic Khyber Pass, and was feted by the prime minister. He publicly emphasized Pakistan's strategic position, and declared that she "had to play an important role in the world fight against Communism."[15] On the other side of the equation, the Soviet Union and Communist China, which initially had shunned India and Pakistan as stooges of imperialism, had begun to treat Indian foreign policy with greater appreciation.

India, Pakistan, and the Great Powers

During more than a century of British connection the Indian subcontinent's intercourse with the outside world had consisted mainly of exchanges with Great Britain. India's economy had become dependent on the imperial power and her external defense was controlled entirely by London. Though Indians had been permitted to hold high civil posts, the king's commission in the armed forces was the last avenue opened to them. Consequently, there were but few senior officers in the Indian army, and not one of them had attained the rank of general when the hour of independence struck. In the civil and police administrations, too, the key positions had been held by British officers.

A sudden break with the past, under the circumstances, was a sheer impossibility. Independent India and Pakistan were compelled to appoint British officers to head all three branches of their armed services besides having to retain literally hundreds of them in other positions; and Britain

Independent India and Pakistan

remained their sole source of war matériel till other avenues gradually opened up. On the civil side a large number of British officers were similarly kept on, India — as we have seen — even retained as governor general the last of the proconsuls who had ruled her as Britain's appointees. The existing pattern inevitably continued in trade and commerce as well. The United Kingdom had incurred a huge debt for goods and services supplied by India during World War II. These "sterling balances," jointly due to India and Pakistan, amounted to £1,160 million. Since the release of this sum, as well as the conversion to other currencies, was restricted, it had the effect of tying the creditor countries the more closely to the British market. That under the partition scheme India and Pakistan started their lives as dominions within the British Commonwealth ipso facto meant that their first contacts with the outside world would be with, and through, the United Kingdom. As Nehru put it, "If we dissociate ourselves completely from the Commonwealth, then for the moment we are completely isolated."[16]

Because the Congress party had been rebellious during the independence movement, the British government had viewed the Muslim League with greater benevolence. After independence, however, it was clearly more advantageous for Britain to cultivate friendly ties with India, which was economically and politically much more promising than Pakistan, whose future seemed bleak. The very nature of the Commonwealth was transformed under British guidance to accommodate republican India within its structure. Hitherto the basic bond between the various nations of the Commonwealth had been their "common allegiance" to the crown but India was allowed to continue her membership upon accepting the king (not the crown) as a "[mere] symbol" of the free association of the member nations "and as such the Head of the Commonwealth."[17]

In foreign policy matters India and the United Kingdom often acted in harmony. In her prompt recognition of Communist China, for instance, Britain was greatly influenced by India. And New Delhi and London concerted their pressures on the United States during the Korean war, as well as at the Geneva Conference, which considered the conflicts in Korea and Indochina.[18] There were occasional irritations along the way over such matters as India's Kashmir policy and her invasion of Hyderabad but it was not till the Anglo-French Suez invasion of 1956 that Indo-British relations suffered their first palpable setback.

Any hopes Pakistan might have entertained that the Muslim League's

THE FIRST MOVES (1947–53)

preferential relationship with the British government would be transferred to her after 1947 were soon frustrated. Britain and other Commonwealth countries turned a deaf ear to Pakistan's appeals to use their good offices for bringing under control the carnage which continued after partition and in March 1948, under pressure from Mountbatten, who was still governor general of India, the British government modified its position on the Kashmir dispute in the United Nations Security Council to make it more acceptable to India. Many Pakistanis had secretly hoped that India would carry out her long-standing pre-independence pledge to leave the Commonwealth, for Pakistan's continued membership, in that case, would have given her an edge on her rival. But the decision to retain India within the Commonwealth, at the cost of modifying the very ideology of that body, finally convinced Pakistanis that India would always pull greater weight in the Commonwealth than their own country and that they must look elsewhere for comfort and protection. When Britain devalued the pound in September 1949, India reduced the par value of the rupee correspondingly, but Pakistan, partly as an assertion of independence from Britain's tutelage, refused to follow suit.

India's and Pakistan's relations with the United States make an interesting subject for scholarly research. Over the years their reality has become obscured by the overgrowth of subjective evaluation. India has exerted an almost mesmeric attraction for American liberals (indeed for liberals everywhere) because of her ancient civilization, pursuit of democracy, striving for secularism, and gift of moralization. She has, therefore, been seen through a romantic haze. Moreover, in terms of population, she is the world's second most substantial nation. All these factors have worked to the disadvantage of Pakistan which is smaller, has been under military dictatorship during half her independent existence, is outspoken, and is uncompromisingly Muslim.

India certainly is unique among the newly independent countries in that she has staged regular elections and effected changes of government peacefully. But the facts remain that one and the same political party has wielded power so far and, but for the brief regime of the innocuous Shastri, the disparate elements of her vast population have been held together by the charisma of just two members of the same family, Jawaharlal Nehru and his daughter Indira Gandhi.[19]

Whatever basic likenesses there might be between the political systems of India and the United States, often honorifically referred to as the two

INDEPENDENT INDIA AND PAKISTAN

greatest democracies in the world, they have not succeeded in producing much similarity in their attitudes toward international problems. How little India's vaunted joint worship with America at the shrine of democracy has influenced the formulation of Indian foreign policy was well brought out in a *Daily Telegraph* (8 March 1955) diagnosis of the reason underlying India's preference, at that time, for totalitarian China over democratic United States: "The Chinese may be prisoners of an ideology which he [Nehru] dislikes: but they are Asians. The Americans may be democratic: but they are not Asians, and must, therefore, not interfere in Asia." Apart from this feeling of Asianism Indians have been influenced by the conviction that capitalism is the natural mother of international exploitation and war. Indo–American relations were the least abrasive in the years 1958 to 1965 during which the United States came to India's rescue first with money, when the latter was facing financial collapse, and later with weapons, when she was routed by the Chinese in the Himalayan skirmishes.

Before 1947, India had been the close preserve of the British government and Americans had little direct knowledge of the deep differences between Hindus and Muslims. Having themselves forged a single nation out of many diverse elements, they could not understand why the Muslims wanted to break up India into two nations. President Franklin D. Roosevelt thought of the Indian freedom movement "in terms of the thirteen colonies fighting George III" and, wishing to enlist Indian popular support for the war against Japan, urged Churchill more than once during World War II to set up a temporary dominion government "headed by a small representative group, covering different castes, occupations, religions and geographies." In other words, he pressed Churchill to hand over power to the Congress leaders, who alone claimed to represent all classes, faiths, and regions. Churchill rejected the proposal because he did not wish to break with the Muslims, who were a hundred million strong and constituted the main army elements.[20]

For a proper appreciation of India's and Pakistan's relations with the United States in the opening phase of their independence it is necessary briefly to sketch the main features of the international scene immediately following World War II. Those who today ridicule the American policy of preventing the expansion of Communism during the period immediately following World War II should ask themselves what the world would have looked like in subsequent years if the United States had

The First Moves (1947–53)

stood aside and allowed the militant monolithic Communism of those days to have a free hand in Western Europe, Greece, Turkey, Iran, Korea, and Indochina. Ours is a rapidly changing international climate. Yesterday's policies, no doubt, are now outmoded; nevertheless it is in the context of the situation then prevailing that they must be appraised.

Though it is now fashionable to underrate the Communist menace of those days, and to single out John Foster Dulles as the chief architect of the fight against Communism, this is not sound history. In reality President Eisenhower and Secretary Dulles simply accepted the logic and pattern of the policy firmly enforced by the Truman administration. "In early 1946 Russian activities in Iran threatened the peace of the world," recalls President Harry S. Truman in his memoirs, because, instead of leaving Iran on the appointed date, the Russian forces attempted to install a "revolutionary government" in Azerbaijan and vacated Iran only after the United States had sent "a blunt message to Premier Stalin." In July of the same year Russia made an "open bid to obtain control of Turkey" by proposing that the Dardanelles be placed under joint Turkish-Russian defense. With American encouragement Turkey rejected the Russian demands and showed determination to resist if Russia used force. Early in 1947 it seemed that the Communist faction in Greece, which had been receiving assistance from Moscow and the Balkan satellite countries, would seize the country. "America could not, and should not, let these free countries stand unaided. To do so would carry the clearest implications in the Middle East and in Italy, Germany, and France. The ideals and the traditions of our nation demanded that we come to the aid of Greece and Turkey and that we put the world on notice that it would be our policy to support the cause of freedom wherever it was threatened. . . . The new menace facing us seemed every bit as grave as Nazi Germany and her allies had been." Later, the Truman administration also treated the war in Korea and the war in Indochina against the French as prongs of the worldwide Communist thrust to dominate the world. A communiqué marking the visit to Washington of the French minister for the Associated States in Indochina expressed "the common recognition" that the French effort in Indochina was "an integral part of the worldwide resistance by the Free Nations to Communist attempts at conquest and subversion. . . . The United States assumes a large share of the burden in Korea while France has the primary role in Indochina." The economic and military support to the French in Indochina, which

INDEPENDENT INDIA AND PAKISTAN

Truman first approved in May 1950, in time resulted in the United States taking the place of France on the battlefields of Indochina. The developments in Asia led the Truman government to extend to that region the *cordon sanitaire* it had already built against Communism in Europe. Defense treaties were signed with Australia and New Zealand, the Philippines, and Japan. Thus, when Secretary Dulles set up SEATO and the Baghdad Pact he was merely extending the rampart his predecessors had begun.[21]

But let us return to the question of the Communist threat to Turkey and Greece. America's response to that challenge came on 12 March 1947 in the form of an address by President Truman to a joint session of the Congress. This statement, soon to acquire the appellation of "Truman Doctrine," though made in the context of the threat to Turkey and Greece in fact laid down the general "policy of the United States to support free peoples who are resisting attempted subjugation by armed minorities or by outside pressures." Truman said "every nation" was now faced with a choice between "alternative ways of life," one of which was "based upon the will of the majority" and guaranteed individual freedom, while the other relied on "terror and oppression" and the suppression of personal freedoms. Some days later he emphasized, "The world today looks to us for leadership. The force of events makes it necessary that we assume that role."[22] Though afterwards it became customary to say that it was Dulles who embarked the United States on a worldwide crusade against Communism, it was clearly Truman who had originated such a policy.

After the inauguration of the Marshall Plan in 1947 to reconstruct the war-ravaged economy of the European countries and the establishment of NATO in April 1949 to protect them against direct attack, the situation in Europe became easier but new worries for the United States soon cropped up in Asia. With the fall of Tientsin and Peiping in January 1949, it became increasingly evident that the Communists under Mao Tse-tung would emerge victorious in China against the Nationalists under Chiang Kai-shek. A new Communist giant in Asia was now seen as complementing the Russian colossus in Europe in the struggle for world hegemony, and India, the next largest country on the same continent, seemed to the Americans the only potential counterpoise to new China.

In a column entitled "America in Asia," Walter Lippmann raised the question of American policy in Asia, "now that Nationalist China, the

The First Moves (1947–53)

Netherlands and France are so manifestly unable to play the role in Asia which we had supposed they would play." He believed America would be "well advised" to enter into "intimate consultation" with Nehru, who was "certainly the greatest figure in Asia." Writing about the Middle East a few weeks later he said it was "elementary prudence" that America should establish no military policy in that region "without consulting India and recognizing her interests and influence." Inside the Senate, Hubert H. Humphrey strongly urged that "India should be brought into the councils of democratic world organization we are forming around the framework of the Atlantic Pact."[23]

President Truman invited Nehru to visit the United States, but the latter's tour, in October 1949, merely emphasized the gap between America's eagerness to enlist India on her side in the confrontation against Communism and the Indian prime minister's determined view that a grouping of the world into two hostile camps simply increased the chances of war. Liaquat Ali Khan had not been invited to the United States at first but was asked to come after the Soviet Union had invited him to visit that country. He never went to the U.S.S.R., and in the United States he worked hard to assure Americans that "in a world of conflicting ideologies," at least one nation — Pakistan — did not suffer such confusion and her people were "free from disintegrating doubts and clashes."[24] However, American hopes were still centered on India, and Liaquat's visit roused far less interest than Nehru's. When the Pakistani leader arrived to address the Senate, it lacked a quorum and the proceedings started half an hour late.

Mainly, it was the Korean war and the question of the Japanese Peace Treaty which finally alienated the United States from India and brought Pakistan and America closer. There were sharp differences between India and the United States on both the real cause of the Korean War and the best way to terminate it. To Americans it was yet one more instance of the Communist offensive to gain world supremacy. Indians, on the other hand, believed that China had entered the lists to defend her borders against the advancing United Nations forces. By saying that there would not have been any war in Korea at all if Communist China had been allowed to occupy her rightful place in the United Nations,[25] Nehru, in effect, heaped the whole blame for the outbreak on the United States, which was chiefly responsible for excluding China from the world organization.

Independent India and Pakistan

In identical letters to Stalin and Acheson, Nehru proposed that the conflict in Korea be resolved by negotiations in the Security Council after China had been invited to sit there. Acheson rejected the recommendation on the ground that the decision between the competing claimants to China's seat in the United Nations had to be reached on the merits and "should not be dictated by an unlawful aggression."[26] In a related development, the General Assembly, at American urging, on 3 November 1950 passed the Uniting for Peace Resolution, giving itself authority to consider questions which might become deadlocked in the Security Council by the exercise of a veto by a permanent member. Though of general scope, the immediate purpose of this measure was to prevent the Soviet Union from impeding the United Nations' effort in Korea. Prime Minister Nehru angrily denounced the move saying that it seemed to be converting the United Nations into a larger edition of the Atlantic Pact.[27]

The Peace Treaty with Japan, sponsored chiefly by the United States, was signed by forty-eight nations at San Francisco on 8 September 1951. India not only rejected the invitation to sign the document but joined Russia and China in condemning its contents for the reason, among others, that it made no provision for the return of Formosa to China.[28] Pakistan had promptly offered to send troops to Korea but refrained from doing so in the end because the United States would not give the undertaking to assist her if India attacked her.[29] Nevertheless, she fully cooperated with the United States on other important issues. She was one of the co-sponsors of the General Assembly resolution which impliedly authorized the United Nations forces to cross the 38th parallel in pursuit of the Communists, and she also voted for the Uniting for Peace Resolution.

Though the grant of United States military assistance to Pakistan predictably had the effect of greatly increasing the friction between India and the United States, there is little justification for the popular refrain that all was well between the two countries till Dulles upset the apple cart. Two notably sober members of the Truman administration were highly critical of India's attitude toward the Korean war. General Marshall sarcastically said that India "was trying to perform the rope trick,"[30] and Acheson, obviously irritated by what he felt were unrealistic assumptions on the part of Indian statesmen, pungently wrote, "I have never been able to escape wholly from a childhood illusion that, if the world is round, the Indians must be standing on their heads — or, perhaps vice

THE FIRST MOVES (1947–53)

versa."[31] Referring to Nehru's uninhibited criticism of the Dutch in Indonesia and the French in Indochina and to the Indian prime minister's own self-righteous attitude toward Kashmir, Acheson said that Nehru "was one of the most difficult men with whom I have ever had to deal."[32] Truman, given to plain speaking, minced no words. He explained that he did not attach much importance to the message of the Indian ambassador to China, K. M. Panikkar, that China would come to the aid of North Korea if the United Nations forces crossed the 38th parallel because "Panikkar had in the past played the game of the Chinese Communists fairly regularly."[33] For Nehru, personally, the president had just one word, the dirtiest in the American political vocabulary of the day: "Communist."[34]

At the bottom of these differences on concrete issues, of course, were the deep differences in the American and Indian outlooks. To Americans the main problem of the day was Communism; to Nehru it was colonialism. Americans believed that Communists respected only armed strength; Nehru believed an armament race only increased tension. Americans wished to build up a coalition of the free world against the Communist states; Nehru thought marshaling the world into two blocs would only make war more probable. Americans viewed socialism as the road to Communism; Nehru looked upon capitalism as the parent of imperialism and fascism.

Indian spokesmen made no secret of their belief that the United States was the main culprit in the cold war. Panikkar said that the course of the cold war was being determined by the "opportunist policies of the U.S."[35] And Vice-President Radhakrishnan declared: "at present there is a group of Western nations trying to crush Russia. If Hitler were alive today, he would have considered the present moment a supreme triumph of his philosophy."[36] On account of their view that imperialism is the natural offspring of capitalism, Indians looked upon America as "even more imperialist than Britain."[37] Krishna Menon told Lord Mountbatten that the United States wished to create an economic, political, and military vacuum in India which America herself would fill.[38]

The Pakistani view, as expressed by Liaquat, was the reverse of the Indian. Russia's policy, he said, "is quite definite. It is one of expansionism; to create trouble; even to promote a revolution because Communism thrives on chaos." But America had no colonies, and no territorial ambitions. In fact, Americans were "the world's greatest philanthropists."[39]

Soviet commentators reflecting the prevailing official line, called the partition of India "a new manoeuvre of British imperialism to retain its positions in India" and characterized the acceptance of the partition plan by the Indian parties as a "deal between the Indian bourgeoisie and British imperialism." That India and Pakistan remained dependent on Britain for so many essential services was seen as further proof of the hollowness of their independence. India's decision to remain within the Commonwealth meant "perpetuating the dependent status of India as a component part of the British Empire." By inviting Nehru to the United States the latter was offering him "the vacancy left behind by Chiang Kai-shek." Pakistan was still worse because the "reactionary elements in Pakistan were stronger than in Hindustan."[40] That Liaquat had preferred to go to America, though he had been invited by the Soviet Union first, only confirmed Russia's poor opinion of Pakistan.

Mao's China, too, subscribed to the theory that India and Pakistan were still subservient to Britain. In a message to the Communist party of India in October 1949 Mao stated that "the imperialist reactionary era" would end only when "like free China," India emerges in "the socialist and People's Democratic family."[41]

Relatively, however, India was a source of greater worry to China and Pakistan to Russia. This was because India seemed to be the bigger culprit in Tibet, which China regarded as her own territory, and Pakistan in Kashmir and the Middle East, which the Soviet Union believed were eyed by the United States and the United Kingdom as highly desirable bases for attacking the U.S.S.R.

Jenmin Jih Pao published an article, stated to have been written by a Tibetan, which exhorted all Tibetans to "rise against the plot to annex Tibet of British and American imperialism and its lackey, Nehru." The imperialists and their "running dog," the Indian premier, were accused of having "manufactured the so-called anti-Communist incident in Tibet of 8 July [1949] in order to prevent the Tibetan people from attaining its long-awaited liberation and to turn the 1,200,000,000 sq. km. of Tibetan territory into a colony of foreign aggressors."[42]

Russia alleged that Britain and America wanted Pakistan to get Kashmir because they "aimed to convert Kashmir into a link in the chain of military bases with which they are doing their best to surround the So-

THE FIRST MOVES (1947–53)

viet Union." Since it was clear that Pakistan "would be entirely dependent upon British and American support" the latter two felt that, "if they were to retain Kashmir as a strategic military base, they must get it included in Pakistan." Pakistan's efforts to forge Muslim unity were seen by Moscow as aiming at "a Moslem military and political bloc . . . [a] new variant of an anti-Soviet bloc of Middle Eastern countries."[43]

Indians remained surprisingly silent about Russian imperialism in Central Asia and overlordship in Eastern Europe, and about the revival of Chinese imperialism in Tibet. They also reacted far more strongly to Western criticism than to Communist abuse. But it was not till India had positively demonstrated her usefulness to the Soviet Union and China, during the Korean war and the Japanese Peace Treaty proceedings, that her forbearance toward the Communist powers began to pay off.

Nehru's peace proposal for Korea, which Acheson had rejected out of hand, was well received by Stalin, who replied: "I welcome your peaceable initiative. I fully share your point of view as regards the expediency of the peaceful regulation of the Korean question through the Security Council with the obligatory participation of the representatives of the five great powers, including the People's Government of China.[44] The *People's China* ascribed the Indian government's denunciation of the Japanese Peace Treaty to the pressure of public opinion which was "well aware of the dangers of U.S. policy" and called it "a development of the greatest importance."[45] Stalin, who had utterly ignored the presence in Moscow of Nehru's sister, Mrs. Pandit, while she was ambassador there from 1947 till 1949, opened the door to her successor, Radhakrishnan, and assured him that East-West problems could be solved.[46] In the Security Council the Soviet representative in making his first substantive intervention in the Kashmir debate took a stand clearly favorable to India. The problem of accession, he asserted on 17 January 1952, should be solved by the Constituent Assembly of Kashmir. After Stalin's death, in March 1953, the pace of Indo-Soviet conciliation gathered further speed.

The Bid for Leadership

With Japan lying helplessly at the feet of the Allies, and China caught in the throes of an exhausting civil strife, Gandhi and Nehru's India, at the close of World War II, seemed to be the only rallying point for the Afro-

INDEPENDENT INDIA AND PAKISTAN

Asians. Two conferences summoned at New Delhi — the Asian Relations Conference and the Conference on Indonesia — were interpreted by the international community as Indian initiatives to seize the leadership which rightfully belonged to India.

The Asian Relations Conference was held from 23 March to 2 April 1947, before India was actually free. Its formal host was the Indian Council of World Affairs but it was lost on no one that the moving spirit behind the whole effort was Jawaharlal Nehru, who held the external affairs portfolio in the viceroy's Executive Council and was virtually functioning as India's foreign minister. It was attended by twenty-four Asian countries and Egypt. In his inaugural speech Nehru politely said that there were "no leaders and no followers" in the conference but the other parts of the oration made it amply clear that he regarded India as "the natural centre and focal point of the many forces at work in Asia." He also declared: "We of Asia have a special responsibility to the people of Africa. We must help them to their rightful place in the human family." The Muslim League held itself aloof from the conference, viewing it as "a thinly disguised attempt on the part of the Hindu Congress to boost itself politically as the prospective leader of Asiatic peoples."[47]

The Conference on Indonesia took place in January 1949 to consider the crisis resulting from the recently renewed Dutch military action against Indonesia. This was an official gathering with the government of independent India as the host. Pakistan, whose policy in respect to Indonesia was similar to India's, was represented by her foreign minister. In his presidential speech Nehru warned that "Asia, too long submissive and dependent and a plaything of other countries, will no longer brook any interference with her freedom."[48] The *Economist* commented that Asia was reclaiming her place in the world's councils under "Indian leadership" and commended Nehru for perceiving "that the vacuum caused by the withdrawal of British power can be filled only by India, which has inherited all — and more than all — of Britain's spiritual means, as well as the best army and administration in the area between France and the Pacific."[49]

Two months after the conference on Indonesia, New Delhi invited the fellow Commonwealth countries of the United Kingdom, Australia, Ceylon, and Pakistan to confer together on the problems facing strife-torn

THE FIRST MOVES (1947–53)

Burma. The *Economist* made these laudatory observations concerning India's role:

> The device of a Commonwealth conference is as appropriate as it is novel, and once again shows Mr. Nehru as a statesman of daring and original constructive genius. Having assembled the nations of Asia for consideration of the Indonesian question, and incidentally taken the wind out of Russia's anti-imperialist sails by giving leadership to Asian opinion on the subject, he has now brought together a family council of the Commonwealth in such a way that neither is Britain exposed to the charge of reviving imperialism by intervention in Burma, nor is India left alone to cope with the very unpleasant situation on its eastern borders.[50]

One of the resolutions of the Conference on Indonesia had enjoined upon the conferees that they should "instruct" their representatives at the United Nations "to consult among themselves."[51] This was the origin of the Arab-Asian group in the United Nations which afterwards expanded into the Afro-Asian group. In a speech at the Indian Council of World Affairs on 22 March 1949, Nehru said he did not like it when people talked "rather loosely" about India becoming the leader of Asia but it was true that "a certain special responsibility is cast on India. India realizes it, and other countries realize it also. The responsibility is not necessarily for leadership, but for taking the initiative sometimes and helping others to co-operate." Mrs. Pandit, however, felt no compunction in telling the same legislature that "whether the Prime Minister wishes to assume leadership or not, India has assumed leadership."[52] However, the expectation that India would seize the leadership of the Afro-Asian world was palpably frustrated at the Bandung Conference in 1955 (see chapter 6).

That some Muslim countries had a poor view of the pre-partition Indian Muslims and their aspirations has already been mentioned. Independent Pakistan's opening moves in her declared program to forge Muslim unity did little toward improving that estimate. Some Pakistanis grandiosely referred to Pakistan as the biggest Muslim country of all, and the natural leader of the family of Muslim nations. All this did not sit well with other Muslim countries, proud of their own ancient heritage. Though the love of Pakistanis for Islam was genuine, their ill-concealed ambition to lead the Muslim world along a new path was wholly unrealistic and their tactics manifestly amateurish. A great deal of irritation was consequently caused. It was not until 1949 that the stresses and strains of the partition problems permitted Liaquat to travel to any other Muslim countries for the purpose of establishing personal contacts with their leaders. In that year, following the April meeting of the Commonwealth prime ministers in London, the Pakistani prime minister undertook a trip which included Egypt, Iraq, and Iran.

Efforts were now made to give more concrete form to Pakistan's inner wish to promote a sense of unity among the various members of the Islamic world. *Dawn* reported in its issue of 30 May 1949 that Pakistan had invited the members of the Arab League as well as other Muslim countries to a government-level Islamic Conference at Karachi to be held in the following winter for the purpose of signing treaties of formal alliances with them. But the conference never materialized, evidently because sufficient support for the idea was not forthcoming. Pakistan, however, managed to stage some other Islamic conferences.

The first Motamar-e-Alam-e-Islami had been held at Mecca in 1926 under the auspices of Sultan Abdul Aziz Ibn Saud. A delegation from India included the Ali brothers. At the meeting Maulana Muhammad Ali proposed that Mecca and Medina be declared international territory and become the spiritual capital of all the Muslims of the world. The proposal, however, was not accepted. The second Motamar was held at Jerusalem in 1931. The Indian delegation on this occasion was led by the poet Muhammad Iqbal.[53] During the turmoil of World War II, and the years immediately following it, the Motamar remained dormant till revived by Pakistani efforts. It then held its third session at Karachi in February 1949 with delegations from seventeen countries. The fourth session, also at Karachi, in February 1951 was even better attended. Thirty-six countries participated on this occasion and the inaugural address was delivered by Prime Minister Liaquat Ali Khan. He commended the Motamar for having adopted as their motto the edict of the Holy Quran "verily, all Muslims are brethren" and affirmed that to Pakistanis nothing was dearer than the prospect of the strengthening of the worldwide Muslim brotherhood.[54] Of all the conferences convened by Pakistan the Motamar has proved to be the most enduring. Yet another session was held at Karachi on 29 April 1967, presided over by the grand mufti of Palestine, al-Haj Sayyid Amin al-Hussaini, and attended by representatives from fifteen countries.[55]

The International Islamic Economic Conference met at Karachi from

THE FIRST MOVES (1947–53)

25 November to 5 December 1949 and was attended by delegations from North Africa, the Middle East, Turkey, Iran, and Afghanistan, representing twenty-one countries in all. A notable absentee was the large and populous Muslim country of Indonesia. Among those who attended were Habib Bourgiba of Tunisia and Aden Abdullah Osman of Somalia, both destined to become the first presidents of their respective countries upon achieving independence. In his presidential speech Finance Minister Ghulam Muhammad of Pakistan asked the Muslim countries to go beyond economic cooperation and "become an organic whole in which each part strengthens the whole and the whole imparts life to each part" and also to "develop a system of collective bargaining and collective security."[56] While the conference was in session the *Economist* commented that the wider question behind the whole meeting was "whether Pakistan will be able to assume the leadership of widely flung peoples who, however much they may have in common, have hitherto been more noted for their 'agreement to disagree' than for any effective cooperation. Pakistan undoubtedly has ambitions of this sort."[57]

Despite the high expectations raised at its inauguration, the International Economic Conference did not have lasting results. The International Islamic Economic Organization, set up by the conference, convened its next session at Tehran. At the third meeting, held at Karachi in May 1954, Foreign Minister Zafrulla Khan in his presidential address said it was "a profound pity" that progress toward the attainment of the aims of the organization had not been in keeping with the immensity of the initial inspiration. The objectives set forth at the time of inauguration were redefined to give new life to the body but it was in vain. After the 1954 meeting the conference silently expired.

Other conferences staged in Pakistan were the Ehtifalul Ulema-i-Islami (1952) to which *ulema* from different countries were invited, and the International Assembly of Muslim Youth (1955).

A rather unfortunate effort was that of Chaudhuri Khaliquzzaman, then holding the important office of president of the ruling Muslim League party, who set out on a two-month tour of the Middle East in September 1949 for the purpose of sounding "public opinion for the formation of a peoples' organisation representing all the Muslim countries of the world with a view to discussing common factors among themselves as also evolving if necessary a common policy which may benefit Islam and the Muslim World as a whole."[58] The Muslim League chief's itin-

INDEPENDENT INDIA AND PAKISTAN

erary took him to Iran, Syria, Iraq, Saudi Arabia, and Cairo and in the course of his travels he met the Iraqi premier, King Ibn Saud of Arabia, the Egyptian premier, the secretary general of the Arab League, the grand muftis of Egypt and Palestine, and the leaders of the Majlis-i-Istaqbal party in Iraq and the Wafd party in Egypt.

Though professedly he had started with the purpose of cementing solidarity on a people-to-people basis, the Muslim League leader during the trip came out with a more ambitious project to which he gave the title of United Islamistan. At Cairo he described Islamistan as an "Atlantic Pact" embracing all the countries of the Middle East from Pakistan to Turkey. "If and when Islamistan is formed," he declared, "it will be an iron curtain against foreign ideologies." After explaining his plan for an Islamic bloc to the leaders and peoples of the Middle Eastern countries, the Pakistani leader went on to London to discuss Islamistan with "responsible British officials."[59]

Khaliquzzaman himself seemed pleased with the result of his endeavors but, in fact, all was not well. Under the caption "Caution Islamistan" *Dawn* published an editorial "to reassure all those in the Middle East and elsewhere in whose minds doubts and question marks may have arisen" that Khaliquzzaman's vision of Islamistan as a basis for a Muslim security pact did not have the support either of the Muslim League or of the government of Pakistan. Propagation of Islamistan in the manner it was done had created suspicions that Pakistan was aspiring to the leadership of an Islamic bloc. "However well-intentioned Chaudhuri Khaliquzzaman's 'Islamistan tour' might have been, it has actually resulted in far more harm than good to Pakistan."[60] That Khaliquzzaman had gone to London at the conclusion of his tour was seen by many as proof that his project in reality had been conceived by Western imperialism. Several years afterwards Khaliquzzaman himself "confessed" that he had been wrong in carrying his mission to the Middle East only two years after the creation of Pakistan. Indian propaganda about Pakistan's ability to survive had affected the Arab world, no less than other countries, and he had found the Arabs "completely ignorant of all we had done for Palestine and other Muslim countries."[61]

Pakistan's ambition to seize the leadership of Muslim countries may be taken to have petered out in the summer of 1952, when she was compelled to abandon the project of convening a Muslim prime ministers' conference at Karachi on account of lack of adequate response from the

The First Moves (1947-53)

invitees. The Karachi correspondent of the *Economist* contributed a perceptive feature to the 24 May 1952 issue of the magazine and captioned it "Pakistan Comes Back to Earth." It observed that Pakistan's latest venture in international politics — the proposal for a Muslim prime ministers' conference — appeared to have ended in disappointment and a halt was likely to be called to the Pan-Islamic trend in Pakistan. It quoted the rector of Cairo's world-famous Al Azhar University as having "observed drily that too many Islamic conferences had been called in Pakistan" and also revealed that the Turkish government had replied, in so many words, that it was not interested in the setting up of the proposed system of consultation because political alignments based on religion did not attract the Turks. The article went on to state that a change in the economic situation had also helped to bring Pakistan back to earth. For the past two years Pakistan had kept consistently hitting the jackpot with her economic policy but during the last two months she had been sharply brought up against the realities of a world gutted with the primary commodities which Pakistan had for sale. Pakistan, the writer said presciently, may, under the circumstances, take a leaf out of the Turkish book and turn its face westwards again. The *Round Table* reported that of the twelve Muslim countries invited by Pakistan, seven had accepted the proposal, at least in principle, but others including Turkey, Lebanon, and Afghanistan had declined.[62] The Pakistani foreign minister told Parliament on 30 September 1953 that "on account of changed circumstances in some of the countries the idea could not be pursued further." A Pakistani writer observed plainly some years later that owing to lack of enthusiasm for it, the project had to be abandoned.[63]

So far as Pakistan's relations with individual Muslim countries are concerned, they were friendly with Turkey from the very beginning and with Iran they were decidedly close. When the first Turkish ambassador to Pakistan presented his credentials to the Quaid-i-Azam on 4 March 1948 the latter pointed out that there was a "unique significance" about the ceremony because "right from the very birth of political consciousness amongst the Muslims of this great sub-continent, the fortunes of your country were observed by us with deep sympathy and interest." The Muslims of Pakistan, the governor general added, entertained sentiments of affection and esteem for Turkey and now that Turkey and Pakistan were both free they could strengthen their ties still further for the good of both.[64]

Iran not only adjoins Pakistan but culturally is closest to Pakistan. More students in Pakistan read Persian than any other foreign language. The Urdu and Persian alphabets are identical and Pakistanis have been greatly influenced by Persian literature and art. "All Muslim countries," declared Prime Minister Liaquat Ali Khan at Tehran on 15 May 1949, "are our affectionate friends but Iran is the closest to our heart."

Such special feelings toward Turkey and Iran were in no small measure responsible for the formal ties which were later forged between these three geographically linked countries in the form of the Baghdad Pact and the RCD. It must be added, however, that, unlike the situation in Pakistan, "the drive of Islam as a polity, as a way of life, is not to be found in either of them."[65]

Pakistan's most painful experience, of course, was the continuous tension for several years with her closest Muslim neighbor, Afghanistan, which laid claim to a large slice of Pakistani territory under the cover of sponsoring the independent state of "Pakhtunistan," and the situation did not begin to ease till the hard-liner Premier Daud, a cousin of King Zahir Shah, resigned office in March 1963.[66] Also disappointing at first were Pakistan's relations with Egypt and Indonesia.

There were three basic reasons why Pakistani-Egyptian relations got off to a poor start. First, apart from the fact that the Egyptians were unable to understand the rationale of the demand for Pakistan, they could scarcely help being affected by the prevailing view that India was going to be a world power while Pakistan might very well be a transitory phenomenon on the world scene. In November 1951 the Egyptian foreign minister, Salah el Din Pasha, told an Indian correspondent in Cairo that Egypt looked to India for moral support in her struggle for national liberation.[67] However, Pakistan, for her part, was as sentimentally attached to Egypt as to any other Muslim country. At a reception given at Karachi by the Egyptian ambassador to Pakistan to celebrate the birthday of King Faruq on 11 February 1951, Khwaja Nazimuddin, governor general of Pakistan, said, "We are not celebrating the birthday of a foreign Monarch in the conventional sense of the word, but of the Head of a State to which Pakistan is bound by unbreakable ties of brotherhood and deep affection."[68] But the same King Faruq was reported to have ridiculed Pakistan's devotion to Islamic causes by saying to his courtiers,

The First Moves (1947–53)

"Don't you know that Islam was born on 14 August 1947?"[69] Secondly, faithful to the Quranic injunction that all Muslims are brothers, Pakistanis fervently believed that the individual problems of the various Muslim countries were the joint concern of all the Muslims of the world, but Egyptian leaders held a different view. Azzam Pasha, the first secretary general of the Arab League, declared, "We are Egyptians first, Arabs second and Muslims third."[70] President Gamal Abdel Nasser also placed Islamic brotherhood in the third and last circle, after the Arab circle and the African Continent circle.[71] He told Pakistanis to their face that he was opposed to the formation of a Muslim bloc because "I do not want to use Islam in international politics."[72] Thirdly, the general belief that Pakistan aspired to the leadership of all the Muslim countries irritated Egypt even more than it did the others because Egypt, on account of her preeminence among the Arabs, already regarded herself the most important country in the Muslim world.

With regard to Indonesia, the Muslim League's deep concern for Indonesia's fight for freedom from Dutch rule has already been referred to. After independence the Muslims of Pakistan were able to exert themselves still more effectively in support of Indonesia. The news of the Dutch "police action" against Indonesia in December 1948 raised a storm of protest in Pakistan and the matter was raised in Parliament on 23 December by means of a motion for adjournment. Foreign Minister Zafrulla Khan described the Dutch action as "crass stupidity and incredible folly" and "an affront to the soul of Asia and an outrage against human decency." He said he found it hard to believe that a nation which only recently had "passed through the furnace of invasion and occupation" by the Nazis should resort to methods that were strangely reminiscent of the Nazis. The fact that over 90 percent of the people of Indonesia were Muslims made their suffering and misery Pakistan's own. He informed the house that the Pakistan government had already suspended with effect from 1 A.M. the license of the Dutch civil airline KLM whose aircraft were being used in aid of the Dutch military action in Indonesia. As a demonstration against the Dutch aggression, the publication of all daily newspapers in Pakistan was suspended on 6 January. Later during the same month, at the New Delhi conference called by Nehru to consider the Indonesian situation, Zafrulla once more bitterly criticized the Netherlands for her military offensive against the Indonesian freedom fighters. On 25 January he said, in a poignant statement to the press,

Independent India and Pakistan

that newly independent countries like Pakistan, looking at the Indonesian struggle for independence, "felt like a bird, one of whose wings was free but the other was still nailed to the ground," and that that feeling would persist till all Asian countries became completely free.[73] When Indonesian independence was at last recognized, Pakistan celebrated the day as a public holiday.

Indonesia, however, at that time felt much closer to India than to Pakistan. Religion had not been an issue in Indonesia's fight for freedom and, though Indonesia's masses and orthodox Muslim elements were sympathetic to Pakistan, the governing leaders proclaimed their country a secular state, committed to a policy of socialism at home, just as Nehru had done. Muhammad Hatta, first prime minister of Indonesia, described Nehru as the "second father of the Republic of Indonesia."[74] On 17 March 1950 Nehru stated in parliament that Indonesia and India were becoming more and more intimately connected "not by formal treaties and alliances and pacts but by bonds which are much more secure, much more binding — the bonds of mutual understanding and interest and, if I may say so, even of mutual affection." When Nehru visited Indonesia in June 1950 he was greeted with tremendous enthusiasm. At a mass meeting at Djakarta, President Soekarno said that people affectionately called him father Soekarno but politically Nehru "is my father."[75]

Indonesia's poor opinion of Pakistanis was ruefully related by a member of the Pakistani Parliament in the course of a foreign affairs debate on 23 March 1950: "I have met many Indonesians, high and low, in Karachi, in Calcutta and Rangoon. Many of them still hold the mistaken notion, so ridiculously spread by Bharati propagandists, that the Muslims of this subcontinent have made no sacrifices for the freedom of their country and that it is the Congress and the Hindus alone who fought against foreign domination."

CHAPTER 6

Panchsheel vs. Defense Alliances (1954-58)

President Eisenhower's announcement in Washington, D.C., in February 1954 that the United States would extend military assistance to Pakistan is treated by some writers on South Asian affairs as a sudden break with the past and the beginning of an entirely new era. It is suggested that Pakistan never felt any danger from Communism and tricked a gullible America into giving her weapons which she wished to use against India only. America, thus, lost India's friendship for nothing. Pakistanis, for their part, complain that by openly siding with the United States they suffered the ill-will of the Communist powers without ever gaining real protection from the United States against India. The Soviet Union henceforth gave India outright support on Kashmir, using her veto several times to Pakistan's detriment.

Both India and Pakistan further allege, at times, that the Nehru-Bogra parleys on Kashmir were nearing success when the United States arms aid to Pakistan created an utterly new situation and upset all chances of Indo-Pakistani conciliation. Pakistanis employ this argument to reinforce their assertion that the price Pakistan had to pay for alliance with America was much higher than what their country received for it in return, and Indians find it useful for taunting Pakistanis that they let Kashmir slip through their fingers by foolishly alienating India at a crucial moment.

There can be no question that the sanction of military assistance by the United States to Pakistan was a highly important event but the rec-

INDEPENDENT INDIA AND PAKISTAN

ord makes it abundantly clear that it was the logical outcome of the processes which had been at work in the preceding years, and its effect also was no other than to quicken the trends which were already discernible. It has been pointed out in a previous chapter that, though Pakistan regarded the threat from India as the more immediate one, she feared Communist expansionism and ideology as well. It has been explained, also, that Pakistan's foreign policy was more in tune with that of the United States than India's had been. Immediately following the announcement that Pakistan would get arms from the United States the *Times of Karachi* wrote that "the significance of the aid is . . . that she [Pakistan] has in an ideological conflict that overshadows the world, declared her choice of friends in terms of her natural inclinations and sympathy."[1]

Fearing Indian displeasure, Washington had proceeded cautiously and the final decision to give military assistance to Pakistan was not made till Vice-President Richard Nixon, following a swing through nineteen countries including India and Pakistan, had stressed at a National Security Council Meeting that the policy of the United States must be based on what was best for America and not on fear of Indian reaction. Nixon's recommendation "was eventually carried through as a counterforce to the confirmed neutralism of Jawaharlal Nehru's India."[2] To speak less euphemistically, the United States went ahead with the proposal because she had had enough of India, which professed neutrality but in effect had sided with the Communist countries in the major issues of the day.

On Kashmir the Soviet Union had already taken a stand favorable to India, and, by rejecting all third-party proposals, Nehru had made it plain that India would never release her hold over Kashmir. During the Indian prime minister's visit to America in October 1949, Acheson had noted that "both Nehru's ideas of procedure, which seemed to preclude negotiation, and his notions on the dispute itself made any possibility of settlement dim indeed."[3] In September 1950 the United Nations representative for India and Pakistan, Sir Owen Dixon, after working hard toward a solution, had stated in his report that in the end he "became convinced that India's agreement would never be obtained to demilitarization in any such form" which would permit a free and fair plebiscite in Kashmir.[4]

The real reason why India further hardened her attitude on Kashmir from August 1953 onward was that at that juncture she fell out with

Panchsheel vs. Alliances (1954–58)

Sheikh Abdullah, on whose support her entire Kashmir policy had hitherto been based. Abdullah was peremptorily dismissed from the premiership and clapped in jail because he had begun to talk in terms of independence for Kashmir, and the "blame for the basic change in policy was irrelevantly laid at the door of Pakistan for entering into military pacts with Western powers, particularly with the United States."[5] Nehru's line of complaint against the United States for giving arms to Pakistan was that such a step imperiled the freedom of the Asian countries, that it would upset the existing equilibrium and constituted a form of intervention in Indo-Pakistani problems, and that it was a step toward war, even world war.[6]

The Indian prime minister's fears, at least in one important respect, soon proved groundless. Far from imperiling the freedom of Pakistan, the arms given to Pakistan by America reduced the existing great disparity in the military capabilities of India and Pakistan, and enabled Pakistanis to breathe easier than they ever had done before. As an Indian writer has dramatically put it: "India held the pistol at the head of Pakistan, until, in 1954, the American alliance delivered the country from that nightmare."[7] For more than a decade Indo-Pakistani relations remained free from any real threat of war. In later years Pakistanis aired many grievances against the United States, some of them not unjustified, but at a time nearer the formation of the United States–Pakistani compact a Pakistani author had frankly recognized that "the only guarantee of [Pakistan's] survival was military aid from the United States."[8] Early in 1957 Ayub Khan, who previously had often deplored Pakistan's military helplessness, said confidently that Pakistani forces could now defend "every inch" of Pakistan. If they were "to hit a target today, it will not be the same tomorrow."[9] Peace between India and Pakistan was broken only in and after 1965 when the margin of military power once again had widened in favor of India.

Though the United States had decided to sign up Pakistan on her side, she never ceased to regard India as the most important uncommitted country in the world. It was obvious that as a military power India did not rank high but in the contest for winning men's minds, which the United States and the U.S.S.R. were waging as champions of the two competing ideologies, India's non-Communist millions were the most substantial prize in the world. For fear of driving India completely into the embrace of the Communist powers, the United States continued to practice restraint in the face of Indian criticism of her policies and to assist India economically. The United States also exercised a moderating influence on Pakistan by advising her not to exacerbate her relations with India. Only once during the period under review did Pakistan revive the Kashmir dispute in the Security Council. This was in January 1957, after an enactment of the Constituent Assembly of Kashmir declaring that Kashmir was an integral part of India had raised Pakistani apprehensions. However, the statements of Indian representatives inside the Security Council, as well as outside it, made it obvious that India would permit no interference with the status quo in Kashmir, and the further efforts of Gunnar Jarring and Frank Graham who were appointed by the Council to mediate the dispute failed to change the picture.

The Principles of *Panchsheel*

Of special relevance to the theme of this book is Prime Minister Jawaharlal Nehru's specific response to the United States policy of defense alliances, to which India's neighbor and opponent, Pakistan, had now been linked. The Indian statesman had always maintained that military preparations and hostile groupings generated tension and precipitated war. He had little respect for the foreign policies of other powers. On one occasion he had invited his colleagues in the Constituent Assembly to turn their minds "to any country today and think of its foreign policy — whether it is the U.S.A., the United Kingdom, the U.S.S.R., China or France. . . . [Y]ou will find that there has been a miserable failure in the foreign policy of every great power and country."[10] Nehru saw the United States–Pakistani alliance not only as a direct threat to India's national interests but also as a test for the principles he had so often commended to the rest of the world. The time had obviously arrived for India to demonstrate concretely to the world how the challenges of international life can be best met.

President Eisenhower had announced his government's decision to provide arms to Pakistan on 25 February 1954. India delivered her countercoup on 29 April in the form of a five-point preamble to an agreement she signed with China "On Trade and Intercourse between Tibet Region of China and India." These five principles, soon to be known as *panchsheel*, were (1) mutual respect for each other's territorial integrity and sovereignty; (2) mutual nonaggression; (3) mutual noninterference in

PANCHSHEEL VS. ALLIANCES (1954–58)

each other's internal affairs; (4) equality and mutual benefit, and (5) peaceful coexistence.

When Nehru inaugurated the discussion on the pact with China in the Lok Sabha on 15 May 1954, he called the preamble "the major thing about this Agreement." His joint communiqué with visiting Premier Chou En-lai on 28 June made it clear that *panchsheel* was being offered to all the world as the ideal method of conducting relations between sovereign states: "If these principles are applied not only between various countries but also in international relations generally, they would form a solid foundation for peace and security and the fears and apprehensions that exist today would give place to a feeling of confidence." A similar statement jointly with his Russian counterpart marked the Indian prime minister's visit to the U.S.S.R.: "The wider acceptance of these principles will enlarge the area of peace, promote mutual confidence among nations, and pave the way for greater international cooperation. In the climate of peace thus created it will become possible to seek peaceful solutions of international questions by the methods of negotiation and conciliation." Subscription to *panchsheel*, according to Nehru, created an "area of peace." Such an area, he claimed, had been created between India and China and he wished that "this area of peace could be spread over the rest of the world." He expostulated with Prime Minister Muhammad Ali Bogra of Pakistan that "such a declaration [of five principles] gives far greater assurance of security and friendly relations than military pacts or military preparations."[11]

Just as American leaders, at that time, were asking nations to stand up and be counted as devotees of peace by joining the Western system of collective defense, Nehru asked them to come forward and enlist themselves as votaries of the alternative method of winning the peace by mounting the *panchsheel* bandwagon. He called *panchsheel* a challenge to the world and invited every country to say that she agreed with them. "I want them to have the courage to say so," he said, "because I do say that every country, if it is honest to itself and if it is honest to its desire to peace, must accept them; there is no way out." A foreign policy resolution of the Congress party said *panchsheel* "put forward the alternative of collective peace to the preparation for collective war."[12]

Both at home and abroad this was Jawaharlal Nehru's finest hour. The special correspondent of the *Christian Science Monitor* singled him out as the world's most important and influential statesman. In recognition of her importance, India was invited by the international community to head the Neutral Nations (prisoners of war) Repatriation Commission in Korea as well as all the three commissions set up at the Geneva Conference to control and supervise the armistice agreements. The Indian prime minister undertook extensive travels overseas to crusade for *panchsheel* and invited a large number of foreign dignitaries to India. During the years 1954–56 he visited twenty-six countries and played host to forty-one heads of state, heads of government, foreign ministers, and the like. The highlights of these exchanges were Nehru's triumphal visits to China (1954) and Russia (1955), the return visit to India of Premier Bulganin accompanied by the first secretary of the Communist party of the U.S.S.R., Nikita Khrushchev (1955), and visits to India by Premier Chou En-lai. India, the Soviet Union, and China together formed an axis of "collective peace." Bulganin told the Indians that the Soviet people saw India as "a likeminded ally in the struggle for peace" and *New Times* wrote: "Shoulder to shoulder Moscow, Peking and Delhi are fighting the great battle for world peace."[13]

During his visit to the Soviet Union, Nehru said that wherever he had gone in the U.S.S.R. he had found "a passion for peace."[14] An opinion poll conducted by the Indian Institute of Public Opinion found that the favorable opinion of the people toward Chou En-lai added up to 40.5 percent, Nasser to 37.7, Tito to 32.1, and Eisenhower to only 14.9. This contrasted with the returns of the *New York Herald Tribune*–Elmo Wilson World-Poll which found that in twelve of the thirteen countries, including Austria, Sweden, France, Germany, Italy, and Britain, Eisenhower was most trusted as "the leader doing most to keep the peace." Columnist Roscoe Drummond, who analyzed these results, commented that Indian public opinion had been "persuaded, perhaps unintentionally by its own Premier, that it should distrust America and trust the Communists."[15]

Panchsheel, however, had its critics too. While conceding that *panchsheel* provided "impeccable principles," the *Daily Telegraph* pointed out that "the whole problem of preserving peace is to make sure that practice accords with profession." Referring to Nehru's claim that his policy was a constructive and positive one, leading to collective peace, the paper asked, "Can it prevent aggression, even against the non-aligned themselves?"[16] The *Times* captioned its comments "India's Two Faces":

PANCHSHEEL VS. ALLIANCES (1954–58)

There are two views of Indian foreign policy. Stripped of its aspirations and noble sentiments for Asia and the world at large, the realist might argue, Indian foreign policy amounts to little more than the containment of Pakistan. In this task India has precise aims and they are vigorously pursued. Positions are tenaciously held — as in Kashmir — and at all times policy in relation to Pakistan has had the backing of force and has been quick to recognize and react to the force that might be used against it. In contrast to this precise concern with Indian interest the five principles of coexistence or the cherishing of fellow neutralists, the expanding area of peace or arguments over the lessening of tension are no more than expressions of a moral attitude inherent in the Indian tradition.[17]

To what extent *panchsheel* benefited any members of the human race never became apparent, but it soon became clear that the Sino-Indian Agreement which gave birth to the doctrine had sealed the fate of one attractive and innocent people. By agreeing to the description of Tibet as "the Tibet region of China," India positively endorsed the Chinese claim that Tibet was an integral part of China. In fact Tibet is a vast geographical, ethnic, linguistic, and cultural unit, distinct from any other part of the world, and it had enjoyed virtual independence since the Chinese revolution of 1911, which ended the rule of the Manchurian dynasty. In July 1949, when it became clear that China would soon become a Communist state "the Tibetan Government broke off diplomatic relations with China and made a Chinese representative in Lhasa depart from Tibet. . . . Since then, Tibet has not even maintained formal relations with the Chinese Government and people."[18]

When Communist China invaded Tibet in 1950 to "liberate" her, Nehru himself had pointedly commented: "From whom they were going to liberate Tibet is, however, not quite clear." He contended that "since Tibet is not the same as China, it should ultimately be the wishes of the people of Tibet that should prevail and not any legal or constitutional arguments."[19] But when the Dalai Lama appealed to the United Nations the matter was shelved chiefly because India, the country most affected by the current of events across her 2500-mile border, had expressed confidence that the Tibetan question could be settled peacefully. Finding no redress at the hands of the world organization, Tibet had no option but to acquiesce in whatever terms the Chinese chose to impose upon her. The result was the seventeen-point Sino-Tibetan agreement of 23 May 1951 on "Measures for the Peaceful Liberation of Tibet." The agreement stipulated inter alia that the Tibetans had the "right of exercising national regional autonomy under the unified leadership of the Central People's Government"; that "the Central authorities will not alter the existing political system in Tibet" nor "the established status, functions and powers of the Dalai Lama"; that "freedom of religious belief" would be allowed; and that "in matters related to various reforms in Tibet, there will be no compulsion."[20] All these promises, however, soon came to nought.

Tibet's freedom was obviously sacrificed by India so that the chances of forming special ties between India and China, which Nehru had long desired, would not be jeopardized. It was essential for the success of his program of a resurgent Asia, from which Western influence would have to be eliminated, that India and China, the two largest Asians, should march hand in hand. In his July 1954 letter to the presidents of the State Congress Committees — whom he addressed as "comrades" — Nehru thus explained the "larger context" of his China policy: "You must have read the joint statement that Mr. Chou En-lai and I issued after our talks in Delhi. . . . I believe that these statements are important not only for the countries concerned but also in a much larger context. I believe also that they indicate a certain historic change in the relationship of forces in Asia. . . . The statements have only given expression to something that has been happening for some time, something that is giving Asia a place of her own in world affairs."[21] This was *realpolitik*, not high morality. At the very time when many countries of Asia and Africa, having far less rationale for independent existence than the ancient land of Tibet, were breaking the bonds of their thralldom, Tibet lost even such autonomy as she already possessed.

An attempt is sometimes made to defend India's conduct on the ground that, by conceding China's suzerainty over Tibet, she merely did what Britain had done before her. Two things need to be said about this. In the first place the British, in the words of Lord Curzon, viceroy of India, accepted Chinese suzerainty over Tibet merely as a "constitutional fiction — a political affectation which has only been maintained because of its convenience to both parties."[22] Secondly, independent India was pledged to eradicate vestiges of colonialism and imperialism, not to condone them.

Nor did Pakistan, another professed enemy of colonialism and imperialism, express the slightest concern at the plight of the hapless Tibetans. Though Pakistani-controlled Kashmir had a direct border with

Panchsheel vs. Alliances (1954-58)

Tibet, which later became the subject of a border agreement between Pakistan and China, Liaquat Ali Khan's only comment on the Chinese invasion of Tibet was: "The scene is so far away that I have nothing to say."[23] It was not till 1959, when Pakistan's relations with China were clouded for a while, that Pakistan could spare a word of sympathy for the poor Tibetans.[24]

Though *panchsheel* contained nothing startlingly new, Nehru spoke of it as "India's contribution" toward bringing the countries of the world nearer to one another. Britain's foreign secretary, Lord Home, thought it so easy to accept the generalities of *panchsheel* that he told the Indian Council of World Affairs that all Commonwealth countries subscribed to them. Bulganin, after pleasing Indians by telling them that "it was India which first proclaimed the Panch Shila," claimed in his report to the Supreme Soviet of the U.S.S.R. that "the principle of peaceful co-existence of countries with different social systems" was a basic Leninist principle of Soviet foreign policy. In February 1972 another personage joined the fraternity of *panchsheel.* He was no other than President Richard Nixon of the United States, whose recommendation, as vice-president, to give American weapons to Pakistan had originally contributed toward the formulation of *panchsheel* as a countermove to the American policy of collective defense. The Sino-United States joint communiqué, marking President Nixon's very first contact with Chinese leadership, stated that the two sides had agreed to "conduct their relations on the principles of respect for the sovereignty and territorial integrity of all states, nonaggression against other states, noninterference in the internal affairs of other states, equality, and mutual benefit and peaceful coexistence." In fact Nixon was taking the place vacated by Jawaharlal Nehru who after the Sino-Indian Himalayan skirmishes of 1962 had angrily declared "there is no Panchsheel *vis a vis* China."[25]

What had made Nehru think that *panchsheel* would be a more effective means of preventing war than military preparedness? The answer to this question lies in the basic philosophy of Gandhi, which Nehru admittedly had set out to apply to the foreign affairs of independent India. Nehru believed that it was Gandhi's unique technique of *satyagraha* which had enabled unarmed India to undermine her militarily powerful British overlords. "In *satyagraha*," explains an Indian analyst, "it is not a question of capturing a particular outpost, isolating and overwhelming an army corps, or bombing an industrial town or a military target out of

Independent India and Pakistan

existence. *Satyagraha* seeks to initiate certain psychological changes, first in those who offer it and then in those against whom it is directed."[26] In other words, *satyagraha* does not endeavor to floor an adversary physically by the conventional method of using superior force but aims at converting him to one's own way of thinking by overwhelming him with a sort of "moral jiu-jitsu."

As Nehru saw it, Gandhi's strategy "took its strength from the fact that he undermined his opponents — psychologically speaking — when he treated them as friends. The opponent's aggressiveness just faded away before him. . . . The psychological approach is far more important than either the political or certainly the military." In *panchsheel*, he explained, it was "a question of our following a policy which . . . makes it more and more difficult progressively for the other country to break trust. . . . [W]e can create an environment wherein it becomes a little more dangerous to the other party to break away from the pledges given." On another occasion he stated that *panchsheel* led to the building up of world opinion which gradually makes it difficult even for "evil powers" to misbehave.[27]

Gandhi had claimed that "the twins [of truth and nonviolence] constitute the mightiest force in the world. Before it the atom bomb is of no effect." Prime Minister Nehru said the answer to the threat of weapons of mass destruction was to be found in the Indian experience of winning freedom by nonviolence. If nuclear weapons were opposed by spiritual and moral strength, their use would become difficult.[28]

Undercurrents of Transition

Though scarcely visible at the time, *panchsheel* in fact had begun to erode almost immediately after its clamorous debut. A government of India publication retrospectively bemoaned: "In July 1954, within three months of the agreement on trade and intercourse between India and Tibet, the Chinese laid claim to an Indian territory for the first time by protesting against the presence of our troops in Barahoti which is a part of the Indian state of Uttar Pradesh. A year later, their troops camped on the camping ground of Barahoti and in September 1955 they even pushed 10 miles south of Niti Pass to Damzan. More intrusions followed in the summer of 1956 in the same sector of the India-China border."[29] In September 1957 the government of India learned that the Chinese

Panchsheel vs. Alliances (1954-58)

had completed the Sinkiang-Tibet highway which passed through the Aksai Chin area claimed by India as her territory.

At the Bandung Conference (April 1955), despite Nehru's strenuous pleading, his fellow Afro-Asians including Chou En-lai, representing twenty-eight other countries, refused to limit themselves to *panchsheel* and approved instead ten principles, including the right of collective defense of which Muhammad Ali Bogra of Pakistan was the principal sponsor. Bandung clearly revealed that Asia had many voices and no acknowledged leader. India henceforth viewed all proposals for a second Bandung type of meeting with marked coolness and confined her preference to the more congenial gathering of nonaligned states where the well-known Nehru-Nasser-Tito troika would set the pace. It made little sense after Bandung to talk any more of India's being the natural leader of the Afro-Asian countries.

Sino-Pakistani relations, never so tense as Pakistani-Soviet relations, entered a period of further relaxation as a result of the personal encounter at Bandung of the prime ministers of Pakistan and China. During 1956 the prime ministers of the two countries exchanged friendly visits. In direct contrast to the open support the Soviet Union gave to India on Kashmir, and to Afghanistan on "Pakhtunistan" during these years, China, despite vociferous Sino-Indian demonstrations of friendship, never took a definite position on either issue, thus leaving perpetually open the door for a cordial relationship with Pakistan. So impressed was Suhrawardy by China's friendliness that he prophetically declared in Parliament: "I feel perfectly certain that when the crucial time comes China will come to our assistance."[30]

An Indian writer marks July 1958 as the time after which Sino-Indian relations began to deteriorate. In August, the Chinese turned down India's offer to mediate the Sino-United States crisis over the offshore islands, and in the autumn Nehru's scheduled visit to Lhasa had to be abandoned at China's behest.[31]

The years 1956-58 also witnessed some other far-reaching developments of which the import became clearer in subsequent years. Khrushchev's denunciation of Stalin in 1956 proved to be the start of the Sino-Soviet ideological schism. The Chinese called it repudiation of true "Marxism-Leninism." In his July 1958 proposal for a conference of world powers to consider the Middle East crisis, the Soviet premier suggested that the participants should be only the U.S.S.R., the United

INDEPENDENT INDIA AND PAKISTAN

States, the United Kingdom, France, and India. He pointedly omitted Communist China from the list of invitees even though, according to the Soviet Union's own repeated assertions, she was rightfully one of the five permanent members of the Security Council and, therefore, entitled to great-power status.

Contemporaneously, a thaw began to be felt in Indo–United States relations. Nehru made the most successful of his three visits to America in the aftermath of the Suez crisis. In a somewhat sentimental radio and television broadcast from Washington, D.C., he talked of a mold in brass of Abraham Lincoln's right hand which an American professor had given him as a gift. "It is a beautiful hand," he told the vast audience touchingly, "strong and firm and yet gentle. It has been kept ever since on my study table, and I look at it every day, and it gives me strength." He praised the United States for "upholding worthily the principles of the Charter of the United Nations" in the recent upheavals in Hungary and Suez. Anticipating India's financial crisis and the need for vastly increased economic assistance, he said, "We plead for your friendship, and your co-operation and sympathy in the great task that we have undertaken in our own country."[32]

Worrying events in India soon caused the United States to bestir herself on the former's behalf. In the general elections in early spring (1957), the Communist party more than doubled its vote in the Lok Sabha, and in the state of Kerala it won an absolute majority and formed the government. Secretary Dulles called this "a dangerous trend." The fear of further Communist inroads was greatly aroused in May when the finance minister, while presenting the general budget in Parliament, disclosed India's fast deteriorating economic position and a mounting foreign exchange crisis. In 1958 the rate of economic growth in Communist China, with whom democratic India was supposed to compete, was at least three times that of India.[33] The United States not only made a heavy contribution herself to avert disaster, but also organized a consortium of the leading non-Communist countries to assist India on a long-term basis. A zealous figure in this effort was Senator John F. Kennedy, destined in the not-too-distant future to become the chief executive of the United States. As Chester Bowles observed, the American policy of fighting Communism turned "a good healthy Communist minority" into a valuable natural resource which a country could cash "right in at the American Treasury."[34]

Panchsheel vs. Alliances (1954–58)

Nor was the economy of India the only sector in which Nehru's magic touch was beginning to falter. During the concurrent crises in Suez and Hungary his foreign policy also, for the first time, came under serious fire at home. Several critics noted that India's condemnation of the Anglo-French invasion of Egypt had been immediate and vigorous, while her criticism of the Soviet incursion into Hungary was slow and cautious. Jayaprakash Narayan, for instance, complained that the government was following a double standard: "One standard of measurement for Egypt, and another for Hungary."[35]

America's economic aid to India shot up to $364.8 million in 1957 from only $92.8 million in 1956. As aid to Pakistan remained at about the same level ($162.5 million in 1956 and $170.7 million in 1957),[36] Pakistanis began to ask what special advantage they derived from being allies of the United States. The Americans, for their part, increasingly expressed disappointment at Pakistan's continued political instability and poor economic performance. It was felt that United States military aid to Pakistan had intensified an armament race between the two South Asian countries, greatly depleting the funds needed for raising the living standards of their poor peoples.

Pakistan and the Muslim World

Pakistan's relations with the Muslim nations during this period followed the existing lines but the trends were greatly accelerated because of Pakistan's alliance with the Western countries. With Turkey and Iran the ties became closer and more concrete, and with Afghanistan and the Arab countries they got far worse than before.

As a step toward integration with the Western defense system, Pakistan, on 2 April 1954, signed an agreement with Turkey which envisaged cooperation in different spheres, including the important field of defense. This was followed by a United States–Pakistani Mutual Defense Assistance Agreement (19 May). Pakistan joined SEATO on 8 September 1954 and the Baghdad Pact (later named CENTO) on 23 September 1955. In the last named she had the Muslim states of Turkey and Iran as fellow members, besides the United Kingdom. The United States did not join the pact formally but worked for its formation and took an active part in the various committees.

The prospect of Pakistan becoming militarily stronger was an unwelcome one for Afghanistan because of the "Pakhtunistan" controversy be-

INDEPENDENT INDIA AND PAKISTAN

tween the two adjoining countries. Pakistan's decision in 1955 to turn the various provinces in the western wing of the country into "One Unit" especially angered Afghanistan because it meant a further erosion of the distinct identity of the Pathans of the Northwest Frontier Province. The Pakistani embassy and consulates in Afghanistan were ransacked by mobs as a result of which diplomatic ties were severed and the Pakistani-Afghan border was sealed, closing the avenue through which most of Afghanistan's commerce and intercourse with the outside world flowed. These incidents enabled the Soviet Union to ingratiate herself into Afghanistan's favor by supporting the latter's stand on "Pakhtunistan" and rendering her economic assistance. Though Pakistan and Afghanistan reopened diplomatic missions in each other's country after some months, and the border traffic was resumed, Pakistan's relations with Afghanistan on the whole remained under considerable strain.

With respect to Arab countries there were signs in the early 1950s that Pakistan was beginning to win their esteem on account of Pakistani Foreign Minister Zafrulla Khan's brilliant espousal of Muslim causes in the United Nations. However, before this thaw could lead to any fruitful result, Pakistan joined the Baghdad Pact and this plunged Pakistani-Arab relations virtually to a cold-war level. Nasser bitterly complained that by inviting Iraq to join the Baghdad Pact the Western powers had dealt a severe blow to Arab unity and also that by emphasizing the Communist danger to the Middle East from the North, they had camouflaged the much nearer danger from their own protégé, Israel. During the days of her zealous membership in the Western system of defense, Pakistan was shunned as a camp follower of Western imperialism.

Saudi Arabia called Pakistan's subscription to the Baghdad Pact "a stab in the heart of the Arab and Muslim states."[37] Pakistanis were further upset when King Saud, during a seventeen-day state visit to India in November and December 1955, publicly certified that the fate of Indian Muslims was "in safe hands."[38] When Nehru visited Saudi Arabia, in the following September, he was welcomed with chants of *marhaba rasool al salam* which literally means "welcome, messenger of peace" but which bore a marked similarity to the description of the Prophet Muhammad in the *kalima*: *Muhammad-ur-Rasool Allah* (Muhammad, the messenger of God). This raised a storm of protest in Pakistan which was not a whit becalmed by the explanation of the Saudi Arabian embassy that the greeting simply meant "welcome, messenger of peace" and not "welcome,

Panchsheel vs. Alliances (1954–58)

Prophet of Peace." *Dawn* (27 September 1956) editorialized that "most Muslims in this country know what the literal meaning of the word *rasool* is, but they also know that it has acquired a sacred connotation since the advent of the Holy Prophet whom the *kalima* specifically describes as *Muhammad-ur-Rasool Allah*." The article advised Pakistanis to restrain their expectations from the "so-called Muslim world" and realize that "for the present," Pakistanis themselves were the sole champions of the ideology of Islam.

Pakistani-Egyptian acrimony reached its highest point during the Suez crisis. Nasser publicly complained that Foreign Minister Hamidul Haq had personally assured him of Pakistani support at the forthcoming First London Conference but had gone back on his word.[39] The Egyptian president humiliated Pakistanis by rejecting the offer of Pakistani troops to join the United Nations Emergency Force in the Middle East, while welcoming the inclusion of an Indian contingent, and by making it known that Prime Minister Suhrawardy, who was contemplating a visit to Cairo, would not be welcome there. Perhaps his unkindest cut was to declare that Suez was as dear to Egypt as Kashmir was to India.[40]

In the National Assembly of Pakistan Suhrawardy questioned Egypt's claim to be a champion of the Arab causes against Israel. He argued that Pakistan had not recognized Israel, and will "never" recognize her. India, on the other hand, had recognized Israel, and had "amicable relations" with her. Even so Nasser had accepted Indian troops on Egyptian soil but had spurned the offer of Pakistani troops.[41] On a later occasion Suhrawardy alleged that Egypt favored the reunion of Pakistan with India and regarded Kashmir as a part of India. He averred that Pakistan could get closer to Egypt only if she became a secular state like the latter and deleted Islam from her constitution. Pakistan, he thought, should think twice before she adopted a step "in the right direction for forming a Muslim combination."[42]

Dawn joined the fray with some vitriolic editorials. It warned against attaining Muslim unity by taking the Muslim Middle East "bound hand and foot, to Cairo's modern little Pharaoh, to be commanded at his will, or to become collectively the satellite of Moscow and be damned both in body and soul, as Hungary's thousands of escaped refugees can tell how."[43] A few days later, another *Dawn* leader captioned "So This Is Nasser!" said that Nasser's "hatred of Pakistan and love for Bharat" was conditioned by "insensate bias and blind prejudice the source of which

INDEPENDENT INDIA AND PAKISTAN

might well be examined by psychiatrists" and regretted that "in the veins of this turbulent egotist not the blood of Islam should seem to flow but the turbid waters of the Nile. Nasser will never be our friend."[44]

Egyptian news media sustained a fierce campaign against Suhrawardy, calling him "the tail of colonialism" and "a mercenary who has sold himself and his country to the devil." *Dawn*'s Cairo correspondent noted that during Suhrawardy's visit to America an official line of attack was handed over to each editor by the chief of propaganda in Egypt, who functioned directly under Nasser. Newspapers were forbidden to publish any corrections issued by Suhrawardy or repudiations emanating from the Pakistani embassy. Pakistan was pictured as Egypt's enemy number one which must be cowed before the West could be effectively tackled. The Indian embassy was assisting the Egyptians by giving them ideas and suggesting suitable lines of propaganda.[45]

Though angry with Nasser as an individual, Pakistanis did not waver in their concern for Egyptians as fellow Muslims. *Dawn* used harsh language against Nasser personally in the "So This Is Nasser!" article but concluded: "Let none of us forget that Nasser is but an incident that will pass while Egypt and Egyptians will always abide. Despite Nasser, therefore, our support and sympathy should continue to be extended to our brethren there in their hour of trial [during the Suez crisis]."

When the United States inaugurated a program of massive economic aid to India, following the Indian foreign exchange crisis of 1957–58, Pakistanis, who always had the feeling that the United States was less solicitous toward her ally Pakistan than toward neutral India, received a further shock. On the rebound their thoughts reverted to their first love, the sister Muslim countries, and there was a general desire to regain the ground lost by Pakistan's overly close association with the West. Asserting that "blood is thicker than water," *Dawn* said that Pakistan truly belonged to the Muslim world. "A brother with whom we may have fallen out is still a brother and nearer to us than a stranger. Lured by the blandishments of the insincere West we had strayed from this truth. Now we have relearned it the hard way and our policies and outlook must be accordingly readjusted."[46]

The hour of Pakistani-Arab reconciliation, however, had not yet arrived. In the Middle East crisis of 1958 Pakistan caused further offense to the Arab states by joining her Baghdad Pact allies, Iran and Turkey, in voicing approval of the dropping of British paratroops in Jordan and

PANCHSHEEL VS. ALLIANCES (1954–58)

the landing of American marines in Lebanon. India criticized the Western powers for interfering in the affairs of other countries but the tone was less strident than in the past. Clearly, increased American assistance had already begun to pay some return.

Revolution in Pakistan

The Muslims of Pakistan, so keen to forge the unity of Muslims all over the world, at home continued to squabble among themselves. Not only did the two wings of Pakistan move further apart from each other, but inside each wing the never-ending factional feuds and rivalries were fast sapping the country's vitality.

East Pakistanis viewed the One Unit scheme as the West Pakistani counterstroke to the overwhelming victory of the United Front over the Muslim League in the East Pakistani elections. A constitution for the new state of Pakistan, which had been lying on the anvil since 1947, was nearing completion. East Pakistanis believed that West Pakistanis, especially the Punjabis who dominated West Pakistan, had constituted themselves into One Unit to enable them to talk to their compatriots in the eastern part with one voice to nullify the latter's numerical superiority and prevent them from capturing power at the center. During the debate on the One Unit bill in Parliament, a Bengali member quoted the following interesting excerpt from a document which was being secretly circulated among West Pakistani leaders: "A fragmented West Pakistan has really nothing to ask from East Pakistan because the realities of the situation in any conceivable constitutional pattern would already have given East Pakistan an incontrovertible superiority."[47]

Nehru alluded to the turmoil and instability inside Pakistan at a news conference on 4 June 1958, at which he discussed recent incidents on the Indo-Pakistani border. He said the difficulty about protesting to Pakistan currently was that India did not quite know whom to address in that country and wondered whether the authorities in Pakistan exercised any control over those manning the border.[48] By October 1958 conditions in both parts of Pakistan had reached a state of chaos. In the words of General Ayub, who assumed absolute power by staging a revolution: "Ever since the death of the Quaid-e-Azam and Mr. Liaquat Ali Khan, politicians started free-for-all type of fighting in which no holds were barred. . . . They used provincial feelings, sectarian, religious and racial differences to set a Pakistani against a Pakistani. . . . The coun-

Independent India and Pakistan

try and people could go to the dogs as far as they were concerned. . . . A perfectly sound country has been turned into a laughing stock. . . . We have to put this mess right and put the country on an even keel."[49]

As the commander in chief of the army Ayub had been one of the original architects of the alliance with America. He now earnestly set about the task of rehabilitating that loosening tie. A statement typical of his opening years read: "Pakistan has openly and unequivocally cast its lot with the West. . . . We do not believe in hunting with the hound and running with the hare."[50]

CHAPTER 7

Warclouds over South Asia: Sino-Indian Conflict (1959-62)

The Cold War

The thirty-first of March 1959 proved to be a landmark in South Asian affairs, for it was on that day that the Dalai Lama escaped into India after an adventurous two-week march from Lhasa. This event started a chain reaction of which the force has still not been spent. It immediately set off a cold war between India and China, which eventually escalated to the brief Himalayan war between them. Directly or indirectly, it contributed to the widening of the split between the Soviet Union and China, to the cooling off of relations between Pakistan and the United States, to the creation of common interests between Pakistan and China, and to the Indo-Pakistani wars of 1965 and 1971.

It was fear for his safety and freedom that caused the Dalai Lama to flee from his homeland. By 1955 the Tibetans, specially the Khampas and Amdowas in the eastern region, had started an open struggle against the Chinese occupation forces, and before long the clashes assumed the proportions of a rebellion. In early March 1959 tension spread to Lhasa itself, where thousands of tribesmen from the east had been collecting. When the commander of the local Chinese garrison invited the Dalai Lama to a cultural show, asking the latter to leave behind his customary armed escort, there was speculation that the Chinese wished to take the god-king prisoner and spirit him away to China. Thereupon, the Dalai Lama, disguised as a soldier and accompanied by his mother and other

INDEPENDENT INDIA AND PAKISTAN

relatives and a group of his most trusted followers, set out for India in the darkness of the night.

Upon entering Indian territory he was greeted by a telegram of welcome from Prime Minister Nehru which read: "My colleagues and I welcome you and send you greetings on your safe arrival in India. We shall be happy to afford the necessary facilities for you, your family and entourage to reside in India. The people of India who hold you in great veneration will no doubt accord their traditional respect to your personage."[1] A crowd of journalists and photographers awaited the celebrated refugee at the railhead of Tezpur and splashed the account of his escape as "the story of the year." From Tezpur he was taken to Mussoorie by a special train, provided by the government of India.

In his statements made at Tezpur as well as at Mussoorie, the Dalai Lama bitterly attacked the Chinese for their cruelties in Tibet.[2] He alleged that, though the seventeen-point agreement of 1951 had been forcibly imposed upon Tibet, the Tibetans had decided to abide by it to save themselves "from the danger of total destruction." The Chinese, however, contravened the terms of the pact from the very beginning. Contrary to their undertaking, they undermined his — the Dalai Lama's — authority, and proceeded to exterminate the Tibetan race and destroy the religion and culture of Tibet. Sixty-five thousand Tibetans had been killed since 1956 and 1000 monasteries had been destroyed during the 1959 rebellion. He was still prepared for a peaceful settlement provided "such a solution guarantees preservation of the rights and powers which Tibet has enjoyed and exercised without any interference prior to 1950."

On 9 September the Dalai Lama cabled an appeal to the secretary general of the United Nations, his second such effort, and the matter came before the General Assembly in the form of a motion sponsored by Ireland and Malaya. The resolution expressed grave concern at reports that "the fundamental human rights and freedoms of the people of Tibet" had been denied to them and called for "respect for the fundamental human rights of the Tibetan people and for their distinctive cultural and religious life."[3]

Nehru had advised the Dalai Lama not to take the matter to the United Nations, saying that no good would come of it. The Indian delegation, therefore, abstained in the vote on the resolution. Because of the poor state of relations between Pakistan and China at that time, Pakistan, however, strongly supported the motion and voted for it, in com-

Sino-Indian Conflict (1959-62)

pany with the United States. Prince Aly Khan, the Pakistani representative, declared that the people of Pakistan had been greatly concerned over the unfortunate events in Tibet. "The Pakistan delegation rejects any cynical opinion that there is very little the United Nations can do about the situation in Tibet," he went on, because the Assembly did have an effective means at its disposal, namely, world opinion. Above all, the Tibetan question raised a profound question of conscience for all members of the United Nations.[4] The resolution was carried by a vote of 45 to 9, with 26 abstentions.

The Chinese were furious at the worldwide condemnation of their conduct in Tibet and thought India was a secret party to the conspiracy against them. They had long believed that Kalimpong in India was a base for the insurrection in Tibet.[5] They renewed this charge, besides alleging that the Dalai Lama had been abducted to India, that he was being held there under duress, and that his statement from Tezpur had been "imposed on him by foreigners." They also strongly protested to the government of India against an incident on 20 April outside the Chinese Consulate General at Bombay, in the course of which a portrait of Mao Tse-tung had been pelted with tomatoes and rotten eggs.

On 6 May 1959 the *Renmin Ribao* (People's Daily) published a lengthy article, "The Revolution in Tibet and Nehru's Philosophy."[6] Though the article hoped for continued good relations with India, it blamed India for having interfered in the "internal affairs" of China since 1950. "The Indian Government intervened through diplomatic channels in October 1950," the article asserted, "when the Chinese Government ordered its troops to enter Tibet. . . . The Indian Government delivered . . . three notes to the Chinese Government. . . . [S]uch interference still continues in certain forms." It said that the impressive welcome extended to the Dalai Lama and the visit to Mussoorie by the Indian prime minister were equivalent to "giving a welcome to, and holding a meeting with, the leader of a rebellion in a friendly country." It complained, further, that the Indian government had "never pursued a clear-cut policy of non-interference." Nehru felt greatly disturbed by the charges against himself and his country and said the Chinese had "used the language of the cold war regardless of truth and propriety."[7]

The Border Dispute

The Chinese and the Indian governments had been exchanging notes on

INDEPENDENT INDIA AND PAKISTAN

border incidents since July 1954 but Nehru had not revealed these differences to the Indian public or Parliament, hoping to resolve the problem by quiet diplomacy. However, his hand was forced by a serious incident at Longju, and a news item published in the *Assam Tribune* of 26 August 1959 that 1000 Chinese troops, equipped with the most modern weapons, had entered the Northeast Frontier Area (NEFA) and hoisted the Chinese flag there. In response to a short-notice question and an adjournment motion in the Lok Sabha on 28 August, the prime minister said that the report in the *Assam Tribune* was not correct but he conceded that there had been some Chinese intrusions into Indian border areas for the past two or three years and at one place (Aksai Chin) the Chinese had built a road which traversed Indian territory. He admitted, further, that a clash involving a picket of about 38 Indian soldiers and a detachment of "some hundreds, 200 or 300 or, maybe, even more" Chinese troops had taken place on 25 and 26 August at Longju in NEFA, and that the Indians had been forced to abandon the position. On a later occasion he told Parliament that Indian authorities had come to know about the Aksai Chin road in September 1957, when a Chinese government statement announced its completion.

The fat was now in the fire and resentment ran high. On 31 August one member of Parliament asked, "Will not the Government of India at least consider the advisability of bombing the road built in our territory out of existence?"[8] A more serious incident, at Kongka Pass in Ladakh on 20–21 October 1959, in which nine Indian soldiers were killed, caused tempers to rise still higher.

At a public meeting on 24 October Nehru admitted that the Sino-Indian border conflict was causing "grave anxiety" but appealed to the people to remain calm. The *Indian Express* observed that the prime minister's appeal for calmness was not only dangerous but foolish. The *Hindustan Times* wrote that it was "fatuous" to continue the "sham debate" on what China was up to. "It would appear," the editorial continued, "that the Chinese have been carrying out probing actions and seizing territory at will on no better claim than that no Indian opposition was met. . . . [T]he need to do something is peremptory. Mr. Nehru has warned us against brave talk and action taken in anger. Let us warn him in turn that he may not have many more opportunities to unite the country behind him, if China is allowed to go on heaping contumely and humiliation on us." A *New York Times* dispatch summed up the Indian

SINO-INDIAN CONFLICT (1959–62)

scene in these words: "Mr. Nehru is receiving sharp criticism for his meek response to Communist China's pressure. Newspaper editorials throughout India have expressed bitter resentment and forthright condemnation of the Government's policy. Never before has Mr. Nehru been so sharply criticized."[9]

An ugly public demonstration took place in front of the Chinese embassy on 17 November 1959. The mob shouted slogans such as *Chini luteron hai hai* (Curse be on the Chinese robbers), *Chou En-lai murdabad* (May Chou En-lai perish), and *Mao Tse-tung hai hai* (Curse be on Mao Tse-tung). Straw effigies of Mao Tse-tung and Chou En-lai were burned at the spot. In Parliament, Acharya Kripalani, a past president of the Congress party, criticized the promise that *panchsheel* "will usher in perpetual peace and that everybody will live happily ever after." The conception of coexistence "implies mutuality," he argued. "A nation coexists with another nation. If the other nation does not want to co-exist with it, how can there be co-existence?" He also ridiculed the government's puerile past posture toward China: "The people were encouraged to keep shouting '*Hindi-Chini bhai bhai*,' when in fact aggression was taking place. The Chinese must have laughed in their sleeves at this strange and infantile exhibition of childish sentimentality. Today the people feel humiliated and they look ridiculous."[10] Nehru now "had to reckon with the wave of anti-Chinese feeling which made national prestige rather than national interest the main determinant of policy towards China."[11]

Already, on 4 September 1959, Nehru had impliedly recognized that the theory of balance of power, which he had belittled so often in the past, had its uses in the game of international power politics. "Natural friendship," he had observed, "does not exist if you are weak and if you are looked down upon as a weak country. . . . It is only when people are more or less equal, when people respect each other that they are friends. So also nations." After the Kongka Pass clash of arms he said that the border issue with China had now become a military issue and would be dealt with by the army. A "forward policy" was adopted to counter what was seen as the Chinese threat to India's entire border. Essentially it consisted of establishing small military posts, mostly in the wasteland of the Ladakh region, for the purposes of staking India's claim, checking Chinese advance, and getting behind Chinese posts to cut off their lines of communication and regain lost ground. But it was naively

INDEPENDENT INDIA AND PAKISTAN

assumed that India would get what she wanted without serious retaliation from the Chinese. Krishna Menon, who was the defense minister at the time, conceived the policy as "showing the flag and so on, largely depending upon our hope that good sense would prevail."[12]

In the meantime the war of words continued unabated. The Chinese alleged that the Indians had encroached upon China's territory at several places since the Sino-Indian Agreement of 1954, and they claimed that the Longju and the Kongka Pass encounters had taken place on their land and they had acted defensively. Premier Chou En-lai's letter of 8 September 1959 specially alarmed Nehru. In it he not only restated the Chinese position that the "Sino-Indian boundary has never been formally delimited," but emphatically asserted that "the so-called McMahon Line" was the product of the British policy of aggression against the "Tibet region of China" and had never been recognized by any Chinese central government. It was "decidedly illegal" and the Chinese government "absolutely" did not recognize it. Even more disturbing was the specific claim he advanced to 90,000 square kilometers of "the Tibet region of China" south of the McMahon Line, which were in India's possession.[13]

Nehru, responding on 26 September, said that Chou En-lai's letter had "greatly surprised and distressed" him and claimed that the boundaries of India were "settled for centuries by history, geography, custom and tradition." He recognized that the 35,000-kilometer-long India-China border had never been demarcated on the ground and minor disputes could arise at some places. But he was adamant that no discussions could be fruitful "unless the posts on the Indian side of the traditional frontier now held by the Chinese forces are first evacuated by them." The door was thus slammed against a negotiated settlement on a give-and-take basis. India refused to negotiate seriously unless the Chinese first vacated what India unilaterally claimed to be her areas. China's proposal, made in Chou En-lai's letter of 7 November 1959, that China and India each withdraw 20 kilometers from the McMahon Line in the east, and from the line of actual control in the west, was not accepted. Nehru demanded, instead, that in the western sector each side withdraw behind the boundary shown on the other side's maps. As he himself explained later, this really meant that the Chinese should vacate the territory India claimed as hers.[14]

Though China had formally laid claim to a large tract in NEFA, she was in fact willing to accept the McMahon Line as the de facto border

Sino-Indian Conflict (1959-62)

in that sector, provided India did not disturb her possession of the Aksai Chin, through which the important road from Sinkiang ran into Tibet. This was clear from Chou En-lai's letter of 7 November just cited as well as from what he publicly said in New Delhi when he met Nehru there in April 1960. China "absolutely" could not recognize the illegal McMahon Line, repeated the Chinese premier in the course of his press conference in the Indian capital; "nevertheless, pending a settlement of the Sino-Indian boundary question, we are willing to maintain the present state and will not cross this line." With regard to the western sector he said he had asked the Indian government to adopt an attitude similar to the attitude of the Chinese government toward the area in the eastern sector but the Indian government had not agreed to this.[15] In his own separate remarks to the press Nehru confirmed that the differences on the western sector had constituted the real stumbling block, and he criticized the Chinese wish to "link their acceptance of the actual position in N-EFA with Indian recognition of the fact of Chinese occupation in Ladakh."[16]

In their joint communiqué (25 April 1960) the two conferees stated that their "talks did not result in resolving the differences that had arisen" but added that the officials of the two sides would hold meetings from June to September 1960, study the material on which each side relied, and report to both governments. After their discussions the officials, to no one's surprise, produced sharply dissenting reports.

During the officials' meetings China had refused to discuss "the boundary west of the Karakoram Pass between China's Sinkiang and Kashmir" because "of the present actual situation in Kashmir."[17] This came as a shock to the Indians, who had hitherto assumed that China recognized their claim to the whole of Kashmir. "China has now come out openly on the Kashmir issue," lamented the Indian team, "and declined to recognize the accession of Kashmir to India."

The Himalayan War

After the officials' reports the negotiations reached an impasse, and it was only a question of time before the provocative moves and countermoves of the parties on the disputed border resulted in a serious passage of arms.

Prime Minister Jawaharlal Nehru reassured his countrymen, from time to time, that India's position on the border was improving and the Chinese were losing ground. "Progressively the situation has been changing from a military point of view and from other points of view, in our favour," he told the Lok Sabha on 28 November 1961, "and we shall continue to take steps to build up these things, so that ultimately we may be in a position to take action to recover such territory as is in their possession." On 20 June 1962 he repeated that "the position as it is, is more advantageous to India than it was previously, and the advantage is growing." Two months later he said, once more, that India had been strengthening her position "by building road communications and the rest and by putting up posts" and that "in the military sense" she was much stronger than she was a year or two previously. Because of her posts, India had regained control of 2500 square miles. At the same time, however, he vehemently rejected all suggestions that India should request military assistance from any other country to meet the Chinese challenges. "Personally I do not think," he argued, "that we shall maintain our independence for long if we go about seeking military aid from others to defend ourselves." A few days afterwards he rejected the idea of seeking military aid on the ground that it would be "basically and fundamentally opposed to a non-alignment policy. Taking military help means practically becoming aligned to that country."[18]

By the summer of 1962 it had become fairly evident that a major clash between the Indian and Chinese forces could not be long delayed. In a note sent to India on 30 April 1962 China warned that if India did not withdraw her "aggressive posts" the Chinese frontier guards would be "compelled to defend themselves." It stated further that the Chinese "frontier guards" had been ordered to resume patrols in the sector from Karakoram Pass to Kongka Pass which they had unilaterally stopped and would be asked to do the same along the entire border if Indian intrusions and harassment did not cease.[19]

The phase which led to the brief Sino-Indian border war from 20 October till 21 November 1962 opened on 8 September. According to the Indians the Chinese that day crossed the McMahon Line at Thagla Ridge in NEFA and infested the Indian post at Dhola. The Chinese said that the disputed site was in the "Che Dong area" which was on the Chinese side of the McMahon Line and the Indians had been provocatively intruding into it since June.[20] Be that as it may, the Indians decided to dislodge the Chinese from the disputed territory but the same disregard of reality which had characterized India's China policy from the very beginning was apparent in the way she made light of the task of

Sino-Indian Conflict (1959–62)

evicting her powerfully entrenched antagonist. A report in the *Times* of 12 October noted: "Observers in a position to know better are still speaking lightly of a swift action to eject the '300 or 400' Chinese. Official accounts of continued strengthening of the original Chinese force have been ignored."[21] On the same day Nehru told the press that the army had been instructed to eject the Chinese from NEFA.[22] Defense Minister Krishna Menon vowed even more dramatically, on the following day, that India was determined to throw out the Chinese from Indian soil and would fight "to the last man, to the last gun."[23]

At this stage the Chinese took up the gauntlet and on 20 October large-scale fighting broke out in the eastern as well as the western sector of the frontier. The Chinese easily overran the Indian positions, rounding up some 4000 prisoners; the Indians could not catch even one Chinese soldier. On 24 October China made a three-point peace proposal, suggesting that the existing positions of the two sides on the boundary be frozen. India, however, insisted that the situation as it had prevailed before 8 September 1962 must be restored. This proved, the Chinese remarked, that "since 1959 the Indian Government has seized by force large tracts of Chinese territory."[24]

The rapid advance of the Chinese forces, specially into NEFA, where they threatened Tezpur and could have easily cut off Assam from the rest of India, greatly demoralized the Indians. November 20, to use the words of an eyewitness, Ambassador Kenneth Galbraith, "was the day of ultimate panic." One widely believed rumor had it that 500 Chinese paratroopers were about to swoop upon New Delhi. However, the situation was eased on the following day by a Chinese government proclamation that the Chinese "frontier guards" would observe a cease-fire that midnight all along the line, and withdraw to positions twenty kilometers behind the line of actual control as it had existed on 7 November 1959. Specifically, they would take up positions twenty kilometers north of the McMahon Line in the eastern sector and a like distance from the line of actual control on their side of the middle and western sectors.[25] Both sides stopped fighting at the appointed hour, and in time the Chinese withdrew to the promised positions.

What, then, was the net result of all the tension since 1959 and the war in 1962, in which the Indian "forward policy" apparatus, constructed so laboriously over a space of some three years, crumbled like dust in a matter of days? Simply this: that eventually India had to acquiesce

Independent India and Pakistan

in a settlement which the Chinese had been amicably offering her since 7 November 1959 and now had imposed by force of arms. This alignment was by no means unreasonable and India would have been wise to have accepted it peacefully in the first place.

The sector of the boundary really vital for India was the eastern because it was closer to India's population centers and industrial and oil-producing locations. Here the objection of the Chinese to the McMahon Line had been one of principle only. To them it was a legacy of those humiliating days when stronger powers could impose on weaker China the borders of their own choice. They would have been satisfied with the existing alignment, provided it was made the subject of a fresh treaty between free India and new China.[26]

In the western sector, too, which was the real bone of contention, the stand of the Chinese seems to have been reasonable. Their main concern there was to preserve possession of the road which passes through Aksai Chin. On 12 September 1959, Nehru himself had said, "The Aksai Chin area is in our maps, undoubtedly. But it is a matter for argument as to what part of it belongs to us and what part of it belongs to somebody else. I have frankly to tell the House that the matter has been challenged for a hundred years. There has never been any delimitation there."[27] On a later occasion he stated in Parliament that at one time India had been willing to let the Chinese use the Aksai Chin road as an interim arrangement because it "is an old caravan route . . . because it was there before too."[28] But in his letter dated 26 September 1959 to Chou En-lai he referred to the proposal the British had made to China in 1899 that the Macartney-MacDonald Line be accepted as the boundary, and asserted that "this signified beyond doubt that the whole of Aksai Chin area lay in Indian territory."

Alastair Lamb finds that, even according to the 1899 proposal, the Chinese road through Aksai Chin falls on the Chinese side of the frontier.[29] The Chinese point out that the Aksai Chin area is the only traffic artery linking Sinkiang with western Tibet, because the Gobi Desert to its northeast is almost impassable. The route, they say, is hundreds of years old and, from March 1956 to October 1957, 3000 workers had labored on the site to turn it into a motor road. Altogether the highway is 1200 kilometers long, and 180 kilometers of it runs through Aksai Chin. The very fact that the Indians remained unaware of the road construction activities, they emphasize, shows that the area had been under

SINO-INDIAN CONFLICT (1959–62)

Chinese jurisdiction, not under Indian control. This desolate tract, observes an American author, while important to the Chinese, "is not strategically important for the defense of India. India's natural defense line in this area is Karakoram Mountains, which run south of Aksai Chin from northwest to southeast. Therefore an agreement which recognized Indian claims along the northeastern frontier and those of China to the Aksai Chin would meet the strategic requirements of both countries."[30]

India's swift defeat in battle was accompanied by a palpable reverse on the ideological front. Nehru eagerly accepted military assistance from other countries, which, according to his own comparatively recent pronouncement, was "basically and fundamentally" inconsistent with a policy of nonalignment. The Indians not only asked for United States transport planes but, "in further modification of the non-alignment policy," also wished American pilots and crews to fly the machines. After the cessation of hostilities the Indians raised the question of a "tacit air defense pact" with the United States in case the Chinese resumed their offensive. The Indians would commit their tactical aircraft and the Americans would defend their cities. They also agreed to the visit of a big American aircraft carrier off South India.[31]

Nehru himself, of course, continued to insist that India's policy of nonalignment had remained unaffected and claimed that even major aligned countries like the United States and the Soviet Union "want it to be continued." Galbraith also tried to console Indians by telling them that "India's foreign policy had achieved a substantial measure of success."[32]

Whatever the appearances, the fact of the matter was that, with the failure of Nehru's policy of special friendship with the major fellow-Asian state of China, the main pillar of his foreign policy edifice had collapsed. And this hurt no one more than its proud and highly sensitive architect. After 1959 Nehru was never again his old confident and dominant self. When he visited John F. Kennedy in the White House in November 1961 he gave the impression of being "an old man, his energies depleted, who heard things as at a great distance and answered most questions with indifference." Kennedy, who had earlier wished "India to be a free and thriving leader of a free and thriving Asia," said that to converse meaningfully with Nehru was "like trying to grab something in your hand, only to have it turn out to be just fog. . . . [Nehru] had stayed around too long, and now it was all going bit by bit."[33]

The 1962 military debacle completed the destructive process. "It affected him deeply; it had a very bad effect on him," recalls Nehru's longtime friend and associate Krishna Menon; "it demoralized him very much. Everything he had built was threatened. India was to adopt a militarist outlook which he did not like." On 27 May 1964, the day of Nehru's death, a friend remarked, "He died on the day the Chinese crossed our frontier."[34]

Before examining the repercussions of the Sino-Indian confrontation in other countries, let us revert briefly to an occurrence which was a by-product of the rising tempo of Sino-Indian acrimonies.

India's Invasion of Goa

No one will deny that the tiny Portuguese possessions of Goa, Damao, and Diu were anachronistic disfigurements on the map of free India, which had to go one day, but India's impetuous military conquest of them in December 1961 raised much legitimate criticism. The incursion having been mounted during the high tide of the campaign for the forthcoming general elections, had all the appearance of a sop given to the public to divert their attention from the failure of the government's China policy. As Frank Moraes, the well-known Indian journalist, picturesquely put it, "It was a little like stamping on a mouse in the kitchen when there was a tiger at the door."[35]

What made the whole thing look worse was that the Indian leaders had beforehand tied themselves into moral knots over this fairly simple political issue. They had pointedly singled out the case of Goa as a test for their peaceful pretensions. "The fact that a war [against the Portuguese possession of Goa] is a little war does not make it less than a war," Nehru had impressively stated. "You may call it by any name you like. If a little war is justifiable under [certain] circumstances, a big war is also justifiable under certain other circumstances." On the same subject Menon had declared: "In this problem of Goa the test is not so much for Portugal as for us. It is one of those things where there is a sort of challenge that we have thrown out to the world that every problem is capable of being resolved by negotiations, that it is possible to bring about the liquidation of an authoritarian and imperial regime in any country by the use of non-violent and peaceful methods. Other methods are foreign to us and inapplicable to the situation. There is also no way of our proving it to the world except by example." After the event, however, both Nehru and Menon justified the invasion of Goa. Nehru con-

Sino-Indian Conflict (1959–62)

tended that India's use of military force in Goa had not violated Gandhi's principles of nonviolence and reminded his fellow countrymen that Gandhi had approved India's action in Kashmir which was not nonviolent; and Menon asserted that India had not abjured violence in regard to any country which violated her interests.[36]

International Reaction to the Sino-Indian Conflict

PAKISTANI REACTION

To the security-conscious military regime of Ayub Khan in Pakistan the happenings on India's northern borders in 1959 appeared highly ominous. Less than a month after the Dalai Lama's arrival in India, Ayub made the first of his repeated offers that India and Pakistan together should defend the subcontinent which was their joint home, and less than a week after the Longju encounter he arranged to make a stop at the New Delhi airport on his way to Dacca, met Nehru there, and repeated the offer.[37]

Statements made at the time by responsible Pakistanis clearly indicate how concerned they really felt about the seeming threat to India and Pakistan. At a news conference, on 23 October 1959, Ayub said that the import of the happenings in Tibet and the Russian road-building activities in Afghanistan was that in five years the subcontinent would become vulnerable to a two-pronged Sino-Soviet drive southwards. Foreign Minister Manzur Qadir said expansionist tendencies were more noticeable in China than in Russia. Two high Pakistani officials declared, on 19 June 1960, that the Communist threat to South Asia was growing. One of them, a Cabinet minister, insisted that "the Chinese are on the march." The other, an unnamed senior civil servant, confirmed that Pakistan had taken physical steps to make her northern frontiers secure.[38]

Owing to Nehru's deep aversion to military pacts, nothing came of Pakistani offers of joint defense, but Ayub's conciliatory gestures sufficiently improved the climate of Indo-Pakistani relations for the two neighbors to solve most of their border issues in two minister-level conferences in October 1959 and January 1960. More importantly, the chronic Indus Waters dispute was finally settled by a treaty to which Nehru and Ayub appended their signatures at Karachi on 19 September 1960. After concluding the Indus treaty, Nehru stayed on in Pakistan till 23 September, and he and Ayub conferred at length on the Kashmir dispute. However, they could make no progress toward the settlement of

INDEPENDENT INDIA AND PAKISTAN

that intractable problem, and, though Ayub kept on repeating his offer of joint defense, it was now simply a question of time before the transitory Indo-Pakistani amity would give way to the customary tension between the two countries. All Nehru could offer to Pakistan was a reiteration of his proposal that India and Pakistan subscribe to a "no war" declaration or pact. "How can there be a no war declaration if urgent issues remain unresolved?" responded Foreign Minister Manzur Qadir.[39]

The Goa walkover caused the volatile Indian morale to bubble up with overconfidence and responsible voices began to demand a similar chastisement of the two remaining villains, China and Pakistan. "If the Chinese will not vacate the areas occupied by her," threatened the normally mild-mannered Lal Bahadur Shastri, "India will have to repeat what she did in Goa."[40] No less a person than the president of the ruling Congress party declared that India was determined to get Pakistani and Chinese aggression vacated. The whole country was behind the government's aim to liberate Pakistan-occupied Kashmir.[41] Fearing an Indian assault, Pakistan appealed to the Security Council, but even a resolution asking no more than that India and Pakistan start fresh negotiations on the Kashmir issue was vetoed by the Soviet Union. An uneasy stalemate between India and Pakistan thus existed at the time hostilities broke out between India and China and the Western countries instituted an arms airlift to India. The effect of this important development on Indo-Pakistani relations will be described in chapter 8.

SOVIET REACTION

The worsening of the Sino-Indian border situation in 1959 came at an awkward time for Nikita Khrushchev. Ever since the Twentieth Party Congress of the CPSU (February 1956), at which he had denounced the "personality cult" practiced by Stalin and obtained the party's endorsement for the view "that there was a real possibility of averting wars in the present-day international conditions,"[42] he had been working toward a relaxation of the East-West cold war. Eight days after the Longju incident, President Eisenhower announced that the Russian premier would visit the United States that fall. Khrushchev arrived in America on 15 September, and on 27 September he and Eisenhower stated from Camp David that all international problems should be solved by peaceful means.

At the end of the month Khrushchev went to Peking and, at a reception in his honor, lectured his hosts on the undesirability of using force.

172

Sino-Indian Conflict (1959–62)

That the visit was not marked by the issuance of the usual joint communiqué was interpreted by many observers as an indication that all was not well. Not long afterwards the bloody incident of Kongka Pass took place. The Soviet Union alleged later that "the Chinese leaders [had] got themselves involved in an armed clash on the Indian-Chinese border" with the object of "torpedoing the relaxation of international tension" which had taken place as the result of Khrushchev's visit to the United States.[43]

In the summer of 1959 the Russians declined to pass on to the Chinese the technical data for the manufacture of nuclear arms, which they had previously promised.[44] The first public Russian comment after Longju came in the form of a Tass statement issued on 9 September which expressed the hope that India and China would settle their disputes "in the interests of both countries."[45] Since the statement referred to Sino-Soviet bonds as those of "fraternal friendship" and to Indo-Soviet ties as those of "friendly cooperation" only, some commentators detected in it a shade of partiality toward China. However, to the Chinese who, as comrades in the Communist family, expected wholehearted support from the U.S.S.R. it seemed that the latter was merely "assuming a facade of neutrality" and in fact was favoring India and condemning China.[46] Khrushchev's statement after the Kongka Pass skirmish calling for "negotiations to the mutual satisfaction of both sides"[47] was viewed by the Chinese with similar disapproval because "it brushed aside India's responsibility for the provocation."[48] As the beginnings of the Sino-Soviet split were not yet apparent, the Indians were greatly pleased to find that Russia had not sided with the sister Communist state of China. Nehru said in the Lok Sabha on 27 November 1959 that there was no country more anxious for peace than the Soviet Union and hardly any country which cared less for peace than China.

Another source of irritation to the Chinese was the growing volume of Soviet economic assistance to India and of Indo-Soviet trade. A fresh Soviet commitment of rupees 180 crores toward India's Third Five-Year Plan was announced in September 1959, just when the Sino-Indian border trouble was becoming acute. The Indians also obtained from the Soviet Union equipment which they could use to improve their position vis-à-vis the Chinese in the Himalayas. In February 1961 Defense Minister Krishna Menon disclosed that practically all the equipment required for constructing roads in the northern border regions had been procured from the Soviet Union. If it had been the intention of the Soviet Union

INDEPENDENT INDIA AND PAKISTAN

to support China, he surmised, she could have refused to sell this machinery to India. In April it was reported that the recently purchased Soviet AN-12 heavy-duty transport aircraft had begun to fly in Ladakh. On 5 May 1962 it was announced in New Delhi that India had arranged to purchase from the Soviet Union two squadrons of the latest MIG supersonic fighters and eventually to manufacture them under license in India.[49]

The outbreak of the large-scale fighting on the Sino-Indian frontier in October 1962 coincided with the U.S.S.R.–United States crisis over the Russian guided missiles in Cuba. On 22 October President Kennedy ordered a partial blockade of Cuba and the searching of Russian ships at sea. A war between the two superpowers seemed imminent. At this hour of peril the Soviet Union needed the support of all Communist states, specially that of China which is the largest of them all. For the moment, therefore, the Soviet Union veered round to a position of clear support for China. An editorial in *Pravda* (25 October) called China's peace proposals of the previous day to India "constructive" and infused with a desire to end the conflict. It echoed the Chinese assertion that the "notorious" McMahon Line had never been recognized by China, and described the Soviet Union's ties with China as "brotherly" and with India as merely "friendly."[50]

After Khrushchev agreed to dismantle the missile sites, the United States blockade of Cuba was lifted on 20 November and the Cuban crisis subsided. The Chinese castigated Khrushchev both for his recklessness in installing the missiles in Cuba in the first place and for his docile retreat afterwards in the face of the American challenge. For their part, the Russians gradually assumed a position of pointed partiality toward India against China. With publication of the Chinese letter of 14 June (1963) criticizing the concept of "peaceful co-existence," the Chinese and the Russians began to trade charges in full view of the rest of the world and the point of no return in Sino-Soviet differences was reached. The U.S.S.R. and United States now openly began to pursue parallel policies designed to strengthen India against their common enemy, China.

UNITED STATES REACTION

While it was not quite clear at first whether, and to what extent, the Soviet Union would side with India, there was no such doubt with regard to the United States, which had always wished to build up India as the

SINO-INDIAN CONFLICT (1959-62)

natural counterpoise to China in Asia. Thus to start with Washington was the only sure major source of aid and comfort to New Delhi. For a time, therefore, New Delhi's relations with Washington, which had begun to improve when America rescued India from financial collapse in 1957-58, became more cordial than those with Moscow.

In 1954 Nehru had spurned the personal assurance of Eisenhower that the arms aid to Pakistan did not affect friendship with India, but in the case of the United States-Pakistan Bilateral Agreement of March 1959 he readily accepted a routine clarification that the agreement could not be invoked against India because he felt "sure" that the United States had "nothing but goodwill for us." During his visit to India in December 1959, Eisenhower, who had figured so low as a man of peace in the 1957 Indian public opinion poll, was publicly hailed by the Indian prime minister as one who had "raised the banner of peace in the world" and "found a place in our hearts."[51]

India contributed combat troops for service under the United Nations in the Congo when several African nations decided to withdraw their contingents and the United Nations peacekeeping role was under severe criticism by the U.S.S.R. The early batches arrived in United States planes "thus symbolizing the joint Indo-American purpose."[52] India also opposed Khrushchev's proposal of a "troika" of three secretaries general to head the secretariat of the United Nations, instead of one. At the Belgrade conference of nonaligned nations, Nehru, who in the past had declared colonialism to be one of the main issues facing the contemporary world, advised fellow neutralists to turn their thoughts from this vanishing evil to the more imminent problem of preventing war. In an analysis of the Belgrade proceedings, presidential adviser Walt W. Rostow assured Kennedy that nonaligned countries, in their stance on international issues, did take into account where their aid came from.[53]

On the specific question of the Sino-Indian boundary, Secretary of State Christian Herter, making the first official United States statement on 12 November 1959, said that American authorities had "no firsthand knowledge of a definitive border which could rightly be claimed by either side." Galbraith did not get Washington's clearance to support the Indian stand on the McMahon Line till 27 October 1962. About the western sector he conceded that "the Chinese have a serious claim to the Aksai Chin Plateau." However, on the question who was responsible for the actual breach of the peace on the border, Washington placed the

INDEPENDENT INDIA AND PAKISTAN

entire blame on China from the very beginning and the United States response to the Indian request for arms was unhesitating. Nehru said on 29 October 1962 that some arms from the United States and the United Kingdom had already arrived and more were expected.[54]

A high-powered Anglo–United States team, headed by W. Averell Harriman and Duncan Sandys, reached New Delhi in the fourth week of November to assess India's needs. To pacify the fears of their ally Pakistan at India's increasing armed strength, the Americans and the British (1) successfully pressed Nehru to open negotiations with Pakistan for the settlement of Kashmir, (2) took a written undertaking from India that the arms supplied to her would be used only against "Chinese aggression" and any equipment no longer needed for that special purpose would be returned to the supplying country.[55]

REACTION OF NEUTRAL COUNTRIES

To most Indians a greatly disappointing feature of the world reaction to their troubles was the noncommittal attitude which their fellow unaligned Afro-Asians adopted toward the whole affair. Only Malaya, the neutral with a Western bias, sided with India. The rest of them steered a strictly middle course on the merits of the case, and concerned themselves solely with trying to extinguish the embers of war between the two South Asian giants. Two of the neutrals, in fact, expressed definite unhappiness at the alacrity with which the Western powers had responded to India's cry for help. At the Colombo Conference of six nonaligned countries, convened to work out proposals for a peaceful resolution of the problem, Mrs. Sirimavo Bandaranaike, prime minister of Ceylon, said: "We have seen how India has been obliged to seek arms assistance from Western powers and the eagerness with which this has been given. This kind of entanglement with Power blocs would be contrary to the cardinal principles of non-alignment." And Ghana protested to the United Kingdom that the latter's spontaneous rush of arms to India amounted to "dangerously prejudging the issue."[56]

CHAPTER 8

Warclouds over South Asia: Indo-Pakistani Conflict (1963-February 1974)

Erosion of United States–Pakistani Alliance

Pakistan did not oppose the arms aid to India by her principal Western allies, per se. What she urged was that India should not be militarily strengthened unless she made a compensatory concession to soothe Pakistani fears. Ayub wrote to Kennedy: "Only a speedy and just Kashmir settlement can give us any assurance that the contemplated increase of India's military power is not likely to be employed against Pakistan in future."[1]

Under combined persuasion from the United States and the United Kingdom India held six rounds of talks with Pakistan but, American and British spokesmen having publicly declared that military assistance to India was not dependent upon a Kashmir settlement,[2] India was under no real pressure to budge from her long-standing position that the existing cease-fire line in Kashmir, with some minor adjustments, should be confirmed as the permanent dividing line between India and Pakistan. Not surprisingly, the negotiations collapsed at the sixth session in May 1963. A few weeks later a joint Kennedy-Macmillan communiqué from Macmillan's country house, Birch Grove, proclaimed that military assistance to India would continue in order "to strengthen her defences against the threat of renewed Chinese Communist attack."[3]

Pakistan's alliance with the United States from this point lingered on in name only. The United States would have preferred that India and Pakistan jointly confront China in Asia but, if that was not feasible and

INDEPENDENT INDIA AND PAKISTAN

a clear choice had to be made between larger India and smaller Pakistan, India obviously would be a weightier counterpoise and must be preferred.

Pakistan Shifts to "Bilateralism"

"WALKING ON A TRIANGULAR TIGHTROPE"

To counterbalance the erosion of her special relationship with the United States, Pakistan quickly moved to mend her connection with the two neighboring great powers, China and Russia. In his book *Friends Not Masters,* Ayub has explained how his mind had worked when "the force of events" compelled him to reappraise Pakistan's foreign policy. He premised that the major countries interested in Pakistan were India, the Soviet Union, China, and the United States. The prospects of establishing "normal" relations with India did not "appear to be in sight," but he was hopeful of success with regard to the remaining three. All this would be "like walking on a triangular tightrope" and called for the "strategy" of setting up "bilateral equations with each one of them, with the clear understanding that the nature and complexion of the equation should be such as to promote our mutual interests without adversely affecting the legitimate interests of third parties."[4]

"NORMALIZATION" OF SINO-PAKISTANI RELATIONS

China's own antipathy to India having brought her down on the same side of the fence as Pakistan, Sino-Pakistani relations improved more quickly than Soviet-Pakistani relations.

At Pakistan's initiative a Sino-Pakistani boundary agreement was signed on 2 March 1963 in respect to the 300-mile border between Sinkiang and Pakistani-controlled Kashmir. Once the possibility of border differences was thus eliminated, Pakistan's ties with China improved rapidly. On 17 July 1963 Foreign Minister Bhutto was able to reassure his countrymen, who had been feeling forlorn after their alliance with the United States had come under strain, that "God forbid . . . if India in her frustration turned her guns against Pakistan, the international situation is such to-day that Pakistan would not be alone in that conflict. . . . An attack by India on Pakistan involves the territorial integrity and security of the largest state in Asia."[5]

In August Pakistan and China signed a civil aviation agreement, followed by a barter agreement in September. Before the year (1963)

Indo-Pakistani Conflict (1963–74)

closed China had become the largest buyer of Pakistani cotton. During his visit to Pakistan in February 1964, Prime Minister Chou En-lai joined Ayub in expressing the hope that the Kashmir dispute would be settled "in accordance with the wishes of the people of Kashmir."[6] Not long afterwards China offered Pakistan an interest-free loan of $60 million. Upon arrival in Peking on a state visit, in March 1965, Ayub was given a tremendous welcome. China marked the occasion by reaffirming her support to the Pakistani position on Kashmir and Pakistan returned the favor by criticizing, for the first time, "the schemes [of the United States] for creating two Chinas."[7]

"NORMALIZATION" OF SOVIET-PAKISTANI RELATIONS

Pakistani efforts to "normalize" relations with the Soviet Union moved forward at a comparatively slower pace first because there was a greater residue of bad feeling between Russia and Pakistan than there was between China and Pakistan and secondly because Russia had no desire to improve relations with Pakistan at the cost of her existing friendship with India and perforce had to move with caution.

Pakistani-Soviet relations had touched their nadir in May 1960, when a U2 spy plane, having taken off from Peshawar in Pakistan, was shot down in the U.S.S.R. At a diplomatic party in Moscow Khrushchev, now premier, threatened the Pakistani *chargé d'affaires* that the Soviet Union would pulverize Peshawar with rockets if the provocation was repeated. Though Pakistanis put up a bold front against the Russian threats, they had, in fact, been compelled to consider harder than ever whether their alliance with distant America had really benefited them sufficiently to risk destruction at the hands of the next-door nuclear superpower. From now on Pakistanis laid increasingly less emphasis on their ideological affinity with the West and increasingly more on their geographical proximity to Russia and China.

Not long after the U2 incident Ayub called United States governmental machinery "cumbersome, sluggish and a clumsy juggernaut" and he doubted its capacity to respond rapidly to an attack. At the same time he abruptly modified Pakistani policy toward aid from Communist sources. He had emphasized recently that "unlike several other countries around us, we have shut ourselves off almost completely from the possibility of any major assistance from the Communist bloc." But now he said there was no reason why Pakistan could not "do business" with the

INDEPENDENT INDIA AND PAKISTAN

Soviet Union.[8] A start was made on 4 March 1961 with a Pakistani-Soviet agreement under which Pakistan was granted a loan of $30 million as well as technical assistance for exploration of oil.

After the Sino-Indian war several factors combined to make the Soviet Union still more receptive to the idea of improving relations with Pakistan. First, it had become evident that India could not stand up to China effectively while the enervating Indo-Pakistani hostility continued. The Soviet Union, like the United States before her, therefore began to favor conciliation between the two principal southern neighbors of China. In January 1966 she had the satisfaction of hosting the India-Pakistan summit at Tashkent. Secondly, the Soviet Union no longer felt confident that India could resist being drawn into the American orbit. With the rise of tension between China and India in 1959, Nehru's foreign policy had come under increasing criticism from the rightists in India, some of whom pressed for an open alliance with the West. This trend gathered further momentum after India's military defeat at the hands of Communist China. Many Indians argued that all Communists were undependable and India's real well-wishers were the Western democracies. A visible casualty of the assault by the right was Nehru's long-time friend and adviser Defense Minister Krishna Menon, who was compelled to abandon his important post in the middle of the Sino-Indian war. Early in 1963 the *New Times* noted that 900 persons "prominent in public life" had been arrested in different parts of India at the instigation of the "ultra-reactionary parties" and that the leaders of the Jan Sangh and Swatantra parties were calling for an abandonment of India's neutralism.[9] This anxiety, about where the rightists in India might take the country, was not appreciably relieved till Mrs. Gandhi's convincing election victory in March 1971. Thirdly, the more Pakistan withdrew from her commitments to the West the more acceptable her foreign policy became in Russian eyes, and, of course, the Soviet Union did not wish Pakistan to leave the Western embrace only to be totally enfolded by Chinese arms.

During 1963 Russia advanced to Pakistan a further loan to the tune of £11 million sterling and concluded with her a barter agreement and an air transport agreement. In the course of the Security Council debate on Kashmir in 1964, the Soviet Union visibly softened her pro-Indian stance on the dispute. The real breakthrough, however, came when Ayub made a state visit to the Soviet Union in April 1965. This event was im-

INDO-PAKISTANI CONFLICT (1963-74)

mediately marked by the grant of another Soviet loan amounting to $50 million, a trade agreement, and a cultural exchange agreement but its fuller implication became evident later in the year when the Soviet Union assumed a middle position in the Indo-Pakistani wars.

PAKISTAN AND THE AFRO-ASIAN WORLD

During the period in which Pakistan improved her relations with the two principal Communist powers, she was also able to furbish her image in the Muslim countries (except in Malaysia) as well as in the Afro-Asian world generally. This was principally because she was at last putting up a more impressive performance in various ways than her rival, India. Under Ayub Pakistan had attained political stability and since 1959 she had been registering a greater rate of economic growth than India. Ayub, moreover, was shedding the country's subservience to the Western countries and steering her toward a more independent foreign policy. Beginning with her foreign exchange crisis in 1957-58, India, on the other hand, had been losing ground. In 1959 her relations with China deteriorated, and in 1962 she was worsted by China in battle.

With respect to Muslim countries an additional factor which assisted Pakistan toward a better understanding with them was that Pakistan had learned not to harp overmuch upon the ties of Islam and her own importance. Ayub conceded that "The upsurge in other Muslim countries by and large, is racial, is linguistic, is territorial, is anti-imperialist, anti-colonial; it is very little religious. I should, therefore, think that when we expect other Muslim countries to agree entirely with us in principle [that Islamic ideology should govern affairs of state and formulation of foreign policy] we find that we are disappointed. I believe it is our fault in not judging or reading the situation correctly. . . . [W]hen Pakistan came into being a lot of people started bragging about Pakistan being the biggest Muslim country. . . . We have enormous problems, and any talk about leading others is sheer nonsense."[10]

Chiefly through Ayub's initiative, Pakistan, Iran, and Turkey in July 1964 founded the Regional Cooperation for Development. Its purpose was declared to be collaboration in the spheres of communications, agriculture, industry, mineral resources, education, health, regional development, technical cooperation, and cultural exchanges. Though RCD has not measured up to its sweeping aspirations, it has been functioning steadily, assisted by a permanent secretariat at Tehran, and has progressed in various directions, especially toward setting up "Joint Purpose

Independent India and Pakistan

Enterprises," i.e. industrial and manufacturing projects jointly run by two of the partners or by all three of them.[11]

The coolness between Pakistan and Malaya — which, together with Singapore, North Borneo, and Sarawak, formed the Federation of Malaysia in September 1963 — resulted from their differing attitudes toward India and China. During the Himalayan war between China and India, Tunku Abdul Rahman, prime minister of Malaya, happened to be in India and immediately came out strongly in favor of the host country. When Malaysia came into being, Indonesia viewed the new state as an instrument for perpetuating British imperialism in the area and President Soekarno vowed to "crush" it. India requited Tunku's earlier good turn by befriending Malaysia while China took Indonesia's side. Indonesia, irritated by India's support to Malaysia, came around to support Pakistan on Kashmir. China, Pakistan, and Indonesia thereupon formed an axis and worked together to stage a second Bandung-type Afro-Asian conference, hoping to humiliate India among her peers by ganging up on her in the proposed gathering.[12]

Pakistani spokesmen began to talk in what, for them, was a new language. In his address at the Afro-Asian Seminar at Lahore on 11 February 1965, Bhutto said that the primary purpose of Afro-Asian solidarity was to promote "the liberation of the countries of Asia and Africa from all the evils of colonial rule."[13] Ayub, almost in the words of a Nehru of a bygone era, declared, "For too long have the nations of this vast and ancient continent [of Asia] been the playthings of forces beyond their control."[14] India no longer claimed that colonialism was the paramount issue of the times; Pakistan seemed to have filled her place in the neutralist-Communist crusade to eliminate all vestiges of imperialism from the face of the earth.

Ayub's star reached its zenith early in April 1965. He had successfully "normalized" relations with the two neighboring Communist giants and earned the respect of most fellow Afro-Asians. At home things seemed to be going well. The economy continued on the upswing, and in January that year he had won a convincing though not an overwhelming victory in the presidential election over Miss Fatima Jinnah, sister of the respected Quaid-i-Azam, whom the Combined Opposition parties had put up as a candidate.[15]

TENSING OF PAKISTANI–UNITED STATES RELATIONS

At this stage one of the sides of Ayub's tightrope triangle began to

INDO-PAKISTANI CONFLICT (1963–74)

sag; Pakistan's relations with the United States dramatically worsened. The United States had no serious objection to Pakistan's mending her fences with the Soviet Union because the two superpowers, having attained a balance of terror, themselves were once more edging toward a better understanding with each other after the temporary setback to the spirit of Camp David resulting from the U2 incident. But Pakistan's growing cordiality with China was another matter. In American estimation at the time this meant consorting with the enemy.

Up to and including the Sino-Pakistani border agreement, the United States had viewed the changing scene tolerantly but the civil aviation agreement and Chou En-lai's visit to Pakistan evoked critical comments from Washington, and Ayub's enthusiastic China visit altogether exhausted President Johnson's patience. On 16 April (1965) he suddenly and unilaterally "postponed" Ayub's official visit to the United States which had been scheduled to commence on 25 April. That Johnson, at the same time, had postponed Prime Minister Shastri's visit, which was to have taken place more than two months later, was generally taken to mean that he did not wish the insult to Ayub to look too pointed. In July he put further pressure on Pakistan by getting the meeting of the Pakistan Aid Consortium put back by two months. It was now Ayub's turn to get angry. At a meeting of the Muslim League Council he animatedly declared that his foreign travels were undertaken to find new friends, not masters. If friendship with the United States impinged on the sovereignty of Pakistan, Pakistan no longer desired such friendship. He had explained his viewpoint to the United States many times but without effect because "power drunk" countries often did not listen to smaller countries.[16]

Pakistanis later complained that their "ally," the United States, had let them down during the September war against India. In doing this they overlooked the fact that the spirit in which the United States–Pakistani alliance had been conceived had evaporated before the outbreak of Indo-Pakistani fighting. "In our conflict in 1965," recalled President Bhutto in his address to the National Assembly on 14 July 1972, "whenever we said that we were not being given assistance, or that the treaties were not being complied with, we were told that we were passive members, we were not really [functioning] members of the organization [i.e., of the Western system of defense alliances] and so how could they fulfil their part of the commitment."[17]

INDEPENDENT INDIA AND PAKISTAN

Indo-Pakistani Wars of 1965

Let us now survey the march of events, subsequent to the breakdown of the Indo-Pakistani dialogue in the summer of 1963, which culminated in a minor armed collision between India and Pakistan in the spring of 1965 and a major one in September.

Serious trouble first made its appearance in the eastern part of the subcontinent. Pakistan alleged India was evicting Muslims in large numbers from Assam and Tripura and driving them into East Pakistan. India said she was merely expelling Muslims who had trespassed into India from Pakistan. The problem had attained serious enough proportions by September 1963 for Foreign Minister Bhutto to refer to it with concern in his address to the General Assembly of the United Nations.

Inside Kashmir, the Kashmiris, already angry at the October announcement by the outgoing premier of Kashmir that the state would be brought constitutionally closer to India, took to open rioting when a sacred relic, a hair of the Prophet Muhammad, was mysteriously stolen on 27 December 1963 from a mosque near Srinagar. This worsened the already ominous situation in East Pakistan and Indian Bengal where killings began, accompanied by an alarming exodus of refugees in both directions. At Pakistan's request the Security Council once more debated the Kashmir question intermittently from 3 February till 18 May 1964 but was unable to pass any resolution because neither of the two superpowers wished to cause offense to India whose representative, M. C. Chagla, reiterated that Kashmir had become an integral part of India and warned the members that the passing of resolutions was "likely only to aggravate feelings." The Council proceedings petered out with a summation by the president of the views expressed by various members.

While the Security Council was still seized of the Kashmir question, Nehru, in a surprise move on 8 April 1964, released Abdullah from prison, where he had been languishing since his arrest in 1953 except for a brief period of freedom in 1958, and sent him to Pakistan to open negotiations with Ayub. A clue to Nehru's thinking at the time can be found in his address to the Central Committee of the Congress party at Bombay on 16 May. He said that he had discussed with Abdullah the problem of achieving Indo-Pakistani friendship without which India and Pakistan would "continue to react to each other" with retaliatory religious persecutions and India would have to carry the burden of continuing conflict with Pakistan. In Pakistan Abdullah declared on 26 May

INDO-PAKISTANI CONFLICT (1963-74)

that Ayub and Nehru would meet soon but Nehru's death on the next day ended his mission inconclusively. However, it is doubtful whether the feud between India and Pakistan would have ended even if Nehru had lived longer because all Abdullah had offered to Ayub was that India, Pakistan, and Kashmir should together form a confederation. To Pakistanis this meant "the destruction of Pakistan."[18]

The shock of Nehru's death temporarily becalmed the atmosphere as everyone paused to take stock of the new situation but tension reappeared on 21 December 1964, when an Indian presidential order tied Kashmir closer to India by enabling the president to govern Kashmir directly if he thought the constitutional machinery of the state had failed and to pass laws by assuming the powers of the state legislature.[19] Kashmiris were offended further by the announcement on 9 January 1965 that the local National Conference party would be dissolved and the Indian National Congress would establish a branch in Kashmir. At the behest of the Plebiscite Front of Abdullah, 15 January was observed as Protest Day. Despite repression the agitation continued and hundreds of members of the Plebiscite Front were taken into custody.

THE KUTCH WAR

Tension from Kashmir, as usual, spread to India and Pakistan and on 9 April fighting between them suddenly broke out on the disputed border in the Rann of Kutch. Though this small undeclared war was brought to a close by the successful intercession of the British prime minister, Harold Wilson, it had the unfortunate effect of adding to the itch of the armed forces on both sides to have a real showdown. That they had performed better than the Indians in the Kutch fighting buoyed up the existing feeling of the Pakistanis that they could beat the Indians on the battlefield any day. And the Indians, already smarting under their defeat at the hands of the Chinese, had more salt rubbed into their wounds during the inconclusive Kutch skirmishes and began to yearn more than ever for another chance to prove their prowess.

THE SEPTEMBER WAR

The Kashmir situation was aggravated by the arrest of Abdullah on 8 May when he landed in India after a two-and-a-half-month tour of the Middle East and Western Europe, in the course of which he had propagated the right of the Kashmiris to self-determination. He had also contributed an article, "Kashmir, India and Pakistan," to the April 1965

Independent India and Pakistan

issue of the prestigious American quarterly *Foreign Affairs*, suggesting that India, Pakistan, and Kashmir should get together around a table and find a solution which would concede to Kashmiris "the substance of their demand for self-determination but with honour and fairness to both Pakistan and India." Abdullah's apprehension led to a fresh wave of disturbances in Kashmir which continued till they merged with the larger Indo-Pakistani conflict of August and September.

Ayub was under tremendous pressures of various kinds to do something tangible to relieve the worsening situation. First of all there was India's dual move, on the one hand, progressively to absorb Kashmir within her polity and, on the other, to keep the door to negotiations with Pakistan tightly shut. What Nehru had said earlier in a different context was equally applicable to the predicament in which India had now placed Pakistan: "When you shut the door, what remains? Either sitting sullenly and doing nothing, just cursing like an old woman or going out sword in hand or whatever weapon you have, and fighting. There is nothing else left."[20] Time, too, seemed to be working against Pakistan. After her China war, India had embarked on a tremendous effort to increase her military strength. On 8 April 1963 the Indian defense minister had stated that the strength of the army would be doubled[21] and on 21 September 1964 he gave fuller details of India's impressive five-year defense plan (April 1964–March 1969) for strengthening and expanding all the three branches of the fighting forces, the army, the navy, and the air force, with help from the United States, the U.S.S.R., and the United Kingdom.[22] Compared to this Pakistan could not feel certain of being able to maintain even her existing level of defense preparedness. Her main source of military supplies had been the United States, and that source could no longer be counted upon. Then there was the ever-present domestic outcry in Pakistan not to abandon the Kashmiris to their fate. During Ayub's presidential campaign against Miss Jinnah a point frequently made in his favor was that he, the tough field marshal, not his frail female opponent, was the proper person to lead the nation to meet the perpetual threat from India. Was it not high time to counter India's moves, it was asked. Finally, the Azad Kashmiris were straining at the leash. They were a fighting people, unlike the Kashmiris of the Valley who are given more to demonstration than to warlike action. Thousands of them had served in the ranks of the British Indian Army during World War II. By early 1965 the Azad Kashmir authorities had at their disposal

INDO-PAKISTANI CONFLICT (1963–74)

a well-trained force numbering about 20,000 and they began increasingly to press Ayub to let them launch an "Algerian style" struggle to liberate their brothers on the Indian side of the cease-fire line.[23]

Firing incidents along the cease-fire line in Kashmir which had been increasing in number for the last few months reached serious proportions in May and on the 17th of that month the Indian regular forces, making the first major move, occupied three posts in Azad Kashmir statedly to protect the strategic Srinagar-Leh road against Pakistani interference. These units returned to their own side of the line on 30 June when the Kutch agreement was signed but tension continued.

On 5 August armed "infiltrators" in civilian clothes began to cross the cease-fire line from the Pakistani side to assist the rebellious Kashmiris, the high-water mark of whose effort was expected to be reached on 8 August, the anniversary of Abdullah's dismissal and arrest in 1953. This proved to be the prelude to open war between India and Pakistan. The Indians alleged that the guerrillas were regular Pakistani troops dressed as civilians and the operation was "a thinly disguised armed attack" by Pakistan on India. Pakistanis claimed the infiltrators were Azad Kashmiris wishing to assist fellow Kashmiris, who had risen in revolt against Indian oppression. Whatever the exact identity of the raiders, the fact remains that the ultimate control over Azad Kashmir rests in Pakistani hands and Pakistan, therefore, could have restrained the men from crossing the line if she had exerted herself to do so. Ayub had evidently succumbed to the pressures already described and decided to take the attendant risks.

However, expectations that the Kashmiris would rise with sufficient ferocity seriously to threaten the Indian occupation forces and that the upheaval would remain confined to Kashmir proved fallacious. In the end not only did Kashmir remain in Indian hands but the shock of war also released various disruptive forces within Pakistan, causing the country to slide downhill, losing East Pakistan on the way. It is only proper to add that opinion in West Pakistan was overwhelmingly in favor of assisting the Kashmiris in their desperate struggle and it is not fair to heap the entire blame on Ayub's shoulders for miscalculating the full consequences of such a move.

This is not to say that India was an innocent victim. She had created a situation in which Pakistan found herself between the proverbial devil and the deep blue sea. India's basic advantage lay in the fact that she

INDEPENDENT INDIA AND PAKISTAN

was already in occupation of what she wanted. If Pakistan wished to change the status of the disputed territory it was for her to do something about it and risk seeming belligerent. Outsiders, having no direct stakes in a given international situation, are prone to treat the maintenance of the status quo as peace and its disturbance by either side, even for good reasons, a move toward war. "Because India shut the door for negotiations," pronounced Sheikh Abdullah, "Pakistan, being a party, had sent the infiltrators."[24]

Indian regular forces in Kashmir responded to the guerrilla incursions with a fierce offensive at several points along the cease-fire line and made considerable dents in it. All-India radio and other Indian sources referred to the newly occupied positions as "liberated" areas, suggesting that India was not aiming merely at eliminating the infiltrators but had undertaken a "war of liberation" against the whole of Pakistani-controlled Kashmir.

On 1 September Pakistani armored units advanced across the cease-fire line in the Chhamb area, aiming to cut off the only road which links India with Kashmir. Early on the morning of 6 September India responded with an offensive against Lahore in West Pakistan and followed this up with two more thrusts, one in the direction of Sialkot and the other in Rajasthan. By changing the character of the conflict from one limited to the disputed state of Kashmir to one violating settled international frontiers, India lost most of the sympathy she had accumulated by blaming Pakistan for sending the infiltrators into Kashmir. Even trusted friends, such as Kosygin and Nasser, criticized her for carrying the war into West Pakistan.[25]

When hostilities commenced, India enjoyed a decisive quantitative superiority over Pakistan in personnel and arms. Her army was at least four times that of Pakistan, which numbered between 160,000 and 180,000. Pakistan was believed to possess superior weapons and better fighting men. As pointed out by a Pakistani commentator on military affairs, Pakistan's best hope lay in inflicting "a knock-out blow in the Mohammad Ali Clay style."[26] Pakistani armed forces fought well, inflicting heavier losses in men, material, and territory than they suffered, but they failed to overwhelm their massive opponent. India, too, failed to take Lahore or Sialkot or to sever the vital north-south rail and road communication artery which serves West Pakistan. The war, thus, reached a stalemate. India could have easily overrun poorly defended East Paki-

Indo-Pakistani Conflict (1963-74)

stan, but reportedly refrained from doing so because China had warned her against such an assault.[27]

The United States and the U.S.S.R. took a neutral position on the merits of the Indo-Pakistani controversy and coordinated their efforts toward bringing about a cease-fire through the Security Council. The United States, in addition, cut off all military supplies and economic assistance to both sides. Since Pakistan was almost wholly dependent on America for war material, while India had other sources of supply, besides possessing a more highly developed arms industry of her own, the American ban on weapons hurt Pakistan much more than it did her antagonist. Pakistan's capacity to fight a prolonged war was seriously curtailed. The United States also warned China not to intervene in the conflict.[28] The U.S.S.R., in addition to engaging in diplomacy within the United Nations, invited Indian and Pakistani leaders to confer with each other on her soil.

China supported Pakistan's action in crossing the cease-fire line in the Chhamb area, saying that Pakistan was forced to hit back in self-defense after Indian troops had "poured" across the cease-fire line. When India attacked West Pakistan, Peking issued a long statement blaming India for enlarging "the local conflict between India and Pakistan in Kashmir into a general conflict between the two countries." But what really shook India, and caused a flurry in the Security Council, was China's ultimatum to India on 16 September, giving the latter three days in which to dismantle all her "military works" on the border, and return the inhabitants and livestock she had seized.[29] China also supplied some tanks and aircraft to Pakistan but these arrived after the fighting was over.

The Security Council's first two resolutions simply called for a cease-fire and withdrawal of forces to positions held before 5 August, but after the Chinese ultimatum to India the Council passed a stronger resolution "demanding" that the cease-fire take effect within a specified time and promising to consider steps for "a settlement of the political problems, underlying the present conflict."[30] On 23 September the parties ceased firing but the Council's undertaking, to tackle the "political problems" (Kashmir) which had led to the war, was soon forgotten.

So far, the parties had only stopped fighting; the forces had not withdrawn to their original stations. The latter step was accomplished in fulfillment of the Tashkent Declaration, which President Ayub and Prime Minister Shastri signed on 10 January 1966 in the presence of Premier

INDEPENDENT INDIA AND PAKISTAN

Kosygin. Under that declaration the two sides also agreed to "continue meetings at the highest and at other levels on matters of direct concern to both countries."[31] However, after the first minister-level meeting at Islamabad in March had ended in a deadlock, "the spirit of Tashkent" gradually faded away.

Of the Muslim majority countries, Malaysia alone sided with India. Iran gave Pakistan jet fuel and gasoline, besides providing night shelter at Tehran to the airliners of the Pakistan International Airlines to save them from Indian air bombing; Turkey sent guns and ammunition; Jordan and Saudi Arabia subscribed to Pakistan's Defense Fund; and Indonesia dispatched some naval vessels to Karachi. An Arab Summit Conference, in which the United Arab Republic was a participant, commended the principle of self-determination in its communiqué and asked India and Pakistan to settle their differences in accordance with the resolutions of the United Nations (which had promised a plebiscite in Kashmir).[32] Afghanistan officially remained neutral, but at a popular level there was visible sympathy for Pakistan.

Fall of Ayub

Ayub continued to perform well in external affairs after the war with India but the internal situation in Pakistan got out of hand in March 1969 and brought him down.

The United States resumed economic aid to both Pakistan and India in February 1966, and on 12 April 1968 she removed the restrictions on the sale of spare parts for equipment previously supplied. However, military assistance on a grant basis remained blocked. Continuing the mediatory role he had played at Tashkent, Premier Kosygin urged India to settle the Farakka Barrage dispute with Pakistan on the lines of the Indus Waters Treaty, and to open negotiations on Kashmir. A few days later the Soviet Union announced that she would sell arms to Pakistan. These moves annoyed the Indians. Prime Minister Indira Gandhi declared that India would not brook any third-party interference in Farakka and she denounced the Russian decision to supply arms to Pakistan as "fraught with danger."[33]

The United States and the U.S.S.R. also made parallel efforts to persuade India and Pakistan to cooperate with each other on the economic front. America urged the South Asian neighbors to undertake joint ventures and Russia floated the idea of regional cooperation between India,

INDO-PAKISTANI CONFLICT (1963–74)

Pakistan, Afghanistan, Iran, and herself. India was not averse to these feelers but Pakistan rejected them on the ground that it was unrealistic to talk of Indo-Pakistani collaboration while serious disputes existed between the two countries. For declining the idea of regional cooperation Pakistan advanced the further reason that the proposal smacked of the wish to build an anti-Chinese front.

The Pakistani economy showed remarkable resilience in the face of problems caused by the war with India, reduction in foreign aid, and two poor harvests. President Lyndon Johnson stated in his State of the Union message on 10 February 1967 that Pakistan had "an outstanding economic record" and the future was "brighter still." Pakistan's trade with China and Russia continued to grow and she received an increasing amount of economic assistance from them. The war with India, however, brought trouble for Ayub inside both parts of Pakistan, though for different reasons.

On account of the great distance of Kashmir from their own motherland, East Pakistanis were less emotionally involved in the dispute over it than West Pakistanis. Moreover, if Kashmir had joined Pakistan, it would have increased the area and population of the western wing, tilting still further the balance of power in favor of that region. Interruption of Indo-Pakistani trade too hurt East Pakistan more than West Pakistan. During the hostilities East Pakistan had been totally cut off from its western counterpart and lay at the mercy of India. That India held off because China had warned her not to attack East Pakistan was poor consolation for East Pakistanis. They began to clamor for full autonomy, including self-sufficiency in defense, more loudly than ever.

In West Pakistan the war itself was popular and the population there displayed considerable patriotic fervor during the trial. But many regarded Tashkent a sell-out. Having been led to believe that Pakistani forces were poised for a decisive victory when Ayub accepted a cease-fire, they were disappointed that the Tashkent Declaration did not contain a plan which would enable the Kashmiris to join Pakistan. No one came forward openly to state what Ayub privately said to a Pakistani writer: "We could not win Kashmir on the battlefield; how could we do that on the conference table [at Tashkent]?"[34] There were disorderly demonstrations against Tashkent in various towns in West Pakistan in which students took a prominent part.

It was during this period of comparative turmoil in West Pakistan, the

Independent India and Pakistan

main source of Ayub's power, that the East Pakistani Awami League chief, Mujibur Rahman, made bold to revive the twenty-one-point program of his party, in the garb of his six points.[35]

East Pakistanis had been feeling increasingly frustrated as the years passed. The grant of United States arms to Pakistan had strengthened the position of the predominantly West Pakistani army and the constitution of 1956 as well as of 1962 had been based on the principle of parity of East and West Pakistani representation within the national Parliament, depriving the eastern part of its numerical superiority. The Ayub regime no doubt had inaugurated a more vigorous program for the economic uplift of East Pakistan than any previous administration but any healing effects which this might have generated were more than offset by the further emotional disintegration caused by the almost total concentration of power in the West Pakistani–dominated civil-military bureaucratic complex at the center. But Ayub was too well-entrenched in the seat of power, till the war with India, for East Pakistanis to launch any significant movement to wrest power from his hands.

Mujib publicly put forward his six points for the first time in February 1966 at a political convention in Lahore. Briefly, his demands were these: (1) Pakistan shall be a federation on the basis of the Lahore Resolution; (2) the federal government shall deal only with defense and foreign affairs; (3) there shall either be two separate but freely convertible currencies or one currency with constitutional provisions to prevent the flight of capital from East Pakistan; (4) the power of taxation shall vest in the federating units which shall contribute toward the expenditure of the federal government; (5) each wing shall control its own foreign exchange earnings and both shall contribute toward the foreign exchange requirements of the federal government; (6) a militia or a paramilitary force shall be set up for East Pakistan. On the plea of "justice for the different regions and units of Pakistan" Mujib also supported those West Pakistanis who wanted the One Unit to be broken up into its original constituents.[36] Such a measure would have, of course, made it easier for him to form a coalition with one or more of the disgruntled units in West Pakistan, enabling him to dominate the central government.

He and his associates elaborated upon East Pakistani aspirations and grievances from time to time — East Pakistan must be made self-sufficient in defense; the surest method of eradicating economic disparity between the two wings was to "kill the germ of disparity at its birth" by

INDO-PAKISTANI CONFLICT (1963-74)

taking away from the center the right to tax and trade and earn foreign exchange and giving it to the provinces; the principle of parity was "promptly implemented" only so far as representation in the legislature was concerned "but the benefit of parity in representation in the other organs of the state, including the civil, foreign and defence services, was never extended to East Pakistan"; representation in the federal legislature should be on a population basis, otherwise the federal capital and defense headquarters should be shifted to East Pakistan to put a stop to over 70 percent of the central budget being spent in West Pakistan; the disparity in real per capita income between East and West Pakistan had been increasing, instead of decreasing, and was more than 60 percent.[37]

In January 1968 Mujib was implicated, along with several other persons, in the Agarthala conspiracy case and clapped into jail. The charge against the accused was that they were "plotting to deprive Pakistan of its sovereignty over a part of its territory [East Pakistan] by an armed revolt with weapons, ammunitions and funds provided by India." Since some of the accused were stated to have visited Agarthala, in India, to hatch the conspiracy, the case was given that name.

For a while things calmed down on the surface and it seemed that Ayub had ridden out the storm but it was only a question of time before the situation boiled over once more. His basic weakness was that he had never identified himself with the masses. His contemporary in Egypt, Colonel Abdel Gamal Nasser, lost two wars but died a hero. Nasser became a man of the people, convincing the latter that he trusted them and their welfare was uppermost in his thoughts. No one ever suspected him of corruption. Ayub on the other hand remained a typical generalissimo till the last. His dictatorship was of the South American variety, benefiting only the thin upper crust of business tycoons and the civil and military bureaucracy. The politicians, the intellectuals, and the people all felt left out in the cold.

He had begun impressively enough. At home the administration was toned up and the economy began to grow. Abroad Pakistan at last began to be respected. But he took the wrong turning just when it seemed as if he would make the grade. In 1962 he introduced a paternal constitution based on a restricted electoral college of 80,000 "basic democrats" who in practice became yet another layer of corrupt functionaries between himself and the common man. Had he, at that time, established a rapport between the masses and himself by conceding universal adult suffrage and tried to conciliate the alienated classes mentioned above, he might well have become a truly national leader. In subsequent years his prestige was further undermined by allegations of corruption against his family and his administration. Then came the war with India, and early in 1968 he suffered an embolism of the lung, which permanently impaired his hitherto robust constitution.

Ironically, the psychological climate for the overthrow of Ayub Khan was prepared by his own administration. The celebrations of the Decade of Development which were meant to bring home to the people the benefits of Ayub's rule had the reverse effect of irritating the masses by highlighting the fact that, while a handful of their countrymen had grown very rich, their own lot had remained as miserable as ever. To make matters worse, when the festivities ended on 27 October 1968 (the tenth anniversary of the day on which Ayub assumed power), the country found itself woefully short of a daily necessity which sweetens the bitter existence of the poor everywhere, sugar. At this juncture ruffled tempers needed but an excuse to vent themselves on the hollowness of the hyperbolic claims made during the Decade of Development extravaganza. This was provided by the events of 7 November, which normally might have passed unnoticed by the country at large.

Some students of a college in Rawalpindi were arrested that day after they had purchased certain goods from the notorious black market at Landi Kotal. This led to a riotous demonstration and one student was killed by police bullets. The army had to be called out but vandalism and violence not only continued in Rawalpindi but spread to other West Pakistani towns. Students were soon joined by workers. At a public meeting in Peshawar on 10 November a young man fired two pistol shots at Ayub Khan. Ayub was physically unhurt but the incident underlined the mood of the country. Three days later Zulfikar Ali Bhutto, chairman of the People's party, and Wali Khan, president of the National Awami party, were taken into custody. All the leading opponents of Ayub were now behind bars but their cudgels were taken up by fresh volunteers such as Air Marshal Asghar Khan (retired), General Azam Khan (retired), and S. M. Murshed, former chief justice of East Pakistan.

Before proceeding further a word of explanation is necessary with respect to Bhutto, who was destined to play a leading role in the affairs of his country before long. He had left the foreign ministership on 17 June 1966, two days after the United States had announced the resump-

INDO-PAKISTANI CONFLICT (1963–74)

tion of full-scale economic aid to Pakistan. It was believed that he had been ousted by Ayub under American pressure because of his frankly pro-Chinese policy. It transpired later that he had also felt unhappy at the terms Ayub had accepted at Tashkent. In November 1967 he founded the People's party with the slogans "Islam is our faith," "democracy is our polity," "socialism is our economy." In foreign affairs he advocated nonalignment and resignation from the SEATO and CENTO alliances because they had failed to live up to their promises. During his tenure as foreign minister he had proved himself a brilliant spokesman and this plus his own comparative youthfulness had built him a following among the frustrated idealistic young intellectuals of West Pakistan, especially the students, which stood him in good stead in the December 1970 general elections.

Bhutto's arrest added the crown of martyrdom to his other attributes. On 7 February 1969, he declared that he would undertake a hunger strike unto death if the state of emergency, which had been imposed in September 1965 because of the war with India, was not lifted within a week. His prestige went up several notches when Ayub Khan ordered his release on 13 February, just before the fast was due to commence, and lifted the state of emergency four days later.

Meanwhile, the disturbances which had commenced in West Pakistan in November 1968 had spread to East Pakistan in the following month. On 7 December two persons were killed in Dacca by police fire. The city life was completely paralyzed and at various points crowds battled with the police using bottles and brickbats. Maulana Bhashani, the fiery chief of the National Awami party, called for a general strike. Further fuel to the fire was added when, on 15 February 1969, Sergeant Zahurul Haq, one of the accused in the Agarthala conspiracy case, was shot to death in jail under suspicious circumstances. At the funeral meeting on the following day, Bhashani exhorted, *Bangla jago, agun jalo* (Bengalis wake up and kindle the fires).[38] In rural areas "people's courts" staged executions of petty officials, including policemen and "basic democrats."

Ayub Khan now made a series of concessions. He called a round table conference of opposition leaders in February 1969 to which most came but some, including Bhutto and Bhashani, did not; he withdrew the Agarthala conspiracy case against Mujib and others to enable the former to join the round table conference; he declared that he would not be a candidate in the presidential elections in 1970; and he conceded the demands for universal adult suffrage and a parliamentary system of government. But the sweet smell of success simply spurred his opponents toward the final kill. On 17 March 2.5 million workers in West Pakistan observed a strike and on 19 March the *Times* correspondent reported from East Pakistan that "hundreds of villages in East Pakistan have been razed, thousands of Bengalis left homeless and more than 150 persons have been killed in 10 days of mob executions."[39] The economy which had gone into a tailspin when the disturbances began continued its downward plunge.

In a broadcast on 25 March 1969, Ayub conceded that the situation was "no longer under the control of the government" and announced that he was handing over power to the commander in chief of the army, General Yahya Khan. That a West Pakistani army chief, without any support in East Pakistan, had once more grabbed power caused a young Bengali to prophesy: "This is the end of Pakistan. It may take 10 years or 15 years, but this is the end."[40] In the event, it took a much shorter time than that for the two parts of Pakistan to fall apart.

Rise of Indira Gandhi

During the closing years of Nehru's life, the question "After Nehru, who?" was freely debated. Many believed that after the departure of that dominant figure in Indian politics the Congress party, which under his unifying influence had provided national leadership since independence, would disintegrate into quarrelsome factions, leading to a period of uncertainty and confusion in India.

Upon Nehru's death there was, indeed, some behind-the-scenes rivalry between Lal Bahadur Shastri and the leader of the right wing, Morarji Desai, but the latter was outmaneuvered by the Congress president, Kamraj, who effectively pleaded for a unanimous choice in the national interest. Thereupon the middle-of-the-road Shastri, who was a conciliator by temperament, and was believed to have been groomed by Nehru as his successor, emerged as the party's sole choice.

However, the question of succession could not be settled so smoothly when Shastri suddenly died of a heart attack, at Tashkent, within a few hours of subscribing to the Tashkent Declaration. There were, this time, at least five visible aspirants to the office of chief executive. Three of them quit the arena before the final contest, leaving Mrs. Indira Gandhi, daughter of Jawaharlal Nehru, and Desai to fight each other to the last.

INDO-PAKISTANI CONFLICT (1963–74)

The crucial office in the party hierarchy was that of the leader of the Congress Parliamentary party, with which went the post of prime minister. Mrs. Gandhi easily defeated her rival by 355 votes to 169 in the contest for that position, but the tradition of unanimous selection had been broken, and the twice-thwarted Desai simply bided his time to renew the bid for leadership.

Mrs. Gandhi did not bring with her to the office of prime minister the established charisma of her father and could not dominate the party, the Parliament, or the public to the same extent. That the general election was only a year away made many ambitious politicians especially restive. Mrs. Gandhi's first year in office, in fact, turned out to be an exceptionally difficult one for India.

The war with Pakistan, in the previous year, had adversely affected economic planning and the failure of the monsoon rains, for two successive years, created drought conditions and a severe shortage of food grains. Prices soared. There were widespread riots in the streets by students and by those who demanded a complete ban on cow slaughter. Inside Parliament disorderly scenes became a common occurrence, causing many Indians to wonder whether the system of parliamentary democracy was suited to the genius of the Indian people. "The most important cause of the decline of Governmental authority," diagnosed a well-known commentator, "seems to be that the ruling party has become a house divided against itself."[41] Broadcasting on the eve of Republic Day in January 1967, President Radhakrishnan called the past year "the worst since independence." The unruly behavior of the members of the legislature and the public, he said, had "raised, in many minds, doubts about the stability of a united democratic India." He warned the nation that the "prospect of a revolution" was "inescapable" if violence did not end.[42]

In the February 1967 general elections the Congress party paid heavily for its internal dissensions. Its majority in the Lok Sabha was slashed by eighty-one seats, and it was rejected locally by eight states. Among the many Congress stalwarts who lost the election was the party boss, Kamraj, whose victorious adversary was a mere student. A notable feature of the election was that the parties of the left and the right both increased their strength, presaging increased friction between the two opposites. The issue of whether free enterprise or socialism was the more suitable economic philosophy for India began to be debated with increas-

INDEPENDENT INDIA AND PAKISTAN

ing heat. Since the right had fared better in the election than the left, and most defectors from the ranks of the Congress had taken that direction, it was generally believed that the trend toward the right would continue. Desai again sought the office of prime minister but in the end settled for deputy premiership, with the portfolio of finance.

Matters came to a head in May when the Congress Working Committee, under the prodding of the prime minister with Desai opposing, adopted a program to accelerate "the attainment of a democratic socialist society," including "social control" of the banks and removal of privileges of ex-rulers. The inevitable showdown between Mrs. Gandhi and the rightist "Syndicate" within the Congress party took place in 1969, in the form of dramatic moves and countermoves by the contending factions. At the Bangalore session of the All-India Congress Committee, Mrs. Gandhi, on 9 July, renewed her pressure in favor of socialist measures. Desai argued there should be no talk of nationalization at least for the next two years.[43] Four days later, the Congress Parliamentary Board humiliated the prime minister by rejecting her nominee, Jagjivan Ram, as the Congress candidate for president and nominated Sanjeeva Reddy. Mrs. Gandhi retaliated by depriving Desai of the portfolio of finance, whereupon the latter resigned from his deputy prime ministership also and left the Cabinet. She followed this up by nationalizing fourteen major banks, through an ordinance issued by the acting president, V. V. Giri, on 19 July.[44] On the following day Giri himself resigned and, with Mrs. Gandhi's tacit blessing, presented himself as a candidate in presidential election, defeating the "Syndicate" candidate. Though he had stood as an "independent," everyone treated Giri's victory as a triumph for Mrs. Gandhi. The break between the two warring sections became complete in November, when the "Syndicate" expelled Mrs. Gandhi from the party. As a consequence the once monolithic Congress party was split into two parts, the Congress (R), headed by Mrs. Gandhi, and the Congress (O), consisting of her opponents.

Though the economy, especially the agricultural sector, had begun to recover since 1967–68, other problems such as high prices, friction between the center and the states, and public violence continued. An amendment to the constitution to pave the way for the abolition of privy purses and privileges of the princes was thrown out by the Rajya Sabha, and a presidential order seeking the same result was struck down by the courts.

In the spring of 1967 a movement by peasants to seize land by force

Indo-Pakistani Conflict (1963–74)

of arms cropped up in some villages of the mountainous district of Darjeeling, near Tibet. It came to be known as the Naxalbari movement, because one of the affected villages bore the name Naxalbari. Home minister Chavan said picturesquely that "local Maoism was raising its ugly head" in Naxalbari while China "with Red Book in one hand and a sword in the other" was "dancing outside." By June 1970 not a single district of West Bengal was free from Naxalite acivities.[45] On Lenin's 100th birthday (22 April 1969) a new Communist party of India (Marxist-Leninist), avowedly based on Mao's philosophy of armed revolution, was founded at Calcutta, and in September savage communal riots, directed against the Muslims, broke out in Gandhi's home district of Gujarat, just as the country was celebrating the Mahatma's centenary.

The only way in which Mrs. Gandhi could hope effectively to override the continuing opposition of the "Syndicate," and rally the forces of law and order in the country was to go back to the electorate and seek a clear mandate for her policies. The Lok Sabha was, therefore, dissolved before its full term ended and new elections were held to fill its seats.

The result of the poll which took place in the first ten days of March 1971 came as a pleasant surprise even to the prime minister's own followers. Her party won 350 seats, while the Congress (O) was reduced to a miserable rump of 16. Mrs. Gandhi had waged an extensive whirlwind campaign, comparable to the best of her illustrious father's. Though the four right-wing parties had joined hands during the election, the only joint election cry they could come up with was *Indira Hatao* (remove Indira). Mrs. Gandhi countered this with the more positive rhyming slogan *Gharibi Hatao* (remove poverty). Many in the electorate began to picture her enemies as a bloated coterie which wished to prevent Jawaharlal's valiant daughter from serving the poor in the best traditions of her family. India, it seemed, had found her new leader.

The Soviet Union Forges Ahead of the United States in the Competition to Win India's Favor

Parallel to the struggle for power between the parties of the right and the left in India ran the rivalry between Washington and Moscow for greater influence in New Delhi. India's need for foreign aid, and her divisive politics, laid her open to outside interference.

Predictably, the United States favored the rightists and free enterprise,[46] while the U.S.S.R. made no secret of her sympathy for the leftists

INDEPENDENT INDIA AND PAKISTAN

and remained adamant that her assistance was available for the public sector only. Indira Gandhi tried to steer the middle course by declaring that India's "concept of socialism and democracy is and must remain Indian" and in their "march towards socialism" Indians did not wish to be "prisoners of dogma."[47]

When the right wing was in the ascendant in India, the *New Times* approvingly quoted Krishna Menon's statement that "after the death of Jawaharlal Nehru the reactionary forces have dominated the party and the government." As the general elections of 1967 approached, the same periodical apprehensively noted that "reactionary forces" were specially active in the campaign and no fewer than 100 maharajas and maharanis were candidates. After the election, *International Affairs* asked, "Given the present balance of forces in the Indian National Congress, is not the election victory a triumph for big monopoly capital?"[48]

In the meantime Indo–United States relations were running into difficulties of their own. During her visit to Moscow in July 1966, Mrs. Gandhi was promised a billion dollars of economic aid for India over the next five years. In the Indo-Soviet communiqué she joined her hosts in demanding that the United States bombing of North Vietnam "should be stopped immediately," and in declaring that the international situation had deteriorated "as a result of the aggressive actions of imperialist and other reactionary forces." There was no mention in the joint statement of some suggestions which Mrs. Gandhi herself had made only a few days previously — that the Geneva Conference be revived and the halt in American bombing be followed by a cessation of hostilities "on all sides throughout Vietnam." The United States protested that the Indian prime minister had shifted her position perceptibly closer to that of the Soviet Union. At a news conference President Johnson displayed his annoyance. "I do not think," he said, "that we should spend all our time . . . examining what the Government of the United States might be willing to do without any regard to what the enemy might be willing to do." When Johnson deferred action on an Indian request for wheat, the *New York Times* wrote that the Indians suspected that "the hold-up may be partially due to President Johnson's displeasure with Prime Minister Gandhi's recent call for a halt in the bombing of North Vietnam."[49]

In September 1968, the New Delhi correspondent of the *New York Times* reported that there was a growing conviction in India "that neither of the biggest powers [the United States and the U.S.S.R.] can be

INDO-PAKISTANI CONFLICT (1963–74)

regarded any more as a dependable friend."⁵⁰ Indo-Soviet relations, in fact, had reached their lowest point that summer. India had been visibly annoyed by Kosygin's proddings that she should settle the Kashmir and Farakka disputes with Pakistan and by the U.S.S.R.'s decision to supply weapons to Pakistan.⁵¹

In March 1969 the situation suddenly changed, causing the Soviet Union to court India more assiduously than ever before. On the second and the fifteenth of that month clashes took place between the armed forces of the U.S.S.R. and China at the Ussuri River, worsening the already tense situation between the two Communist neighbors. Just as America had once sought allies to surround China, Russia now began to do so with even greater urgency.

The first Ussuri passage of arms had coincided with the arrival in India of the Soviet defense minister, Marshal Grechko, "and before leaving he reportedly held talks with Indian officials on the coordination of policy toward China." On 7 June party leader Leonid Brezhnev publicly declared that the course of events was "putting on the agenda the task of creating a system of collective security in Asia." Peking denounced the Russian plan as "some trash" which "Soviet revisionist social-imperialism . . . has picked up from the garbage heap of the notorious warmonger Dulles . . . to rig up a ring of encirclement round China." Brezhnev's proposition was evidently discussed when the Indian foreign minister, Dinesh Singh, visited Russia in September, for both the *New Times* and *International Affairs* noted with satisfaction that Dinesh Singh had stated on his return home that India welcomed the Soviet proposal.⁵²

Because of India's much-proclaimed commitment to nonalignment, a formal Indo-Soviet treaty with defense overtones did not emerge till India was faced with war with Pakistan but, in the meantime, the U.S.S.R. had the satisfaction of observing that the balance of power inside India was gradually shifting to the left, paving the way for closer relations between the two countries. Giri's victory in the presidential election showed that forces of the left were "becoming an important factor in Indian politics" and "the main result of the [March 1971] general election was the smashing defeat inflicted on the reactionary forces." It was noted that the two Communist parties had become the second and third largest parties in Parliament after Mrs. Gandhi's.⁵³

On the economic front industrial enterprises built with Soviet assistance before the close of 1971 were providing India "with 30 per cent of

Independent India and Pakistan

the entire output of steel, 35 per cent of the extracted oil, 20 per cent of the electric power, 60 per cent of the electrical equipment and 80 per cent of heavy machinery."[54] In the summer of 1970 Mrs. Gandhi denied point-blank that New Delhi had increasingly been turning to Moscow and emphatically asserted that "it is, in fact, Moscow which has turned more towards us."[55] This was not surprising. On account of her large size, geographical proximity to China, and hostility toward China, India was the ideal instrument for furthering Russia's anti-Chinese designs.

The U.S.S.R. had already discovered the futility of trying to persuade India to settle her disputes with Pakistan, and India's continuing protests against the supply of Russian military supplies to Pakistan made it clear that that program also must be terminated if the Soviet Union really wished to please India. A Russian embassy note, issued in New Delhi on 7 July 1971, assured Indians that no Russian arms had been given to Pakistan since April 1970, when deliveries contracted for in 1968 had been completed.[56] Since a pipe line takes a while to dry up, the decision not to supply any more war material to Pakistan was probably taken by the Russian leadership in 1969, when it began to urge India to join the Soviet-sponsored Asian collective security system. Russian military hardware to India, however, continued to flow in increasing quantities. The United States having ceased to be a source of arms to any appreciable degree, the field was clear for Russia to become India's chief provider of that important material. In 1962 India had received only 10 percent of her imported arms from the U.S.S.R. By September 1971 the percentage had shot up to 90.[57]

On the other side of the equation, the United States and Pakistan tried to recapture some of their lost friendship. This move was facilitated by India's continuing criticism of American policies in Indochina, and by the substitution of Richard Nixon for Lyndon Johnson in the White House. In August 1969, Nixon was given an enthusiastic welcome in Pakistan as one of the architects of the United States–Pakistani alliance of the 1950s, and he assured Pakistanis that, as president, he would again work for friendship between his country and theirs.[58] On 9 October 1970, Washington decided, as "an exception to the general rule," to supply Pakistan some items of military equipment to replace those previously supplied.

At the same time the first signs of a thaw appeared in the long frozen Sino-American relations. While the United States had been occupied in

Indo-Pakistani Conflict (1963–74)

Vietnam and China had been engrossed in her cultural revolution (1966–68), the Soviet Union had been expanding her influence in the Middle East and Asia. Since her retreat in the Cuban crisis, the U.S.S.R. had made special efforts to strengthen her navy and, thanks to concessions provided by the United Arab Republic, had built up a considerable presence in the Mediterranean, which washes the shores of Europe, Africa, and the oil-rich Middle East and links together the Atlantic and Indian oceans. Now she seemed to be successfully wooing Asia's second largest state, India. After the Russian invasion of Czechoslovakia in August 1968, on the pretext of saving the socialist system there, the Chinese began anxiously to wonder whether the U.S.S.R. would next turn upon them, with a similar excuse. These fears were heightened during the following summer, when Moscow reportedly sounded "European Communist leaders as to their reactions to a Soviet attack, either an invasion or a 'surgical strike,' against the Chinese nuclear installations."[59]

Though the United States has no need to take sides in the struggle between the two Communist neighbors, it is obviously not in her interest that the Soviet Union should cut down China's stature. Her purpose is better served if China remains a salutary counterpoise to Russia in Asia. By 1969, therefore, circumstances were pushing the United States as well as China toward a reappraisal of their relations. That summer the United States commenced the liberalization of her policies with respect to trade with China and travel of American citizens to that land. A few days later Secretary of State William P. Rogers said, "We . . . look forward to a time when we can enter into a useful dialogue and a reduction of tensions [with China]."[60]

The outlines of the Indo-Soviet versus the Sino-Pakistani–United States alignment, which became manifest during the Indo-Pakistani confrontation of 1971, were thus already beginning dimly to take shape.

The East Pakistani Crisis and Indo-Pakistani War

Upon assuming power General Yahya Khan said his sole ambition was to restore law and order and transfer power to the representatives of the people so that they could give a workable constitution to the country and solve other national problems.[61]

He announced on 28 November 1969 that general elections in Pakistan would be held on 5 October 1970, on the basis of one-man-one-vote[62] and that the One Unit in West Pakistan would be dissolved. A

INDEPENDENT INDIA AND PAKISTAN

Legal Framework Order, published on 30 March 1970, laid down the manner in which the National Assembly and the various provincial assemblies would be elected and the National Assembly would enact a new constitution. The National Assembly would consist of 313 members, 169 from East Pakistan and 144 from West Pakistan.[63] Because of heavy floods in East Pakistan during the rainy season, it was announced on 15 August that elections would be postponed till 7 December.

On 12 November East Pakistan was hit by a massive cyclone, the greatest national calamity of modern times, which left behind more than 200,000 dead and inflicted untold damage on the countryside. There was some talk of postponing the elections once more but the idea was abandoned chiefly because Mujibur Rahman expressed himself against it. The disaster had two effects on the developing political situation. First, it further alienated East Pakistanis from the West Pakistan–based central administration because the former felt that the government had been unsympathetic and tardy in administering relief. Mujib said the new experience had "only brought into sharp focus the basic truth that every Bengali has felt in his bones, that we have been treated so long as a colony and a market." The feeling now pervaded in every village and every slum that Bengalis must rule themselves. Asked if he was considering secession, he replied, "Not yet."[64] Secondly, it roused the sympathy of other countries for the plight of East Pakistanis and highlighted the latter's standing grievances against the West Pakistanis.

The elections were duly held on 7 December 1970, except that voting for 9 National Assembly seats and 21 Provincial Assembly constituencies in the cyclone-affected area took place on 17 January 1971. Mujib's Awami League captured 167 seats in the National Assembly, giving it a clear over-all majority in that chamber, while Bhutto's People's party won 85 seats, which gave it a dominant position in West Pakistan. The purely regional character of the two parties was emphasized by the fact that neither could win any seat at all outside its own region.

During the election campaign Mujib had uncompromisingly stuck to his six points but he had denied that he wanted East Pakistan to break away from its western counterpart. Obviously referring to the fact that East Pakistanis constituted the majority within Pakistan, he had said, "West Pakistan can think of separation, not we." Most West Pakistanis, however, felt convinced that the acceptance of the six-point formula would lead to a complete split between the two wings. Had the Awami

Indo-Pakistani Conflict (1963–74)

League failed to win the majority of seats in the National Assembly, there would have been some hope of preventing Mujib from framing a constitution on the basis of his demands. But after his party's overwhelming victory in the election, which he called a "referendum" on his program, there was nothing to stop the East Pakistani leader from getting his way. He asserted that his party, as the majority party in the National Assembly, had "the democratic right to give the country a constitution"; also, that only the Awami League had the right to form the government at the center.[65]

Bhutto, as the leader of the majority party in West Pakistan, pressed for an adjustment of the six points and also demanded that power at the center should not be handed over to the Awami League, which represented East Pakistan only, but to the majority parties of both wings. He argued that in the important matter of framing a constitution it was essential to evolve a consensus of all the federating units.[66]

These differences proved irreconcilable and the drama proceeded toward its unhappy climax. When Yahya summoned the National Assembly to meet at Dacca on 3 March 1971, Bhutto announced that his party would not attend the session because Mujib's attitude had made it clear that, if the People's party were to go to Dacca, it would be doing so merely to "accept" a constitution, not to frame it.[67] On 1 March Yahya postponed the meeting of the Assembly to an unspecified "later date."

Mujib retaliated by calling a general strike in East Pakistan and launching a "nonviolent noncooperation movement" and a no-tax campaign. On 6 March Yahya announced that the National Assembly would meet on 25 March but Mujib continued to issue "directives" to intensify the campaign of noncooperation. On 10 March the East Pakistani leader claimed: "All branches of the Government including the Secretariat, Government and semi-Government agencies, courts, railways and ports are complying with the directives issued by us in the name of the people of Bangla Desh."[68] The Dacca correspondent of the *New York Times* reported that East Pakistanis were "in effect governing themselves." Yahya flew to Dacca on 15 March and he and several West Pakistani leaders held further discussions with Mujib but to no purpose. The parleys broke down on 25 March, whereupon Yahya banned the Awami League and ordered the Pakistani army "to do their duty and fully restore the authority of the Government." Mujib was arrested for treason and was flown to West Pakistan. The insurgents proclaimed independence on 26 March.

Was this total separation of East and West Pakistan avoidable? After Mujib's election victory it was avoidable only upon Mujib's terms, which meant virtual independence for each of the two wings of Pakistan, with only loose confederal arrangements nominally holding them together. This was bound to give a powerful fillip to the separatist tendencies in the various regions of West Pakistan and could very well have spelled the total disintegration of Pakistan. Any West Pakistani leader who conceded the six points to East Pakistan, therefore, would have been at once stigmatized as a traitor in his own part of the country. At the same time Mujib had become a prisoner of his own electoral victory. Having received an overwhelming mandate for his platform, he could not very well relinquish it without angering his constituents.

The truth of the matter is that by early 1971 the situation had assumed the character of a classical tragedy, in which the actors had become helpless playthings of historical forces reaching back to the early days of Pakistan. East Pakistanis had joined the movement for Pakistan to escape Hindu domination, only to fall under the heel of their fellow Muslims of West Pakistan. As Yahya himself conceded, the people of East Pakistan had the "feeling that they were not being allowed to play their full part in the decision-making processes at the national level and in certain important spheres of national activity. In my view they were fully justified in being dissatisfied with this state of affairs."[69] Most East Pakistanis, however, had long lost faith in the fancy words of West Pakistanis. By breaking down the control of the central government during the closing part of Ayub's tenure, they had already tasted a victory of sorts. When Yahya balked at handing over power to Mujib, they concluded that the lawless tactics they had recently employed with such effect were the only means at their disposal to depose the West Pakistani bogy once and for all.

Yahya's resort to the use of massive military power against the people of East Pakistan was bound to aggravate an already grave situation. Nothing rouses bestiality in human beings more than a civil war. There were excesses on both sides. In the opening phase the Bengalis killed off thousands of non-Bengali Muslims who had settled in East Pakistan after partition and West Pakistanis who had gone there on business. Then the Pakistani army, composed of West Pakistanis, wrought havoc.

Indo-Pakistani Conflict (1963–74)

The Pakistanis estimate that Bengalis slayed some 100,000 non-Bengalis and West Pakistanis. Mujib says the Pakistani army slaughtered 3 million Bengalis, rendered 25 million homeless, and caused 10 million to take refuge in India. Pakistani spokesmen in the United Nations have placed the figure of refugees in India at 2 million, and President Bhutto has stated that between 20,000 and 30,000 Bengalis were killed. The *New York Times* has pointed out that some diplomats and relief workers place the number of East Pakistanis killed at 25,000. Pakistanis allege, further, that much of the damage to property and the network of communications was inflicted by Indian-supported guerrillas. Whatever the statistics, the extent of human suffering was appalling. Peter Preston of the *Guardian* called the unleashing of the army by Yahya Khan "the act of a mindless sergeant-major."[70] After the surrender of the Pakistani army in East Pakistan in December the non-Bengalis there, chiefly of Bihari origin, were subjected to another wave of terrorism and murders. The Pakistani army chief's decision was also a military blunder of the first magnitude because, given all the circumstances, anyone could see that an armed clash with India was a distinct probability.

After the Indo-Pakistani war of 1965 the balance of military power had decisively shifted in favor of India. Pakistan had found it difficult to replace the heavy equipment lost during that conflict while her adversary, despite her economic and political problems, had been determinedly building up her strength. The accompanying tabulation shows the relative defense expenditures of the two countries during the years 1965–70 in million rupees.[71] By 1967 India had "achieved a considerable mea-

	India	*Pakistan*
1965	8,058	1,263
1966	8,848	2,855
1967	9,086	2,294
1968	9,684	2,187
1969	10,332	2,427
1970	11,047	2,761

sure of self-sufficiency in meeting the growing demand of the armed forces."[72] Since 1965 the Soviet Union and her Eastern European allies had furnished India arms worth $730 million. China, in the same period, could supply to Pakistan similar material worth only $133 million.[73] Congressional circles and the liberal press in the United States leveled considerable criticism at the sending of American arms supplies to Pak-

INDEPENDENT INDIA AND PAKISTAN

istan during these years. In fact, however, American military deliveries to both India and Pakistan, in all the six years following the embargo on heavy arms imposed during the 1965 war, amounted to a mere $70 million, and these were restricted to non-lethal equipment and spare parts for equipment previously supplied.[74]

Pakistan, moreover, was a house divided against itself, while India had just given Indira Gandhi a resounding vote of confidence in the general elections. And East Pakistan, the prospective main theater of war, was hundreds of miles away from West Pakistan, which was the country's main bastion. The core of the resistant elements in East Pakistan consisted of about a hundred and fifty thousand Bengali members of the Pakistani army, paramilitary border forces, and police who had revolted and taken to irregular warfare.[75] They were assisted in various ways by the bulk of the population.

Within a week of the final break between Yahya and Mujib both houses of the Indian Parliament unanimously assured East Pakistanis that their struggle would receive the wholehearted support of the people of India.[76] A few days later the All-India Congress Committee (R) expressed "solidarity" with East Pakistanis and expressed the hope that their "historic upsurge would triumph."[77] Both these resolutions pointedly referred to East Pakistan as East Bengal. Indian spokesmen demanded a solution acceptable to Mujib's party which, by this time, meant complete independence for East Pakistan.

Indian practical assistance to the cause of the East Pakistanis initially consisted of giving the guerrillas arms, training, sanctuary, and covering fire and infiltrating some personnel of the Indian Border Force into East Pakistan. It was hoped that the rebels would be able to gain a foothold inside East Pakistan, set up a provisional government there, and gradually render the position of the Pakistani army untenable. However, by May, the Pakistani armed forces had established control over the main population centers and systems of communication and it became clear that the insurgents could not hold a base within East Pakistan without direct military intervention by India. Anticipating an Indian assault, Yahya warned that, if India tried to seize any part of East Pakistan, he would declare war, and he added, ominously, that Pakistan would not stand alone.[78]

The Indians did not doubt their own capacity to handle the Pakistani army but the prognostication that Pakistan would have outside help

INDO-PAKISTANI CONFLICT (1963–74)

alarmed them, especially in the light of contemporaneous moves elsewhere on the diplomatic chessboard. Only a few days previously Nixon had announced that he would visit China before the following May. The Chinese invitation to him had materialized from a visit to China by Henry Kissinger, for which arrangements had been made by the government of Pakistan. These developments were generally taken to mean that a United States–China–Pakistan axis could be in the offing. The only power strong enough to reassure India in the face of this frightening prospect was the Soviet Union. Mrs. Gandhi, therefore, quickly moved to conclude the treaty which Russia had been pressing on India for the preceding two years.

THE INDO-SOVIET TREATY

The most important article of the "Treaty of Friendship and Cooperation" which the U.S.S.R. and India signed at New Delhi on 9 August 1971 was the ninth which stipulated that "in the event that any of the Parties is attacked or threatened with attack, the High Contracting Parties will immediately start mutual consultations with a view to eliminating this threat and taking appropriate effective measures to ensure peace and security for their countries." President Giri fancifully hailed the treaty as "a major step in furtherance of our policy of non-alignment." Foreign Minister Swaran Singh, too, at first denied point-blank that the treaty was a defense pact or a military alliance. But, when confrontation with Pakistan became imminent, he assured his countrymen that India could count upon "total support" from the Soviet Union.[79]

Nonofficial Indian and Soviet sources, however, commented on the pact more realistically. The *Statesman* thought the agreement was "almost indistinguishable from a defense pact." Former Foreign Minister Chagla declared unequivocally that nonalignment was "dead" and the Anglo-Indian leader Frank Anthony felt happy that the ineffective policy of nonalignment had been abandoned and India now had one friend. *New Times* quoted with approval the observation of the Delhi weekly *Link* that the Indo-Soviet treaty "could become the first step towards the establishment of a system of collective security in Asia."[80]

To complete the story it may be stated here that India is not the only country with whom the Soviet Union has made a compact of mutual defense. She has entered into similar covenants with the United Arab Republic (27 May 1971) and with Iraq (9 April 1972) and has unsuccessfully sought such ties with at least three other countries — Afghanistan,

Independent India and Pakistan

Indonesia, and Pakistan. With respect to the Soviet-Iraqi pact, *International Affairs* has affirmed in Dullesian terms that it "serves the purposes of uniting the progressive Arab states on an anti-imperialist basis." To these Soviet-sponsored security arrangements Bangladesh is linked by her Treaty of Friendship, Cooperation, and Peace with India (19 March 1972). The Soviet Union is also outperforming the United States in supplying arms to the countries of the Third World.[81]

THE INDO-PAKISTANI WAR

Mrs. Gandhi's next major move, after consummating the Indo-Soviet alliance, was to undertake two extensive diplomatic journeys, covering the Soviet Union and some other European countries and the United States. Kremlinologists noted that her visit was the first occasion in recent times on which the three top Russian leaders had simultaneously conferred with a visiting prime minster. In the United States she met President Nixon. On her return to New Delhi (13 November) the Indian leader said that the world now had a better appreciation of the seriousness of the crisis in the subcontinent.[82]

In the meantime, toward the end of October, India had invoked article 9 of the Indo-Soviet Treaty. The New Delhi correspondent of the *New York Times* commented on 28 October that the parade of high Soviet offices to New Delhi, which had been "heavy" since the Indo-Soviet Treaty had been signed, in recent weeks had become "almost frenetic." On 8 November the same observer reported that Indian officials acknowledged that "a few" Soviet transport planes, carrying arms, had arrived in India in the last week and that "some ships may be on the way." The new purchases and the delivery speed-ups, the Indians explained, were an outgrowth of the recent visits of Soviet Deputy Foreign Minister Nikolai P. Firyubin and the Soviet air chief, Pavel S. Kutakhov.[83]

At about the same time Indian regular forces began to operate inside East Pakistan. On 7 November "unimpeachable Indian sources" admitted that Indian troops had crossed into East Pakistan to silence Pakistani guns that had been shelling Indian territory. Five days later it was reported that in at least one area inside East Pakistan Indian troops had dug in. The Pakistani foreign secretary, S. M. Khan, stated on the same day that there was a virtual state of war along the Indo-Pakistani border. On 18 November Mrs. Gandhi informed the secretary general of the United Nations that Pakistan was "seriously preparing to start a large-

Indo-Pakistani Conflict (1963–74)

scale armed conflict with India" and the latter had, therefore, to take all necessary "defensive measures." Three days later India invaded East Pakistan in strength, and open war between the two countries broke out. An Indian government spokesman explained away the Indian onset in these interesting terms: "Pakistani tanks were noticed advancing menacingly towards Indian territory. The Indian Army went into action immediately and succeeded in repulsing the attack. . . . 13 Pakistani Chafee tanks were knocked out. The shooting down of the three Sabre jets also came in the wake of this incident although the exact purpose that brought the Pakistani fighters into Indian territory is not known."[84]

During the crisis India had also rejected all suggestions for toning it down while Pakistan had responded favorably to them. These included the proposal of the United States that both sides should pull back troops from the border, and the offer of the secretary general of the United Nations to place his good offices at the disposal of the parties.[85]

Indian armed units rapidly advanced into East Pakistan. On 3 December 1971 the Pakistani air force opened the western front by bombing Indian airfields. Three days later India recognized Bangladesh, whereupon Pakistan severed diplomatic ties with her. Upon the fall of Dacca to Indian troops, on 16 December, India declared a cease-fire on both fronts. Pakistan, having little choice, accepted on the next day, and the brief Indo-Pakistan war came to an end. The independence of Bangladesh, which had been proclaimed on 26 March, thus became a practical if not yet a legal reality. Pakistan's defeat cost her the permanent loss of her more populated half. India also rounded up some 93,000 prisoners in East Pakistan, including 15,000 civilian men, women, and children. On the western front each side captured a few hundred prisoners but Pakistan lost more territory.

During the crisis the efforts of the United States were directed toward persuading the parties to arrive at a peaceful settlement. Though Nixon's critics made much of the American "tilt" in favor of Pakistan, in fact the United States was not insensitive to the reality that "a lasting political solution [of the problem] could be found only on the basis of some form of autonomy for East Pakistan . . . and made clear to all parties" that she favored such a solution. Far from condoning military action in East Pakistan, the United States, early in April 1971, stopped issuing or renewing licenses for military supplies to Pakistan and ceased new commitments for economic development loans. This shut off arms worth $35

Independent India and Pakistan

million and permitted shipment to Pakistan of spare parts worth less than $5 million which were already in the pipe line. By the beginning of November, i.e., before the outbreak of the Indo-Pakistani war, the pipe line had dried up completely.[86] Arms licenses and economic aid to India, on the other hand, were not suspended till India had openly invaded East Pakistan.

After war had broken out the United States worked for a cease-fire. At her initiative the Security Council convened on 4 December but a resolution calling for a cessation of hostilities was vetoed by the U.S.S.R. A similar resolution was frustrated in the same fashion on the following day. The question was then shifted to the General Assembly which, on 7 December, by a vote of 104 to 11, called for an immediate cease-fire and withdrawal of forces to their own territories. Only after the fighting was over did the Soviet Union let the Security Council pass a resolution, on 21 December 1971, demanding a withdrawal of forces to their own territories and "to positions which fully respect the cease-fire line in Jammu and Kashmir." It further called for the observance of the Geneva conventions of 1949 and other provisions with regard to prisoners of war and related matter.[87]

Ambassador Bush expressed the view of the United States in the 4 December meeting in these words: "The very purpose which draws us together here — building a peaceful world — will be thwarted if a situation is accepted in which a government intervenes across its borders in the affairs of another with military forces in violation of the United Nations Charter." The United States also ordered an American flotilla, headed by the carrier *Enterprise*, to sail into the Bay of Bengal. Revealing the purpose and effect of this show of strength, President Bhutto said that the Indian onslaught upon West Pakistan and Azad Kashmir would have continued "if the United States had not given a firm ultimatum warning that hostilities must cease. I know this is true. I have just been in Peking and Chou En-lai confirmed this to me. . . . [T]he United States . . . did put its foot down." Nixon, too, has publicly stated that the Soviet Union persuaded India to declare a cease-fire after East Pakistan had gone down.[88]

Some other aspects of the Nixon administration's realistic handling of the South Asian conflagration need to be brought out, because they have been befogged by the "credibility gap" which caused public opinion to

INDO-PAKISTANI CONFLICT (1963–74)

accept criticism of the administration but to overlook the propriety of any of its actions:

1. Nixon ordered the units of the United States fleet into the Bay of Bengal as a response to the additional warships sent into those waters by the Soviet Union.[89]

2. When American intelligence reported both Mrs. Gandhi and Yahya as saying, at one stage, that the Chinese were on the point of intervening along India's northern borders, White House press secretary Ronald L. Ziegler stated in Washington on 14 December 1971 that if war expanded into West Pakistan it would "very definitely affect the world peace."[90] It is not easy to assess the amount of reality behind international threats which fail to materialize, but the action of the American president, in extinguishing the danger to West Pakistan, was certainly a wise precaution. If nothing else, it did prevent a continuance of death and destruction.

3. Nixon was much criticized for calling India the aggressor but this charge was patently true. In invading her neighboring sovereign state, India did violate the United Nations charter. That Yahya had earlier committed the cruel blunder of setting the army upon the civilian population of East Pakistan did not convert India's subsequent wrong into right.

4. As amply demonstrated by the voting pattern in the General Assembly resolution of 7 December 1971, United States policy was in tune with the view of the majority of the members of the United Nations, especially with that of the Afro-Asian family of nations to which India and Pakistan belong.

5. Intercession by the United States played a significant part in saving the life of Mujibur Rahman, who subsequently was able to head the government of Bangladesh. In August 1971, Secretary of State Rogers had conveyed to the Pakistani ambassador in Washington "the concern of the United States over the fate of Sheik Mujibur Rahman," and had also transmitted to the ambassador an appeal by 11 senators and 58 representatives for compassion for Mujib.[91] President Nixon confirmed afterwards that the United States "obtained assurance from President Yahya that Sheikh Mujibur Rahman would not be executed."[92] Had the United States reproved Yahya publicly, she would not have enjoyed sufficient influence with him to extract the promise that Mujib would not be sentenced to death as a traitor.

6. The United States was the largest contributor, by far, toward the relief of East Pakistani refugees in India.

INDEPENDENT INDIA AND PAKISTAN

7. The United States has already generously aided Bangladesh to the tune of $320 million while the Soviet Union has given only $62 million.[93] The efforts of the Soviet Union during the war were directed toward enabling India to humble her weaker adversary without let or hindrance. Besides blocking action in the Security Council till India had conquered East Pakistan, the U.S.S.R. was willing to make military moves to deter China on India's behalf. Obviously referring to the protective disposition of Soviet forces, President Giri assured the Governors' Conference at New Delhi, on 26 November 1971, that "states . . . on our borders have taken the necessary steps to meet any contingency that might arise to threaten our national integrity."[94] The Soviet ambassador to India also assured his host country that the Soviet fleet in the Indian Ocean would not "allow" the United States Seventh Fleet to intervene on Pakistan's side.[95]

China gave Pakistan enthusiastic verbal support but it can never be definitely known whether she would have actually gone to war to save West Pakistan. On both the occasions that the People's Republic has hitherto taken up arms (the Korean war and the Himalayan war against India) she did so only when her own borders were directly menaced, and in both cases she desisted from fighting after her limited objectives had been attained. Be that as it may, President Bhutto's verdict is that "within limitations, China did what she could. . . . We have not lost confidence in China's friendship or in China's words."[96]

The Muslim countries rendered Pakistan moral as well as material support. During the East Pakistani crisis a twenty-two-nation Charter Committee of the Islamic Conference, meeting at Jeddah in June 1971, unanimously expressed "full support and backing to sisterly Pakistan" in the struggle to maintain her solidarity and territorial integrity and condemned "foreign interference in Pakistan's internal affairs."[97] Saudi Arabia "loaned" to Pakistan 75 American military aircraft and Libya sent "a number of" Northrup F-5 jets, and Jordan "some" F-104s. President Sadat protested against the transfer by Russians of some planes from Egypt to India and complained bitterly that Moscow supported India actively in her war but refused to back Egypt decisively against Israel. The president of Libya said that by supporting India against Pakistan, the Soviet Union had acted like "an imperialist state." Iran's assistance was the most substantial of all. She permitted Pakistani civil aircraft to use Irani airfields during the war, provided fire-extinguishing apparatus

INDO-PAKISTANI CONFLICT (1963-74)

and experts when the oil storage tanks in Karachi were hit by Indian bombs, and alleviated shortages of ammunition, oil, and aircraft.[98]

After the war a communiqué issued by the Conference of Foreign Ministers of Islamic Countries declared "full support" for Pakistan's "territorial integrity, national sovereignty and independence" and called upon the governments of India and Pakistan to withdraw their troops in obedience to the General Assembly resolution of 7 December 1971 and the Security Council resolution of 21 December 1971 and repatriate prisoners as required by the Geneva convention.[99]

Postwar Diplomacy

After the fiasco of his policies, Yahya could not very well continue in office any longer. On 20 December 1971, he stepped down, handing over the presidency to Zulfikar Ali Bhutto. Mrs. Gandhi's new opposite number, being an accomplished politician, played the poor hand he had inherited from his predecessor with notable skill. Before agreeing to hold a meeting with the Indian prime minister, Bhutto tested the ground carefully by making two whirlwind journeys covering twenty-two Afro-Asian countries that had been sympathetic toward Pakistan during the recent confrontation with India, and also paid visits to Pakistan's most important neighbors, China and the Soviet Union. At home he revived the democratic process by summoning the national and provincial assemblies, having an interim constitution approved, and terminating martial law. The National Assembly forthwith legitimatized and strengthened his position by unanimously according him a vote of confidence. He also released Sheikh Mujibur Rahman, who flew to Dacca via London and New Delhi and assumed the office of prime minister of Bangladesh.

India, hitherto, had uniformly stood for settling the smaller differences first,[100] on the ground that such a process would improve the climate for tackling the more difficult questions. However, to cash in on her recent victory, she now pressed for an over-all settlement. Most importantly, she wished to bury the Kashmir question once and for all by making Pakistan accept the cease-fire line as the permanent boundary, and she wanted Pakistan to recognize Bangladesh. Pakistan, on the other hand, advocated a step-by-step approach, which meant leaving aside the Kashmir question till a more opportune moment. The immediate questions, from her point of view, were the withdrawal of forces from areas occupied during the recent war and the release of the Pakistani prisoners of war.

215

INDEPENDENT INDIA AND PAKISTAN

With regard to Kashmir Bhutto stressed that the right of self-determination of the Kashmiris "has not been bestowed on them either by India or Pakistan — it is their inherent right which no one can take away,"[101] and on the question of prisoners India adopted the position that they had surrendered to the joint India-Bangladesh command and could not, therefore, be released by India without the concurrence of Bangladesh. Not surprisingly, these two questions remained unresolved when Bhutto and Indira Gandhi conferred at Simla from 28 June till 3 July 1972.

Under the "Agreement of Bilateral Relations between the Government of India and the Government of Pakistan" published on 2 July 1972, the parties decided to withdraw their armed forces to their own sides of the international border. In Kashmir they agreed to respect "the line of control resulting from the ceasefire of 17 December 1971 . . . without prejudice to the recognized position of either side." They also promised to "meet from time to time" to "normalize relations between the two countries, step by step."[102] It had been stipulated in the agreement that withdrawals would be completed within thirty days of the coming into force of the accord but it was not till 7 December that the two sides could agree on the line of control in Kashmir, and accordingly not till 20 December that withdrawals were completed (in all areas, except a few snowbound spots in Kashmir).

Initially, the Simla agreement was well received in both countries but, by the end of 1972, much of the optimism that it might be the harbinger of a new relationship between India and Pakistan had evaporated. The change for the worse was partly due to the delay in the withdrawal of forces but mainly it resulted from the continuing deadlock over the release of some 93,000 Pakistani prisoners of war, including 15,000 civilian men, women, and children, captured in East Pakistan (the few hundred prisoners captured by each side on the western front were exchanged on 1 December 1972). India will not release the prisoners, so the argument went, till Bangladesh also agrees to do so, Bangladesh will not discuss this or any other matter with Pakistan till the latter recognizes her, and Pakistan will not recognize Bangladesh till Mujib has conferred with Bhutto. The matter was further complicated by Mujib's declared determination to try some 1500 prisoners for war crimes.

Bhutto personally is in favor of recognizing Bangladesh but he has insisted upon seeing Mujib before taking the final step in that direction, because many sections in Pakistan are opposed to endorsing Bangla-

Indo-Pakistani Conflict (1963–74)

desh's independence and he considers it essential to prepare an acceptable "package deal" to override the opposition. The main questions to be considered would be the kind of new relations Pakistan and Bangladesh should have with each other; the apportionment of foreign debts, assets, and liabilities; Bangladesh's assurance that Pakistani prisoners would be freed and none of them would be tried in Bangladesh; and the fate of non-Bengali elements in Bangladesh accused of having collaborated with the West Pakistani administration during the East Pakistani crisis. The Pakistani leader probably would like to make sure also that Bangladesh will not later come out with extravagant claims for war damage and past exploitation by West Pakistan. Bhutto has revealed that, before leaving Pakistan upon his release, Mujib placed his hand on the Quran and promised to meet the former as soon as possible. Before his own countrymen Bhutto has argued that recognition of Bangladesh would be greatly to Pakistan's advantage because it would give Pakistan a voice in Dacca, without which the field would remain clear for India to extend her hegemony over the new state and because recognition would facilitate the return of prisoners. And he has told them bluntly that Bangladesh would not disappear if Pakistan did not recognize her.[103] On 9 July 1973 Bhutto was able to receive authorization from the National Assembly to recognize Bangladesh when such a step would be in the best national interest.

The Pakistani president has offered to try, by court-martial in Pakistan, armed personnel guilty of excesses in East Pakistan. He has expressed the fear that trials in Bangladesh would be in the nature of a "big tamasha [carnival], palm tree justice. . . . The story will come to this side and things will become unmanageable." On another occasion he warned more explicitly that, if Mujib keeps aside any prisoner "for the guillotine," there would be retaliation (against some 400,000 Bengalis, including 30,000 soldiers and 17,000 civil servants, who are stranded in West Pakistan).[104]

According to international law India, clearly, should have released the Pakistani prisoners of war directly after the fighting stopped. Article 118 of the Third Geneva Convention of 1949 demands unambiguously that "prisoners of war shall be released and repatriated without delay after the cessation of active hostilities." When the Security Council, in its resolution of 21 December 1971, called upon the parties to observe the Geneva convention of 1949 it impliedly ruled that the case of the Pakistani

INDEPENDENT INDIA AND PAKISTAN

prisoners falls within the ambit of that convention and India, which alone has custody of the prisoners, is not competent to attach any conditions to the release of the captives. The International Commission of Jurists also, for the same reasons, urged India to liberate the Pakistani detainees immediately.[105]

That India was using the captives for pressuring Pakistan to recognize Bangladesh was obvious. But from time to time Indians also revealed two less publicized but equally real reasons which governed their thinking. The first of these was that the longer they could hold the prisoners the more chances there would be for the latter to become brainwashed or otherwise rusty as a fighting machine. Mrs. Gandhi stated, on 14 May 1972, that it would not be wise on the part of India "to return a large number of crack-trained troops and face aggression again in a few months." Secondly, the Indians tried to use the prisoners as a lever to obtain a final Kashmir settlement to their own liking. After the Simla summit the Indian prime minister declared that the question of repatriation of prisoners "cannot arise until we are assured that there will be durable peace."[106]

When Bangladesh applied for membership in the United Nations, in the summer of 1972, Pakistan and China urged that the question be deferred till Bangladesh had complied with the General Assembly and Security Council resolutions of 7 December and 21 December 1971. China barred Bangladesh's entry into the world body by casting her first veto in the Security Council on 25 August 1972.[107]

Some days before the Security Council vote, President Bhutto had said that Bangladesh believed she had "a kind of veto over the release of our prisoners" but "there is a veto in our hands also" and he forecast that the doors of the United Nations would be closed to Bangladesh. He confirmed later that Pakistan had requested China to use the veto "if you are our friend" but he contended that Pakistan's and China's position was based "on principles." Obliquely referring to the Soviet Union, which had bitterly criticized China's veto, he recalled that "one great power had exercised about 107 vetoes. Some of these vetoes had fallen on the right of self-determination of the people of Jammu and Kashmir, while others had neutralized meaures to prevent aggression [during the 1971 Indo-Pakistani war]."[108]

The question of Bangladesh's membership in the United Nations was also debated in the General Assembly but that body neatly got out of the predicament by adopting two interdependent resolutions, one of which called for the return of Pakistani prisoners and the other expressed the "desire" that Bangladesh would be admitted to membership at an early date. "The effect," commented the *New York Times*, was "to toss the problem of peace back to the parties themselves, denying them the luxury of using the world forum to score points against each other while avoiding necessary compromises at home."[109] On the whole, however, Pakistan and China had greater cause for satisfaction than India and Bangladesh, because the former's objective of postponing the question had been attained, while the latter's attempt to secure Bangladesh's entry into the United Nations without delay was foiled.

With none of the parties in a mood to surrender an advantage without a quid pro quo, the obvious way to move toward a normalization of relations between India, Pakistan, and Bangladesh was to work out a mutually acceptable arrangement on the basis of the age-old maxim of give-and-take. A joint India-Bangladesh declaration issued on 17 April 1973 seemed to open the possibility for just such a deal. It stated that "the two Governments are ready to seek a solution to all humanitarian problems through simultaneous repatriation of the Pakistani prisoners of war and civilian internees, except those required by the Government of the People's Republic of Bangladesh for trial on criminal charges, repatriation of the Bangalees forcibly detained in Pakistan and repatriation of the Pakistanis in Bangladesh, that is, all non-Bangalees who owe allegiance and have opted for repatriation to Pakistan." According to Indian estimates this would mean that (1) about 400,000 Bengalis (including some 35,000 disarmed Bengali soldiers) detained in Pakistan would go home to Bangladesh; (2) about 260,000 non-Bengalis (out of a total of about 600,000) in Bangladesh "who are citizens of Pakistan" would be repatriated to Pakistan; (3) about 90,000 Pakistani prisoners of war "who surrendered to the Joint Command of India and Bangladesh" would return home to Pakistan.[110]

A Pakistani government statement issued three days later rejected the right of the authorities in Dacca to try any among the prisoners of war on criminal charges, because "the alleged criminal acts were committed in a part of Pakistan" by citizens of Pakistan, but expressed Pakistan's readiness "to constitute a judicial tribunal of such character and composition as will inspire international confidence" to try the persons charged with offenses. The statement warned that, if the authorities in Dacca pro-

Independent India and Pakistan

ceeded to hold the threatened trials, it would become impossible for the government of Pakistan to refrain any longer from "bringing to trial those Bengalis in Pakistan against whom there is evidence of the commission of such acts as subversion, espionage and high treason." The Pakistani reply also criticized the Indo-Bangladeshi proposal relating to "Pakistanis in Bangladesh" on the ground that it advanced "the unique doctrine that an ethnic, linguistic or political minority can be persecuted, offered an 'option' under pain of loss of jobs, property or even life and arbitrarily expelled from its place of domicile, creating an obligation for Pakistan to receive its members." Any humanitarian problem which may arise in relation to the unfortunate persons in question "should be a concern of humanity" and Pakistan would be willing to participate in the effort to alleviate "this human plight." Pakistan, however, kept the door open for negotiations and invited the representatives of the government of India to Islamabad for obtaining "clarification of the implications" of the proposals and "to explore further possibilities for the implementation of the Simla agreement."[111]

The Indo-Bangladeshi offer had wisely left out political matters, such as recognition of Bangladesh and her admission to the United Nations and the Kashmir dispute and had confined itself to the interlocked humanitarian problems left behind by the conflict of 1971. Statements made by Pakistani spokesmen made it evident that there was room for a realistic compromise on the questions of trial of Pakistani prisoners and repatriation from Bangladesh to Pakistan of persons of non-Bengali origin who wish to retain Pakistani citizenship. Pakistani Minister of State for Foreign and Defense Affairs Aziz Ahmed publicly said that Pakistan was willing to set up an international tribunal to try prisoners of war accused of having committed excesses and would be prepared to associate representatives of Bangladesh with the proceedings. With regard to the repatriation of non-Bengalis to Pakistan President Bhutto stated that the problem was open to negotiation but "we cannot open the floodgates and say send as many as you want."[112] The fate of Bengalis stranded in Pakistan has got linked with that of the Pakistani prisoners of war and non-Bengalis in Bangladesh. Should the remaining issues be settled, there no longer would be any reason for holding Bengalis in Pakistan.

It is Bangladesh's insistence upon trying Pakistani prisoners of war in Bangladesh by Bangladeshi judges that constitutes the main hurdle in the path of reconciliation between the three states of the subcontinent. On the

INDO-PAKISTANI CONFLICT (1963–74)

very day on which India and Bangladesh made their joint proposal for a three-way exchange of the detainees, the Bangladeshi foreign minister, Kamal Hossain, declared at Dacca that 195 Pakistani prisoners would be brought to Dacca and prosecuted for genocide and other crimes. Though the figure of 195 represented a substantial numerical concession over the original count of 1500, the question remained whether Bangladesh had any jurisdiction over the Pakistani prisoners. Aziz Ahmed reiterated that "the holding of such trials would lead to a point of no return" because "under no circumstances" could Pakistan accept the position that any Pakistani prisoner can be tried by Bangladesh. This verbal warning was backed up with two practical moves. On 6 May it was reported from Islamabad that Bengali officials, who had been occupying official quarters which had been allotted to them when serving the government of Pakistan, had been shifted to "repatriation accommodation pending their return to Dacca." Indian Foreign Minister Swaran Singh condemned this "mass arrest" of Bengalis and their transport to "internment camps in some obscure places." Secondly, Pakistan filed a petition in the International Court of Justice on 11 May asking the court to issue an order restraining India from transferring any prisoners to Bangladesh. "At the time the acts in question were alleged to have been committed," argued the attorney general of Pakistan at the hearing on 4 June, "the territory now constituting Bangladesh was universally recognized as part of Pakistan and, therefore, Pakistan has the exclusive jurisdiction to hold such trials." India declined to appear before the tribunal but sent a letter contending that the court had no jurisdiction to entertain Pakistan's suit.[113] While the case before the International Court of Justice was still pending, it was announced on 12 July that Indian and Pakistani representatives would meet at Islamabad on 24 July to discuss problems left behind by the war of 1971.

India previously had taken the position that she was willing to negotiate only the manner of implementing the proposals contained in the joint Indo-Bangladeshi statement and Pakistan must accept their substance before any talks could get under way. Bangladeshi Foreign Secretary Enayet Karim had asserted that there was no question of modifying the Indo-Bangladeshi offer. Indian spokesmen had also charged that in taking the question to the International Court of Justice Pakistan had committed a breach of the Simla agreement under which the parties had undertaken to settle their differences by bilateral negotiations, but

INDEPENDENT INDIA AND PAKISTAN

Pakistanis legitimately asked how any matters in dispute can be settled by bilateral discussions if one of the two sides makes a proposal on a take it or leave it basis and declines an invitation from the other party to talk any further about it. That India had agreed to enter into negotiations with Pakistan without any preconditions was generally taken as a sign that she and Bangladesh were willing to accommodate the Pakistani point of view to a reasonable extent. The Pakistani and Indian delegations, led respectively by Minister of State Aziz Ahmed and Mrs. Gandhi's former principal secretary, P. N. Haksar, met at Islamabad on the prescribed date and conferred together for a week. A joint communiqué issued on 31 July 1973 stated that the meeting had to be adjourned because "certain issues" required further consideration and that the two sides would meet again at New Delhi on 18 August.[114] It is not improbable that the discussions remained inconclusive because Mujibur Rahman, being out of the subcontinent on a visit to Europe and Canada, was not available to the Indian delegation for final consultation. The comparatively short postponement raised the hope that both sides at last felt that the humanitarian problems in question ought to be tackled without further unnecessary delay.

Aziz Ahmed and Haksar conducted another intense round of talks in New Delhi from 18 to 28 August 1973 and arrived at an agreement on the following lines: Repatriation of all Pakistani prisoners of war (other than the 195 which Bangladesh wishes to try for war crimes) and civil internees, all Bengalis in Pakistan, and "a substantial number" of non-Bengalis who wish to migrate from Bangladesh to Pakistan shall commence as soon as logistic arrangements can be completed. It has been laid down that the principle of simultaneity will be observed in the matter of repatriation of all categories of persons. The question of the 195 Pakistani prisoners of war shall be settled by a discussion between Bangladesh, India, and Pakistan and that of moving a further number of non-Bengalis to Pakistan shall be decided by a meeting between Bangladesh and Pakistan. Bangladesh has made it clear that she will partake in meetings with Pakistan only on the basis of "sovereign equality." In making logistic arrangements the governments concerned may seek the assistance of international humanitarian organizations and others. The government of Bangladesh (which did not participate in the talks) conveyed its concurrence in the agreement through the Indian representative.[115]

Since each of the three sides can claim a measure of success all of

INDO-PAKISTANI CONFLICT (1963–74)

them have expressed themselves pleased with the outcome of the Indo-Pakistani negotiations. That Bangladesh will negotiate with Pakistan only on the basis of "sovereign equality" means that Pakistan will have to recognize her at some stage in order to get back the 195 prisoners of war. China's recognition would automatically follow Pakistan's and this in turn would clear the way for Bangladesh's entry into the United Nations. India would get rid of the Pakistani prisoners of war whose continued illegal detention had subjected her to much embarrassing criticism. The responsibility for resolving the outstanding issues now chiefly rests on the shoulders of Bangladesh and Pakistan. Pakistan has good reason to hope that Bangladesh eventually would give up her insistence upon trying the remaining 195 prisoners and that a satisfactory compromise would be reached on the question of the number of non-Bengalis which she would be called upon to absorb within her territories. Above all, the agreement could prove to be the breakthrough toward a more relaxed relationship among the three major states of the South Asian subcontinent which have already suffered untold damage by mutual strife. The exchange of detainees commenced on 19 September 1973 and has proceeded reasonably smoothly till now (February 1974).

Tension between the United States and India, because of the Nixon administration's "tilt" in favor of Pakistan during the Indo-Pakistani war, continued for some time after the fighting had ceased. In the United States–Chinese communiqué of 27 February 1973, marking the American president's visit to China, both parties called for the withdrawal of Indian and Pakistani forces to their own territories and to their own sides of the cease-fire line in Kashmir. China, in addition, reiterated her support for "the people of Jammu and Kashmir in their struggle for the right of self-determination." Mrs. Gandhi expressed apprehension that the mention of the "so-called Kashmir dispute" in the Sino-American statement might mean that "some mischief against India" was "in the offing."[116] Thereafter, both the United States and India occasionally expressed a wish to improve the tone of their relations but there has been little change for the better so far.

As a matter of fact further irritation was caused when responsible Indians, in the fall of 1972, complained that the American CIA was active in Orissa, and Congress President S. D. Sharma alleged that the CIA and "certain foreign powers" were trying to "throttle" the economy of India. The Congress president proclaimed that his accusations against

INDEPENDENT INDIA AND PAKISTAN

the CIA were based on "evidence that is in our possession," but his prime minister conveniently observed that it was not for India to prove that the CIA was active in India but "for the CIA to prove that it is not active in India."[117]

While the air was still clouded with these damaging allegations, Foreign Minister Swaran Singh suddenly came out with a bid for "friendly and cooperative" relations between India and the United States. The stated reason for this change of heart was not a meeting of minds on any concrete issues of the day but the useful general thesis, which both sides trot out for want of having anything specific to say, that "we cherish common values of an abiding nature such as our belief in democracy and a democratic way of life, individual liberty and human dignity." A somewhat startled *New York Times*, trying to diagnose the real reason behind this unexpected "Indian Love Call," divined that "the sober second thoughts reflected in Mr. Singh's friendly overture may have been induced by a serious crop failure in India which requires the Indians to seek grain imports that only the United States could provide."[118]

Before the Indian overture could bear any fruit, Mrs. Gandhi nullified it by criticizing American heavy bombing of North Vietnam to end the war and posing the question whether "this sort of war or the savage bombing" would have been tolerated for so long had the victims been European. A State Department spokesman testily protested that it was "inadmissible" to suggest that the bombings "were motivated out of any racial considerations." Through a letter to the *New York Times* a Muslim "humbly" asked Mrs. Gandhi: "Would this sort of illegal detention of 90,000 Pakistani men, women and children have been tolerated for so long had the people been other than Pakistanis?"[119]

As a manifestation of displeasure at Mrs. Gandhi's remarks on the bombing of North Vietnam, the Nixon administration delayed the departure for India of Ambassador-designate Daniel Moynihan. When the envoy eventually arrived in New Delhi he appealed for "a new realism in the relationship between the two largest of the world's democracies." He glossed over their "differing perceptions of the import of events" by calling them the mark of open society wherein resides "the strength of our democracies." But Moynihan had hardly settled down in his new post when a fresh worry emerged. This resulted from the announcement in Washington that the White House had decided to modify the total embargo on arms supplies to India and Pakistan by permitting the sale

INDO-PAKISTANI CONFLICT (1963–74)

of "non-lethal" equipment and spare parts to India as well as Pakistan. Under the new rule Pakistan would be able to obtain spare parts, parachutes, and reconditioned aircraft engines worth $1.2 million which she had ordered but could not get after the embargo of 1971. She would also be able to complete the purchase of 300 armored personnel carriers worth $13 million, for which she had made a down payment before the embargo. India could, similarly, purchase $91 million worth of communications equipment for an air defense system which had been blocked by the embargo.[120]

A storm of intemperate protest immediately broke out in India. Foreign Minister Swaran Singh alleged that arms shipments to Pakistan "will once again pose a grave threat to India's security." In Parliament several members termed the American decision "hostile" and called for the cancellation of Mrs. Gandhi's appointment with the American ambassador which had been fixed several days previously.[121]

The agitation gradually subsided after Moynihan assured the Indian prime minister that the United States had taken a "conscious decision" not to supply lethal weapons in future to any country in the subcontinent and President Nixon pointed out the unreality of Indian objections at a press conference which coincided with the announcement that India would receive $83 million worth of economic aid that had been withheld because of the Indo-Pakistani war. "Look at the numbers," Nixon said; "$83 million in economic assistance to India and $14 million in military assistance to Pakistan. . . . There were contracts that had been made, the materials had already been, in effect, sold, and under the circumstances, we felt that it was time to clean the slate. . . . India's superiority is so enormous that the possibility of Pakistan being a threat is absurd. . . . India, as you know, purchases quite significant amounts of arms from the Soviet Union, and also has an arms capability itself."[122]

On 13 May 1973 the Congress president, Sharma, resumed his attack on the United States. Without bothering to disclose any specific instances of American misconduct he sweepingly accused the United States of planning "revenge" on India and warned his countrymen against the "vicious designs" of America. Mrs. Gandhi did not deny the truth of her party chief's allegations but tried to dilute their venom with the general observation that India's national interests were not served by speaking against any particular country because India desired friendship with all nations. Atal Behari Vajpayee, the Jana Sangh leader, however, called upon the Congress president either to prove his "wild allegations" or to withdraw them. If the United States was really plotting against India, he said, then all talk of strengthening friendly ties with that country must stop.[123]

On 13 December 1973 the United States and India were able to remove a long standing irritant from their relationship. It was agreed that out of the more than $3 billion which the United States government had accumulated in Indian currency over the years by selling wheat to needy Indians, $2.3 billion would be gifted to India for utilization in development projects under the Fifth Plan while the remaining $1 billion would be expended by the United States to defray embassy expenses in India and to finance American economic assistance to Nepal.

However, only a few days earlier, during Soviet party leader Leonid Brezhnev's visit to India (26 to 30 November 1973), the Soviet Union had scored a much more spectacular success in the form of a fifteen-year Indo-Soviet agreement to further strengthen cooperation "in the fields of industry, power, agriculture, geological surveys, training of personnel, and trade, as well as in all other branches of the economy of the two countries where the necessary economic prerequisites are favourable for rapid development." Mrs. Gandhi acknowledged the "invaluable help that Indo-Soviet co-operation has brought to us in our advance towards a self-reliant modern industrial economy" and emphasized that a special feature of Soviet assistance was that it flows into the State Sector to which a special role has been assigned in Indian planning. Brezhnev, who had been greeted in India with chants of "Hindi Russi bhai bhai," reminiscent of the famous Bulganin and Khrushchev visit of 1955, called the new agreement "a qualitatively new positive advancement" in the collaboration between the two countries while S. D. Sharma, president of the ruling Congress party, said that as a result of the Soviet chief's visit Indo-Soviet friendship had become "more human and more emotional."

In his address to a joint session of the two houses of the Indian Parliament Brezhnev openly canvassed for Indian participation in a system of collective security in Asia but his effort brought forth no visible fruit in that respect. However, Mrs. Gandhi bestowed high praise on Soviet foreign policy in the joint Indo-Soviet Declaration referring to it as one "consistently aimed at consolidating world peace, at strengthening peaceful co-operation among states, at supporting the peoples struggling against colonialism and striving to consolidate the political and economic inde-

INDO-PAKISTANI CONFLICT (1963–74)

pendence of their countries." The communiqué also expressed the satisfaction of both sides "with the coincidence of proximity of positions of the U.S.S.R. and India on crucial questions of the international situation."

With regard to Indo–United States relations, Foreign Minister Swaran Singh, on 21 December 1973, praised the United States for having accepted the Indian point of view on the question of wheat funds but added in the same breath: "We may have differences in the political field with many countries but we have always endeavored to keep, whenever we can, our economic relationships somewhat on a different level." In other words, though India would expect the United States, no less than the Soviet Union, to continue to extend economic assistance to herself, political dividends from India, at least for the time being, are likely to continue to flow mainly in the direction of the Soviet Union.[124]

Of course, the Soviet Union's current desire to cultivate India's friendship could dramatically change if a faction inside China favoring Sino-Soviet rapprochement gains the upper hand after the dominating father figure of Mao Tse-tung disappears from the Chinese scene. In fact the post-Mao era could bring forth a number of unpredictable surprises because China has not yet attained the economic breakthrough or the political stability which the Soviet Communist system has achieved with a head start of three decades.

The aforementioned Indian agitation against the American decision to resume the sale of non-lethal weapons and spare parts to India and Pakistan, which President Bhutto called a "quite uncalled for storm in a teacup," well illustrates the kind of difficulties which have prevented India and Pakistan from getting closer. Since India's victory over Pakistan in 1971, Indian spokesmen have been talking with two different voices. Deputy Foreign Minister Pal Singh says that India has chalked out a "special and decisive role" in South Asia, and a senior Foreign Ministry official has insisted that, if the United States wishes to improve relations with India, she must treat India as the "dominant power" in that region. At the same time Mrs. Gandhi has tried to assure Pakistanis that her country does not have any big-power ambitions but desires to cultivate the goodwill and friendship of all nations "as equals." She has appealed to Pakistanis to cross the "psychological barrier" which the past has built between them and their Indian neighbors.[125]

Of course, this formidable mental block will be cleared only when both sides are able to view matters less subjectively. Stronger India should realize that weaker Pakistan has as much right to purchase American spare parts as India herself has to buy Russian lethal weapons and Pakistan should get rid of the old fear that India can snuff out her independent existence at will. Since 1957, when her economy faltered, India has been beset by various troubles of her own and her capacity to digest Pakistan has progressively decreased. In the matter of East Pakistan, India merely took advantage of the openings provided by Pakistan's own follies. The best way of slowing down the mutually baneful armament race is for both countries to try to improve the hostile climate in which they live. To keep one's own lines of military supplies open, while endeavoring to block the other party's, only increases suspicion and makes reconciliation more difficult.

With East Pakistan gone, SEATO became irrelevant for Pakistan and she withdrew from it on 8 November 1972. Pakistan at the same time recognized North Vietnam and decided to establish diplomatic ties with North Korea. An official spokesman explained that these simultaneous decisions reflected the government's determination to follow an "independent foreign policy." Some days later Pakistan also resigned her membership on the United Nations Commission for Unification and Rehabilitation of Korea as a mark of "disengagement from cold war machinery in Asia.[126]

With respect to CENTO Bhutto, who as the opposition leader had pledged to leave all alliances, has asserted that the situation has changed, because of loss of East Pakistan and India's alliance with the Soviet Union. "If India should renounce the defense treaty with Moscow," he has offered, "Pakistan would pull out of the Central Treaty Organization." Another reason for staying on in CENTO, of course, is the presence in that alliance of Pakistan's Muslim friends, Iran and Turkey, which have always stood by their ally in the hour of need. There are clear indications that an Iran–Pakistan–United States axis is emerging to counteract the U.S.S.R.-Iraq-India influence in the Persian Gulf–Arabian Sea–Indian Ocean route through which most of the Middle Eastern oil must pass. Pakistani columnist M. B. Naqvi has noted that American ships had joined Iran-Pakistan exercises. In a joint communiqué issued by Bhutto and the shah of Iran in Tehran on 14 May 1973, the two heads of state pledged that their countries "would resolutely stand by each other in all matters bearing on their national independence and territorial integrity." The Pakistani leader has affirmed explicitly that Pakistan and Iran are

INDO-PAKISTANI CONFLICT (1963–74)

allies with a system of cooperation in defense. During the shah's state visit to Washington, D.C., toward the end of July, President Nixon "pledged United States support for peace and security in the Middle East and Persian Gulf area." Nixon gave a similar assurance to Bhutto when he welcomed the latter at the White House on 18 September 1973. He recalled the "friendship that has bound our two countries together for over a generation" and added that "the independence and integrity of Pakistan is a cornerstone of American foreign policy."[127]

Before the loss of East Pakistan, Pakistan had to look in two opposite directions, toward the Middle East because West Pakistan adjoined it and toward Southeast Asia because East Pakistan belonged to that area. Pakistanis now can wholeheartedly strengthen their ties with the Muslim Middle East with which they have religious and cultural ties besides geographic contiguity. In the Arab-Israeli war of October 1973 Pakistan expressed her solidarity with the Arabs and sent mobile medical teams to Egypt and Syria to tend to the wounded soldiers there. Pakistan's increasing closeness with the Muslim world was further underlined by the decision of the Muslim countries to hold a summit conference at the ancient city of Lahore in Pakistan on 22 February 1974 to deliberate the Arab-Israeli problem.

Pakistan's growing identification with the Muslim Middle East could have important consequences. First, it would bring to Pakistanis an emotional fulfillment for which they have longed so ardently. Secondly, by belonging to an increasingly powerful family of nations, Pakistan would be able to shed some of her haunting feeling of insecurity against India. Thirdly, the Soviet Union, in her continuing desire to woo the Muslim world, would have to show to Pakistan the same consideration she shows the other members of that bloc and this would automatically result in the reduction of her existing pronounced tilt in favor of India.

On 2 February 1973 *Peking Review* published a résumé of Pakistani newspaper reports complaining of intensified activities of Soviet "fishing trawlers," fitted with electronic spying equipment, along the coast of Pakistan. These trawlers visit Indian ports for refueling and exchange of information with the Indian navy which, too, has stepped up its activities. "This shows," commented the Chinese periodical spicily, "that besides stealing fish from Pakistani waters, these trawlers are being used to keep liaison with some political fish as well." Pakistani-Soviet relations suffered a new setback when a large cache of Soviet-made weapons, suitable

INDEPENDENT INDIA AND PAKISTAN

for guerrilla warfare and evidently meant for disaffected elements in Pakistan, was unearthed in the Iraqi embassy in Pakistan on 10 February 1973. Concerning the Soviet Union's proposal for an Asian collective security system, Bhutto has raised the very question which Nehru had put when Sino-Indian relations were worsening and Ayub was suggesting that India and Pakistan should jointly defend the subcontinent: Asian security "against whom?"[128] Nevertheless there is a desire on both sides to avoid unnecessary strain, especially in matters of trade and technical assistance. On 30 December 1973, Prime Minister Bhutto laid the foundation stone of Pakistan's first steel mill, the Karachi Steel Works, which is being constructed with Soviet assistance.

The stock of China, as the only big power Pakistanis currently regard as dependable, continues to stand high in Pakistan. Bhutto has said that, if India "thrusts" another conflict upon Pakistan, "our eyes will have to gaze again across the Karakoram."[129] Sino-Pakistani friendship, which not long ago was the main irrritant between Pakistan and the United States, is becoming an additional source of accord between them because of the recent change for the better in America's own relations with China. Many observers believe that one reason for Nixon's "tilt" toward Pakistan during 1971 was his desire not to jeopardize the success of his forthcoming trip to China. However, China's precise role in the rivalry for supremacy in the Persian Gulf and Indian Ocean areas is not clear. She would naturally oppose the group which includes the Soviet Union but there is no comparison between her military and economic capacity and that of either of the two superpowers. The outcome of the America-Iran-Pakistan versus Soviet Union–India–Iraq contest will, therefore, largely depend upon what the superpowers do. Presently it would seem that totalitarian U.S.S.R. feels freer to aid her dependents than democratic United States which is conducting an agonizing reappraisal of her policy of intervention in Asia and is burdened with domestic issues of serious proportions. But international affairs are in a continual flux and it is difficult to predict their direction with any degree of certainty.

At the dawn of 1972 Mrs. Gandhi was riding high on her success against Pakistan, and in the spring the country gave her another vote of confidence in the states elections. Bhutto, on the other hand, had only just assumed the guardianship of a shattered and deeply demoralized country. Considering the odds in each case, Bhutto has done better than expected and Mrs. Gandhi less well. Apart from the achievements al-

INDO-PAKISTANI CONFLICT (1963-74)

ready mentioned, Bhutto has introduced some economic, labor, education, and land reforms. In May 1972 the Pakistani rupee was realistically devalued from Rs. 4.76 to Rs. 11.00 per United States dollar. Above all, he was able to get a new constitution for Pakistan passed by the National Assembly on 10 April 1973 by 125 votes, with three abstentions but none against. It envisages a parliamentary system under which the prime minister will be the effective head of government and the president the constitutional head of state. Having been elected prime minister by the National Assembly, Bhutto took the oath of that office when the constitution was inaugurated on 14 August 1973, the twenty-sixth anniversary of the country's independence. In India, an experienced, and by no means unsympathetic, observer found, as the year 1972 ended, that the general mood had become "surprisingly bleak, as if the air had gone out of the balloon." A number of disturbing developments made their appearance as the new year (1973) progressed. Relations between the central government and several of the state governments continued to deteriorate resulting in the dismissal of the latter and the assumption of their powers by the central government. Ajit Bhattacharjea, editor of the *Times of India* (Bombay), calculated that in the first seven and one half years after Mrs. Gandhi became prime minister the central government had taken over the administration of states twenty-two times as compared to only ten times during all the previous sixteen years since the inauguration of the constitution. In April there were strong allegations against Indira Gandhi's government that it had undermined the principle of judicial independence by appointing, as chief justice of India, a judge of the supreme court whose political philosophy was more acceptable to the ruling party than that of the three judges who were senior to him, and in May the country was shaken by the mutiny of 20,000 members of the provincial armed constabulary in Mrs. Gandhi's own home state of Uttar Pradesh.[130]

Though Bhutto's performance in many ways is remarkable, his troubles are far from over, especially in the turbulent outlying provinces of the Northwest Frontier and Baluchistan. On 17 July 1973 Muhammad Daud overthrew the monarchy in the neighboring country of Afghanistan and installed himself as president of the new republic. During Daud's premiership from 1953 to 1963 Afghanistan's relations with Pakistan had passed through their worst phase. He had openly fanned the "Pakhtunistan" agitation and taken Afghanistan closer to the Soviet Union. The new Daud administration soon stepped up the "Pakhtunistan" propaganda and also accused Pakistan of promoting subversive activities within Afghanistan.

Clearly, India as well as Pakistan faces awesome difficulties. The only bright spot in the gloomy picture is that they are doing well in exports. This is specially remarkable in the case of Pakistan which has already made up the lag caused by the loss of the East Pakistani market. Both countries, however, continue to labor under the fundamental problems of grinding poverty and disruptive regionalism and "linguism." Despite the much-publicized "green revolution" crops remain at the mercy of the elements which can produce a destructive drought one year and devastating floods the next. And prices keep on soaring. The general frustration readily expresses itself in the form of widespread lawlessness and violence of various kinds. India, of course, still possesses two notable advantages: a tradition of comparative constitutional stability and her larger size which gives her greater bargaining power in the marketplace of international politics.

Next door, in Bangladesh, conditions are almost hopeless. Her inexperienced administration is unable to cope with the colossal task of running and rebuilding a grossly overpopulated and sadly ravaged country.[131] Mujibur Rahman's personal prestige seems to be the chief national asset. Knowing that one of the main causes of Pakistan's political instability was that she did not produce her first constitution till nine years after independence, Mujib wisely arranged for Bangladesh's constitution to be completed within one year of the surrender of the Pakistani army in East Pakistan while the enthusiasm of the country for her newly won independence was still running high and it was relatively easy to obtain a consensus on this basic issue. Elections under the new law were held in March 1973 and resulted in an overwhelming victory for Mujib's party.

But the infant state's desperate need for foreign assistance makes her singularly vulnerable to interference from outside. It is one place where the interests of India and the Soviet Union, the main contenders for Bangladesh's favor, might clash. The first country Mujib visited as prime minister outside the subcontinent was the U.S.S.R. and there he obtained pledges of emergency as well as long-term assistance. It is believed that he was sounded out on the possibility of political ties between the Soviet party and Bangladesh's Awami League. He requested his hosts to dis-

INDO-PAKISTANI CONFLICT (1963–74)

patch a salvage team to clear the mines and sunken vessels from the ports of Chittagong and Chalna and make them navigable again. The Soviet Union sent an expedition of twenty-two ships of various kinds under the command of Rear Admiral Sergei Zuyenko and by September Chittagong was handling "more ships . . . than before the hostilities broke out a year ago." The Soviet experts would not complete the work at Chalna, Zuyenko explained at that time, because "the Bangladesh authorities say that they will be able to handle everything else that remains to be done in Chalna by themselves." However, only a few weeks later it was reported that Chalna would be cleared under the auspices of the United Nations relief operation in Dacca which had employed a consortium of four salvage companies headed by a Dutch concern because "the Russians were experiencing 'considerable difficulties' with the Chittagong operation and could not undertake another one." What could be the real reason why the Soviet Union was not allowed to complete the task she had undertaken? Did India persuade Bangladesh to reduce the Russian naval presence in Bangladeshi waters? Zuyenko denied that a base was being set up at either of the Bangladeshi ports but President Bhutto believes that the Soviet Union has "set up a base more or less in Chittagong. . . . Bangladesh is the backdoor of China." There is little doubt that the Soviet Union would like to bind Bangladesh closer to herself. *New Times* reported that "an international conference on security and co-operation in Asia took place in Dacca, the Bangladesh capital, over May 23–25 . . . within the framework of general preparations for a World Congress of Peace Forces, to convene next autumn in Moscow. . . . Participants in the [Dacca] conference gave much attention to the Soviet proposal of creating an Asian collective security system."[132] Inside Bangladesh, however, her continuing overdependence on India and Russia has begun to produce its own reaction in the form of a growing wish to balance the situation by improving relations with Pakistan, China, and the United States. This probably was the main reason behind the concessions Bangladesh recently made on the issue of the Pakistani prisoners of war, for once ties between Pakistan and Bangladesh are normalized there would be nothing to stand in the way of better relations between Bangladesh and China and America.

Seemingly China has lost the last round in South Asia to Russia and India but the East Pakistani tragedy has underlined Mao's dictum that political power grows out of the barrel of a gun. The turmoil left behind

Independent India and Pakistan

by the recent storm will make it easier for the great powers, especially bordering China, to intensify their penetration of the subcontinent directly as well as indirectly.

Today America is trying to base her Asian policy on China, not on India, as she used to do, and oil-rich Iran appears to be replacing Pakistan as the American favorite around the Arabian Sea. That India should have been bypassed in the bodies set up to implement the January 1973 cease-fire agreements on Vietnam would have been unthinkable in the palmy days of Jawaharlal Nehru. The lesson for both India and Pakistan is clear: It is not sufficient for a country simply to recite the high principles of democracy, socialism, and the like. In international life, no less than in private life, it is actual performance that wins the respect of others in the long run.

CHAPTER 9

Retrospect and Prospect

India and Pakistan Belie High Expectations

When India and Pakistan were ushered by Britain into the international arena to play their parts as independent nations, Western civilization had just emerged from her second devastating civil war within a generation, and already there were rumblings of another ominous big-power confrontation between the West and the East.

It was hoped, especially by the Western powers, that these two new nations, the largest among the newly independent countries, would be major contributors to sanity and stabilization in a troubled era. The twin countries boasted an ancient civilization, they seemed to possess the necessary framework for accelerating economic development, and their peoples individually were strikingly intelligent. India, it was believed, would become a model for all less-developed countries for progress and economic reconstruction by democratic means. And Pakistan was expected to function as a catalyst for Muslim solidarity against godless Communism in the strategic belt reaching from North Africa to Indonesia.

In the event, however, far from reassuring others, India and Pakistan have indulged in four suicidal wars between themselves, and India has fought two additional wars, one with Portugal to take Goa and another with her largest neighbor, China, in assertion of border claims; and this by no means seems to be the end of the trouble. No one talks any more of India and Pakistan as important powers. The acknowledged centers of power today are the United States, the U.S.S.R., Western Europe, China, and Japan.

INDEPENDENT INDIA AND PAKISTAN

The Lesson of History: Progress through Revolution

Do the misfortunes of India and Pakistan simply result from the blunders of their post-independence leaders, or do they inevitably flow from historical deficiencies in their bodies politic?

If we were to look at the past experiences of countries we today categorize as developed and those we broadly label as less developed, we would find that while the former have all been tempered by revolutions of various sorts, religious, intellectual, social, and economic, the latter have missed most such movements and are, in a sense, still living in the past.

As an illustration of what is implied here by progress by revolution it would be best to select Great Britain, for the reason that she is usually held up as the shining example of a levelheaded community which rose by peaceful evolution and managed to avoid the domestic upheavals that racked so many other lands. Those who point to Britain as the embodiment of peaceful advancement, however, are looking only at the more recent phase of her national life; they are disregarding what went before. The truth of the matter is that Britain did undergo painful cataclysms of her own. Her distinction lies in the fact that she passed through the purging ordeals earlier than other countries and was, therefore, able to realize her maximum potential ahead of them and become the first truly global power in the history of mankind.

Britain's revolution was a prolonged three-stage phenomenon. The first of these stages, called the Wars of the Roses, lasted for three decades in the second half of the fifteenth century. Essentially, it was a civil war between two baronial factions which undermined each other's power and, in the process, weakened feudalism and prepared the way for the absolute monarchy of the Tudors. During this period Britain also shared in Europe's Renaissance and Reformation, which were in the nature of intellectual and religious revolutions. The second major stage of Britain's political revolution consisted of another civil war. This one resulted in the dethronement and execution of King Charles I, established the supremacy of Parliament, and set the country on the road to democracy. Finally, Britain had to pass through the throes of an industrial revolution, the appalling conditions during which have been graphically described for posterity by Charles Dickens, and which provided a good part of the inspiration for Marxism.

An examination of the histories of other countries that are in the van-

RETROSPECT AND PROSPECT

guard of progress and prosperity today would show that all the great leaps forward by mankind have been made by the exacting and painful method of revolution. It seems to need a whirlwind to uproot deeply entrenched fallacies and powerful vested interests. The less-developed countries which are in a much greater hurry to move forward than countries in the past, appear destined to suffer correspondingly greater convulsions.

After the Russian and Chinese Communist revolutions, *revolution* became a dirty word in the vocabulary of Western chancelleries, which overlooked the simple fact that their countries had been propelled into the modern age by revolutions of their own. Lately, however, there has been a greater acceptance of the right of every nation to develop along the lines dictated by its own peculiar stresses and strains.

South Asia: The Static Subcontinent

South Asia is an ancient land, with a recorded history of nearly three thousand years, but never, during these millennia, has she felt the rejuvenating effect of any far-reaching socio-religious or popular political revolution. Not that revolutionaries failed to appear on the Indian scene from time to time. They did come but orthodoxy was too well organized for them to be able to make any significant headway against it.

Perhaps the first true revolutionary in Hindu India was the Buddha, who preached the equality of all men in a caste-ridden society, emphasized the excellence of pure deeds over ornate ritual, recognized the equality of the sexes by the ordination of women, and spoke in the vernacular which the people understood best. Hierarchical Hinduism under the patronage of the Gupta rulers, however, managed to stage a counter-revolution and overwhelm the simple faith of the Buddha, which now can be traced mainly in countries other than the land of its conception.

Another outstanding Indian revolutionary was the great Moghul emperor Akbar. He abolished an invidious tax which some of his predecessors had levied on their Hindu subjects, decreed that no Indian of any caste or creed could be turned into a slave, married a Hindu queen, appointed Hindus to the highest offices in the state, and even tried to introduce a new faith, combining the best elements of all the religions, though he compelled no one to accept it. This truly great emperor was not lacking in devotion to God but he was remarkably free from intolerance in a highly intolerant age. He "never for a moment forgot God" and passed "every moment of his life in self-examination or in adoration of

INDEPENDENT INDIA AND PAKISTAN

God."[1] In a letter to the shah of Persia Akbar described his responsibility as a ruler of diverse peoples in these striking terms: "The various religious communities are Divine treasures entrusted to us by God. We must love them as such. It should be our firm faith that every religion is blessed by Him, and our earnest endeavour to enjoy the bliss of the ever-green garden of universal toleration. The Eternal King showers his favours on all men without distinction. Kings, who are 'shadows of God,' should never give up this principle."[2] Akbar's example and efforts, however, had no discernible effect on the traditional religious proclivities and social taboos of the mass of his subjects. Several spiritual leaders also sought Hindu-Muslim unity but made scarcely greater impact than Akbar. The best known among them are Kabir and Nanak, a Muslim and a Hindu respectively by birth.

Nothing typifies India's and Pakistan's intolerance as much as their lack of appreciation for Akbar's highly commendable efforts to create a homogeneous society in India. Prime Minister Jawaharlal Nehru, often cited as the finest example of secularism in India, frequently harped upon the tolerance Asoka displayed in matters of religion, but had the Indian leader been really unbiased, his patron saint would have been Akbar, for it was Akbar's policy of fusion of the Hindu and Muslim cultures that has relevance to the Hindu-Muslim problem which modern India was called upon to face, not Asoka's, which was simply one of embracing Buddhism, a faith indigenous to India, and taking steps to propagate it. Independent India's national emblem is an adaptation from the Sarnath Lion Capital of Asoka, and her national flag also bears the design of the wheel which appears on the abacus of that capital, but Akbar receives no recognition whatsoever in either of these symbols.

In Pakistan Akbar has fared even worse. Though Quaid-i-Azam Muhammad Ali Jinnah paid a handsome tribute in the National Assembly of Pakistan to Akbar's magnanimity, comparing it with the Prophet's generous treatment of the conquered Jews and Christians, the prevailing line is to castigate Akbar for starting the decline of the Moghul empire by foolishly straying from the straight path of Islam and sharing power with his Hindu subjects.[3]

The age of popular governments, instead of inherited or imposed kingdoms and empires, began in 1776 when the "thirteen United States of America" successfully asserted the principle that governments derive "their just powers from the consent of the governed" and, whenever any

RETROSPECT AND PROSPECT

form of government becomes destructive of the inalienable rights of the people, they have the inherent right to alter it. Most progressive countries that were free to shape their own destiny graduated from the monarchical and oligarchical conceptions of government to the ideal of "government of the people, by the people, for the people" during the two centuries that followed the great American Revolution.

But countries that remained immobilized by the shackles of colonialism and imperialism failed to march with the changing times. It suited their masters to maintain the status quo within their possessions by warding off the winds of change. Under British domination India, perforce, missed the tremendous nationalistic, socio-religious, and economic changes which were transforming the face of many other countries, and the religious differences between the Hindus and the Muslims became increasingly exacerbated as they fought for power as rival heirs to the British raj.

Independence: The Untapped Revolution

Independence could have been made the occasion for an entirely fresh start by both India and Pakistan. True, they still carried most of the crushing burdens of their long past, and their massive populations compounded their problems manifold. But the coming of freedom itself was a revolution. It had brought to the fore, for the first time in India's history, popular leadership, committed to modernization and welfare; and the new nations were in a position to profit from the recent successes and failures of many other countries. These assets could have been made the steppingstone for an orderly breakthrough toward social justice, religious sanity, and economic reconstruction. Indeed, if the leaders had redeemed but half the rosy promises of peace and plenty they held out, the entire picture today would have been different.

Indian leaders have impressively talked of an Indian socialism which would combine in itself the best features of all modern economic experiences, and presumably would excel them all in quality and performance, but, in the words of a letter published in the *Statesman Weekly* of New Delhi on 29 January 1972, "All we have got during the last 25 years was a public sector which is capable of looking after neither itself nor the people for whose good it was created." Investigations by the Indian government committees in 1967 revealed that "75 monopoly groups were running the Indian economy," controlling 1536 companies with assets

Independent India and Pakistan

over Rs. 26,000 million, and holding half the productive capital in the private sector. The most powerful of all were "seven giant multi-millionaire families who own 35 per cent of corporate assets."[4]

India's paper homage to secularism in her constitution simply means that the state does not patronize any particular religion. The statutory liberality has not permeated into the daily lives and outlook of her millions, who individually remain as orthodox as ever, and are divided into thousands of castes and subcastes exactly as before. The pernicious practice of untouchability, against which Gandhi waged a lifelong crusade and which independent India has outlawed, still blights the existence of countless Indians.

In Pakistan Jinnah had promised in Parliament that, in the course of time, "angularities" such as belonging to the Hindu community or the Muslim community would vanish because belonging to any religion had nothing to do with the business of the state, but his successors have tenaciously clung to the slogan of a Muslim state. There has been much talk of Islamic socialism but the net result, so far, of all the economic planning has been that most of the wealth of the country has been concentrated in the hands of twenty-odd families. Pakistanis appear to have forgotten the unifying and dynamic qualities of Islam, which, in a short span of time, turned the backward and divided Arab tribesmen of a barren land into a great and progressive people. There is no consensus among them what Islamic socialism and an Islamic constitution mean in twentieth-century terms.[5] Those who shout the loudest about Islam today are the most reactionary elements of all.

Instead of a healthy feeling of well-being and unity making its appearance, the evil forces of lawlessness and disruption are becoming increasingly active in both India and Pakistan, and there is a mood of desperation among the people who are tired of more than a quarter century of unredeemed promises of better days to come.

Meanwhile it has become infinitely more difficult to bring internal revolutions to a natural conclusion by the interplay of indigenous forces. The world has shrunk and any national commotion today immediately becomes the target of international rivalry between the three great powers, the United States, the U.S.S.R., and China, and begets unpredictable consequences under the impact of powerful outside influences.

Internal and external conditions for a secessionist movement in East Pakistan being the most favorable, it has been the first to go its own way.

Retrospect and Prospect

But if there is a Bengali nation its natural boundaries are not limited to the present extent of Bangladesh. Indian Bengal, chafing under the yoke of its own central government, would no doubt wish to join its liberated counterpart. Other provinces in both India and Pakistan contain cores of similar movements. But the chances are that nothing clear-cut will emerge in the foreseeable future. The central governments of India and Pakistan would feel obliged to try to contain, or crush, all movements for regional freedom, and the United States, the U.S.S.R., and China are bound to take a hand in the turbulence and aggravate the situation. An indefinite period of increasing turmoil and confusion in the great subcontinent almost certainly lies ahead, and such a climate is more conducive to the growth of the extreme form of Communism, generally dubbed "Maoism," than of any other visible system. Avowed followers of "Maoism," under the appellation of "Naxalites," already have posed a serious problem in certain parts of India, and the utter disruption of normal life in what was East Pakistan makes that ravaged territory another fertile source of recruitment to the extremist cult. For those who believe in the unity of greater India, Communism would have a special attraction in that it professes to transcend local nationalism, and underplays religious, linguistic, and class distinctions which have long been the curse of Indian society. More and more people in South Asia either by conviction, or in sheer desperation, are, in fact, coming round to the view that the neighboring Russian and Chinese experiments have greater relevance to their own conditions than have the experiences of the more distant Western societies.

In the eyes of the devotees of the goddess democracy it is sacrilegious to say anything disrespectful about the object of their worship, and in India and Pakistan it is particularly offensive to question the capacity of the parliamentary type of government to serve all mankind. As Attlee pointed out, the Asians "believe that the Westminster model is the only real one for democrats." When he was in India, as a member of the Simon Commission, Attlee ventured to suggest that Indians might find the American presidential system more suited to their conditions "but they rejected it with great emphasis. I had the feeling that they thought I was offering them margarine instead of butter."[6]

But two facts concerning democracy as we know it today are incontrovertible. First, it is essentially a young system, barely half a century old, and it is too early to claim that it is infallible under all conditions

Independent India and Pakistan

and is immutable. Even in the mother of parliaments the veto power of the unrepresentative House of Lords was not abolished till 1911. When the twentieth century opened only 28 percent of the population over the age of twenty had the vote in the United Kingdom, and all of them were men. It was not till women had proved their mettle during World War I that part of the demands of the suffragettes were met in 1918; and the same act, for the first time, granted universal suffrage to all men over twenty-one. Thus, as Attlee has emphasized, "Britain did not really become a democracy until after the first world war."[7] Secondly, no modern nation has achieved real democracy before attaining prosperity and literacy. Democracy seems to be the delectable reward for successfully tackling the grim toils of national construction. Have India, Pakistan, and Bangladesh the capacity to reverse this established sequence?

Is there any escape, then, from massive upheavals for these countries in the years to come?

Well, for one thing they could learn from their past blunders, bury the hatchet, and start a friendly and cooperative relationship with one another. They could then bend all their energy to the stupendous revolutionary task of transforming their medieval communities into modern states. It is essential that they build from the base upwards. There is now a general realization that it was a mistake to dream of an industrial revolution before revolutionizing the humbler sector of agriculture but not many have, so far, faced up to the reality that an enlightened modern state cannot be run successfully by a society whose socio-religious precepts and practices have remained stagnant for hundreds of years and are out of tune with the times. Political leaders will talk freely about democracy and economic development but are strangely reticent with respect to socio-religious changes. The reason, of course, is that advocating such changes would enable their opponents immediately to rouse the fury of the ignorant orthodox masses and sweep the present incumbents off the seats of power.

Indeed, the socio-religious sector of the South Asian society has been the most neglected one of all. In their early years the British enforced some socio-religious reforms, such as the abolition of child sacrifice, *suttee*, and *thugee*, but the mutiny of 1857 administered a setback to the healthy trend. The rebels, Hindus as well as Muslims, having successfully exploited the slogan of interference with religion by the foreign Christian rulers, the Queen's Proclamation (1858) promised that there

Retrospect and Prospect

would be no "interference with religious belief or worship of any of our subjects." Only once afterwards did the British commit the error of offending the orthodox Hindus. Lord Lansdown's Age of Consent Bill of 1890, forbidding the consummation of marriage till the wife was twelve years old, roused an opposition "so fierce that Government never again ventured to initiate legislation on any matters which might be deemed, however unreasonably, to impinge on the domain of Hindu religious and social custom."[8]

It was hoped that the governments of free India and Pakistan would be less timid in tackling socio-religious reforms than their foreign predecessor but experience has belied that expectation. The Hindu Marriage and Divorce Bill (1955) and the Hindu Succession Bill (1956) generated such sustained controversy that no comparable legislation has been attempted in India subsequently.[9] In Pakistan Ayub Khan was able to command the passage of the Muslim Family Laws Ordinance (1961) but the measure was widely attacked and there have been no further attempts at similar reform. Some *ulemas* have issued *fatwas* against family planning too.[10]

The great powers, the United States, the U.S.S.R., and China, can help India, Pakistan, and Bangladesh best by ceasing to treat the subcontinent as a part of the arena where they measure their respective capacities for world hegemony and, instead, join hands for the constructive purpose of assisting the three neighbors to compose their differences on a fair and enduring basis. They could, further, give the latter all possible assistance to put them economically on their feet. An obvious way to insulate economic aid from power politics would be to camouflage its origin by channeling it through the United Nations. It is now accepted that, in this liberal age of ours, with equality as its watchword, the very rich and the very poor citizens cannot peacefully coexist within the same state. It will have to be accepted, also, that the affluent and the indigent nations cannot peacefully coexist for any length of time on the face of the same shrunken planet.

World Wars I and II having undermined the legitimacy of imperialism, the small maritime nations no longer can don the mantle of greatness by grabbing territories overseas. Power currently has passed into the hands of continental powers with large populations, extensive territories, and rich resources of their own. The next healthy step would be the rise of arrangements, between the small and medium powers, to offset the crushing dominance of the great powers, and finally there would have to be an effective world organization which would abolish the irrational custom of settling disputes between sovereign states by war, so that the strong and the weak could share the fruits of modern science and technology in peace and harmony.

APPENDIX

The McMahon Line: Its Origin and Significance in the Sino-Indian Boundary Dispute

The revolution in China which resulted in the overthrow of the Ch'ing dynasty and the emergence of a republican form of government in 1911 had its repercussions also in Tibet over which China exercised suzerainty at that time. The Chinese troops in Tibet, some of whom had mutinied, were overwhelmed and expelled from Tibet. There was thus a complete breakdown of Chinese control and the Dalai Lama declared his country independent. The Chinese, however, continued to proclaim Tibet "an integral part of China."

Wishing to stabilize conditions on the border of their Indian empire, the British addressed a memorandum to the Chinese on 17 August 1912 proposing an agreement under which Chinese suzerainty over Tibet would be recognized but China would have no right to interfere in the internal affairs of Tibet or to station an unlimited number of troops there. The memorandum threatened that the British government would not recognize the new Chinese government nor would it allow the Chinese to make use of the route to Tibet through India unless the proposed agreement was concluded.

After much hesitation the Chinese agreed to participate in a conference at Simla in India which was attended by the plenipotentiaries of Great Britain, China, and Tibet. The British representative was Sir Arthur Henry McMahon. The Simla parleys dragged on from October 1913 till July 1914. The Chinese and the Tibetans sharply disagreed on both the main questions at issue, the political status of Tibet and the

245

alignment of the boundary between China and Tibet. The boundary between India and Tibet was not discussed at the tripartite conference but during its pendency the British and the Tibetans held separate negotiations at which the two of them agreed upon an alignment of the border between Tibet and India from northeast Bhutan to the Isu Razi Pass in northern Burma (the eastern sector of the Sino-Indian border). This was shown on a map and came to be known as the McMahon Line because the British delegation in these talks was also headed by McMahon. The agreement was finalized by an exchange of notes between the two parties in March 1914. China was not invited to take part in any of these proceedings.

At the tripartite conference itself the British representative ultimately was able to obtain the initials of all three plenipotentiaries on the draft of a convention which (1) recognized Chinese suzerainty over Tibet but prohibited China from converting Tibet into a province of China and (2) divided Tibet into two zones, Inner Tibet and Outer Tibet. To minimize the Chinese presence in Outer Tibet, which bordered India, it was stipulated that China would be authorized to send to Lhasa only one "Chinese high official" whose escort would not exceed 300 men. The map attached to the draft convention, which was also initialed by all three participants in the conference, showed not only the border between China and Tibet which was relevant to the convention but also the McMahon Line which was extraneous to it. Had China ratified the convention, it might have been argued that she had accepted the Mc-Mahon Line by implication if not by direct affirmation. However, the government of China promptly repudiated the initials of its nominee on the ground that the proposed Sino-Tibetan boundary was unacceptable. Consequently, only the British and the Tibetan plenipotentiaries signed the Simla Convention on 3 July 1914. The same two parties further issued a declaration confirming that they held themselves bound by the terms of the convention and stating that China would be denied the enjoyment of any privileges under the convention so long as she did not sign it. China thus was a party neither to the convention nor to the agreement relating to the McMahon Line. Both these documents, she says, were invalid because Tibet was under the sovereignty of China and had no right to make treaties with any foreign power. India contends that in 1914 Tibet did enjoy treaty-making powers. She asserts, further, that the substance of the agreement relating to the McMahon Line was

Appendix: The McMahon Line

mentioned at the tripartite conference and the Chinese spokesman raised no objection to the alignment then or later till the current Sino-Indian dispute began. China is, therefore, estopped from impugning the validity of the McMahon Line.

The Indians additionally aver that the border indicated by the McMahon Line is inherently valid because it follows ancient custom and tradition and lies along the main watershed which is the natural dividing line. But, rejoin the Chinese, it is the boundary which they themselves claim that has been hallowed by tradition and custom, not that claimed by India. Geographical features, according to the Chinese, are a relevant but not a decisive factor; a traditional customary line is formed over a long period mainly by the extent to which each party has exercised administrative control.

Notes

Notes

Chapter 1. Hinduism and Islam: The "Two Closed Systems" of the Indian Subcontinent

1. Jawaharlal Nehru, *India's Foreign Policy*, p. 80.
2. M. Rafique Afzal, ed., *Speeches and Statements of Quaid-i-Millat Liaquat Ali Khan, 1941–51*, p. 216.
3. Nicholas Mansergh, ed., *Documents and Speeches on British Commonwealth Affairs, 1931–1952*, I, p. 230. Commenting on Gandhi's assertion that the Hindu-Muslim quarrel was coeval with the advent of the British, Coupland wrote, "He could scarcely have intended those words to bear their full meaning, but there was half a truth in them. For the open exhibition of the quarrel, the throwing-off of all restraint, the rioting and fighting — none of this was possible under Mogul rule. Akbar set Hindus on a formal equality with Moslems, but the Hindus would no more have dared in his day than in Aurungzeb's to assert their communal rights or in any way to challenge or provoke the feelings of their rulers. For several reasons the position has been very different under British rule." R. Coupland, *Report on the Constitutional Problem in India*, part I; *The Indian Problem, 1833–1935*, p. 35. A more realistic Gandhi view, expressed elsewhere, was that "the outsider cannot create disunity unless the seeds of disunity are within yourself." Michael Brecher, *India and World Politics: Krishna Menon's View of the World*, p. 197.
4. *Alberuni's India*, trans. Edward C. Sachau, I, pp. 19, 22, 240–241.
5. R. C. Majumdar, *History of the Freedom Movement in India*, I, pp. 52, 37.
6. Reginald Heber, *Narrative of a Journey through the Upper Provinces of India, [and] to Madras and the Southern Provinces*, I, p. 183.
7. *Indian Parliamentary Debates*, vol. V, no. 5, 4 Aug. 1950, col. 375.
8. Jawaharlal Nehru, *An Autobiography*, p. 136.
9. L. S. Amery, *India and Freedom*, p. 100.
10. Sir John Strachey in 1888, quoted by Sasadhar Sinha, *Indian Independence in Perspective*, p. 68.
11. Nehru, *An Autobiography*, pp. 340–341.
12. *Indian Round Table Conference* (First Session, 1931), p. 102.
13. "Shamloo," ed., *Speeches and Statements of Iqbal*, p. 117. "Shamloo" is the pseudonym of Latif Ahmed Sherwani, deputy secretary of the Pakistani Institute of International Affairs.

14. Jawaharlal Nehru, *Discovery of India*, p. 63.
15. Quoted by S. Radhakrishnan, *Eastern Religions and Western Thought*, pp. 312–313.
16. Nehru, *Discovery of India*, p. 63–64. See also Frank Moraes's article "Gandhi Ten Years After," in *Foreign Affairs* for January 1958. Moraes observes that Gandhi's effort to equate nonviolence with Hinduism was "vigorously contested" by many Hindus who cited Krishna's address to Arjuna in the Bhagvad Gita, urging the latter to play his part in the destruction of the enemy in war.
17. Quoted by Sinha, *Indian Independence in Perspective*, p. 109.
18. K. M. Panikkar, *India and the Indian Ocean*, p. 16.
19. S. Radhakrishnan, *The Hindu View of Life*, p. 78. Radhakrishnan, president of India from 1962 to 1967, had earlier been Spalding Professor of Eastern Religions and Ethics at the University of Oxford.
20. S. Radhakrishnan, "Hinduism and the West," in *Modern India and the West*, ed. L. S. S. O'Malley, p. 339.
21. M. K. Gandhi, *Truth Is God*, p. 61.
22. Vijaya Lakshmi Pandit, *The Evolution of India*, p. 6. Mrs. Pandit, sister of Jawaharlal Nehru, was India's ambassador to the U.S.S.R. and the United States.
23. S. Radhakrishnan, "Hinduism," in *The Legacy of India*, ed. G. T. Garratt, p. 268.
24. Radhakrishnan, *Eastern Religions and Western Thought*, p. 313.
25. Radhakrishnan, "Hinduism," p. 276.
26. Quoted by Tibor Mende, *Nehru: Conversations on India and World Affairs*, p. 34.
27. B. R. Ambedkar, *Pakistan, or The Partition of India*, p. 119.
28. Walter Crocker, *Nehru: A Contemporary's Estimate*, p. 34.
29. Wilfred Cantwell Smith, *Islam in Modern History*, p. 268. Muslims in India were not free from sects and castes of their own but ascribed their appearance to the influence of Hinduism. "This is one of the quiet ways," said Iqbal, "in which conquered nations revenge themselves on their conquerors." And, of course, he condemned the practice in no uncertain terms "in the name of God, in the name of humanity, in the name of Moses, in the name of Jesus Christ, and in the name of him — a thrill of emotion passes through the very fibre of my soul when I think of that exalted name — yes, in the name of him [the Prophet Muhammad] who brought the final message of freedom and equality to mankind." Syed Abdul Vahid, ed., *Thoughts and Reflections of Iqbal*, p. 54.
30. "Shamloo," ed., *Speeches and Statements of Iqbal*, p. 31.
31. *Ibid.*, p. 236.
32. Vahid, ed., *Thoughts and Reflections of Iqbal*, pp. 59–60.
33. *Ibid.*, p. 50.
34. Javid Iqbal, ed., *Stray Reflections: A Notebook of Allama Iqbal*, p. 26.
35. *Dawn*, 6 Nov. 1949.
36. Ilyas Ahmad, "Sovereignty in Islam," *Pakistan Horizon*, Dec. 1958, p. 254. Mahatma Gandhi appeared to accept this attitude as normal and proper: "The brave [Ali] brothers are staunch lovers of their country but they are Musalmans first and everything else after and it must be so with every religiously minded man." *The Independent* (Allahabad), dated 2 Oct. 1921, quoted by Majumdar, *History of the Freedom Movement in India*, III, p. 825, n. 16. Other well-known Muslims of the subcontinent who are on the record for having made similar statements are Sheikh Muhammad Abdullah of Kashmir, who likened Islam to the sun and all the other religions to the stars and said he was "Muslim first and Muslim afterwards," and Fazlul Haq, who declared that, though he was at that time heading a coalition government as premier of Bengal, he was a Muslim first and a Bengali afterwards. For Abdullah's assertion see Prem Nath Bazaz, *Inside Kashmir*, pp. 325–326, and for Fazlul Haq's words see Kamruddin Ahmad, *The Social History of East Pakistan*, p. 47.

NOTES FOR PAGES 14–19

37. Aslam Siddiqi, *Pakistan Seeks Security*, p. 160.
38. Quran, 49:10.
39. "Shamloo," ed., *Speeches and Statements of Iqbal*, p. 234.
40. Quoted by Ambedkar, *Pakistan*, p. 296.
41. Jawaharlal Nehru, "India Today and Tomorrow," in Nehru, Arnold Toynbee, and Clement R. Attlee, *India and the World*, p. 11.
42. Arnold Toynbee, *The World and the West*, p. 45.
43. Jamil-ud-Din Ahmad, ed., *Some Recent Speeches and Writings of Mr. Jinnah*, II, p. 173. Though Jinnah's Hindu lineage added barb to Gandhi's question, it also illustrates how easy it is to attain an honored place in the Muslim brotherhood, once one is a member. The slave kings of India and the Mamelukes of Egypt are other examples of Muslims of humble birth who were able to climb the pinnacles of power. Mumtaz Hasan, "The Background of the Partition of the Indo-Pakistan Subcontinent," *The Partition of India*, ed. C. H. Philips and M. D. Wainwright, p. 328.
44. Jamil-ud-Din Ahmad, ed., *Some Recent Speeches and Writings of Mr. Jinnah*, II, pp. 180–181. The difference between Hinduism and Islam "is not only one of religion in the stricter sense, but also of law and of culture. They may be said indeed to represent two distinct and separate civilisations." Joint Committee on Indian Constitutional Reform (Session 1933–34), *Report*, vol. I (part 1), p. 1. "It would be an utter misapprehension to suppose that Hindu-Muslim antagonism is analogous to the separation between religious denominations in contemporary Europe. Differences of race, a different system of law, and the absence of intermarriage constitute a far more effective barrier. It is a basic opposition manifesting itself at every turn in social custom and economic competition, as well as in mutual religious antipathy." *Report of the Indian Statutory Commission*, vol. I: *Survey*, p. 25. In his article "Two Nations in India," published in *Time and Tide* on 9 March 1940, Jinnah also explained that the British conception of "religion as a private and personal matter between man and God" did not apply to Hinduism and Islam, "for both these religions are definite social codes which govern not so much man's relation with his God, as man's relation with his neighbour."
45. Jamil-ud-Din Ahmad, ed., *Speeches and Writings of Mr. Jinnah*, I, p. 230.
46. Jamil-ud-Din Ahmad, ed., *Some Recent Speeches and Writings of Mr. Jinnah*, II, p. 64.
47. Jinnah's speech at Aligarh on 8 March 1944, quoted by M. A. H. Ispahani in *Quaid-i-Azam, as I Knew Him*, p. 107.
48. Afzal, ed., *Speeches and Statements of Quaid-i-Millat Liaquat Ali Khan*, p. 27.
49. Hasan, "The Background of the Partition of the Indo-Pakistan Subcontinent," p. 325.
50. K. M. Panikkar, *A Survey of Indian History*, pp. 130–131.
51. Ambedkar, *Pakistan*, pp. 17–19.
52. A Muslim may marry a Jewess or a Christian woman but not an idol-worshiper. A Muslim woman must marry only a Muslim. Hindus will not marry outside their own caste.
53. Aga Khan, *India in Transition*, p. 251.
54. Quoted by Pyarelal, *Mahatma Gandhi: The Last Phase*, I, p. 63.
55. Gandhi on "Hindu-Muslim unity," quoted by C. F. Andrews in *Mahatma Gandhi's Ideas*, p. 57.
56. M. K. Gandhi, *An Autobiography, or The Story of My Experiments with Truth*, p. 58; Nehru, *An Autobiography*, p. 13.
57. Gandhi in *Young India*, dated 20 Oct. 1921, quoted by Ambedkar in *Pakistan*, p. 140n.
58. Sinha, *Indian Independence in Perspective*, p. 65.
59. Afzal Iqbal, ed., *Select Writings and Speeches of Maulana Mohamed Ali*, I, p. 81.

Notes for Pages 19–27

60. H. N. Brailsford in *Mahatma Gandhi,* by H. S. L. Polak, H. N. Brailsford, and Lord Pethic-Lawrence, p. 219.
61. Though he subsequently emerged as a champion of Muslim nationalism, Iqbal had started his poetical career as a passionate advocate of Hindu-Muslim unity. In his well-known *Tirana-i-Hind* [The Anthem of India] he wrote:

Sare Jehan se uccha Hindustan hamara
Hum bulbulein hein iskee yeh gulsitan hamara
[Our Hindustan is the best country in the world.
We are its nightingales, it is our garden]
Muzhub nahin sekhatha apus mein ber rukhna
Hindi hein hum wattan hai Hindustan hamara
[Religion does not teach us to bear malice toward one another.
We are Hindis and our country is Hindustan]
Kuch bat hai ke husti mit-tee nahin hamari
Sadion raha hai dushman dour-i-zaman hamara
[There must be some inherent strength in us because our individuality has endured though times have been adverse for many centuries]

62. K. M. Panikkar, *Hinduism and the West,* pp. 13–14.
63. Radhakrishnan, "Hinduism and the West," p. 350.
64. Heber, *Narrative of a Journey,* I, p. 187.
65. A. K. Majumdar, *Advent of Independence,* p. 38.
66. Quoted by V. P. Menon, *The Story of the Intergration of the Indian States,* p. 468.

Chapter 2. Origins of Indian and Pakistani Foreign Policies

1. The equivalent of Christendom's *bellum justum.*
2. Aslam Siddiqi, *A Path for Pakistan,* p. 112.
3. Majid Khadduri, *War and Peace in the Law of Islam,* p. 251.
4. Hassan Kaleemi, "The Message of Islam, the Way to Integration," *Dawn,* 5 April 1968.
5. *Ibid.*
6. Ian Stephens, "The Image of Pakistan — II," *Morning News* (Dacca), 25 Feb. 1961.
7. L. F. Rushbrook Williams, *The State of Pakistan,* pp. 118–119.
8. *Dawn,* 14 May 1962.
9. An organization founded jointly by Pakistan, Iran, and Turkey in July 1964.
10. M. Ayub Khan, *Friends Not Masters,* p. 181.
11. Nehru, *India's Foreign Policy,* p. 80.
12. Quoted by R. K. Karanjia, *The Mind of Mr. Nehru,* p. 89.
13. Jawaharlal Nehru, *Speeches,* IV, p. 378.
14. Crocker, *Nehru,* p. 88.
15. T. M. P. Mahadevan, "Indian Philosophy and the Quest for Peace," in *India's Non-aligned Policy: Strength and Weaknesses, Problems in Asian Civilization,* ed. Paul F. Power, pp. 6–7.
16. *Round Table* (London), June 1957, p. 286.
17. H. N. Brailsford, *Subject India,* p. 97.
18. *Parliament of India, Official Report,* 4 Aug. 1950, col. 387.
19. Quoted by Ton That Thien, *India and Southeast Asia, 1947–1960,* p. 348.
20. Quoted by Francis Carnell, "Political Ideas and Ideologies in South and South-East Asia," in *Politics in Southern Asia,* ed. Saul Rose, p. 281.
21. Quoted by A. G. Noorani, *Our Credulity and Negligence,* p. 64.
22. *Dawn,* 11 Mar. 1965.

Notes for pages 27–33

23. *Round Table,* Dec. 1956, p. 21.
24. K. S. Murty, *Indian Foreign Policy,* p. 9. Kautilya, author of the well-known *Arthasastra* [Treatise on Material Gain], was a minister in the court of Chandragupta, a contemporary of Alexander the Great. He is often compared to Niccolo Machiavelli.
25. *Ibid.* Manu was the author of the famous Hindu law book *Manu Smriti.*
26. *Ibid.,* p. 11.
27. Rajendra Prasad, *Speeches of President Rajendra Prasad, 1952–1956,* p. 215.
28. Pandit, *The Evolution of India,* p. 3.
29. *Rajya Sabha Debates,* 17 Sept. 1953, part II, col. 3991.
30. Indian crowds chanted the first slogan during Prime Minister Chou En-lai's visits to India during the middle 1950s when Sino-Indian relations were cordial. The second greeted Bulganin and Khrushchev during their extensive tour of India in November and December 1955.
31. Phillips Talbot and S. L. Poplai, *India and America: A Study of Their Relations,* p. 17.
32. *Constituent Assembly (Legislature) of Pakistan Debates,* 24 May 1948, p. 767.
33. N. V. Rajkumar, ed., *The Background of India's Foreign Policy,* p. 6.
34. Bimla Prasad, *The Origins of Indian Foreign Policy,* p. 51.
35. N. V. Rajkumar, ed., *The Background of India's Foreign Policy,* p. 47; Nehru, *An Autobiography,* p. 361.
36. "Most Indian nationalists never rose above their limited national horizon." Brecher, *Nehru,* p. 111.
37. D. G. Tendulkar, *Mahatma,* V, p. 166.
38. Nehru, *The Discovery of India,* p. 423.
39. For example: "We have endeavoured to follow, in our limited and imperfect way, the teaching of two great sons of India, the Buddha and Gandhi." Nehru, *India's Foreign Policy,* p. 384.
40. Vijaya Lakshmi Pandit, "India's Foreign Policy," *Foreign Affairs,* April 1956. On an earlier occasion, speaking in Parliament on reports that the United States would grant military assistance to Pakistan, Mrs. Pandit conceded that it was natural that "other countries" should be agitated by it but expressed the belief that threats of "this kind" to India's safety could not be met by similar action. India's protection lay in "following those principles which were our guiding light in the days of our independence movement." She said that "one is almost in despair" at the hysteria in some parts of the world owing to this "mad race for armaments." But India was lucky because "having no armaments to speak of, we can only rely on the spirit of the people." *Lok Sabha Debates,* 23 Dec. 1953, cols. 3014, 3016, 3017.
41. Quoted in Nehru, *An Autobiography,* p. 510.
42. *Speeches of President Rajendra Prasad,* p. 214.
43. Quoted by Nehru, *An Autobiography,* p. 522.
44. *Ibid.,* p. 510.
45. *Ibid.,* p. 524.
46. *Ibid.,* p. 526.
47. Nehru, *Speeches,* III, p. 3.
48. *Ibid.,* I, p. 202.
49. V. Nikhamin, "India's Role in World Affairs," in *Studies in Indian Foreign Policy,* ed. K. P. Misra, p. 157.
50. Nehru, *An Autobiography,* p. 84.
51. *Speeches of President Rajendra Prasad,* p. 216.
52. Polak, Brailsford, Pethic-Lawrence, *Mahatma Gandhi,* p. 262.
53. *Report on Indian Constitutional Reforms* (popularly called the Montagu-Chelmsford Report), p. 282.
54. John W. Wheeler-Bennett, *King George VI: His Life and Reign,* p. 703.

55. *House of Commons Debates*, 5 Mar. 1947, cols. 497, 504. Britain, of course, does deserve credit for gracefully accepting the inevitable, instead of intensifying Indo-British tension by trying to hang on to her imperial possessions amid deteriorating conditions. Some other European colonial powers, unfortunately, did not act so wisely. But it is not correct to assert that Britain gave up her empire in India out of benevolence of character. Essentially, she departed from India because the cost of staying there had become unacceptable in terms of expenditure of treasure and human lives.

56. Moraes, "Gandhi Ten Years After." India has fought four wars against Pakistan (the Kashmir war of 1948, the Rann of Kutch war of 1965, the second Kashmir war of 1965, and the East Pakistani war of 1971); she has fought one war with China (the Sino-Indian border war of 1962); and she invaded Junagadh (1947), Hyderabad (1948), and Goa (1961) to amalgamate them with herself.

57. Thien, *India and Southeast Asia*, p. 337.

58. *Round Table*, Sept. 1957, p. 393.

59. Gandhi himself had posed the question of what India should do if "a modern edition of Nero" descended upon her after she had won independence from the British and answered it as follows: "the representatives of the State will let him in but tell him that he will get no assistance from the people. They will prefer death to submission. The second way would be non-violent resistance by the people who have been trained in the non-violent way. They would offer themselves unarmed as fodder for the aggressor's cannon. The underlying belief in either case is that even a Nero is not devoid of a heart. The unexpected spectacle of endless rows upon rows of men and women simply dying rather than surrender to the will of an aggressor must ultimately melt him and his soldiery. Practically speaking there will be probably no greater loss in men than if forcible resistance was offered; there will be no expenditure in armaments and fortifications. The non-violent training received by the people will add inconceivably to their moral height. Such men and women will have shown personal bravery of a type far superior to that shown in armed warfare. In each case the bravery consists in dying, not in killing. Lastly, there is no such thing as defeat in non-violent resistance." M. K. Gandhi, *Satyagraha* [Nonviolent Resistance], p. 386.

60. *Mujahidin* is plural for *mujahid*, which means a person who participates in *jihad*. The movement is popularly called "Wahabi" on account of the mistaken belief that it was the Indian counterpart of Muhammad Abdul Wahab's movement in Arabia. In fact, Syed Ahmed Barelvi, founder of the *mujahidin* movement, drew his inspiration from the eighteenth-century Indian reformer Shah Waliullah and was a protégé of Shah Waliullah's son and successor, Shah Abdul Aziz. Abdul Aziz declared that India had become *dar ul-harb* because the "infidels" had taken control of it and could "abolish or retain the ordinances of Islam according to their pleasure." W. W. Hunter, *The Indian Musalmans*, p. 105. In his *Review on Dr. Hunter's Indian Musalmans*, Sir Syed Ahmed Khan endeavored to prove that the *mujahidin* movement was directed against Sikh rule only, but Syed Ahmed Barelvi's own words, as well as those of his British adversaries, make it clear that the *mujahidin* were against both Sikh overlordship and British domination. For extracts from some letters of Syed Ahmed Barelvi see Q. Ahmad, *The Wahabi Movement in India*, p. 326; for a British view, besides Hunter's, see p. 331 of the same publication. There is no real reason why the facts stated in Hunter's book should not be accepted. As a senior British official he was in the proper position to know the truth. See also Shan Muhammad, *Sir Syed Ahmed Khan*, p. 128, who also refutes Sir Syed's contention. "The fraternity of Islam and the historical tradition of Muslim suzerainty over India, within almost living memory," explains Majumdar, "generated among the Indian Muslims a sort of national feeling which was conspicuous by its absence among the Hindus." Majumdar, *History of the Freedom Movement in India*, I, pp. 281–282.

NOTES FOR PAGES 35–43

61. Hunter, *The Indian Musalmans*, pp. 12, 16.
62. *Ibid.*, p. 27.
63. *Sedition Committee Report* (popularly known as the Rowlatt Report), p. 124.
64. Ishtiaq Husain Qureshi, *The Muslim Community of the Indo-Pakistan Subcontinent*, p. 208.
65. In an article published in the *Civil and Military Gazette* (Lahore), on 14 August 1954 (Independence Day), Hameed ud Din, a noted Pakistani historian, referred to the battle of Balakot, in which Syed Ahmed Barelvi lost his life, as the "first battle for Pakistan."
66. Quoted by Hafeez Malik in *Moslem Nationalism in India and Pakistan*, p. 207.
67. Valentine Chirol, *Indian Unrest*, pp. 5–6.
68. See Lord Hardinge's memoirs, *My Indian Years*, pp. 11, 14, 36–39.
69. Hirendranath Mukerjee, *India's Struggle for Freedom*, p. 126; *Muslim Standard* (London), 9 Mar. 1922. Nehru, *The Discovery of India*, p. 349. "Profoundly stirred, the Indian Mussalman wished to help actively his brothers-in-faith of Turkey but like an enraged lion in an iron cage, he moved round his home and he could not go out to help them actively. And so he collected a magnificent sum for the Ottoman Red Crescent without which sufferings of the Turkish people might have been far more terrible in that crusade of the little nations of Christendom. Indians could get permission from their English rulers to send to Turkey only a medical mission which rendered splendid services to the Muslim wounded." *Muslim Standard*, Mar. 9, 1922. The medical mission was seen off at the Delhi railway station by thousands of Muslims led by Maulana Muhammad Ali. Muslims regard it the first "embassy of practical goodwill" sent by Muslim India to a foreign Muslim country. S. M. Ikram, *Modern Muslim India and the Birth of Pakistan*, p. 161.
70. For a fuller version of the interview which took place on 19 March 1920, see C. H. Philips, *The Evolution of India and Pakistan*, p. 219.
71. *Islamic News* (London), 21 Apr. and 5 May 1921.
72. *Muslim Standard*, Oct. 1922.
73. Ambedkar, *Pakistan*, p. 291n.
74. Valentine Chirol, *India*, p. 222.
75. For further details of these two incidents see *The Memoirs of Aga Khan*, pp. 195–197, and Ikram, *Modern Muslim India and the Birth of Pakistan*, pp. 196–198.
76. Arnold Toynbee, quoted in Pakistan Historical Society, *A History of the Freedom Movement*, vol. III, part II, p. 306, n. 2.
77. "Shamloo," ed., *Speeches and Statements of Iqbal*, p. 205.
78. *Letters of Iqbal to Jinnah*, p. 11.
79. For the text of this resolution and the texts of the foreign policy resolutions of the Muslim League referred to in the paragraphs which follow, see Chaudhuri Khaliquzzaman, *Only If They Knew It!* unless another source is specifically indicated. It is necessary to refer to these resolutions at some length because, while the declarations of the Congress party are comparatively well known, it is not generally realized how deeply concerned the Indian Muslims felt about happenings in the rest of the Muslim world. *Jazirat-ul-Arab* literally means the island of Arabia but "according to Muslim history, tradition, and belief, does not mean the Arabian peninsula alone, but also includes Syria, Mesopotamia, and Palestine. As the name indicates, Arabia is an island with the waters of the Euphrates and the Tigris making its fourth boundary." K. K. Aziz, *The Indian Khilafat Movement, 1915–1933: A Documentary Record*, pp. xxi–xxii.
80. "Shamloo," ed., *Speeches and Statements of Iqbal*, p. 214.
81. *Ibid.*, p. 216.
82. Jamil-ud-Din Ahmad, ed., *Speeches and Writings of Mr. Jinnah*, I, p. 154.

83. *Ibid.*, II, p. 77.
84. *Ibid.*, pp. 306–307.
85. *Ibid.*, p. 313.
86. *Ibid.*, p. 406.
87. Quoted in Majumdar, *History of the Freedom Movement in India*, III, p. 823, n. 6.
88. "About the middle of 1920, anti-British feeling was stronger among the Moslems than among the rest of the Indian population." Subhas Chandra Bose, *The Indian Struggle*, p. 41.
89. Qureshi, *The Muslim Community of the Indo-Pakistan Subcontinent*, p. 276.
90. R. A. J. Nadvi, ed., *Selections from Muhammad Ali's Comrade*, p. 40.
91. "Shibli Nomani" by Mukhtar Zaman, *Morning News* (Karachi), 11 Dec. 1966.
92. *The Memoirs of Aga Khan*, p. 285.
93. *National Assembly of Pakistan Debates*, 29 Nov. 1962, p. 225.
94. Zafar Mansoor, "Pakistan's Contribution to Arabs' Cause," *Dawn*, 14 Aug. 1959.
95. Quoted by Aziz Ahmad, *Studies in Islamic Culture in the Indian Environment*, p. 64.
96. *The Memoirs of Aga Khan*, p. 166.
97. Khaliquzzaman, *Only If They Knew It!* p. 16.
98. *Ibid.*, pp. 29–30.
99. *Constituent Assembly of Pakistan Debates*, 24 May 1948, pp. 763–764.
100. Quoted by Frank Moraes, *Jawaharlal Nehru: A Biography*, p. 326.
101. This resentment comes out whenever Indians feel angry with Britain; for example, after the September 1965 war, Mrs. Pandit alleged that Britain had been sympathetic to Pakistan during the conflict because she still clung to the "old notions" she held when India carried on a successful fight against British imperialism. Pakistan was Britain's protégé. *Hindu Weekly*, 6 Dec. 1965. "The British had a conscientious objection to handing over a minority to a majority. They were not prepared to divide India and create a Pakistan; their objection was moral as well as political. At the same time they were not prepared to leave it to the majority to do what they liked with the minority." Sudhir Ghosh, *Gandhi's Emissary*, p. 154. In July 1947 Jawaharlal Nehru said to Josef Korbel, a member of the United Nations Commission for India and Pakistan, that Pakistan "should never have been created, and it would never have happened had the British not stood behind this foolish idea of Jinnah." Josef Korbel, *Danger in Kashmir*, p. 130.
102. Chester Bowles, *Ambassador's Report*, p. 102.
103. Robert Trumbull, "Behind India's Foreign Policy," *New York Times Magazine*, 5 Oct. 1952.
104. Brecher, *India and World Politics*, p. 9.
105. *India News*, 13 June 1969.
106. Syad Razvi Wasti, *Lord Minto and the Indian Nationalist Movement, 1905 to 1910*; Countess Mary of Minto, *India, Minto and Morley, 1905–1910*, p. 71; Leonard Mosley, *The Last Days of the British Raj*, p. 15.
107. Quoted by Mende, *Nehru*, p. 61.
108. This actually happened at the time of the Indo-Pakistani war of September 1965. On the eve of President Ayub Khan's departure for Washington to see President Lyndon Johnson, after Pakistan's conflict with India, a press release was issued from the Texas White House setting out the framework within which Johnson would discuss America's future relations with India and Pakistan. In his appreciation of the situation, Johnson compared the Indo-Pakistani war to America's own Civil War (*Dawn*, 3 Dec. 1965). Sources close to President Ayub Khan "could not comprehend how the conflict between the two sovereign states

Notes for pages 50-58

of India and Pakistan could be likened by the Americans to their civil war" (*Dawn*, 7 Dec. 1965).

109. See his letter "Islam and Bolshevism," in *Zamindar* (Lahore), dated 23 June 1923, reprinted in *Guftar-i-Iqbal*, ed. M. Rafique Afzal, pp. 5-8.

110. *New York Times*, 13 April 1950.

111. *Constituent Assembly (Legislature) of Pakistan Debates*, 27 Mar. 1952, p. 608.

112. *Dawn*, 31 Mar. 1954.

113. M. Ayub Khan, "Strategic Problems of the Middle East," *Asian Review*, July 1958.

114. Quoted by Prime Minister Chaudhri Muhammad Ali, in a government of Pakistan Handout, E. No. 3486, dated 29 June 1956. Ali said Pakistan's attitude to Western institutions had been greatly influenced by Muslim thinking, specially by Pakistan's national poet, Iqbal.

115. *Dawn*, 8 Apr. 1952.

116. *Ibid.*, 26 Aug. 1953.

117. Husein Rofe, "What Does Islam Mean to Asia?" *Far Eastern Economic Review*, 3 Nov. 1966.

118. K. A. Hakim, *Islam and Communism*, p. 47.

119. Javid Iqbal, *The Ideology of Pakistan and Its Implementation*, p. 135.

120. "Shamloo," ed., *Speeches and Statements of Iqbal*, p. 167.

121. A. K. Sumar, quoted in *Dawn*, 9 Mar. 1965. *Zakat* is a prescribed tax on unconsumed assets and *fitra* or *zakat-ul-fitr* is the charitable gift to the poor at the time of the *eid-ul-fitr* festival which marks the end of the *ramadan*, the month of fasting.

122. *Morning News*, 20 Nov. 1966.

123. Rofe, "What Does Islam Mean to Asia?"

124. M. A. H. Ispahani, "Pacts and Aid," *Pakistan Horizon*, 2nd Quarter 1966, p. 118.

125. M. Ayub Khan, *Friends Not Masters*, p. 166.

126. *New York Times*, 6 Aug. 1969.

Chapter 3. Britain's "Cut and Run" Departure and Its Consequences

1. M. Ayub Khan, *Friends Not Masters*, p. 12.

2. *Report of the Indian Statutory Commission*, vol. I, p. 29. Jawaharlal Nehru expressed the same view in "A Letter to an Englishman": "Obviously no one can say that there was not an inherent tendency towards division in India, and with the prospect of the approach of political power, this was likely to grow." Nehru, *India's Freedom*, p. 88.

3. Ambedkar, *Pakistan*, p. 175.

4. Rajendra Prasad, *India Divided*, p. 392.

5. Quoted by Hector Bolitho, *Jinnah, Creator of Pakistan*, p. 195.

6. Quoted by E. W. R. Lumby, *The Transfer of Power in India*, p. 78.

7. Quoted by Maulana Abul Kalam Azad, *India Wins Freedom*, p. 218.

8. *Jawaharlal's Discovery of America*, p. 144.

9. *Statesman*, 14 Oct. 1947.

10. Sardar Patel's view quoted by Azad, *India Wins Freedom*, p. 242.

11. K. Sarwar Hasan, ed., *Documents on the Foreign Relations of Pakistan: The Transfer of Power*, p. 261.

12. Quoted by V. P. Menon, *The Transfer of Power in India*, p. 382.

13. *New York Times*, 8 Aug. 1947. Noakhali is a district in what was East Pakistan till 1971.

NOTES FOR PAGES 58–64

14. John Connell, *Auchinleck*, pp. 920–922. Auchinleck was commander in chief in India at the time of partition and stayed on there for some months as supreme commander of all British forces still in India. His other duties were to oversee the equitable distribution of the former Indian forces and their equipment between the new dominions of India and Pakistan.
15. Vincent Sheean in *New York Herald Tribune*, 16 Jan. 1948.
16. Quoted by Lord Birdwood, *Two Nations and Kashmir*, p. 120.
17. Eustace Seligman, *What the United States Can Do about India*, pp. 36 and 43.
18. *Times*, 2 June 1956 and 26 June 1956.
19. *Round Table*, Mar. 1960.
20. Kingsley Martin in *New Statesman*, 15 Feb. 1963, cited by Latif Ahmed Sherwani, *Foreign Policy of Pakistan*, p. 13; Selig S. Harrison, "Troubled India and Her Neighbors," *Foreign Affairs*, Jan. 1965, p. 319; Alastair Lamb, *The Kashmir Problem*, p. 14. Lamb is a specialist in Asian territorial disputes.
21. Ian Stephens, *Pakistan*, p. 193.
22. V. P. Menon, *The Transfer of Power in India*, p. 386.
23. Brigadier J. G. Smith in *Asiatic Review*, Jan. 1948, p. 11.
24. Viscount Templewood, "Some Reflections on Recent Indian Constitutional History," *Asiatic Review*, Oct. 1952.
25. Penderel Moon, *Divide and Quit*, p. 81. Moon, a senior member of the Indian Civil Service, was in India at the time of partition.
26. Andrew Mellor in *Asiatic Review*, July 1952, p. 177.
27. Quoted by Connell, *Auchinleck*, p. 879.
28. Alan Campbell-Johnson, "Reflections on the Transfer of Power," *Asiatic Review*, July 1952, pp. 180–181. Campbell-Johnson served as Mountbatten's press attaché during the latter's viceroyalty of India. He kept a diary record of political developments and afterwards published it in book form under the title *Mission with Mountbatten*.
29. Quoted by Connell, *Auchinleck*, p. 908.
30. Sir Cyril Radcliffe, a member of the British bar, was appointed to preside over the two commissions which were charged with the duty of demarcating the boundaries between India and Pakistan in the eastern and the western wings of the subcontinent. Since the Muslim and non-Muslim members of the commissions disagreed with one another, Radcliffe's decision constituted the "award" in both cases.
31. Campbell-Johnson, *Mission with Mountbatten*, p. 152.
32. The British on the whole are a fair-minded people and their rule was markedly more benign than that of any other modern colonial rulers. The criticism here is solely directed toward the manner in which the transfer of power was effected. Gandhi once said that the British Empire had certain ideals with which he had fallen in love. One of them was that each of its subjects has "the freest scope possible for his energies and honour, and whatever he thinks is due to his conscience." This, he thought, was true of the British, as of no other, government. "I am no lover," he concluded, "of any government, and I have more than once said that that government is best which governs least. And I have found that it is possible for me to be governed least under the British Empire." Polak, Brailsford, and Pethic-Lawrence, *Mahatma Gandhi*, p. 97.
33. Quoted by Wheeler-Bennett, *King George VI*, pp. 707–708, 709.
34. *Ibid.*, p. 708.
35. Connell, *Auchinleck*, p. 852.
36. Mosley, *The Last Days of the British Raj*, p. 51.
37. The eastern part of the subcontinent remained relatively less disturbed during this time. At Calcutta, Gandhi, supported by Huseyn Shaheed Suhrawardy, attained remarkable success in not letting the situation get out of hand. On 1

Notes for pages 64–71

September 1947 Gandhi started a fast vowing not to break it till sanity returned to Calcutta and broke it on 4 September, after receiving assurances of good behavior from leaders of both communities. Lord Mountbatten wrote to Gandhi: "In the Punjab we have 55,000 soldiers and large-scale rioting on our hands. In Bengal our forces consist of one man, and there is no rioting. As a serving officer, as well as an administrator, may I be allowed to pay my tribute to the one-man boundary force!" Quoted by Tendulkar, *Mahatma*, VIII, p. 111.

38. Chaudhri Muhammad Ali, *The Emergence of Pakistan*, p. 264.
39. Campbell-Johnson, *Mission with Mountbatten*, p. 87.
40. M. Ayub Khan, *Friends Not Masters*, p. 20.
41. *Ibid.*, p. 21.
42. Major General Fazal Muqeem Khan, *The Story of the Pakistan Army*, p. 41.
43. Quoted by Connell, *Auchinleck*, p. 877.
44. Quoted by V. P. Menon, *The Story of the Integration of the Indian States*, p. 132.
45. *Memoirs of Lord Ismay*, p. 421, and Campbell-Johnson, *Mission with Mountbatten*, p. 354.
46. V. P. Menon, *The Transfer of Power in India*, p. 359.
47. *Ibid.*, p. 360.
48. *Constituent Assembly Debates*, Nov. 1949, quoted by K. L. Panjabi, *The Indomitable Sardar*, p. 155.
49. Afzal, ed., *Speeches and Statements of Quaid-i-Millat Liaquat Ali Khan*, p. 209.
50. Ispahani, *Quaid-i-Azam Jinnah, as I Knew Him*, p. 222. See also by Hatim A. Alavi, "Why Quaid Chose August 14," *Dawn*, 14 Aug. 1968.
51. "Some Reminiscences" by Majid Malik, *Daily Jung* (Urdu), 26 Aug. 1968. Malik was director of public relations in the All-India Muslim League at the time to which his reminiscences belong. Afterwards he rose to be the principal information officer of the government of Pakistan. The *Jung* article was written after he had retired from service.
52. Ray Murphy, *Last Viceroy*, p. 235.
53. Campbell-Johnson, *Mission with Mountbatten*, p. 23.
54. *Ibid.*, p. 56.
55. Quoted by Mosley, *The Last Days of the British Raj*, p. 105.
56. B. L. Sharma, *The Kashmir Story*, p. 22. Sharma was director in charge of Kashmir affairs in the Indian Ministry for External Affairs for over ten years.
57. V. V. Balabushevich and A. M. Dyakov, *A Contemporary History of India*, p. 488.
58. Campbell-Johnson, *Mission with Mountbatten*, p. 120.
59. *The Memoirs of Lord Ismay*, p. 433.
60. Wilfred Russell, *Indian Summer*, p. 105.
61. Mehr Chand Mahajan, *Looking Back*, pp. 188, 268. The words "strategic and tactical reasons" are those of Sardar Patel who was chiefly responsible for deputing Mahajan to Kashmir.
62. "The importance of the Governor-General's functions as set out in section 9 of the Indian Independence Act can scarcely be over-emphasized. He has to superintend the transition, adjust the provisions of the Act of 1935, divide up personnel, assets and liabilities. Of course sovereign power is with the legislatures — the constituent assemblies, engrossed in other business — and ministries will give advice. But where advice had been conflicting, it could have been left to an impartial authority — whom everybody expected to be Lord Mountbatten — to decide." *Round Table*, Sept. 1947.
63. Quoted by H. V. Hodson, *The Great Divide*, p. 331.
64. Nehru, *India's Foreign Policy*, p. 449.

65. Campbell-Johnson, *Mission with Mountbatten*, p. 265.
66. V. P. Menon, *The Story of the Integration of the Indian States*, p. 132.
67. *Ibid.*, p. 391.
68. Hodson, *The Great Divide*, p. 507.
69. Quoted by Connell, *Auchinleck*, p. 864.
70. Though Mountbatten was compelled to concede Pakistan, he referred to it as "this mad Pakistan." Hodson, *The Great Divide*, p. 523.
71. *House of Commons Debates*, 10 July 1947, col. 2445.
72. *Ibid.*, col. 2467.
73. *House of Lords Debates*, 16 July 1947, col. 809.
74. Quoted by Hodson, *The Great Divide*, pp. 512, 513, 535.
75. See paragraphs 5 and 8 of "Form of Instrument of Accession," Appendix VII, Government of India *White Paper on Indian States*. In an address to a special meeting of the Chamber of Princes Mountbatten publicly affirmed that the Instrument of Accession provided that the states accede on three subjects "only" and it contained "an explicit provision that in no other matters has the Central Government any authority to encroach on the internal autonomy or the sovereignty of the States." Speeches of Rear Admiral the Earl Mountbatten of Burma, *Time Only to Look Forward*, p. 55.
76. Quoted by K. P. Karunakaran, *India in World Affairs (August 1947–January 1950)*, p. 3.
77. For further details of this conference see the section entitled "The Bid for Leadership" in chapter 5.
78. *Round Table*, June 1947.
79. Vincent Sheean, *Nehru*, p. 93.
80. Keith Callard, *Pakistan: A Political Study*, p. 303.

Chapter 4. Jawaharlal Nehru: The Personal Factor

1. J. S. Bright, ed., *Before and After Independence* (J. Nehru's speeches, 1922–57), p. 601.
2. "Nehru's approach to most political issues has a strong emotional content." Michael Brecher, *Nehru: A Political Biography*, p. 116.
3. *Ibid.*, p. 564.
4. *India News*, 7 Aug. 1970. Indira Gandhi talks in the same ideological terms as did her famous father, but she has a greater appreciation of the hard facts of international power politics. Most of Nehru's years had been spent as the theorist of India's foreign policy. He became an actual practitioner in that field only upon becoming the prime minister of independent India at the ripe age of nearly 58. Indira, on the other hand, was her father's companion and colleague for several years in the post-independence period and was able to learn from his successes and failures before she was called upon to carry the responsibility directly on her own shoulders.
5. "Proud and lonely, vehement, passionate and determined, he was also introspective and self-questioning, often in doubt and sometimes not far from despair. In many ways he was a Hamlet in action, capable of quick and decisive thrusts but always musing, speculating, querying." Percival Spear, "Nehru," *Modern Asian Studies*, Jan. 1967.
6. Louis Fischer's introduction, "Giants and Men," to Azad, *India Wins Freedom*, p. xxi.
7. Nehru, *India's Foreign Policy*, p. 51.
8. *Ibid.*, p. 40.
9. Nehru, *Speeches*, II, p. 395.
10. For texts of letters on the subject exchanged by the two prime ministers, see *No War Declaration and Canal Waters Dispute, Correspondence between the*

NOTES FOR PAGES 81–86

Prime Ministers of Pakistan and India. This particular quotation has been taken from Liaquat's letter of 14 Feb. 1950. See also Liaquat's statement in *Constituent Assembly of Pakistan Debates*, 28 Nov. 1950, p. 825.

11. The positions first taken up by Nehru and Liaquat have been consistently maintained by their respective successors. Indian spokesmen have asserted, from time to time, that Pakistan has always "rejected" India's offer to subscribe to a no war declaration, but Pakistan has been uniformly willing to partake in the proposed declaration provided India, at the same time, accepts a reasonable method of settling Indo-Pakistani disputes, so that the basic causes of possible wars were also removed. For further details see this author's *Pakistan's Foreign Policy: An Historical Analysis*, pp. 48–53; and "India's Offer of a No War Declaration to Pakistan: Its History and Import," *Pakistan Horizon*, 3rd Quarter 1972.

12. W. F. Van Eekelen, *Indian Foreign Policy and the Border Dispute with China*, p. 53; *Times*, 23 Oct. 1954; *New Times*, No. 45, 1955.

13. *Daily Telegraph*, 8 Mar. 1955.

14. George McT. Kahin, *The Asian-African Conference*, pp. 24, 30.

15. *Jawaharlal's Discovery of America*, p. 26.

16. Willard Range, *Jawaharlal Nehru's World View*, p. 123.

17. At the time of his death India's relations with most of her neighbors were in an unsatisfactory state. With China and Pakistan they were hostile, with Nepal they were uncertain, and with Burma and Ceylon disputes relating to the status of citizens of Indian origin in those countries were still unsolved.

18. Bowles, *Ambassador's Report*, p. 104.

19. "It is increasingly clear that secularism as Nehru conceived of it died with him. . . . Nehru was unable to make secularism more than a thin overlay on the vast Congress organization with its base in orthodox rural India." Selig S. Harrison, "Troubled India and Her Neighbors," *Foreign Affairs*, Jan. 1965.

20. Nehru, *The Discovery of India*, pp. 11–12.

21. *Ibid.*, p. 527.

22. Nehru, *An Autobiography*, p. 469.

23. Nehru, *The Discovery of India*, p. 544.

24. Nehru, *An Autobiography*, p. 118.

25. *Ibid.*, pp. 429–432.

26. Dietnam Rothermund, "Nehru and Early Indian Socialism," in *St. Antony's Papers, No. 18*, ed. S. N. Mukherjee, p. 101.

27. Nehru, *An Autobiography*, p. 596.

28. Quoted by Prem Nath Bazaz, *The History of the Struggle for Freedom in Kashmir*, p. 346.

29. Quoted by Jinnah in *Presidential Addresses of Quaid-i-Azam*, pp. 147–148.

30. *Ibid.*, p. 149.

31. Bose, *The Indian Struggle*, p. 293.

32. Nehru, *An Autobiography*, p. 72.

33. Quoted by Majumdar in *History of the Freedom Movement in India*, I, p. 331.

34. Quoted by Syed Sharifuddin Pirzada, *Evolution of Pakistan*, p. 99.

35. Quoted by Ambedkar, *Pakistan*, pp. 121–122.

36. *Ibid.*, p. 131.

37. For the text of the resolution see Azad, *India Wins Freedom*, p. 79.

38. V. P. Menon, *The Transfer of Power in India*, p. 358.

39. Azad, *India Wins Freedom*, p. 214.

40. *Ibid.*, p. 217.

41. *Ibid.*, p. 219.

42. Quoted by Mosley, *The Last Days of the British Raj*, p. 248.

43. "Long ago," writes Nehru, "right at the commencement of non-co-operation

or even earlier, Gandhiji had laid down his formula for solving the communal problem. . . . [H]e was prepared to agree to everything that the Muslims might demand. He wanted to win them over, not to bargain with them." Nehru, *An Autobiography*, p. 136.

44. "Evidence is slowly accumulating, which will one day prove to be conclusive, that the man who did most to ensure the creation of Pakistan was none other than its uncompromising opponent, Jawaharlal Nehru. It was Nehru, not Gandhi, who saw to it that any *rapprochement* between the Congress and the League, particularly after the reforms introduced under the Government of India Act, 1935, was thwarted." Herbert Feldman, "The Communal Problem in the Indo-Pakistan Subcontinent: Some Current Implications," *Pacific Affairs*, Summer 1969, p. 154.

45. Quoted by Khalid Bin Sayeed, *Pakistan: The Formative Stage*, p. 83.
46. *Ibid.*, p. 84.
47. Chaudhuri Khaliquzzaman, *Pathway to Pakistan*, pp. 156–157.
48. R. Coupland, *Report on the Constitutional Problem in India*, part II: *Indian Politics, 1936–1942*, p. 111.
49. Azad, *India Wins Freedom*, p. 188.
50. Brecher, *Nehru*, pp. 231–232.
51. Quoted by *ibid.*, p. 231.
52. Sir Maurice Gwyer and A. Appadorai, eds., *Speeches and Documents on the Indian Constitution, 1921–47*, II, p. 612.
53. Mosley, *The Last Days of the British Raj*, p. 28.
54. Louis Fischer in his Introduction to Azad's *India Wins Freedom*, p. xvii.
55. *Statesman*, 16 Dec. 1947.
56. Korbel, *Danger in Kashmir*, p. 128.
57. *New York Times*, 2 Mar. 1957.
58. Nehru, *Speeches*, I, pp. 336–337.
59. *Indian Parliamentary Debates, Official Report*, 3 Dec. 1956, col. 1324.
60. *Washington Post*, 19 Dec. 1962.
61. M. Ayub Khan, *Friends Not Masters*, p. 128.
62. *Dawn*, 1 June 1964.
63. *Round Table*, Sept. 1954, p. 358.
64. Campbell-Johnson, *Mission with Mountbatten*, p. 246.
65. *Asian Recorder*, 1964, p. 6161.
66. Jawaharlal Nehru, *A Bunch of Old Letters*, p. 204.
67. *New York Times*, 16 Feb. 1962. For Secretary Acheson's opinion of Nehru see the section "India, Pakistan, and the Great Powers" in chapter 5.
68. Nehru, *Speeches*, I, p. 283.
69. *Lok Sabha Debates*, 14 Aug. 1962, col. 1770.
70. This is Neville Maxwell's conclusion in *India's China War*, p. 141.
71. *Ibid.*
72. United Nations *General Assembly Official Records*, 1 Oct. 1970.
73. *Ibid.*, 5 Oct. 1971.
74. M. K. Gandhi, *An Autobiography, or The Story of My Experiments with Truth*, p. 184. At p. 389 of the same book Gandhi tells us how the word *satyagraha* was coined to describe his unusual technique for combating various forms of injustice. *Sat*, he states there, means truth and *agraha* means firmness. At another place he explains: "Its [*satyagraha*'s] root meaning is holding on to truth, hence *truth*-force. I have also called it *love-force* or *soul-force*. In the application of Satyagraha, I discovered in the earliest stages that pursuit of truth did not admit of violence being inflicted on one's opponent but that he must be weaned from error by patience and sympathy. For what appears to be truth to the one may appear to be error to the other. And patience means self-suffering. So the doctrine came to mean vindication of truth, not by infliction of suffering on

NOTES FOR PAGES 93-101

the opponent, but on one's own self." Quoted by Mahadev H. Desai, *Day-to-Day with Gandhi: Secretary's Diary*, vol. II: *From April 1919 to October 1920*, p. 91.
75. Nehru, *The Discovery of India*, pp. 43-44.
76. *Ibid.*, p. 550.
77. Nehru, *Speeches*, I, p. 237.
78. Thomas A. Bailey, *A Diplomatic History of the American People*, p. 4.
79. *Ibid.*
80. Nehru, *India's Foreign Policy*, p. 22.
81. Jawaharlal Nehru, *Visit to America*, p. 81.
82. Washington's Farewell Address.
83. Nehru, *India's Foreign Policy*, pp. 47-48.
84. *Ibid.*, p. 85.
85. *Ibid.*, p. 40.
86. *Ibid.*, p. 39.
87. Nehru, *Visit to America*, pp. 56-57.
88. *Ibid.*, p. 37.
89. *Ibid.*, pp. 29-30. His complete disregard of bitterness with his immediate neighbor, Pakistan, is remarkable. As several observers noted, he seemed to regard Pakistan a domestic problem.
90. Nehru, *India's Foreign Policy*, p. 65.
91. *Ibid.*, p. 34.
92. Jawaharlal Nehru, *The Unity of India*, pp. 221, 222, 234, 223, 240.
93. Nehru, *The Discovery of India*, p. 571. This book was written by Nehru in 1944, during imprisonment in Ahmadnagar Fort.
94. Quoted by Pyarelal, *Mahatma Gandhi*, II, p. 354.
95. Quoted by Bolitho, *Jinnah, Creator of Pakistan*, p. 206.
96. Nehru, *Speeches*, I, pp. 194-195.
97. Speech in the House of the People, 7 Aug. 1952. Nehru, *Speeches*, II, p. 114.
98. Korbel, *Danger in Kashmir*, p. 149.
99. C. M. Ali, *The Emergence of Pakistan*, p. 299.
100. Bowles, *Ambassador's Report*, p. 102; K. Natwar-Singh, ed., *The Legacy of Nehru*, p. 20.
101. Quoted by Moraes, *Jawaharlal Nehru*, p. 472.
102. Nehru, *The Discovery of India*, p. 425.
103. For the text of the Report see B. Prasad, *The Origins of Indian Foreign Policy*, Appendix I.
104. K. P. S. Menon, *India and the Cold War*, p. 9.
105. Jawaharlal Nehru, *Soviet Russia: Some Random Sketches and Impressions*.
106. From the Presidential Address to the All Bengal Students Conference at Calcutta on 22 Sept. 1928, in *Before and After Independence*, ed. Bright, p. 66.
107. From the Presidential Address to the National Congress, Lucknow, 1936.
108. Quoted by B. Prasad, *The Origins of Indian Foreign Policy*, p. 127.
109. *Ibid.*, p. 123.
110. Jawaharlal Nehru, *Eighteen Months in India*, p. 80. This, of course, was the Communist line, as laid down by Lenin: "Every country with a rapidly developing capitalist industry very soon begins to look about for colonies, for countries, that is, with poorly developed industries . . . where manufactured goods can be sold at a handsome profit. And it is for the sake of this profit of capitalist gangs that the bourgeoise governments have been waging endless wars, keeping large numbers of men in unhealthy tropical areas, spending millions of the people's money and driving the peoples of colonial countries to starvation, despair and revolt. Recall the rebellion of the native Indian population against Britain and the hunger in India, or Britian's present war with the Boers." Anand Gupta, ed., *India and Lenin*, p. 74.
111. Nehru, *The Unity of India*, p. 294.

112. Nehru, *India's Freedom*, p. 45. For a later Nehru view that the Communist regime has brought "some advantages" but at the cost of individual liberty see *Speeches*, IV, p. 376.
113. Nehru, *The Unity of India*, p. 370.
114. Nehru, *The Discovery of India*, p. 555.
115. Brecher, *Nehru*, p. 224.
116. *Ibid.*, p. 587; Mende, *Nehru*, pp. 40, 97.
117. This unit was attached to the Eighth Route Army under the Communist command whose leader, Mao Tse-tung, informed Nehru of his appreciation. B. Prasad, *The Origins of Indian Foreign Policy*, p. 139.
118. Dorothy Norman, ed., *Nehru: The First Sixty Years*, I, pp. 634–635.
119. Winston S. Churchill, *The Second World War*, vol. IV: *The Hinge of Fate*, p. 179; Azad, *India Wins Freedom*, p. 52.
120. Nehru, *Eighteen Months in India*, p. 174, 175.
121. Nehru, *The Unity of India*, pp. 278, 280.
122. *Ibid.*, p. 357.
123. "Gandhi to Chiang Kai-shek," *Nation*, 24 Oct. 1942; Krishna Nehru Hutheesing, ed., *Nehru's Letters to His Sister*, pp. 83–84, quoted by Margaret W. Fisher, "India's Jawaharlal Nehru," *Asian Survey*, June 1967; quoted by G. Eric Hansen, "Indian Perceptions of the Chinese Communist Regime and Revolution," *Orbis*, Spring 1968.
124. *Dawn*, 5 Mar. 1965, an unsigned article, "Sino-Pakistan Relations Rooted in the Past," released from Peking during President Ayub Khan's visit to China.
125. Chen Hang-seng, "China and Pakistan: Old Friendship Recalled," *Dawn*, 18 Feb. 1964.
126. K. M. Panikkar, *In Two Chinas*, p. 101.
127. Sir George Schuster and Guy Wint, *India and Democracy*, pp. 211–212.
128. J. C. Kundra, *Indian Foreign Policy*, p. 22. Not knowing what was to follow a few years later, K. P. S. Menon, the first Indian ambassador to China, when presenting his credentials in Peking, harped on the popular theme of the so-called historical friendship between India and China and said there had never been a war between them, "hardly even a border scramble." On the contrary they had been collaborators in the art of living. *Statesman*, 31 Mar. 1947.
129. Hansen, "Indian Perceptions of the Chinese Communist Regime and Revolution."
130. Nehru in the Lok Sabha on 27 Nov. 1959; Nehru, *India's Foreign Policy*, p. 370.
131. Nehru to Chou En-lai on 27 Oct. 1962, *Notes, Memoranda and Letters Exchanged between the Governments of India and China*, White Paper No. VIII, p. 4.
132. Nehru in the Lok Sabha on 8 Nov. 1962; Nehru, *Speeches*, IV, p. 231.
133. Nehru, *Speeches*, IV, p. 380.
134. *New York Times*, 10 Dec. 1961.
135. W. F. Van Eekelen, *Indian Foreign Policy and the Border Dispute with China*, p. 203. "Our defence policy until the Chinese invaded us," states Krishna Menon who was India's defense minister till he was forced to resign after the Sino-Indian border clash of 1962, "was intended to resist an attack from Pakistan." *India and World Politics*, p. 167.
136. *Asian Recorder*, 1963, p. 4991.
137. Karunakaran, *India in World Affairs*, p. 47.
138. Quoted by R. Palme Dutt, *India Today and Tomorrow*, p. 276.
139. Dutt, *India Today and Tomorrow*, p. 276.
140. Quoted by Panjabi, *The Indomitable Sardar*, p. 198.
141. For the text of this remarkable letter see D. V. Tahmankar, *Sardar Patel*, pp. 288–293.

Notes for pages 108–122

142. Quoted by Panjabi, *The Indomitable Sardar*, p. 243.
143. *Economist*, 5 Aug. 1950.

Chapter 5. The Opening Moves (1947–53)

1. *Dawn*, 6 June 1972.
2. For the texts see Nehru, *Speeches*, I, pp. 1, 315; II, p. 391.
3. A well-known Gandhi statement runs: "They say 'means are after all means.' I would say 'means are after all everything.' As the means so the end. There is no wall of separation between means and end. Indeed the Creator has given us control (and that too very limited) over means, none over the end." M. K. Gandhi, *All Men Are Brothers: Life and Thoughts of Mahatma Gandhi as Told in His Own Words*, p. 81.
4. Government of Pakistan Handout, E. No. 484, 9 Feb. 1951.
5. Afzal, ed., *Speeches and Statements of Quaid-i-Millat Liaquat Ali Khan*, p. 553.
6. Even during Jinnah's lifetime, Feroze Khan Noon, a prominent West Pakistani politician, was warning his colleagues in the Constituent Assembly that "this provincialism is a curse. . . . This provincialism really is going to lead to dictatorship, because of the unreasonableness of certain Members and their pettymindedness and I tell you that today dictatorship is not a bad thing for Pakistan." *Constituent Assembly of Pakistan Debates, Official Report*, vol. III, 1948, 22 May 1948, p. 87. Interestingly, Noon himself was the prime minister of Pakistan in October 1958 when General Ayub Khan assumed dictatorial powers by ousting the tottering civil administration.
7. Mujibur Rahman, founder of Bangladesh, was a zealous member of the Awami League which was one of the main constituents of the United Front. The twenty-one-point manifesto of the United Front later served as a blueprint for Mujib's Six Points, a denial of which by the West Pakistani leadership resulted in the proclamation of independence by East Pakistan. The nineteenth point of the manifesto demanded that East Pakistan become "fully autonomous and sovereign, as envisaged in the historic Lahore resolution," and militarily self-sufficient. It should retain all subjects, including residuary powers, except defense, foreign affairs, and currency. The Lahore resolution, also called the Pakistan resolution, passed by the Muslim League at Lahore on 23 March 1940 had called for a grouping of the Muslim majority areas of northwestern and eastern India "to constitute independent states in which the constituent units shall be autonomous and sovereign." A Muslim Legislators Convention, on 9 April 1946, resolved that the two Muslim majority wings of India be constituted into a single sovereign state but East Pakistanis contended that such a meeting had no authority to modify a resolution passed at a plenary session of the organization.
8. *New York Times*, 23 May 1954.
9. For the text of the letter see Korbel, *Danger in Kashmir*, p. 83.
10. Nehru's broadcast on 2 Nov. 1947. The text is in *White Paper on Jammu and Kashmir*, p. 53.
11. *Parliamentary Debates, House of the People, Official Report*, 17 Sept. 1953, col. 3989.
12. Nehru, *India's Foreign Policy*, p. 421; Krishna Menon's speech in United Nations *General Assembly Official Records*, 10 Dec. 1956.
13. Afzal, ed., *Speeches and Statements of Quaid-i-Millat Liaquat Ali Khan*, p. 436; M. Ayub Khan, *Friends Not Masters*, pp. 22, 40.
14. *New York Times*, 13 Nov. 1953.
15. *Dawn*, 10, 11, 12, and 13 Nov. 1952.
16. Nehru, *Speeches*, I, p. 285.
17. For the text of the joint declaration made by the prime ministers of all

Commonwealth countries, including India and Pakistan, on 27 April 1949, see Mansergh, ed., *Documents and Speeches on British Commonwealth Affairs, 1931–1952*, II, p. 846.

18. Dean Acheson, *Present at the Creation*, p. 335, and Patrick Gordon Walker, *The Commonwealth*, p. 315; "Anglo-Indian Peace Initiatives" in Acheson's *Present at the Creation*, p. 416; Walker, *The Commonwealth*, p. 318. Walker states that at the Geneva Conference the British government "co-operated extremely closely with India. There was indeed an Anglo-Indian front against the United States."

19. In his presidential address to the Jana Sangh General Council, on 6 May 1972, Atal Behari Vajpayee complained of the "personality cult" of the Indian prime minister and attributed the overwhelming success of the Congress party in the elections to the fact that the Congress in effect put forward "just one candidate [Mrs. Gandhi]" for all seats and its only manifesto was to strengthen her hands. Neither the Congress nor the party president, or any other leader of the party, figured anywhere in the election. *Asian Recorder*, 1972, p. 10804. See also Milton Israel's comment that "Mrs. Gandhi successfully advanced the proposition that she was, in effect, India's only 'national' leader." Milton Israel, "The Indian Party System and the 1971 Parliamentary Elections," *International Journal*, Summer 1972. Measuring Nehru's importance to India, Acheson had stated that "if he did not exist — as Voltaire said of God — he would have to be invented." Acheson, *Present at the Creation*, p. 336. Before the Nehrus, the Congress party had been subject to Gandhi's one-man rule. "Mahatma Gandhi occupies the same position among Congressmen," declared one of the Mahatma's followers in an open session of the Congress, "as that held by the leadership of Mussolini among Fascists, Hitler among Nazis and Stalin among Communists. . . . The various struggles for independence . . . were started, carried out and terminated in accordance with his dictates. . . . [A] practice has grown up to elect as the Congress president the person upon whom Mahatma's choice falls. . . . In brief, he is all in all in the Congress." S. C. Biswas, ed., *Gandhi, Theory and Practice, Social Impact and Contemporary Relevance*, p. 366.

20. Churchill, *The Second World War*, vol. IV: *The Hinge of Fate*, pp. 181–182, 184–185, 190.

21. Harry S. Truman, *Memoirs*, vol. II: *Years of Trial and Hope*, pp. 93–101; *United States Department of State Bulletin*, 30 June 1952. At least one State Department official, John Ohly, had the foresight to warn at the time that such situations had a way of snowballing and the United States could become a scapegoat for the French and be sucked into direct intervention. Acheson, *Present at the Creation*, p. 674.

22. Truman, *Memoirs*, vol. II: *Years of Trial and Hope*, pp. 105–107.

23. *New York Herald Tribune*, 10 Jan. and 14 Mar. 1949; *Congressional Record*, 81st Congress, 1st Session, 25 Apr. 1949, Senate, Appendix, vol. 95, part 13, p. A 2374.

24. Liaquat Ali Khan, *Pakistan, the Heart of Asia*, p. 16.

25. For example, in Parliament on 3 Aug. 1950 and 29 Sept. 1954.

26. For the text of Nehru's proposals addressed to Premier Stalin and Secretary Acheson and Acheson's response see *United States Department of State Bulletin*, 31 July 1950, pp. 170–171.

27. Charles H. Heimsath and Surjit Mansingh, *A Diplomatic History of Modern India*, p. 69.

28. For texts of Indo–United States exchanges on the subject see *United States Department of State Bulletin*, 3 Sept. 1951, pp. 385–388.

29. M. A. H. Ispahani, "The Foreign Policy of Pakistan, 1947–1964," *Pakistan Horizon*, 3rd Quarter 1964.

30. Truman, *Memoirs*, vol. II: *Years of Trial and Hope*, p. 424.

31. Acheson, *Present at the Creation*, p. 420.
32. *Ibid.*, p. 336.
33. Truman, *Memoirs*, vol. II: *Years of Trial and Hope*, p. 362.
34. Interview with Supreme Court Justice William O. Douglas, reported in *Parade Magazine* of the *St. Paul Sunday Pioneer Press*, 6 Aug. 1967.
35. Panikkar, *In Two Chinas*, p. 168.
36. V. V. Ba'abushevich and A. M. Dyakov, *A Contemporary History of India*, p. 564.
37. C. R. Attlee and Francis Williams, *Twilight of Empire: Memoirs of Prime Minister Clement Attlee*, p. 238.
38. Hodson, *The Great Divide*, p. 243.
39. Afzal, ed., *Speeches and Statements of Quaid-i-Millat Liaquat Ali Khan*, p. 181; Liaquat Ali Khan, *Pakistan*, pp. 76, 108.
40. *New Times*, No. 3, 1948, No. 3, 1949, No. 42, 1949, No. 3, 1948.
41. Heimsath and Mansingh, *A Diplomatic History of Modern India*, p. 186.
42. B.B.C. Monitoring Service, No. 21, 13 Sept. 1949, Part V (The Far East).
43. *New Times*, No. 40, 1948, No. 47, 1949.
44. Quoted by R. Palme Dutt, *The Crisis of Britain and the British Empire*, p. 215.
45. *People's China*, 16 Sept. 1951.
46. Arthur Stein, *India and the Soviet Union*, p. 30.
47. Nehru, *Speeches*, I, pp. 297–304; *The Indian Annual Register*, January–June 1947, p. 298.
48. Nehru, *Speeches*, I, p. 325.
49. *Economist*, 5 Feb. 1949.
50. *Ibid.*, 5 Mar. 1949.
51. For the text of the resolution see D. N. Sharma, *Afro-Asian Group in the U.N.*, p. 351.
52. Nehru, *India's Foreign Policy*, p. 44; *Parliamentary Debates of India*, 23 Dec. 1953, col. 3013.
53. For information relating to the 1926 and 1931 sessions of the Motamar see "Pakistan's Role in Uniting World Muslims," by Inamullah Khan in *Dawn*, 23 Mar. 1968.
54. Government of Pakistan Handout, No. 484, 9 Feb. 1951.
55. Hafeez Malik, "Foreign Relations of Pakistan: An Interpretation," presented on 18 Nov. 1967, to a symposium on Pakistan: The Modernization of an Islamic State, at Syracuse University, Syracuse, N.Y.
56. *Civil and Military Gazette*, 26 Nov. 1949, quoted by Siddiqi, *Pakistan Seeks Security*, pp. 89–90.
57. *Economist*, 3 Dec. 1949, p. 1228.
58. *Dawn*, 7 Sept. 1949.
59. *Ibid.*, 29 Oct. 1949, 31 Oct. 1949.
60. *Ibid.*, 15 Nov. 1949.
61. Khaliquzzaman, *Only If They Knew It!* pp. 31–32.
62. *Round Table*, June 1952, p. 259.
63. Hafeez-ur-Rahman Khan, "Pakistan's Relations with U.A.R.," *Pakistan Horizon*, 3rd Quarter 1960, p. 212.
64. Quaid-i-Azam Mahomed Ali Jinnah, *Speeches as Governor-General of Pakistan, 1947–1948*, p. 69.
65. Foreign Minister Zulfikar Ali Bhutto, in *National Assembly of Pakistan Debates*, 27 Nov. 1962, p. 131.
66. The present author has dealt with the question of "Pakhtunistan" more fully at pp. 68–90 of *Pakistan's Foreign Policy*.
67. *Indian Press Digests*, 16 Sept. to 15 Nov. 1951, vol. I, no. 2, p. 29.
68. Government of Pakistan Handout, E. No. 506, 11 Feb. 1951.

69. *Dawn*, 27 Sept. 1956. Power was transferred to Pakistan at a ceremony at Karachi on 14 Aug. 1947, presided over by Mountbatten as the representative of the British crown.
70. Quoted by M. S. Agwani, "India, Pakistan, and West Asia," *International Studies* (Delhi), July–Oct. 1966, p. 159.
71. Gamal Abdel Nasser, *The Philosophy of the Revolution*, pp. 69–70.
72. *Dawn*, 15 April 1960.
73. *Pakistan Affairs* (Washington, D.C.), 8 Feb. 1949.
74. Quoted by B. V. Keskar, Indian deputy minister for external affairs, in *Statesman*, 6 Dec. 1949.
75. *Ibid.*, 9 June 1950.

Chapter 6. *Panchsheel* vs. Defense Alliances (1954–58)

1. *Times of Karachi*, 26 Feb. 1954, quoted in *Pakistan Affairs*, 12 Mar. 1954.
2. Ralph de Toledano, *Nixon*, p. 164.
3. Acheson, *Present at the Creation*, p. 336.
4. *Report of Sir Owen Dixon to the Security Council*, 15 Sept. 1950, paragraph 52.
5. Prem Nath Bazaz, *Kashmir in Crucible*, p. 69. Bazaz, a Kashmiri pandit, has written extensively on Kashmir.
6. *Negotiations between the Prime Ministers of Pakistan and India Regarding the Kashmir Dispute*, p. 74; *Parliamentary Debates, House of the People*, 23 Dec. 1953, col. 2983, and 1 Mar. 1954, col. 971; R. P. Stebbins, *The United States in World Affairs*, p. 324.
7. Nirad C. Chaudhuri, *The Continent of Circe*, p. 244.
8. Mushtaq Ahmad, *The United Nations and Pakistan*, p. 140.
9. *Dawn*, 30 Jan. 1957.
10. Nehru, *India's Foreign Policy*, p. 29.
11. For the text of the agreement see H. E. Richardson, *Tibet and Its History*, p. 278; *Foreign Policy of India (Texts of Documents 1947–64)*, pp. 295, 486–487; *Lok Sabha Debates*, 15 May 1954, col. 7496; *Negotiations between the Prime Ministers of Pakistan and India Regarding the Kashmir Dispute*, p. 85.
12. *Lok Sabha Debates*, 31 Mar. 1955, col. 3900–3901; All-India Congress Committee, *Indian National Congress Resolutions on Foreign Policy, 1947–57*, p. 34.
13. M. S. Rajan, *India in World Affairs, 1954–56*, pp. 634–635; N. A. Bulganin and N. S. Khrushchev, *Visit of Friendship to India, Burma and Afghanistan*, p. 92; *New Times*, No. 45, 1955.
14. Nehru, *India's Foreign Policy*, p. 574.
15. Roscoe Drummond, "What India Thinks," *New York Herald Tribune* (European ed.), 14 Nov. 1957.
16. *Daily Telegraph*, 24 Dec. 1954.
17. *Times*, 2 June 1956.
18. Dalai Lama, *My Land and My People*, p. 230.
19. Nehru, *India's Foreign Policy*, pp. 302–303. At a later date — 4 Sept. 1959 — he said categorically, "For all practical purposes, ever since the Manchu Dynasty fell or a little after that, Tibet was practically independent." *Prime Minister on Sino-Indian Relations*, vol. I: *In Parliament*, p. 110.
20. The text is in *Concerning the Question of Tibet*, p. 14.
21. *Round Table*, Sept. 1954.
22. Quoted by Girilal Jain, *Panchsheela and After*, p. 33.
23. Afzal, ed., *Speeches and Statements of Quaid-i-Millat Liaquat Ali Khan*, p. 495.
24. See the section "The Cold War" in chapter 7.

NOTES FOR PAGES 149-161

25. Nehru, *Speeches*, III, p. 306; *Hindu*, 24 Oct. 1955; Bulganin and Khrushchev, *Visit of Friendship to India, Burma and Afghanistan*, pp. 58 and 226; *New York Times*, 28 Feb. 1972; Noorani, *Our Credulity and Negligence*, p. 104.
26. Biswas, ed., *Gandhi*, p. 497.
27. Mende, *Nehru*, pp. 141-142; *Lok Sabha Debates*, 29 Sept. 1954, col. 3683, quoted by Heimsath and Mansingh, *A Diplomatic History of India*, p. 192; *Hindu*, 20 Jan. 1957.
28. M. K. Gandhi, *Towards Lasting Peace*, p. 205; *Hindu*, 6 Apr. 1955, quoted by Rajan, *India in World Affairs*, p. 97, n. 5.
29. *India's Fight for Territorial Integrity*, p. 5.
30. *National Assembly of Pakistan Debates*, 25 Feb. 1957, p. 1097. For a fuller version of China's relations with Pakistan from 1947 to 1964 see S. M. Burke, "Sino-Pakistani Relations," *Orbis*, Summer 1964.
31. Karunakar Gupta, *India in World Politics: A Period of Transition, Fall 1956 to Spring 1960*, p. 2.
32. Nehru, *India's Foreign Policy*, pp. 597-599.
33. John F. Kennedy, *The Strategy of Peace*, p. 48.
34. Chester Bowles, "Evaluation of American Foreign Policy," *India Quarterly*, July-Sept. 1961.
35. *Hindu*, 18 Nov. 1956, quoted by Stein, *India and the Soviet Union*, pp. 91-92. Narayan is a prominent Socialist leader in India. At one time he was looked upon as a possible successor to Nehru.
36. Burke, *Pakistan's Foreign Policy*, p. 255.
37. Broadcast from radio Mecca reported in *Dawn*, 26 Sept. 1955.
38. *Hindu*, 11 Dec. 1955, quoted by Rajan, *India in World Affairs*, p. 478.
39. *Times*, 3 Sept. 1956.
40. *Round Table*, Mar. 1957, p. 172.
41. *National Assembly of Pakistan Debates*, 25 Feb. 1957, p. 1099.
42. *Ibid.*, 4 Sept. 1958, pp. 373-374.
43. *Dawn*, 25 Nov. 1956.
44. *Ibid.*, 1 Dec. 1956.
45. *Ibid.*, 11 Aug. 1957.
46. *Ibid.*, 31 Mar. 1958.
47. *Constituent Assembly of Pakistan Debates*, 7 Sept. 1955, p. 558.
48. *Hindu*, 5 June 1958, quoted by K. Gupta, *India in World Politics*, p. 219.
49. G. W. Choudhury, *Documents and Speeches on the Constitution of Pakistan*, pp. 486-487.
50. M. Ayub Khan, "Pakistan Perspective," *Foreign Affairs*, July 1960.

Chapter 7. War Clouds over South Asia: Sino-Indian Conflict (1959-62)

1. Dalai Lama, *My Land and My People*, p. 194.
2. For the Dalai Lama's statement at Tezpur and his first statement at Mussoorie see *Asian Recorder*, 1959, pp. 2659-60, and for his prepared statement and observations at a press conference at Mussoorie on 20 June 1959, see *Asian Recorder*, 1959, p. 2758, and the *New York Times*, 21 June 1959.
3. Dalai Lama, *My Land and My People*, pp. 206-207.
4. United Nations *General Assembly Official Records*, 20 Oct. 1959.
5. This allegation was not without force. The rebellious Khampas "maintained some sort of liaison with the disgruntled Tibetan nobles, led by the demoted Tibetan Prime Minister, Mr. Lukhangwa, who had settled in the Indian border town Kalimpong." K. Gupta, *India in World Politics*, p. 2. See also pp. 74, 76, 85, 86, 88, 98, 106, and 307 of the same book.

6. For the text of the article see *Concerning the Question of Tibet*, pp. 239–276. This article purported to have been prepared by the editorial department of the newspaper but is believed to have been written personally by Mao Tse-tung (see K. Gupta, *India in World Politics*, p. 117n).
7. Nehru, *India's Foreign Policy*, p. 321.
8. *Ibid.*, p. 333.
9. *Asian Recorder*, 1959, p. 2999; *New York Times*, 27 Oct. 1959; *Hindustan Times*, 26 Oct. 1959; *New York Times*, 27 Oct. 1959.
10. *Lok Sabha Debates*, 25 Nov. 1959, cols. 1733–34.
11. K. Gupta, *India in World Politics*, p. 3. The author's conclusion is endorsed in the Introduction by K. P. S. Menon, a former ambassador of India to China and the U.S.S.R.
12. *Prime Minister on Sino-Indian Relations*, vol. I: *In Parliament*, p. 116; *Asian Recorder*, 1959, p. 2999; Brecher, *India and World Politics*, p. 151.
13. *Documents on the Sino-Indian Boundary Question*, pp. 3–8. For further details regarding the McMahon Line see the Appendix.
14. *Notes, Memoranda and Letters Exchanged between the Governments of India and China*, White Paper No. II, pp. 34, 45, and White Paper No. III, pp. 46, 50; *Rajya Sabha Debates*, 26 Mar. 1962, col. 1148.
15. *Peking Review*, 3 May 1960.
16. *Asian Recorder*, 1960, p. 3302.
17. *Report of the Officials of the Government of India and the People's Republic of China on the Boundary Question*, p. 11.
18. *Lok Sabha Debates*, 28 Nov. 1961, col. 1858, 20 June 1962, col. 11935, 22 Aug. 1962, cols. 2878–79, 2995, 14 Aug. 1962, col. 1754, 22 Aug. 1962, col. 2990.
19. *Peking Review*, 4 May 1962.
20. For China's stand on the border conflict, including the 8 September incident, see "Premier Chou En-lai's Letter to the Leaders of Asian and African Countries on the Sino-Indian Border Question," *The Sino-Indian Boundary Question* (enlarged ed.), pp. 6–37. Neville Maxwell in *India's China War* (p. 295), says that the post in fact was at Che Dong but the Indian commander, who set it up on 4 June 1962, called it Dhola after a pass on the Indian side of the McMahon Line. He states, further, that both Thagla Ridge and the "Dhola post" were on the Chinese side of the McMahon Line. Braj Kumar Nehru, the Indian ambassador to the United States, speaking at the National Press Club, Washington, D.C., on 21 November 1962 stated: "On September 8 this year, the Chinese forces crossed that line [the McMahon Line] and occupied the Thagla Ridge in the North Eastern frontier. The Indian army was thereupon directed for the first time to engage in military action to expel the invaders. This they were not successful in doing; instead, the Chinese started a counterattack in massive strength on the 20th October on both the Eastern and Western fronts and the result up to today has been that they have advanced even beyond the area they claim." The text of this speech was distributed at the time by the Information Service of India, Washington, D.C. See also Nehru's letter dated 14 November 1962 to Chou En-lai and memorandum given by the Ministry of Foreign Affairs, Peking, to the embassy of India in China on 29 December 1962, the full texts of which will be found at pp. 10–13 and 39–46 of *Notes, Memoranda and Letters Exchanged between the Governments of India and China*, White Paper No. VIII.
21. Quoted by Shanti Prasad Varma, *Struggle for the Himalayas*, p. 149.
22. Quoted by Maxwell, *India's China War*, p. 342.
23. *Asian Recorder*, 1962, p. 4910.
24. "Statement of the Government of the People's Republic of China, October 24, 1962," *The Sino-Indian Boundary Question*, pp. 1–5. In his letter of 15 November 1962 to the leaders of the Asian and African countries, Chou En-lai ex-

plained that the essence of these proposals was to restore the state of the Sino-Indian boundary to its 1959 position. "Letter from the Prime Minister of India to the Prime Minister of China, 27 October 1962," *Notes, Memoranda and Letters Exchanged between the Governments of India and China,* White Paper No. VIII, 1963, p. 5; "Premier Chou En-lai's Letter to the Leaders of Asian and African Countries on the Sino-Indian Boundary Question," *The Sino-Indian Boundary Question,* p. 32.

25. John Kenneth Galbraith, *Ambassador's Journal,* p. 487; *Notes, Memoranda and Letters Exchanged between the Governments of India and China,* White Paper No. VIII, p. 19.

26. The Chinese have followed a fairly consistent pattern in their attitude toward border problems. In their border treaties with Burma (28 Jan. 1960), Nepal (21 Mar. 1960), and Pakistan (2 Mar. 1963) they have largely accepted the alignments left behind by the British. In the case of Burma this included a stretch of the McMahon Line. Their declared attitude toward the border dispute with the U.S.S.R. in principle is no different: "It must be confirmed that the treaties relating to the present Sino-Soviet Boundary are all unequal treaties imposed on China by tsarist Russian imperialism. But . . . the Chinese Government . . . is still ready to take these unequal treaties as the basis for determining the entire alignment of the boundary line. . . . What should be done is to hold negotiations for . . . a new equal treaty to replace the old unequal one." *Peking Review,* 30 May 1969.

27. Nehru, *Speeches,* IV, p. 212.

28. *Rajya Sabha Debates,* 26 Mar. 1962, col. 1147.

29. Alastair Lamb, *Asian Frontiers,* p. 108, and *The China-India Border,* p. 103.

30. Barnds, *India, Pakistan and the Great Powers,* p. 320. At p. 320 of his book *The Flying Troika* former Indian ambassador K. P. S. Menon also says that it was unfortunate that China's offer to recognize the McMahon Line, "which no previous Chinese government had ever recognized," in return for the Aksai Chin area was not accepted. This would have served the interests of both the countries. China would have obtained Aksai Chin, which is of special importance to her but of little use to India, and India's contention with respect to the boundary in the eastern sector, which is of vital importance to her, would have prevailed.

31. Galbraith, *Ambassador's Journal,* pp. 481, 504, 501.

32. Nehru, *Speeches,* IV, p. 262. He also said, characteristically, that if India abandoned nonalignment it would be a "terrible moral failure." M. S. Rajan, *Non-alignment: India and the Future,* pp. 35, 110. Galbraith's comment is in *Asian Recorder,* 1962, p. 4932. Krishna Menon found Galbraith "too pro-Indian." See Penderel Moon's review of *Ambassador's Journal* in *Round Table,* July 1970.

33. Arthur M. Schlesinger, Jr., *A Thousand Days,* p. 525; Kennedy, *The Strategy of Peace,* p. 143.

34. Brecher, *India and World Politics,* p. 157; Frank Moraes, *Nehru, Sunlight and Shadow,* p. 116.

35. Quoted by Schlesinger, *A Thousand Days,* p. 529.

36. *Rajya Sabha Debates,* 6 Sept. 1955, col. 2098, and 27 Aug. 1954, col. 578; *Hindu Weekly Review,* 1 Jan. 1962; *Hindustan Times,* 26 Dec. 1961.

37. *Dawn,* 25 Apr. 1959; *Asian Recorder,* 1959, p. 2871.

38. Government of Pakistan Handout, E. No. 2741, 31 May 1960; *New York Times,* 20 June 1960.

39. *Hindu,* 19 Jan. 1960 and 25 Jan. 1960. Ayub's offer of joint defense to India was also a repetition of an idea which Pakistani leaders from Iqbal onwards had been putting forward. See Burke, *Pakistan's Foreign Policy,* pp. 53–56.

40. *Hindu,* 6 Feb. 1962, quoted by Maxwell, *India's China War,* p. 230.

41. Quoted by Zulfikar Ali Bhutto, *The Myth of Independence,* p. 62.

42. *History of the Communist Party of the Soviet Union,* p. 665.

Notes for pages 173–181

43. *A Reply to Peking* (Soviet Booklet No. 122), p. 22.
44. For a fuller account of the origin and early history of Sino-Soviet differences see Edward Crankshaw, "The Polarisation of the Communist World," in Evan Luard, ed., *The Cold War: A Re-appraisal.*
45. *Asian Recorder*, 1959, p. 2886.
46. *The Truth about How the Leaders of the CPSU Have Allied Themselves with India against China*, p. 6.
47. *Asian Recorder*, 1959, p. 2999.
48. *The Truth about How the Leaders of the CPSU Have Allied Themselves with India against China*, p. 7.
49. For a description of Soviet aid to India and of Indo-Soviet trade, see Stein, *India and the Soviet Union*, chapter 7; *Asian Recorder*, 1961, pp. 3865, 3950. A consignment of four fighters arrived in India in February 1963. The program to build MIG factories did not begin to move forward till September 1964. Stein, *India and the Soviet Union*, pp. 205, 207.
50. *Asian Recorder*, 1962, p. 4915; J. A. Naik, *Soviet Policy towards India*, p. 154.
51. Nehru, *India's Foreign Policy*, pp. 476, 601.
52. Heimsath and Mansingh, *A Diplomatic History of Modern India*, p. 502.
53. Schlesinger, *A Thousand Days*, p. 521.
54. Joseph Linus, *The Sino-Indian Border Dispute*, p. 46; Galbraith, *Ambassador's Journal*, pp. 439, 474; *Asian Recorder*, 1962, p. 4915.
55. For the undertakings given by India to the United States and the United Kingdom see *Asian Recorder*, 1962, pp. 4932 and 4944. During the 1965 Indo-Pakistani war India made much of the alleged breach of promise by Pakistan that she would "never" use United States weapons against India but the only restriction placed by the Mutual Defense Assistance Agreement of 1954 on the use of arms supplied to Pakistan in fact was that they would not be used for aggression against any other nation. Both India and Pakistan pleaded self-defense in 1965. Even so, India broke her unequivocal promise to use the war material only against China. Quantitatively Pakistan used more American weaponry because the United States had been her only source of supply. But it was massive United States economic assistance to India that had enabled the latter to divert her own resources toward the purchase of arms in the international market.
56. *Asian Recorder*, 1963, p. 4979; "Chinese Aggression and India," *International Studies*, July–Oct. 1963, p. 67.

Chapter 8. War Clouds over South Asia: Indo-Pakistani Conflict (1963–February 1974)

1. M. Ayub Khan, *Friends Not Masters*, p. 150.
2. For statements on this point by Ambassador Galbraith, Secretary Rusk, and Prime Minister Macmillan, see *Asian Recorder*, 1962, p. 4932, *United States Department of State Bulletin*, 25 Mar. 1963, and *Asian Recorder*, 1963, p. 5317.
3. *Pakistan Horizon*, 3rd Quarter 1963, p. 279.
4. M. Ayub Khan, *Friends Not Masters*, pp. 116–121.
5. *National Assembly of Pakistan Debates*, 17 July 1963, p. 1666.
6. *Pakistan Horizon*, 1st Quarter 1964, p. 4.
7. *Ibid.*, 2nd Quarter 1965, p. 181.
8. *New York Times*, 27 June 1960; M. Ayub Khan, "Pakistan Perspective," *Foreign Affairs*, July 1960 (it takes several months for magazine articles to get into print; this article was obviously written before the U2 incident though it was published after it); *New York Times*, 27 June 1960.
9. *New Times*, No. 5, 1963.
10. M. Ayub Khan, *Speeches and Statements*, IV, p. 82.

11. *Pakistan Horizon*, 3rd Quarter 1964, p. 301; for further information on RCD and a list of Joint Purpose Enterprises see Burke, *Pakistan's Foreign Policy*, pp. 305–307.
12. The Afro-Asian Conference was to open in Algeria on 29 June 1965 but had to be postponed because a few days earlier the host country got involved in a domestic revolution and a bomb exploded at the proposed site of the meeting. In the end, it was never held.
13. Zulfikar Ali Bhutto, *The Quest for Peace*, pp. 32–34.
14. M. Ayub Khan, *Speeches and Statements*, VII, p. 144. In his inaugural speech at the Asian Relations Conference at New Delhi on 23 March 1947, Nehru had said, "Far too long have we of Asia been petitioners in western courts and chancelleries." Nehru, *Speeches*, I, p. 301.
15. Ayub secured the votes of 49,647 basic democrats, who formed the electoral college, while Miss Jinnah polled 28,345 votes.
16. *Dawn*, 15 July 1965.
17. The text was printed in a Government of Pakistan Handout, E. No. 2597R, n.d.
18. *New York Times*, 17 May 1964 and 1 June 1964. That Abdullah had offered confederation is clear from M. Ayub Khan, *Friends Not Masters*, p. 128, and from J. P. Narayan's statement (*Dawn*, 11 Sept. 1964). Five days after releasing Abdullah Nehru himself expressed the hope in the Lok Sabha that India and Pakistan would come "constitutionally" closer. See also *Asian Recorder*, 1964, p. 5952, quoting another statement Ayub made on 31 May 1964.
19. *Asian Recorder*, 1965, p. 6226. Provisions such as these were designed to erode the special status which article 370 of the constitution of India, enacted in 1949, had allowed to Kashmir in recognition of the fact that her future affiliation was not settled.
20. *Prime Minister on Sino-Indian Relations*, vol. I: *In Parliament*, p. 356.
21. *Asian Recorder*, 1963, p. 5207.
22. *Ibid.*, 1964, p. 6099.
23. See Patrick Seale's dispatch in the *Observer* of 10 Oct. 1965.
24. *Hindu Weekly Review*, 22 Apr. 1968.
25. For Kosygin's message to Shastri see *Hindu Weekly*, 20 Sept. 1965, and for Nasser's attitude see Bhutto, *The Myth of Independence*, p. 75.
26. *Dawn*, 6 June 1965.
27. This warning was given in the course of the Sino–United States bilateral talks which used to be held in Warsaw. See Foreign Minister Bhutto's disclosure in *National Assembly of Pakistan Debates*, 15 Mar. 1966, p. 499.
28. *Times*, 17 Sept. 1965.
29. *Dawn*, 5 Sept. 1965; Hasan, ed., *Documents on the Foreign Relations of Pakistan: China, India, Pakistan*, p. 429; *Notes, Memoranda and Letters Exchanged between the Governments of India and China*, p. 44.
30. For the texts of these Security Council resolutions see *Pakistan Horizon*, 4th Quarter 1965.
31. *Asian Recorder*, 1966, p. 6896–6897.
32. *Dawn*, 20 Sept. 1965.
33. *Asian Recorder*, 1968, p. 8468; *Hindu Weekly*, 15 July 1968; *Asian Recorder*, 1968, p. 8467; *Hindu Weekly*, 15 July 1968.
34. Syed Shabbir Husain, *Lengthening Shadows*, p. 105.
35. For the main demands contained in the twenty-one Points see chapter 5, n. 7.
36. See Mujib's speech on 10 March 1969 at the Round Table Conference called by Ayub Khan. The text is in S. M. Zafar, *Through the Crisis*, pp. 221–229.
37. Sheik Mujibur Rahman, *6-Point Formula: Our Right to Live*, p. 14; Kazi Kamal, *Sheikh Mujibur Rahman: Man and Politician*, p. 57; Zafar, *Through the*

Crisis, pp. 221–229. The language controversy had died down with the promulgation of the 1956 constitution which conceded the East Pakistani demand that Bengali be a state language along with Urdu.

38. Tariq Ali, *Pakistan: Military Rule or People's Power*, p. 207.
39. *New York Times*, 18 Mar. 1969; Peter Hazelhurst's dispatch to the *Times*, reproduced in *New York Times*, 20 Mar. 1969.
40. *New York Times*, 27 Mar. 1969.
41. K. Rangaswami, "Can't Congress Get to Sunshine Again?" *Hindu Weekly*, 26 Dec. 1966.
42. *Hindu Weekly*, 30 Jan. 1967.
43. *Statesman Weekly*, 12 July 1969.
44. *Asian Recorder*, 1969, p. 9158.
45. *Hindu Weekly*, 10 July 1967; *Statesman Weekly*, 20 June 1970.
46. See K. Rangaswami, "U.S. Pressure Shows No Abatement," *Hindu Weekly Review*, 5 Sept. 1966, for a description of the various kinds of American pressures.
47. For Kosygin's reiteration that the U.S.S.R.'s "cooperation" followed the channel of the public, not the private, sector and Mrs. Gandhi's observations quoted here see *Hindu Weekly Review*, 25 July 1966.
48. *New Times*, No. 5, 1967, No. 7, 1967, and No. 8, 1967; *International Affairs*, April 1967.
49. *New York Times*, 20 July 1966; *Asian Recorder*, 1966, p. 7209; *New York Times*, 22 July 1966 and 29 Nov. 1966.
50. *Ibid.*, 28 Sept. 1968.
51. For additional comments see "India: Disenchantment with the Soviet Union," *Round Table*, Jan. 1969.
52. Harold C. Hinton, *The Bear at the Gate*, p. 24; *International Affairs*, July 1969; *Peking Review*, 4 July 1969; *New Times*, No. 39, 1969; *International Affairs*, Jan. 1970.
53. *New Times*, No. 35, 1969, and No. 12, 1971.
54. *International Affairs*, Dec. 1971.
55. *India News*, 3 July 1970.
56. *Asian Recorder*, 1971, p. 10270.
57. Barnds, *India, Pakistan and the Great Powers*, p. 229.
58. *Dawn*, 3 Aug. 1969.
59. Hinton, *The Bear at the Gate*, p. 29.
60. *Department of State for the Press*, No. 238, 8 Aug. 1969.
61. *Pakistan Affairs*, 1 April 1969.
62. This meant, in effect, that the principle of parity of representation between East and West Pakistan would go and East Pakistan would have a majority in the National Assembly.
63. For the text of the Legal Framework Order 1970 see Government of Pakistan, *White Paper on the Crisis in East Pakistan*, Appendix B.
64. *New York Times*, 27 Nov. 1970.
65. For the text of the Awami League Manifesto see *Dawn*, 24, 25, 26 June 1970; *Pakistan Affairs*, 4 July 1969; for example, see Bhutto, *The Great Tragedy*, p. 13: "In essence, the Six Point formula was meant to strike at the roots of our nationhood. Initially it would have created two Pakistans, and later might well have brought five independent States into being." *Dawn*, 16 Feb. 1971.
66. *Ibid.*; see also Bhutto, *The Great Tragedy*, p. 36.
67. *Dawn*, 16 Feb. 1971.
68. *Dawn*, 12 Mar. 1971.
69. Government of Pakistan, *White Paper on the Crisis in East Pakistan*, Appendix A.
70. Government of Pakistan, *Summary of the White Paper on the Crisis in East Pakistan*, p. 10; *New Times*, No. 11, 1972; *Dawn*, 17 Nov. 1972; *New York*

NOTES FOR PAGES 207–214

Times, 24 June 1972; Pran Chopra, ed., *The Challenge of Bangladesh*, p. 57.
71. Barnds, *India, Pakistan and the Great Powers*, p. 306.
72. *Hindu Weekly Review*, 3 July 1967.
73. Richard M. Nixon, *U.S. Foreign Policy for the 1970's: A Report to the Congress, February 9, 1972*, p. 147.
74. *Ibid.*, p. 146.
75. Pakistan Embassy, *The Ambassador Addresses a Press Conference, National Press Club, Washington, August 30, 1971*, p. 15.
76. *Asian Recorder*, 1971, p. 10158.
77. *Ibid.*
78. *Statesman Weekly*, 24 July 1971.
79. *Ibid.*, 21 Aug. 1971 and 14 Aug. 1971; *Asian Recorder*, 1971, p. 10501.
80. *Statesman Weekly*, 14 Aug. 1971; G. Kudin and A. Usvatov, "Soviet-Indian Treaty in Action," *New Times*, No. 39, 1971 (see also in the same issue O. Borisov, "For Peace and Security in Asia").
81. *Asian Recorder*, 1972, pp. 10749, 10794; "A Talk with Pakistan's President Bhutto," *Newsweek*, 3 Apr. 1972; *International Affairs*, June 1972; Walter Sullivan, "Survey Says Soviet Leads in Sending Arms to Third World Nations," *New York Times*, 14 June 1972.
82. *Asian Recorder*, 1971, p. 10419; *Statesman Weekly*, 20 Nov. 1971.
83. M. S. Rajan, "Indo-Soviet Treaty and Non-alignment," *India News*, 10 Mar. 1972; *New York Times*, 29 Oct. 1971, 9 Nov. 1971.
84. *New York Times*, 8 Nov. 1971 and 13 Nov. 1971; *Asian Recorder*, 1971, p. 10512; *Statesman Weekly*, 27 Nov. 1971.
85. Nixon, *U.S. Foreign Policy for the 1970's*, p. 146.
86. *Ibid.*, pp. 145, 142.
87. For the texts of General Assembly Resolution 2793 (XXVI) and Security Council Resolution 307 (1971) see *Pakistan Horizon*, No. 1, 1972.
88. *New York Times*, 13 Feb. 1972; "An Interview with the President," *Time*, 3 Jan. 1972 (see also "Soviet Aide Talks with Mrs. Gandhi" in *New York Times*, 13 Dec. 1971, and "Political Commentary" by S. Viswam in *Statesman Weekly*, 18 Dec. 1971).

Indian spokesmen deny that India had declared a cease-fire under Soviet pressure but no Soviet representative has controverted Nixon's positive statement. It stands to reason that, having the upper hand in the fighting, India should have liked to inflict a decisive defeat on the Pakistani forces on the western front also, and to occupy Pakistani-controlled Kashmir which she claims belongs to her. These actions would have been the most effective way of reducing Pakistan's capacity to cause concern to India in the future.

On 17 October 1971, when war was imminent, the Indian defense minister had declared that "we shall go right up to Lahore and Sialkot [in West Pakistan] and shall not come back whatever the consequences." *Asian Recorder*, 1971, p. 10467. The same official admitted, after the cease-fire, that arrangements had been made to rush troops from the Bangladesh front to the western theater of war "for the final kill" but Mrs. Gandhi's decision to declare a cease-fire changed the situation. *Boston Globe*, 31 Jan. 1972.

89. Jack Anderson, "Why I Blew the Whistle," *St. Paul Pioneer Press Parade Magazine*, 13 Feb. 1972; Benjamin Welles, "U.S. Says Soviet Moves Vessels to Indian Ocean," *New York Times*, 13 Dec. 1971.
90. Anderson, "Why I Blew the Whistle"; *New York Times*, 16 Dec. 1971.
91. *New York Times*, 12 Aug. 1971.
92. Nixon, *U.S. Foreign Policy for the 1970's*, p. 145.
93. *Minneapolis Tribune*, 29 Nov. 1972; *New York Times*, 4 Oct. 1972.
94. Nixon, *U.S. Foreign Policy for the 1970's*, p. 150; *India News*, 3 Dec. 1971.
95. *New York Times*, 31 Dec. 1971.

Notes for pages 214–222

96. *Dawn*, 20 Feb. 1972.
97. *Dawn*, 2 July 1971; *Asian Recorder*, 1971, p. 10298.
98. *Asian Recorder*, 1971, p. 10473; *New York Times*, 31 Mar. 1972; *Weekly Commentary and Pakistan News Digest*, 11 May 1973.
99. *Dawn*, 5 Mar. 1972.
100. For instance see Mrs. Gandhi's statement to this effect made as recently as December 1970: *India News*, 25 Dec. 1970.
101. In the National Assembly on 14 Apr. 1972 (*Pakistan Affairs*, 16 May 1972).
102. For the text of the Simla agreement see *Pakistan Horizon*, No. 3, 1972.
103. *Weekly Commentary and Pakistan News Digest*, 22 Sept. 1972; *Dawn*, 20 Dec. 1972.
104. *Dawn*, 15 Sept. 1972 and 4 Dec. 1972. For the figures given here see *Asian Recorder*, 1972, p. 10616, and *New York Times*, 17 Apr. 1972, and President Bhutto's article, "Pakistan Builds Anew," in *Foreign Affairs*, Apr. 1973. The vicious circle of revenge and counterrevenge would also put in mortal danger the lives of settlers of Bihari origin and others in Bangladesh believed to have sided with the West Pakistani army. Many Biharis have already been slaughtered in cold blood. And this is not all. Zillur Rahman, secretary general of the Awami League, has threatened that if Bengali officials are put on trial in Pakistan, Bangladesh would ask India to hand over all civilian Pakistani prisoners for trial in Bangladesh (*Dawn*, 9 June 1973). Pakistanis would also demand that the Bengalis who terrorized and murdered West Pakistanis and other non-Bengalis be tried for their atrocities.
105. *Pakistan Affairs*, 1 Sept. 1972; see also editorials in the *New York Times*, dated 22 Mar. 1972 and 31 Jan. 1973, stating that India's detention of the Pakistani prisoners contravenes international law.
106. *Statesman Weekly*, 20 May 1972 and 15 July 1972. See also the statement of the Chinese representative in the Security Council on 10 Aug. 1972 quoting Mrs. Gandhi as having said that, pending the "final settlement" of the Jammu and Kashmir dispute, she would not permit the repatriation of Pakistani prisoners of war.
107. The People's Republic of China had been seated in the United Nations, in place of Nationalist China, in October 1971, a few weeks before the Indo-Pakistani war.
108. President Bhutto's press conference on 10 Aug. 1972 (transcript distributed by the Embassy of Pakistan, Washington, D.C.); *Weekly Commentary and Pakistan News Digest*, 24 Nov. 1972; *Peking Review*, 8 Sept. 1972.
109. *New York Times*, 2 Dec. 1972.
110. *India News*, 27 Apr. 1973.
111. *Pakistan Affairs*, 1 May 1973.
112. *Dawn*, 24 Apr. 1973; "Pakistan, Time for Forgiveness," *Time*, 23 July 1973.
113. *Statesman Weekly*, 21 Apr. 1973; *Dawn*, 26 Apr. 1973; *Pakistan Times*, 7 May 1973; *India News*, 18 May 1973. Swaran Singh estimated the number of these Bengalis to be between 5000 and 6000 (*Statesman Weekly*, 12 May 1973). A Pakistani official statement gave the number as 211 (*Pakistan Affairs*, 16 June 1973); *Pakistan Affairs*, 1 June 1973 and 16 June 1973; *Statesman Weekly*, 16 June 1973.
114. *Dawn*, 12 May 1973 and 22 May 1973; *Pakistan Affairs*, 1 June 1973; *India News*, 1 June 1973; *New York Times*, 1 Aug. 1973. The relevant passage in the Simla agreement reads: "The two countries are resolved to settle their differences by peaceful means through bilateral negotiations or by any other peaceful means mutually agreed upon between them."
115. For the text of the agreement which was released simultaneously in New Delhi and Rawalpindi on 29 August 1973 see the *Times*, 30 Aug. 1973.

Notes for pages 223–234

116. *Statesman Weekly*, 11 Mar. 1972.
117. *Ibid.*, 21 Oct. 1972, 28 Oct. 1972, 30 Sept. 1972, and 7 Oct. 1972.
118. *India News*, 8 Dec. 1972; editorial, "Indian Love Call," *New York Times*, 6 Dec. 1972.
119. *New York Times*, 8 Feb. 1973 and 20 Feb. 1973.
120. *India News*, 9 Mar. 1973; *New York Times*, 15 Mar. 1973.
121. *India News*, 23 Mar. 1973; *Statesman Weekly*, 17 Mar. 1973.
122. *Statesman Weekly*, 17 Mar. 1973; *New York Times*, 16 Mar. 1973. Economic aid to Pakistan had been resumed on 19 June 1972 (*New York Times*, 20 June 1972).
123. *Statesman Weekly*, 19 May 1973.
124. *India News*, 21 Dec. 1973 and 4 Jan. 1974; *Statesman Weekly*, 1 Dec. 1973; *New Times*, No. 49, 1973. See also Smith Hempstone, "Seeds of Foreign Aid Produce a Bitter Harvest," *Minneapolis Tribune*, 29 July 1973: "Of all the billions of dollars of the American taxpayers' money that profligate administrations have sown around the world in the past quarter-century, none has reaped such a bitter harvest as the $10 billion pumped into India since 1950."
125. *India News*, 12 May 1972; *New York Times*, 1 Dec. 1972; *India News*, 9 Feb. 1973 and 1 Dec. 1972.
126. *Dawn*, 10 Nov. 1972; Pakistani spokesman quoted in *Peking Review*, 1 Dec. 1972.
127. *Weekly Commentary and Pakistan News Digest*, 23 June 1972; *Dawn*, 13 Nov. 1972; *Pakistan Affairs*, 1 June 1973; *Weekly Commentary and Pakistan News Digest*, 18 May 1973; *New York Times*, 26 July 1973 and 19 Sept. 1973. See also Bernard Weinraub's article "India and Pakistan Vying in Mideast" in *New York Times*, 5 July 1973.
128. *Pakistan Affairs*, 1 Mar. 1973; *Weekly Commentary and Pakistan News Digest*, 9 Mar. 1973. Soviet-backed Iraq and United States–backed Iran are rivals for influence in the Persian Gulf and there has been tension between them because of a dispute relating to territory on the Shatt al-Arab near Abadan and Iran's occupation of three islands in the Persian Gulf. It was disclosed in Washington on 21 February 1973 that Iran in recent months had contracted to buy more than two billion dollars' worth of military equipment. This, State and Defense Department officials stated, would reinforce "a point of stability" in the Persian Gulf area. *New York Times*, 22 Feb. 1973. Iraq's growing ties with India were underscored by the conclusion between them of seven economic agreements in one sitting on 7 April 1973. One of these stipulated the supply to India of 30 million tons of Iraqi crude oil over a period of ten years. *Asian Recorder*, 1973, p. 11396. For Nehru's question "Against whom is this common defense policy?" see *Rajya Sabha, Official Report*, 4 May 1959, col. 1676.
129. *Dawn*, 4 Dec. 1972.
130. Phillips Talbot, president of the Asia Society, New York, in *Asia Society Calendar*, Jan. 1973; Ajit Bhattacharjea, "Misuse of President's Rule, Waning Confidence in Democracy," *Times of India*, 16 July 1973; *Statesman Weekly*, 28 Apr. 1973 and 26 May 1973. See also Bernard Weinraub's dispatches from New Delhi, "India's Problems Growing Worse," in *New York Times*, 8 June 1973, and "India Marks Her 26th Year of Independence in an Air of Gloom," in *New York Times*, 15 Aug. 1973; and Kuldip Nayar's article, "Between the Lines, Return of Old Frustrations," in *Statesman Weekly*, 26 May 1973.
131. See "Graft, Confusion Peril Bengalis," *New York Times*, 4 Oct. 1972; "Waldheim Reports Bangladesh Faces Threat of Famine Again," *New York Times*, 2 Jan. 1973; Khushwant Singh, "Bangladesh, After the First Year: Will It Ever Be a Workable Country?" *New York Times Magazine*, 21 Jan. 1973; "Rising Bangladesh Unrest Marked by 2000 Killings," *New York Times*, 11 June 1973.
132. *New York Times*, 6 Mar. 1972 and 25 Oct. 1972; *New Times*, No. 37, 1972; *Dawn*, 3 Mar. 1973; *New Times*, No. 22, 1973.

Chapter 9. Retrospect and Prospect

1. Radhakrishnan, *Eastern Religions and Western Thought*, p. 340.
2. Quoted by S. Abid Husain, *Indian Culture*, p. 38.
3. For instance see Qureshi, *The Muslim Community of the Indo-Pakistan Subcontinent*, pp. 167–168.
4. N. Savelyev, "Monopoly Drive in India," *International Affairs*, No. 4, 1967.
5. According to President Ayub Khan there is no specific mention of any particular system of government in the Quran and a country should have "that democratic type of the government, which was in the line of the people's thinking, environment and circumstances and [best] for the solution of the people's problems." *Dawn*, 21 Sept. 1968.
6. Clement R. Attlee, *Empire into Commonwealth*, p. 41.
7. Clement R. Attlee in *Freedom in a Democracy*, p. 9.
8. Chirol, *India*, p. 99. The opposition to the bill was spearheaded by the most popular Hindu leader of the time, Bal Gangadhar Tilak, whose epithet, Lokamanya, meant "respected by the people."
9. For a good account of the enormous difficulties which the Nehru government encountered in getting these bills passed see Gene Overstreet, "The Hindu Code Bill," in James B. Christoph, ed., *Cases in Comparative Politics*, pp. 413–440. Among those opposed to the proposed changes were such stalwarts from the upper echelon of the ruling Congress party itself as the Congress president, Sitaramayya, and the president of India, Rajendra Prasad.
10. *Dawn*, 29 Oct. 1966.

Bibliography of Sources Cited

Bibliography of Sources Cited

Books

Acheson, Dean. *Present at the Creation.* New York: W. W. Norton, 1969.
Afzal, M. Rafique, ed. *Guftar-i-Iqbal* [Words of Iqbal]. Lahore: Research Society of Pakistan, University of the Punjab, 1969.
———. *Speeches and Statements of Quaid-i-Millat Liaquat Ali Khan, 1941–51.* Lahore: Research Society of Pakistan, University of the Punjab, 1966.
Ahmad, Aziz. *Studies in Islamic Culture in the Indian Environment.* Oxford: Clarendon Press, 1964.
Ahmad, Jamil-ud-Din, ed. *Speeches and Writings of Mr. Jinnah.* Vol. I. 6th ed. Lahore: Muhammad Ashraf, 1960.
———. *Some Recent Speeches and Writings of Mr. Jinnah.* Vol. II. 1st ed. Lahore: Muhammad Ashraf, 1947.
Ahmad, Kamruddin. *The Social History of East Pakistan.* Dacca: Crescent Book Center, 1967.
Ahmad, Mushtaq. *The United Nations and Pakistan.* Karachi: Pakistan Institute of International Affairs, 1955.
Ahmad, Q. *The Wahabi Movement in India.* 1st ed. Calcutta: Firma K. L. Mukhopadhyay, 1966.
Ali, Chaudhri Muhammad. *The Emergence of Pakistan.* New York: Columbia University Press, 1967.
Ali, Tariq. *Pakistan: Military Rule or People's Power.* New York: William Morrow, 1970.
All-India Congress Committee. *Indian National Congress Resolutions on Foreign Policy, 1947–57.* New Delhi, n.d.
Ambedkar, B. R. *Pakistan, or The Partition of India.* Bombay: Thacker, 1946.
Amery, L. S. *India and Freedom.* London: Oxford University Press, 1942.
Andrews, C. F. *Mahatma Gandhi's Ideas.* New York: Macmillan, 1930.
Attlee, Clement R. Attlee, earl. *Empire into Commonwealth.* London: Oxford University Press, 1961.
———. *Freedom in a Democracy.* Modern World Series. London: Central Office of Information, n.d.
——— and Francis Williams. *Twilight of Empire: Memoirs of Prime Minister Clement Attlee.* New York: A. S. Barnes, 1962.

BIBLIOGRAPHY

Azad, Maulana Abul Kalam. *India Wins Freedom.* New York: Longmans, Green, 1960.
Aziz, K. K. *The Indian Khilafat Movement, 1915–1933: A Documentary Record.* Karachi: Pakistan Publishers, 1972.
Bailey, Thomas A. *A Diplomatic History of the American People.* 7th ed. New York: Appleton-Century-Crofts, 1964.
Balabushevich, V. V., and A. M. Dyakov. *A Contemporary History of India.* New Delhi: People's Publishing House, 1964.
Barnds, William J. *India, Pakistan and the Great Powers.* New York: Praeger, 1972.
Bazaz, Prem Nath. *The History of the Struggle for Freedom in Kashmir.* New Delhi: Kashmir Publishing Co., 1954.
———. *Inside Kashmir.* Srinagar: Kashmir Publishing Co., 1941.
———. *Kashmir in Crucible.* New Delhi: Pamposh Publications, 1967.
Bhutto, Zulfikar Ali. *The Great Tragedy.* Karachi: People's Party, 1971.
———. *The Myth of Independence.* London: Oxford University Press, 1969.
———. *The Quest for Peace.* Karachi: Pakistan Institute of International Affairs, 1964.
Birdwood, Christopher Bromhead Birdwood, baron. *Two Nations and Kashmir.* London: Robert Hale, 1956.
Biswas, S. C., ed. *Gandhi, Theory and Practice, Social Impact and Contemporary Relevance.* Simla: Indian Institute of Advanced Study, 1969.
Bolitho, Hector. *Jinnah, Creator of Pakistan.* London: John Murray, 1954.
Bose, Subhas Chandra. *The Indian Struggle.* London: Asia Publishing House, 1964.
Bowles, Chester. *Ambassador's Report.* New York: Harper & Row, 1954.
Brailsford, H. N. *Subject India.* New York: John Day, 1943.
Brecher, Michael. *India and World Politics: Krishna Menon's View of the World.* New York: Praeger, 1968.
———. *Nehru: A Political Biography.* London: Oxford University Press, 1959.
Bright, J. S., ed. *Before and After Independence* (J. Nehru's speeches, 1922–57). New Delhi: Indian Printing Works, n.d.
Bulganin, N. A., and N. S. Khrushchev. *Visit of Friendship to India, Burma and Afghanistan.* Moscow: Foreign Languages Publishing House, 1956.
Burke, S. M. *Pakistan's Foreign Policy: An Historical Analysis.* London: Oxford University Press, 1973.
Callard, Keith. *Pakistan: A Political Study.* London: George Allen & Unwin, 1957.
Campbell-Johnson, Alan. *Mission with Mountbatten.* London: Robert Hale, 1951.
Chaudhuri, Nirad C. *The Continent of Circe.* London: Chatto & Windus, 1965.
Chirol, Valentine. *India.* London: Ernest Benn, 1930.
———. *Indian Unrest.* London: Macmillan, 1910.
Chopra, Pran, ed. *The Challenge of Bangladesh.* Bombay: Popular Prakashan, 1971.
Choudhury, G. W. *Documents and Speeches on the Constitution of Pakistan.* Dacca: Green Book House, 1967.
Christoph, James B., ed. *Cases in Comparative Politics.* Boston: Little, Brown, 1965.
Churchill, Winston S. *The Second World War,* vol. IV: *The Hinge of Fate.* Boston: Houghton Mifflin, 1950 (reprinted New York: Bantam Books, 1962).
Connell, John. *Auchinleck.* London: Cassell, 1959.
Coupland, R. *Report on the Constitutional Problem in India,* part I: *The Indian Problem, 1833–1935.* London: Oxford University Press, 1943.
———. *Report on the Constitutional Problem in India,* part II: *Indian Politics, 1936–1942.* London: Oxford University Press, 1943.
Crocker, Walter. *Nehru: A Contemporary's Estimate.* London: George Allen & Unwin, 1966.

BIBLIOGRAPHY

Dalai Lama. *My Land and My People.* London: Weidenfeld & Nicholson, 1962.
Desai, Mahadev H. *Day-to-Day with Gandhi: Secretary's Diary,* vol. II: *From April 1919 to October 1920.* Rajghat, Varanasi: Sarva Seva Sangh Prakashan, 1968.
De Toledano, Ralph. *Nixon.* New York: Henry Holt, 1956.
Dutt, R. Palme. *The Crisis of Britain and the British Empire.* London: Lawrence & Wishart, 1957.
―――. *India Today and Tomorrow.* London: Lawrence & Wishart, 1955.
Galbraith, John Kenneth. *Ambassador's Journal.* Boston: Houghton Mifflin, 1969.
Gandhi, M. K. *All Men Are Brothers: Life and Thoughts of Mahatma Gandhi as Told in His Own Words.* Paris: UNESCO, 1958.
―――. *An Autobiography, or The Story of My Experiments with Truth.* Ahmedabad: Navajivan Publishing House, 1945.
―――. *Satyagraha* [Nonviolent Resistance]. Ahmedabad: Navajivan Publishing House, 1951.
―――. *Towards Lasting Peace.* Bombay: Bharatiya Vidya Bhavan, 1956.
―――. *Truth Is God.* Ahmedabad: Navajivan Publishing House, 1969.
Garratt, G. T., ed. *The Legacy of India.* Oxford: Clarendon Press, 1951.
Ghosh, Sudhir. *Gandhi's Emissary.* Boston: Houghton Mifflin, 1967.
Gupta, Anand, ed. *India and Lenin.* New Delhi: New Literature, 1960.
Gupta, Karunakar. *India in World Politics: A Period of Transition, Fall 1956 to Spring 1960.* Calcutta: Scientific Book Agency, 1969.
Gwyer, Sir Maurice, and A. Appadorai, eds. *Speeches and Documents on the Indian Constitution, 1921–47.* Vol. II. London: Oxford University Press, 1957.
Hakim, K. A. *Islam and Communism.* Lahore: Institute of Islamic Culture, 1962.
Hardinge, Charles Hardinge, baron. *My Indian Years.* London: John Murray, 1948.
Hasan, K. Sarwar, ed. *Documents on the Foreign Relations of Pakistan: China, India, and Pakistan.* Karachi: Pakistan Institute of International Affairs, 1966.
―――. *Documents on the Foreign Relations of Pakistan: The Transfer of Power.* Karachi: Pakistan Institute of International Affairs, 1966.
Heber, Reginald. *Narrative of a Journey through the Upper Provinces of India, [and] to Madras and the Southern Provinces.* Vol. I. London: John Murray, 1849.
Heimsath, Charles H., and Surjit Mansingh. *A Diplomatic History of Modern India.* Calcutta: Allied Publishers, 1971.
Hinton, Harold C. *The Bear at the Gate.* Washington, D.C., and Stanford, Calif.: American Enterprise Institute for Public Policy Research and Hoover Institution on War, Revolution and Peace, Stanford University, 1971.
Hodson, H. V. *The Great Divide.* London: Hutchinson, 1969.
Hunter, W. W. *The Indian Musalmans.* Lahore: Premier Book House, 1964.
Husain, S. Abid. *Indian Culture.* Bombay: Asia Publishing House, 1963.
Husain, Syed Shabbir. *Lengthening Shadows.* Rawalpindi: Mujahid Publications, 1970.
Hutheesing, Krishna Nehru, ed. *Nehru's Letters to His Sister.* London: Faber & Faber, 1963.
Ikram, S. M. *Modern Muslim India and the Birth of Pakistan.* Lahore: Sh. Muhammad Ashraf, 1965.
Iqbal, Afzal, ed. *Select Writings and Speeches of Maulana Mohamed Ali.* Vol. I. Lahore: Sh. Muhammad Ashraf, 1963.
Iqbal, Javid. *The Ideology of Pakistan and Its Implementation.* Lahore: Sh. Ghulam Ali & Sons, 1959.
―――, ed. *Stray Reflections: A Notebook of Allama Iqbal.* Lahore: Sh. Ghulam Ali & Sons, 1961.
Iqbal, Muhammad. *Letters of Iqbal to Jinnah.* Lahore: Sh. Muhammad Ashraf, n.d.

BIBLIOGRAPHY

Ispahani, M. A. H. *Quaid-i-Azam, as I Knew Him*. Karachi: Forward Publications Trust, 1966.
Jain, Girilal. *Panchsheela and After*. Bombay: Asia Publishing, 1960.
Jinnah, M. A. *Presidential Addresses of Qaid-e-Azam*. Delhi: All India Muslim League, 1946.
———. *Speeches as Governor-General of Pakistan, 1947–1948*. Karachi: Government of Pakistan, [1948].
Kahin, George McT. *The Asian-African Conference*. Ithaca, N.Y.: Cornell University Press, 1956.
Kamal, Kazi. *Sheikh Mujibur Rahman: Man and Politician*. Dacca: Kazi Giasuddin Ahmed, 1970.
Karanjia, R. K. *The Mind of Mr. Nehru*. London: George Allen & Unwin, 1960.
Karunakaran, K. P. *India in World Affairs (August 1947–January 1950)*. London: Oxford University Press, 1952.
Kennedy, John F. *The Strategy of Peace*. New York: Harper & Row, 1960.
Khadduri, Majid. *War and Peace in the Law of Islam*. Baltimore: John Hopkins Press, 1962.
Khaliquzzaman, Chaudhuri. *Only If They Knew It!* Karachi, 1965.
———. *Pathway to Pakistan*. Lahore: Longmans, Green, 1961.
Khan, Aga [Sultan Muhammad Shah]. *India in Transition*. Bombay: Bennett Coleman, 1918.
———. *The Memoirs of Aga Khan*. New York: Simon & Schuster, 1954.
Khan, Major General Fazal Muqeem. *The Story of the Pakistan Army*. Karachi: Oxford University Press, 1963.
Khan, Liaquat Ali. *Pakistan, the Heart of Asia*. Cambridge, Mass.: Harvard University Press, 1950.
Khan, M. Ayub. *Friends Not Masters*. London: Oxford University Press, 1967.
———. *Speeches and Statements*. Vols. IV and VII. Karachi: Pakistan Publications, Government of Pakistan, n.d.
Khan Bahadur, Syed Ahmed. *Review on Dr. Hunter's Indian Musalmans: Are They Bound in Conscience to Rebel against the Queen?* Lahore: Premier Book House, n.d.
Korbel, Josef. *Danger in Kashmir*. Princeton, N.J.: Princeton University Press, 1966.
Kundra, J. C. *Indian Foreign Policy*. Groningen (Netherlands): J. B. Wolters, 1955.
Lamb, Alastair. *Asian Frontiers*. New York: Praeger, 1968.
———. *The China-India Border*. London: Oxford University Press, 1964.
———. *The Kashmir Problem*. New York: Praeger, 1966.
Linus, Joseph. *The Sino-Indian Border Dispute*. Singapore: Malaysia Publications, 1965.
Luard, Evan, ed. *The Cold War: A Re-appraisal*. New York: Praeger, 1964.
Lumby, E. W. R. *The Transfer of Power in India*. London: George Allen & Unwin, 1947.
Mahajan, Mehr Chand. *Looking Back*. New York: Asia Publishing House, 1963.
Majumdar, A. K. *Advent of Independence*. Bombay: Bharatiya Vidya Bhavan, 1963.
Majumdar, R. C. *History of the Freedom Movement in India*. Vols. I and III. Calcutta: Firma K. L. Mukhopadhyay, 1962, 1963.
Malik, Hafeez. *Moslem Nationalism in India and Pakistan*. Washington, D.C.: Public Affairs Press, 1963.
Mansergh, Nicholas, ed. *Documents and Speeches on British Commonwealth Affairs, 1931–1952*. 2 vols. London: Oxford University Press, 1953.
Maxwell, Neville. *India's China War*. London: Jonathan Cape, 1970.
Mende, Tibor. *Nehru: Conversations on India and World Affairs*. New York: Braziller, 1956.

BIBLIOGRAPHY

Menon, K. P. S. *The Flying Troika: Extracts from a Diary by K. P. S. Menon, India's Ambassador to Russia, 1952–61*. London: Oxford University Press, 1963.
———. *India and the Cold War*. Bombay: Bharatiya Vidya Bhavan, 1966.
Menon, V. P. *The Story of the Integration of the Indian States*. Bombay: Orient Longmans, 1961.
———. *The Transfer of Power in India*. Princeton, N.J.: Princeton University Press, 1957.
Minto, Mary, countess of. *India, Minto and Morley, 1905–1910*. London: Macmillan, 1934.
Misra, K. P. *Studies in Indian Foreign Policy*. Delhi: Vikas Publications, 1969.
Moon, Penderel. *Divide and Quit*. London: Chatto & Windus, 1962.
Moraes, Frank. *Jawaharlal Nehru: A Biography*. Bombay: Jaico Publishing House, 1962.
———. *Nehru, Sunlight and Shadow*. Bombay: Jaico Publishing House, 1964.
Mosley, Leonard. *The Last Days of the British Raj*. London: Weidenfeld & Nicholson, 1961.
Mountbatten, Louis Mountbatten, earl. *Time Only to Look Forward*. London: Nicholas Kaye, 1949.
Muhammad, Shan. *Sir Syed Ahmad Khan*. Meerut: Meenakshi Prakashan, 1969.
Mukerjee, Hirendranath. *India's Struggle for Freedom*. Calcutta: National Book Agency, 1962.
Mukherjee, S. N., ed. *St. Antony's Papers, No. 18*. London: Oxford University Press, 1966.
Murphy, Ray. *Last Viceroy*. London: Jarrolds, 1948.
Murty, K. S. *Indian Foreign Policy*. Calcutta: Scientific Book Agency, 1964.
Nadvi, R. A. J., ed. *Selections from Muhammad Ali's Comrade*. Lahore: Muhammad Ali Academy, 1965.
Naik, J. A. *Soviet Policy towards India*. Delhi: Vikas Publications, 1970.
Nasser, Gamal Abdel. *The Philosophy of the Revolution*. N.p.: National Publishing House, 1954.
Natwar-Singh, K., ed. *The Legacy of Nehru*. New York: John Day, 1965.
Nehru, Jawaharlal. *An Autobiography*. London: Bodley Head, 1958.
———. *A Bunch of Old Letters*. New York: Asia Publishing House, 1960.
———. *Discovery of India*. London: Meridian, 1960.
———. *Eighteen Months in India*. Allahabad: Kitabistan, 1938.
———. *India's Foreign Policy*. Delhi: Publications Division, Government of India, 1961.
———. *India's Freedom*. London: George Allen & Unwin, 1962.
———. *Jawaharlal's Discovery of America*. Delhi: East and West Publishers, 1950.
———. *Soviet Russia: Some Random Sketches and Impressions*. Bombay: Chetana, 1929 (reprinted, 1949).
———. *Speeches*. Vols. I–IV. Delhi: Publications Division, Government of India, 1958, 1963, 1964.
———. *The Unity of India*. New York: John Day, 1942.
———. *Visit to America*. New York: John Day, 1950.
———, Arnold Toynbee, and Clement R. Attlee. *India and the World*. New Delhi: Allied Publishers, 1962.
Noorani, A. G. *Our Credulity and Negligence*. Bombay: Ramdas G. Bhaktal, 1963.
Norman, Dorothy, ed. *Nehru: The First Sixty Years*. 2 vols. London: Bodley Head, 1965.
O'Malley, L. S. S., ed. *Modern India and the West*. London: Oxford University Press, 1941.
Pakistan Historical Society. *A History of the Freedom Movement*. Vol. III, part II. Karachi: Pakistan Historical Society, 1961.

Bibliography

Pandit, Vijaya Lakshmi. *The Evolution of India.* London: Oxford University Press, 1958.
Panikkar, K. M. *Hinduism and the West.* Chandigarh: Punjab University Publication Bureau, 1964.
———. *India and the Indian Ocean.* London: George Allen & Unwin, 1945.
———. *In Two Chinas.* London: George Allen & Unwin, 1955.
———. *A Survey of Indian History.* London: Asia Publishing House, 1960.
Panjabi, K. L. *The Indomitable Sardar.* Bombay: Bharatiya Vidya Bhavan, 1964.
Philips, C. H. *The Evolution of India and Pakistan.* London: Oxford University Press, 1962.
——— and M. D. Wainwright, eds. *The Partition of India.* London: George Allen & Unwin, 1970.
Pirzada, Syed Sharifuddin. *Evolution of Pakistan.* Lahore: All-Pakistan Legal Decisions, 1963.
Polak, H. S. L., H. N. Brailsford, and Lord Pethic-Lawrence. *Mahatma Gandhi.* London: Odhams Press, 1949.
Power, Paul F., ed. *India's Non-aligned Policy: Strength and Weaknesses, Problems in Asian Civilization.* Boston: D. C. Heath, 1967.
Prasad, Bimla. *The Origins of Indian Foreign Policy.* Calcutta: Bookland Private, 1962.
Prasad, Rajendra. *India Divided.* Bombay: Hind Kitabs, 1947.
———. *Speeches of President Rajendra Prasad, 1952–1956.* Delhi: Government of India, 1958.
Pyarelal. *Mahatma Gandhi: The Last Phase.* 2 vols. Ahmedabad: Navajivan Publishing House, 1956, 1958.
Qureshi, Ishtiaq Husain. *The Muslim Community of the Indo-Pakistan Subcontinent.* The Hague: Mouton, 1962.
Radhakrishnan, S. *Eastern Religions and Western Thought.* 2nd ed. New York: Oxford University Press, 1940 (reprinted in Galaxy edition, 1959).
———. *The Hindu View of Life.* London: George Allen & Unwin, 1965.
Rahman, Sheikh Mujibur. *6-Point Formula: Our Right to Live.* Dacca: Pioneer Press, 1966.
Rajan, M. S. *India in World Affairs, 1954–56.* London: Asia Publishing House, 1964.
———. *Non-alignment: India and the Future.* Mysore: University of Mysore, 1970.
Rajkumar, N. V., ed. *The Background of India's Foreign Policy.* Delhi: Navin Press, 1952.
Range, Willard. *Jawaharlal Nehru's World View.* Athens: University of Georgia Press, 1961.
Richardson, H. E. *Tibet and Its History.* London: Oxford University Press, 1962.
Rose, Saul, ed. *Politics in Southern Aisa.* London: Macmillan, 1963.
Russell, Wilfred. *Indian Summer.* Bombay: Thacker, 1951.
Sachau, Edward C., trans. *Alberuni's India.* Lahore: Government of West Pakistan, 1962.
Sayeed, Khalid Bin. *Pakistan: The Formative Stage.* Karachi: Pakistan Publishing House, 1960.
Schlesinger, Arthur M., Jr. *A Thousand Days.* Boston: Houghton Mifflin, 1965.
Schuster, Sir George, and Guy Wint. *India and Democracy.* London: Macmillan, 1941.
Seligman, Eustace. *What the United States Can Do about India.* New York: New York University Press, 1956.
"Shamloo" (pseudonym of Latif Ahmed Sherwani), ed. *Speeches and Statements of Iqbal.* Lahore: Al-Manar Academy, 1948.
Sharma, B. L. *The Kashmir Story.* New York: Asia Publishing House, 1967.

Bibliography

Sharma, D. N. *Afro-Asian Group in the U.N.* Allahabad: Chaitanya Publishing House, 1969.
Sheean, Vincent. *Nehru.* London: Victor Gollanz, 1960.
Sherwani, Latif Ahmed. *Foreign Policy of Pakistan.* Karachi: Allies Book Corporation, 1964.
Siddiqi, Aslam. *Pakistan Seeks Security.* Lahore: Longmans, Green, 1960.
———. *A Path for Pakistan.* Karachi: Pakistan Publishing House, 1964.
Sinha, Sasadhar. *Indian Independence in Perspective.* Bombay: Asia Publishing House, 1964.
Smith, Wilfred Cantwell. *Islam in Modern History.* Princeton, N.J.: Princeton University Press, 1957 (reprinted, New York: New American Library Mentor, 1959).
Stebbins, R. P. *The United States in World Affairs.* New York: Harper, 1956.
Stein, Arthur. *India and the Soviet Union.* Chicago: University of Chicago Press, 1969.
Stephens, Ian. *Pakistan.* London: Ernest Benn, 1963.
Tahmankar, D. V. *Sardar Patel.* London: George Allen & Unwin, 1970.
Talbot, Phillips, and S. L. Poplai. *India and America: A Study of Their Relations.* New York: Harper, 1958.
Tendulkar, D. G. *Mahatma.* Vols. III, V, VIII. Delhi: Publications Division, Government of India, 1961, 1962, 1963.
Thien, Ton That. *India and Southeast Asia, 1947–1960.* Geneva: Librairie Droz, 1963.
Toynbee, Arnold. *The World and the West.* New York: Oxford University Press, 1953.
Truman, Harry S. *Memoirs*, vol. II: *Years of Trial and Hope.* New York: Doubleday, 1956.
Vahid, Syed Abdul, ed. *Thoughts and Reflections of Iqbal.* Lahore: Sh. Muhammad Ashraf, 1964.
Van Eekelen, W. F. *Indian Foreign Policy and the Border Dispute with China.* The Hague: Martinus Nijhoff, 1964.
Varma, Shanti Prasad. *Struggle for the Himalayas.* Delhi: University Publishers, 1965.
Walker, Patrick Gordon. *The Commonwealth.* London: Mercury Books, 1965.
Wasti, Syed Razvi. *Lord Minto and the Indian Nationalist Movement, 1905 to 1910.* London: Clarendon Press, 1964.
Wheeler-Bennett, John W. *King George VI: His Life and Reign.* New York: St. Martin's Press, 1958.
Williams, L. F. Rushbrook. *The State of Pakistan.* Rev. ed. London: Faber & Faber, 1966.
Zafar, S. M. *Through the Crisis.* Lahore: Book Center, 1970.

Articles

Agwani, M. S. "India, Pakistan, and West Asia," *International Studies* (Delhi), July–Oct. 1966, pp. 158–166.
Ahmad, Ilyas. "Sovereignty in Islam," *Pakistan Horizon*, Dec. 1958, pp. 244–257.
Alavi, Hatim A. "Why Quaid Chose August 14," *Dawn*, 14 Aug. 1968.
Anderson, Jack. "Why I Blew the Whistle," *St. Paul Pioneer Press Parade Magazine*, 13 Feb. 1972.
Bhattacharjea, Ajit. "Misuse of President's Rule, Waning Confidence in Democracy," *Times of India*, 16 July 1973.
Bhutto, Zulfikar Ali. "Pakistan Builds Anew," *Foreign Affairs*, Apr. 1973, pp. 541–554.
Borisov, O. "For Peace and Security in Asia," *New Times*, No. 39, 1971.

BIBLIOGRAPHY

Bowles, Chester. "Evaluation of American Foreign Policy," *India Quarterly*, July–Sept. 1961, pp. 215–226.
Burke, S. M. "India's Offer of a No War Declaration to Pakistan: Its History and Import," *Pakistan Horizon*, 3rd Quarter 1972, pp. 22–37.
———. "Sino-Pakistani Relations," *Orbis*, Summer 1964, pp. 391–404.
Campbell-Johnson, Alan. "Reflections on the Transfer of Power," *Asiatic Review* (London), July 1952, pp. 163–182.
Carnell, Francis. "Political Ideas and Ideologies in South and South-East Asia," in Saul Rose, ed., *Politics in Southern Asia*. London: Macmillan, 1963.
Crankshaw, Edward. "The Polarisation of the Communist World," in Evan Luard, ed., *The Cold War: A Re-appraisal*. New York: Praeger, 1964.
Drummond, Roscoe. "What India Thinks," *New York Herald Tribune* (European ed.), 14 Nov. 1957.
Feldman, Herbert. "The Communal Problem in the Indo-Pakistan Subcontinent: Some Current Implications," *Pacific Affairs*, Summer 1969, pp. 145–163.
Fisher, Margaret W. "India's Jawaharlal Nehru," *Asian Survey*, June 1967, pp. 363–373.
Gandhi, M. K. "Gandhi to Chiang Kai-shek," in "Political War," ed. J. Alvarez del Vayo, *Nation*, 24 Oct. 1942, pp. 411–412.
"Graft, Confusion Peril Bengalis," *New York Times*, 4 Oct. 1972.
Hameed ud Din. "First Battle for Pakistan at Balakot," *Civil and Military Gazette*, 14 Aug. 1954.
Hang-Seng, Chen. "China and Pakistan: Old Friendship Recalled," *Dawn*, 18 Feb. 1964.
Hansen, G. Eric. "Indian Perceptions of the Chinese Communist Regime and Revolution," *Orbis*, Spring 1968, pp. 268–293.
Harrison, Selig S. "Troubled India and Her Neighbors," *Foreign Affairs*, Jan. 1965, pp. 312–330.
Hasan, Mumtaz. "The Background of the Partition of the Indo-Pakistan Subcontinent," in C. H. Philips and M. D. Wainwright, eds., *The Partition of India*. London: George Allen & Unwin, 1970.
Hempstone, Smith. "Seeds of Foreign Aid Produce a Bitter Harvest," *Minneapolis Tribune*, 29 July 1973.
"Interview with the President, An," *Time*, 3 Jan. 1972.
Ispahani, M. A. H. "The Foreign Policy of Pakistan, 1947–1964," *Pakistan Horizon*, 3rd Quarter 1964, pp. 231–252.
———. "Pacts and Aid," *Pakistan Horizon*, 2nd Quarter 1966, pp. 117–126.
Israel, Milton. "The Indian Party System and the 1971 Parliamentary Elections," *International Journal*, Summer 1972, pp. 437–447.
Jinnah, M. A. "Two Nations in India," *Time and Tide*, 9 Mar. 1940.
Kaleemi, Hassan. "The Message of Islam, the Way to Integration," *Dawn*, 5 Apr. 1968.
Khan, Hafeez-ur-Rahman. "Pakistan's Relations with U.A.R.," *Pakistan Horizon*, 3rd Quarter 1960, pp. 209–226.
Khan, Inamullah. "Pakistan's Role in Uniting World Muslims," *Dawn*, 23 Mar. 1968.
Khan, M. Ayub. "Pakistan Perspective," *Foreign Affairs*, July 1960, pp. 547–556.
———. "Strategic Problems of the Middle East," *Asian Review*, July 1958, pp. 220–228.
Mahadevan, T. M. P. "Indian Philosophy and the Quest for Peace," in Paul F. Power, ed., *India's Non-aligned Policy: Strength and Weaknesses, Problems in Asian Civilization*. Boston: D. C. Heath, 1967.
Malik, Hafeez. "Foreign Relations of Pakistan: An Interpretation." Presented on 18 Nov. 1967 to a symposium on Pakistan: The Modernization of an Islamic State, at Syracuse University, Syracuse, N.Y.

Bibliography

Malik, Majid. "Some Reminiscences," *Daily Jung* (Urdu), 26 Aug. 1968.
Mansoor, Zafar. "Pakistan's Contribution to Arabs' Cause," *Dawn*, 14 Aug. 1959.
Moraes, Frank. "Gandhi Ten Years After," *Foreign Affairs*, Jan. 1958, pp. 253–266.
Nayar, Kuldip. "Between the Lines, Return of Old Frustrations," *Statesman Weekly*, 26 May 1973.
Nikhamin, V. "India's Role in World Affairs," in K. P. Misra, ed., *Studies in Indian Foreign Policy*. Delhi: Vikas Publications, 1964.
Overstreet, Gene. "The Hindu Code Bill," in James B. Christoph, ed., *Cases in Comparative Politics*. Boston: Little, Brown, 1965.
"Pakistan, Time for Forgiveness," *Time*, 23 July 1973.
Pandit, Vijaya Lakshmi. "India's Foreign Policy," *Foreign Affairs*, Apr. 1956, pp. 432–440.
Radhakrishnan, S. "Hinduism," in G. T. Garratt, ed., *The Legacy of India*. Oxford: Clarendon Press, 1951.
———. "Hinduism and the West," in L. S. S. O'Malley, ed., *Modern India and the West*. London: Oxford University Press, 1941.
Rajan, M. S. "Indo-Soviet Treaty and Non-alignment," *India News*, 10 Mar. 1972.
Rangaswami, K. "Can't Congress Get to Sunshine Again?" *Hindu Weekly*, 26 Dec. 1966.
———. "U.S. Pressure Shows No Abatement," *Hindu Weekly Review*, 5 Sept. 1966.
Rofe, Husein. "What Does Islam Mean to Asia?" *Far Eastern Economic Review*, 3 Nov. 1966, pp. 257–260.
Savelyev, S. "Monopoly Drive in India," *International Affairs*, No. 4, 1967, pp. 35–40.
Singh, Khushwant. "Bangladesh, after the First Year: Will It Ever Be a Workable Country?" *New York Times Magazine*, 21 Jan. 1973.
"Sino-Pakistan Relations Rooted in the Past," *Dawn*, 5 Mar. 1965.
"Soviet Aide Talks with Mrs. Gandhi," *New York Times*, 13 Dec. 1971.
Spear, Percival. "Nehru," *Modern Asian Studies*, Jan. 1967, pp. 15–29.
Stephens, Ian. "The Image of Pakistan—II," *Morning News* (Dacca), 25 Feb. 1961.
Sullivan, Walter. "Survey Says Soviet Leads in Sending Arms to Third World Nations," *New York Times*, 14 June 1972.
"Talk with Pakistan's President Bhutto, A," *Newsweek*, 3 Apr. 1972, p. 42.
Templewood, Viscount. "Some Reflections on Recent Indian Constitutional History," *Asiatic Review*, Oct. 1952, pp. 243–248.
Trumbull, Robert. "Behind India's Foreign Policy," *New York Times Magazine*, 5 Oct. 1952.
Usvatov, Kudin, and A. Usvatov. "Soviet-Indian Treaty in Action," *New Times*, No. 39, 1971.
Viswam, S. "Political Commentary," *Statesman Weekly*, 18 Dec. 1971.
"Waldheim Reports Bangladesh Faces Threat of Famine Again," *New York Times*, 2 Jan. 1973.
Weinraub, Bernard. "India and Pakistan Vying in Mideast," *New York Times*, 5 July 1973.
———. "India's Problems Growing Worse," *New York Times*, 8 June 1973.
Zaman, Mukhtar. "Shibli Nomani," *Morning News* (Karachi), 11 Dec. 1966.

Official Documents

INDIA

Foreign Policy of India (Texts and Documents, 1947–64). Lok Sabha Secretariat, 1966.

BIBLIOGRAPHY

Indian Round Table Conference (12 November–19 January 1931). Cmd 3778. London: His Majesty's Stationery Office, 1931.
India's Fight for Territorial Integrity. Government of India, 1963.
Joint Committee on Indian Constitutional Reform (Session 1933–34). *Report*. Vol. I (part 1). London: His Majesty's Stationery Office, 1934.
Lok Sabha Debates.
Notes, Memoranda and Letters Exchanged between the Governments of India and China, White Papers, Nos. II, III, VIII, XII. Published by the Manager of Publications, Delhi.
Prime Minister on Sino-Indian Relations, vol. I: *In Parliament*. External Publicity Division, Ministry of External Affairs, 1961.
Rajya Sabha Debates.
Report of the Indian Statutory Commission (popularly called the Simon Commission), vol. I: *Survey*. Cmd 3568. London: His Majesty's Stationery Office, 1930.
Report of the Officials of the Government of India and the People's Republic of China on the Boundary Question. Government of India, 1961.
Report on Indian Constitutional Reforms (popularly called the Montagu-Chelmsford Report). Cd. 9109. London: His Majesty's Stationery Office, 1918 (reprinted, 1925).
Sedition Committee Report (popularly called the Rowlatt Report), 1918.
White Paper on Indian States. Government of India, 1950.
White Paper on Jammu and Kashmir. New Delhi: Government of India, 1948.

PAKISTAN

Ambassador Addresses a Press Conference, National Press Club, Washington, August 30, 1971, The. Washington, D.C.: Pakistan Embassy, n.d.
National Assembly of Pakistan Debates.
Negotiations between the Prime Ministers of Pakistan and India Regarding the Kashmir Dispute. Government of Pakistan, 1954.
No War Declaration and Canal Waters Dispute, Correspondence between the Prime Ministers of Pakistan and India. Government of Pakistan, n.d.
Summary of the White Paper on the Crisis in East Pakistan. Government of Pakistan, 5 Aug. 1971.
White Paper on the Crisis in East Pakistan. Government of Pakistan, 5 Aug. 1971.

PEOPLE'S REPUBLIC OF CHINA

Concerning the Question of Tibet. Peking: Foreign Languages Press, 1959.
Documents on the Sino-Indian Boundary Question. Peking: Foreign Languages Press, 1960.
Sino-Indian Boundary Question, The. Enlarged ed. Government of the People's Republic of China, 24 Oct. 1962.
Truth about How the Leaders of the CPSU Have Allied Themselves with India against China, The. Peking: Foreign Languages Press, n.d.

UNITED KINGDOM

Parliamentary Debates (Hansard), House of Commons and House of Lords.

UNITED STATES

Nixon, Richard M. *U.S. Foreign Policy for the 1970's: A Report to the Congress, February 9, 1972*. Washington, D.C.: Government Printing Office, 1972.
United States Department of State Bulletin.

BIBLIOGRAPHY

U.S.S.R.

Reply to Peking, A. Soviet Booklet No. 122. London, Sept. 1963.
History of the Communist Party of the Soviet Union. Moscow: Foreign Languages Publishing House, 1960.

United Nations Documents

General Assembly Official Records, 10 Dec. 1956, 20 Oct. 1959, 1 Oct. 1970, 5 Oct. 1971.
Report of Sir Owen Dixon to the Security Council. 15 Sept. 1950.

Press Digests

Asian Recorder.
Indian Annual Register, The, vol. I, Jan.–June 1947.
Indian Press Digests (University of California).

Miscellaneous

B.B.C. Monitoring Service, No. 21, 13 Sept. 1949, Part V (The Far East).
Nehru, Braj Kumar. "Text of Speech at the National Press Club Luncheon, Washington, D.C.," 21 November 1962. Distributed by the Information Service of India, Washington, D.C.

Index

Index

Abdullah, Sheikh Muhammad: dismissal from prime ministership of Kashmir, 143; sent to Pakistan by Nehru, 184; rearrested, 185; writes article on Kashmir, 185; verdict on Indo-Pakistani war of *1965*, 188; claims he is "Muslim first and Muslim afterwards," 252n36

Acheson, Dean: criticizes Indian logic, 128; criticizes Nehru, 129; criticizes Nehru's attitude toward Kashmir, 129, 142

Afghanistan: relations with Pakistan, 138, 153–154, 231–232

Ahmed, Aziz: negotiates agreement with India for release of internees, 222

Ahmed, Syed (of Rai Bareilly): inaugurates *mujahidin* movement, 34; killed at Balakot, 34

Akbar, the Great Moghul: his religious tolerance, 237–238; India's and Pakistan's poor appreciation of his example, 238

Aksai Chin plateau: China builds road through, 150–151; its importance to China, 165, 169; Indian and Chinese claim to, 168; Galbraith's view, 175

Alberuni: differences between Hindus and Muslims, 8

Ali, Maulana Muhammad: on British policy of "divide and rule," 10; says every Muslim is superior to Gandhi, 15; warns against basing Hindu-Muslim unity on external cause, 18; acts against his own warning, 19; leads Khilafat delegation to London, 38; contemplates suicide out of sympathy for Turkey, 44

All-India Muslim League. *See* Muslim League

Ambedkar, B. R.: restrictiveness of caste system, 13; allows Muslim claim to nationhood, 16; Hindu-Muslim civil war, 56

Amery, L. S.: on Cripps mission, 9

Ansari, M. A.: leads medical mission to Turkey, 37; what pan-Islamism meant to Indian Muslims, 44

Asian-African Conference (at Bandung): end of India's hope for Afro-Asian leadership, 151

Asian Relations Conference: convened by India, 76, 132; shunned by Muslim League, 132

Attlee, Clement (later Earl Attlee): criticizes Wavell plan, 63; says Wavell lacks finesse, 64; favors united India, 72; hopes partition of India will not endure, 73

Auchinleck, Field Marshal Sir Claude: Indian cabinet's hostility to Pakistan, 58; difficulty in defending Pakistan, 66

Awami League: adopts six points, 192; wins absolute majority in National Assembly, 204

Ayub Khan. *See* Khan

INDEX

Baghdad Pact (later Central Treaty Organization): Pakistan joins, 153; criticized by Nasser, 154; why Pakistan continues membership in, 228
Bahadur Shah: extends leadership to Mutiny of *1857*, 35–36
Bandung Conference: end of India's hope for Afro-Asian leadership, 151
Bangladesh: proclaims independence, 206; Treaty of Friendship, Cooperation, and Peace with India, 210; wishes to try Pakistani POWs for war crimes, 216, 220; unsuccessful bid for admission to United Nations, 218; joint statement with India on repatriation of internees, 219; hopeless internal conditions, 232; requests Soviet Union to clear seaports for navigation, 232–233. *See also* East Pakistan
Basic Democracy: failure of, 193
Bazaz, Prem Nath: why India hardened attitude in Kashmir dispute, 143
Bengal: partition of, 36; annulment of partition of, 36–37
Bhai bhai: Indian slogan to greet Russian and Chinese leaders, 49, 226
Bhashani, Maulana: exhorts East Pakistanis to action, 195
Bhutto, Zulfikar Ali: Muslims not perpetrators of religious apartheid in India, 15–16; calls Nehru arrogant, 91; attack on Pakistan would involve security of largest state in Asia, 178; purpose of Afro-Asian solidarity, 182; why Western allies did not assist Pakistan in *1965* war against India, 183; leaves foreign ministry, 194; arrest and release, 194–195; brilliant spokesman, 195; founds People's party, 195; refuses to attend Ayub's Round Table Conference, 195; urges modification of Mujib's six points, 205, 276n65; reason for not attending National Assembly, 205; why United States sent carrier *Enterprise* to Indian Ocean, 212; satisfied with China's support during East Pakistani war, 214; becomes president, 215; whirlwind tour of Afro-Asian countries, 215; holds summit conference with Indira Gandhi, 216; reasons for wishing to confer with Mujib before recognizing Bangladesh, 216–217; why China vetoed Bangladesh's admission to UN, 218; why Pakistan remains in CENTO, 228; says Iran and Pakistan cooperate in defense, 228–229; visits United States, 229; observation on Soviet proposal for Asian collective security, 230; continuing faith in China's friendship, 230; his reforms, 230–231; becomes prime minister, 231; Soviet naval base in Chittagong, 233
Birch Grove communiqué: signals erosion of United States–Pakistani alliance, 177
Bose, Subhas Chandra: secret of Gandhi's success with Indian masses, 84
Boundary Force: failure of, 62
Brezhnev, Leonid I.: proposes system of collective security in Asia, 201; visits India, 226
Buddha, Gautama: his relevance to India's foreign policy, 30, 255n39; his revolutionary innovations, 237
Bulganin, Nikolai A.: visit to India, 146; calls coexistence Leninist principle, 149

Cabinet mission: reasons for rejecting demand for Pakistan, 65; plan torpedoed by Nehru, 87–88
Caste system: its evil effects, 13, 19
Central Treaty Organization (CENTO). *See* Baghdad Pact
China, People's Republic of: Nehru's love for, 102–104; myth of *3000* years of Sino-Indian friendship, 104–107; poor view of independent India and Pakistan, 130; suspects Indian designs on Tibet, 130; agreement with India concerning Tibet, 144; invades Tibet, 147; agreement with Tibet, 147–148; border incidents with India, 150, 162; schism with U.S.S.R., 151–152, 174; growing tension with India, 161–163; border dispute with India, 164–165; refuses to recognize India's claim to Kashmir, 165; war with India, 166–167; supports Pakistan in September *1965* war, 189; criticizes Brezhnev's proposal of system of collective security in Asia, 201; thaw in rela-

298

INDEX

tions with United States, 202–203; attitude during East Pakistani war, 214; vetoes admission of Bangladesh to United Nations, 218; visited by Nixon, 223; consistency in attitude toward boundary disputes, 273n26

Chou En-lai: at Bandung Conference, 151; repudiates McMahon Line, 164; willingness to compromise on border dispute with India, 165; supports Pakistan on Kashmir, 179; calls Nehru implacable, 191

Cold War: origins of, 124–126

Commonwealth: India stays within, 122; Pakistan's disenchantment with, 122–123. *See also* United Kingdom

Communism: Indian view of, 49; Pakistani view of, 50–53; Nehru on, 50; Iqbal on, 50; Liaquat Ali Khan on, 51; incompatibility with Islam, 52

Congress, Indian National: extent of interest in world affairs, 29–30; turned into mass party by Gandhi, 34; accepts partition with reservation, 57; pro-China resolutions, 102; commends *panchsheel,* 145; splits into two factions, 198

Cripps, Sir Stafford: mission to India, 9; why Britain left India, 33

Daily Telegraph: on Nehru's bias toward China, 124; criticizes *panchsheel*, 146

Dalai Lama: on Tibet's independent status, 146, 270n18; escape to India, 159; criticizes Chinese oppression in Tibet, 160; appeals to United Nations against Chinese oppression in Tibet, 160

Daud, Sardar Muhammad: resigns, 138; recaptures power, 231

Dawn: criticizes Communism, 51; criticizes Nasser, 155

Dixon, Sir Owen: says India would not permit fair plebiscite in Kashmir, 142

Dulles, John Foster: misconception regarding his policy, 125, 128; on Communist victory in Kerala, 152

East Pakistan: language controversy with Central Government, 117–118; repudiation of ruling Muslim League party in *1954* election, 118; objection to formation of "One Unit" in West Pakistan, 157; effect of September *1965* war on, 191; growing frustration with West Pakistan, 192; hit by massive cyclone, 204; votes for Mujib's six points, 204; declares independence, 206; invaded by India, 210–211. *See also* Bangladesh and Mujibur Rahman

Egypt: initial coolness toward Pakistan, 138–139; tension with Pakistan during Suez crisis, 155–156. *See also* Nasser

Eisenhower, Dwight D.: calls Nehru complex man, 92; announces military aid to Pakistan, 144; his unfavorable place in Indian opinion poll, 146; praised by Nehru during *1959* visit to India, 175

Faruq, King: ridicules Pakistan's enthusiasm for Islam, 138–139

Galbraith, John Kenneth: panic in New Delhi during Sino-Indian war, 167; praises Indian foreign policy, 169; Krishna Menon calls him "too pro-Indian," 273n32

Gandhi, Indira: nonalignment not negotiable, 79; criticizes U.S.S.R. arms supply to Pakistan, 190; resents Kosygin's advice to settle differences with Pakistan, 190; becomes prime minister, 197; differences with "syndicate," 197–198; wins landslide victory in election, 199; criticizes U.S. bombing of Vietnam, 200, 224; holds summit conference with Bhutto, 216; real reasons for delaying release of Pakistani prisoners of war, 218; resents mention of Kashmir in Sino–United States communiqué, 223; says CIA must prove it is not active in India, 224; praises U.S.S.R. foreign policy, 226; has greater understanding of power politics than Nehru, 262n4

Gandhi, Mahatma Mohandas Karamchand: on cause of Hindu-Muslim differences, 7; definition of Hinduism, 11; on liberality of Hinduism, 12; favors intermarriage between caste Hindus and untouchables, 17; does not favor intermarriage and

INDEX

interdining between Hindus and Muslims, 17; treated as outcast for going to England, 17; why he supported Khilafat movement, 18; owns defeat on forging Hindu-Muslim unity, 19; his relevance to India's foreign policy, 30, 115, 149–150; says Nehru compelled Congress to think of all exploited peoples, 30; dislike for industrialization, 31; failure of India to follow his creed of nonviolence, 33; his greatest legacy to India, 34; says Congress would have to accept partition over his dead body, 57; no politics without religion, 84; his "every fibre" Hindu, 84; secret of his success, 84, 150; criticizes Nehru's arrogance, 91–92; on Nehru's love of China, 104; what free India should do if attacked, 256n59; praises British rule, 260n32; forms "one-man boundary force" in Calcutta, 260–261n37; meaning of *satyagraha*, 264n74

Giri, V. V.: wins presidential election, 198; calls Indo-Soviet treaty furtherance of policy of nonalignment, 209; on Soviet preparedness to protect Indian integrity during East Pakistani war, 214

Goa: Indian invasion of, 170; Nehru and Menon's statements before and after invasion of, 170–171

Great Britain. *See* United Kingdom

Haq, A. K. Fazlul: becomes premier of East Pakistan, 118; claims to be Muslim first and Bengali afterwards, 118; desires independence for East Pakistan, 118

Hatta, Muhammad: calls Nehru "second father" of Republic of Indonesia, 140

Heber, Reginald: notices Hindu-Muslim tension, 8; inhabitants of different provinces in India treated one another as foreigners, 20

Hijrat movement, 44

Hindu Mahasabha: vows to undo partition, 57; its president calls Hindus and Muslims two nations, 85

Hinduism: contrast with Islam, 10–17; Gandhi's definition of and Nehru's comments on, 11; liberality of, 11–12; Radhakrishnan's view of, 11–12; nature of, 11–13; nonviolence in, 11, 252n16; "closed system," 15; its effect on India's foreign policy, 22, 24, 25–29; Hinduism and Communism, 49

Hungarian crisis: Jayaprakash Narain criticizes Indian policy toward, 153

Hunter, William Wilson: on "Wahabi" threat, 35

Hyderabad: relevance to Kashmir dispute, 119

India: penchant for nonalignment, 7, 22, 24, 25–26, 113; lack of unity before British conquest, 20; effect of Hinduism on its foreign policy, 22, 24, 25–29; reluctance to accept partition as settled fact, 58–60; offers no-war declaration to Pakistan, 80; myth of *3000* years of friendship with China, 104–107; foreign policy objectives, 114–116; *1950, 1951* crises with Pakistan, 120; initial dependence on Britain, 121–122; attitude toward Korean War, 127, 131; attitude toward Japanese Peace Treaty, 128–129, 131; basic differences with United States, 129; silence over Soviet and Chinese imperialism, 131; bid for Afro-Asian leadership, 131–133; hardens attitude toward Kashmir dispute, 142–143; agreement with China concerning Tibet, 144; puts forward *panchsheel* as alternative to defense pacts, 145; indifference to fate of Tibet, 147–148; reason for sacrificing Tibet's independence, 148; border incidents with China, 150, 162; setback to leadership at Bandung Conference, 151; foreign exchange crisis, 152; improvement in relations with United States, 152; criticism of U.S. arms aid to Pakistan, 153; greets Dalai Lama, 160; growing tension with China, 161–163; adopts "forward policy" on Chinese border, 163, 165–166; border dispute with China, 164–165; war with China, 166–167; net result of war with China, 167–168; erosion of nonalignment, 169, 209; invades Goa, 170; border settlements with Pakistan,

300

INDEX

171; six rounds of talk with Pakistan, 177; Rann of Kutch war with Pakistan, 185; September *1965* war with Pakistan, 187–188; disenchantment with both superpowers, 200; shift to left, 201; Soviet-assisted industrial enterprises in, 201–202; increase in military strength after *1965*, 207–208; attitude toward crisis in East Pakistan, 208; early promise of assistance to East Pakistani rebels, 208; Treaty of Friendship and Cooperation with U.S.S.R., 209; Treaty of Friendship, Cooperation, and Peace with Bangladesh, 210; invades East Pakistan, 210–211; recognizes Bangladesh, 211; reason for declaring cease-fire, 212, 277n88; summit conference with Pakistan, 216; illegal detention of Pakistani prisoners of war, 217; and real reasons for such detention, 218; joint offer with Bangladesh for release of detainees, 219; agreement with Pakistan on exchange of internees, 222; continuing poor relations with United States, 223–226; "rupee agreement" with United States, 226; internal troubles, 231; belies high expectations, 235; inability to effect socio-religious changes, 242–243. *See also* Indira Gandhi, Jawaharlal Nehru, Mohandas Karamchand Gandhi

Indian Statutory Commission. *See* Simon Commission

Indonesia: conference on, 132; Pakistan's concern for independence of, 139–140; its greater attachment to India, 140; improvement of relations with Pakistan, 182

Indus Waters: dispute, 118; treaty, 171

Iqbal, Sir Muhammad: on basic principles of Islam, 10; calls Islam nationality, 14; Muslim toughness with enemies, 24; importance of Indian Muslims in Asia, 40; incompatibility of Communism and Islam, 50; cultural affinity between Islam and West, 51; *Tirand-i-Hind*, 254n61

Iran: special ties with Pakistan, 137, 138; assistance to Pakistan in *1965* and *1971* wars with India, 190, 214; practically ally of Pakistan, 228

Iraq: Treaty of Peace, Friendship, and Cooperation with U.S.S.R., 209–210; discovery of cache of Soviet-made arms in Iraqi embassy in Pakistan, 229–230; hostility with Iran, 279n128; growing ties with India, 279n128

Islam: basic doctrine of, 10, 13; incompatibility with Hinduism, 10–17; brotherhood in, 13, 14; nationality in, 13–14; "closed system," 14, 15, 16; and Christianity, 15, 51; its effect on Pakistani foreign policy, 22–25, 27–29; incompatibility with Communism, 50, 52–53

Jammu and Kashmir, state of. *See* Kashmir

Japanese Peace Treaty: boycotted by India, 128

Jinnah, Quaid-i-Azam Muhammad Ali: real origin of Pakistan, 15, 16; why Muslims are separate nation, 15; talks with Gandhi, 15; effect of Hindu's conversion to Islam, 15; Muslims required by Islam to maintain separate identity, 16; turns Muslim League into mass party, 40; supports Arabs on Palestine issue, 43; condemns Dutch imperialism in Indonesia, 44; sense of joy upon achieving Pakistan, 56; appeals to India to bury past, 58; offers cooperation to Congress, 86; death of, 117; greets Turkish ambassador, 137; his article "Two Nations in India," 253n44

Jodhpur: its relevance to Kashmir dispute, 119

Johnson, Lyndon B.: postpones Ayub's and Shastri's visits to United States, 183; gets meeting of Pakistani aid consortium postponed, 183; praises Pakistan's economic development, 191; annoyed with Indira Gandhi, 200; likens Indo-Pakistani war to American civil war, 258n108

Joint Committee on Indian Constitutional Reform: differences between Hinduism and Islam, 253n44

Joint Defense: Ayub's offer to India, 171

Jordan: helps Pakistan in *1971* war against India, 214

INDEX

Junagadh: its relevance to Kashmir dispute, 119

Kashmir, State of Jammu and: Nehru's emotional attachment to, 96–98; dispute between India and Pakistan, 118–120; wars between India and Pakistan over, 120, 187–189; in Security Council, 144, 172
Kennedy, John F.: supports increase in U.S. economic aid to India, 152; disappointment with Nehru, 169; issues Birch Grove communiqué with Macmillan, 177
Khaliquzzaman, Chaudhuri: propagates "Islamistan," 135–136
Khan, Aga: on intermarriage, 17; leads Khilafat delegation to London, 38; his mother's wish on burial, 45; asks Indian Muslims to disregard Turkish call for *jihad*, 46
Khan, General Agha Muhammad Yahya: assumes presidency of Pakistan, 196; vows to give democratic constitution, 203; holds general elections, 204; orders Pakistani army to restore order in East Pakistan, 205; concedes East Pakistan not playing full part in decision-making process, 206; his folly in East Pakistan, 206–208; hands over presidency to Bhutto, 215
Khan, Aly: criticizes Chinese oppression in Tibet, 161
Khan, Chaudhry Sir Muhammad Zafrulla: concern for Indonesia's independence, 139–140; brilliant espousal of Muslim causes in United Nations, 154
Khan, Liaquat Ali: origins of Pakistan's foreign policy, 7; difference between lives of Hindus and Muslims, 16; response to India's offer of no-war declaration, 80; Pakistan's foreign policy objective, 116; assassination of, 117; visit to United States, 127; criticizes Communism, 129; praises United States, 129–130; special ties with Iran, 138
Khan, Field Marshal Muhammad Ayub: why Pakistan joined defense pacts, 51; criticizes Communism, 51, 53; Muslim anxiety to win freedom from British as well as Hindus, 55;

early military weakness of Pakistan, 65; Pakistan's increased military strength, 143; assumes power, 157; on alliance with West, 158; offers joint defense to India, 171; fears concerted Sino-Soviet invasion, 171; writes to Kennedy to link arms aid to India with Kashmir settlement, 177; explains shift to "bilateral" foreign policy, 178; visits China, 179; calls U.S. governmental machinery "a clumsy juggernaut," 179; visits U.S.S.R., 180; cause of Pakistan's misunderstanding with Muslim countries, 180; his role in formation of Regional Council for Development (RCD), 181; deplores Asian subservience, 182; wins election against Miss Jinnah, 182; his finest hour, 182; loses prestige after September *1965* war with India, 191; early promise, 193; his basic weakness, 193; compared to Nasser, 193; calls Round Table Conference, 195; quits presidency, 196; enacts Muslim Family Laws Ordinance, 243
Khan, Sir Syed Ahmed: says Khalifa has no jurisdiction in India, 46; discourages *jihad* against the British, 134; on *mujahidin* movement, 256n60
Khilafat: movement, 18, 37–40; agitation increases emotional gap between Hindus and Muslims, 18; abolition of, 39
Khrushchev, Nikita S.: visit to India, 146; denounces Stalin, 151; visits Eisenhower at Camp David, 172; lectures the Chinese on undesirability of using force, 172; criticized by Chinese for role in Cuban crisis, 174; threatens Pakistan with rockets, 179
Kissinger, Henry A.: visits China, 209
Konga Pass: Sino-Indian clash at, 162
Korean War: Nehru blames United States for, 127; Marshall criticizes Indian attitude toward, 128; Pakistan and, 128; Nehru's peace proposal, 131
Kosygin, Aleksei N.: criticizes India for crossing Pakistani border in September *1965* war, 188; mediates between India and Pakistan at Tashkent, 189–190; urges India to

INDEX

settle Farakka and Kashmir disputes with Pakistan, 190
Kripalani, Acharya: criticizes *panchsheel*, 163
Kutch. *See* Rann of Kutch

Lamb, Alastair: "one-nation" and "two-nation" theories, 60
Liaquat Ali Khan. *See* Khan
Lippmann, Walter: India's importance, 126–127
Longju: Sino-Indian clash at, 162

McMahon Line: repudiated by China, 164; Chinese willingness to compromise on, 164–165, 168; its importance to India, 168; view of United States on, 175; origin of, 245–247
Macmillan, Harold: hopes partition of India will not endure, 73; issues Birch Grove communiqué with Kennedy, 177
Malaya: coolness toward Pakistan, 182
Manchester Guardian: calls partition "cut and run" operation, 74; criticizes Yahya's army operation in East Pakistan, 207
Mao Tse-tung: message to Communist party of India, 130
Marshall, General George C.: criticizes India's Korea policy, 128
Martin, Kingsley: Hindu exasperation at partition of India, 59
Menon, K. P. S.: unbroken peace between India and China, 266n128; criticizes Indian rigidity in border dispute with China, 273n30
Menon, V. K. Krishna: Nehru put him on to bait United States, 49; why India accepted partition, 57; says United States wishes to take Britain's place in India, 129; "forward policy," 164; vows India would fight China to last man, 167; rules out use of force in Goa, 170; defends use of force in Goa, 171; loses defense ministership, 180; calls Galbraith "too pro-Indian," 273n32
Montagu-Chelmsford Report: effect of World War I on India's future, 32
Mosley, Leonard: social cordiality between British and Muslims, 49; Mountbatten's "confidence trick of the century," 69; criticizes Nehru for torpedoing Cabinet mission plan, 88
Mountbatten of Burma, Earl: contemplates use of British troops during partition, 62; delays announcement of Boundary Award, 63; friendliness with Nehru, 68; antipathy toward Jinnah, 69; his good turns to Pakistan, 69–72; dislikes partition, 72–73
Moynihan, Daniel: appeals for realism in Indo–United States relations, 224
Mujahidin movement, 34–35
Mujibur Rahman. *See* Rahman
Muslim countries: Pakistan's affinity for, 7, 116; poor appreciation of Pakistan movement by, 46–47; resent Pakistan's wish for leadership, 133; assistance to Pakistan in Indo-Pakistani wars of *1965* and *1971*, 190, 214–215; hold summit meeting in Pakistan, 229
Muslim League: demands separate Muslim homelands, 40; eclipsed by Khilafat movement, 40; foreign policy resolutions of, 41–44; decline of (in Pakistan), 117; defeat in East Pakistani elections, 118

Narayan, Jayaprakash: criticizes Indian attitude toward crisis in Hungary, 153
Nasser, Gamal Abdel: against using Islam for political purposes, 139; criticizes Baghdad Pact, 154; rejects Pakistani contingent for UN Middle East Force, 155; criticizes India for crossing Pakistani border in September *1965* war, 188; compared to Ayub, 193
Naxalbari movement: revolutionary peasant movement in India to seize land, 199, 241
Nazimuddin, Khwaja: dismissal from prime ministership, 118; Pakistani affection for Egypt, 138
Nehru, Pandit Jawaharlal: on non-alignment, 7, 78, 95; why British prevailed in India, 9; comments on Gandhi's definition of Hinduism, 11; his view of Hinduism, 11; calls Hindu society anarchistic, 13; calls Hinduism and Islam "closed systems," 15; why Indians think in terms of isolation, 28; attends International

INDEX

Congress against Imperialism at Brussels, 29, 99–100; visits U.S.S.R., 29, 99–100, 146; relevance of Buddha and Gandhi to Indian foreign policy, 30, 115, 149–150; India's need for industrialization, 31; Congress policy of nonviolence not a creed, 31; why India accepted partition, 57; influence on India's foreign policy, 78; his fine mind, 79; contribution to India's independence, 79; aversion to concrete commitment, 80–81; offers no-war declaration to Pakistan, 80; aversion to war, 81; his secularism, 82–83, 238; underrates Hindu-Muslim problem, 83, 87; secret of Gandhi's success, 84, 150; torpedoes chances of Hindu-Muslim conciliation, 86–88; inability to accept partition as a settled fact, 88–90; his implacability, 91–92; confesses he is difficult to negotiate with, 92; exaggerated view of India's importance, 93; contrasts Indian nonalignment with early American isolationism, 94–95; idealism in India's policy, 95–96; love for Kashmir, 96–98; never professing Communist, 98, 102; on American imperialism, 99; admiration for U.S.S.R., 99–101; love for China, 102–104; visits China, 102, 146; changed view on China, 106–107; objectives of India's foreign policy, 114–116; "ends and means," 115; "psychology of fear," 115, 116; visits to United States, 127, 152, 169; criticizes U.S. arms aid to Pakistan, 143; criticizes foreign policies of big powers, 144; offers *panchsheel* as alternative to defense pacts, 145; "area of peace," 145; his finest hour, 145–146; criticizes Chinese invasion of Tibet, 147; says wishes of Tibetans should prevail over constitutional arguments, 147; why he sacrificed independence of Tibet, 148; why *panchsheel* is more efficacious than military preparedness, 149–150; importance of psychological approach, 150; nuclear weapons versus moral strength, 150; setback at Bandung, 151; greets Dalai Lama, 160; criticized for China policy, 162–163; inflexibility in border dispute with China, 164; rules out military aid for India, 166; orders Indian army to eject Chinese forces, 167; shifts position on Aksai Chin, 168; effect of China's hostility on, 169–170; rules out use of force against Goa, 170; justifies use of force against Goa, 171; at Belgrade nonaligned conference, 175; sends Abdullah to Pakistan, 184; death, 185; insufficient recognition of Akbar's magnanimity, 238

Nixon, Richard Milhouse: urges arms aid to Pakistan as vice-president, 142; visits China, 149, 223; visits Pakistan as president, 202; role in East Pakistani crisis and war, 211–214; pleads for Mujibur Rahman's life, 213; criticizes Indian resentment at sale of U.S. non-lethal weapons to Pakistan, 225; integrity of Pakistan is cornerstone of U.S. policy, 229

No-war declaration: India's offer to Pakistan, 80, 263n11

Nonalignment: natural product of Hindu outlook, 7, 22, 24, 25–26, 113; Nehru on, 7, 78, 95; erosion of Indian policy of, 169, 209

One Unit: resentment of Afghanistan at formation of, 154; resentment of East Pakistanis at formation of, 157; Mujib supports breakup of, 192; dissolution of, 203

Pakistan: desire for special relationship with Muslim countries, 7, 25, 113, 116; effect of Islam on its foreign policy, 22–25, 27–29; demanded by Muslim League, 40; abhorrence for Communism, 49–51; Muslim satisfaction at achieving, 56; early military weakness, 65–66; damaged by hasty partition, 75–77; response to India's offer of no-war declaration, 80; Kashmir wars with India, 120, 187–188; crises of *1950* and *1951* with India, 120; initial dependence on Britain, 121–122; bid for leadership of Muslim world, 133–137; special ties with Iran, 137, 138, 190, 214, 228; friendship with Turkey, 137, 138; initially poor relations with

304

INDEX

Egypt, 138–139; initially poor relations with Indonesia, 140; gets arms from United States, 141, 144, 224–225; indifference to fate of Tibet, 148–149; joins SEATO and Baghdad Pact, 153; tension with Egypt during Suez crisis, 155–156; revolution in, 157; concern at Sino-Indian border tension, 171; offers joint defense to India, 171; border settlements with India, 171; Indus Waters treaty with India, 171; six rounds of talks with India, 177; erosion of alliance with United States, 177; shift to "bilateral" foreign policy, 178; "normalizes" relations with China, 178–179; "normalizes" relations with U.S.S.R., 179–180; improves relations with Muslim countries, 181; coolness toward Malaya, 182; improvement of relations with Indonesia, 182; tensing of relations with United States, 182–183; Rann of Kutch war with India, 185; September *1965* war with India, 187–188; gets arms from U.S.S.R., 190; receives assistance from Muslim countries in *1965* and *1971* wars with India, 190, 214–215; cessation of arms supply from U.S.S.R., 202; crisis and war in East Pakistan, 203–211; dismemberment of, 206; *1971* war with India, 210–211; continuing faith in China's friendship, 214, 230; (Simla) summit conference with India, 216; agreement with India for release of detainees, 222; leaves SEATO, 228; why it remains in CENTO, 228; growing ties with Muslim Middle East, 229; hosts Muslim summit conference, 229; belies high expectations, 235; inability to effect socio-religious changes, 242–243. *See also* Ayub Khan, Bhutto, Jinnah, Liaquat Ali Khan, Mujibur Rahman, East Pakistan

Panchsheel: origin and contents, 144; creates "area of peace," 145; Indian alternative to defense pacts, 145; inefficacy of, 146–147; appears in Sino-American communiqué, 149; erosion of, 149, 150; reason for Nehru's faith in, 149–150; criticized by Kripalani, 163

Pandit, Mrs. Vijaya Lakshmi: on Hinduism, 12; relevance of Buddha and Gandhi to Indian policy, 30; leads Indian delegation to United Nations, 75; India's assumption of leadership, 133

Panikkar, K. M.: on nonviolence in Hinduism, 11; on caste system, 19; why Truman did not heed his message, 129; blames United States for cold war, 129

Partition of India: opposed by Congress leaders, 56–57; Pakistani satisfaction at, 56, 58; Indian resentment at, 58–60; consequences of haste in, 60, 64, 74–77; India desires haste in, 66–67; Pakistan desires less haste in, 67; disliked by British leaders, 72–73

Patel, Sardar Vallabhbhai: calls unification of India distant dream, 20; concedes India had two nations, 86; warns against danger from China, 107–108

People's Republic of China. *See* China

Pethic-Lawrence, Lord: effect of World War II on European domination of Asia, 32

Prasad, Rajendra: India's nonimperialist past, 27; why Congress followed path of nonviolence, 31; what India should do to follow Gandhi's principle of nonviolence, 33; India has not renounced violence, 34; forecasts partition of India would leave bitter legacy, 56

Quran: quoted, 14, 23, 24

Radford, Admiral Arthur W.: visits Pakistan, 121

Radhakrishnan, Sarvepalli: on Hinduism, 11–12; why India could not side with United States or U.S.S.R., 26; Western countries are trying to crush Russia, 129

Rahman, Sheikh Mujibur: his six points, 192, 267n7; supports breakup of One Unit in West Pakistan, 192; elaborates upon East Pakistani demands, 192–193; implicated in Agarthala conspiracy case, 193; released, 195; attends Round Table Conference, 195; criticizes central government for tardiness in cyclone

INDEX

relief, 204; wins election, 204; launches civil disobedience movement in East Pakistan, 205; arrested for treason and taken to West Pakistan, 205–206; his estimate of damage and killings in East Pakistani civil war, 207; United States saves his life, 213; released by Bhutto and becomes prime minister of Bangladesh, 215; refuses to meet Bhutto without recognition of Bangladesh, 216; wishes to try Pakistani prisoners of war for war crimes, 216; visits U.S.S.R., 232; requests U.S.S.R. to clear Bangladesh ports for navigation, 232–233

Rajagopalachari, C. R.: favors acceptance of demand for Pakistan, 85; pleads for alliance with United States, 107

Rann of Kutch: Indo-Pakistani war in, 185

Regional Cooperation Development (RCD): formation of, 180

Roosevelt, Franklin D.: presses Churchill to hand over power to Congress party, 124

Round Table: Indian and Pakistani attitudes after partition, 59

Satyagraha: "moral jiu-jitsu," 150; literal origin, 264n74

Saudi Arabia: criticizes Pakistan for joining Baghdad Pact, 154; praises Indian policy toward Muslims, 154; assists Pakistan in wars against India, 190, 214

Savarkar, V. D.: calls Hindus and Muslims two nations, 85

Seligman, Eustace: reason for India's objection to U.S. arms aid to Pakistan and for denying Kashmir to Pakistan, 59

Sharma, Shankar Dayal: criticizes United States, 223–224, 225; praises results of Brezhnev's visit to India, 226

Shastri, Lal Bahadur: subscribes to Tashkent Declaration, 189

Shibli, Maulana: weeps for Turks, 45

Simon Commission: effect of constitutional reforms on Hindu-Muslim rivalry, 55; nature of Hindu-Muslim antagonism, 253n44

Singh, Swaran: assures countrymen of total U.S.S.R. support, 209; criticizes rounding up of Bengalis in West Pakistan, 221; sudden bid for detente with United States, 224; criticizes sale of U.S. weapons to Pakistan, 225; desires economic relations with United States, 227

Six points: formulated by Mujib, 192, 267n7; form Mujib's election platform, 204

Soekarno, Ahmed: calls Nehru his political father, 140

Southeast Asia Treaty Organization (SEATO): Pakistan joins, 153; Pakistan leaves, 228

Soviet Union. *See* U.S.S.R.

Stalin, Joseph: praises Nehru's Korean peace proposal, 131; begins to view India more benevolently, 131

Stephens, Ian: reason for Pakistan's alliance with West, 24; consequences of hasty partition, 60

Suhrawardy, Huseyn Shaheed: danger from international Communism, 51; forecasts Chinese support to Pakistan, 151; criticizes Egypt, 155

Tashkent Declaration: by India and Pakistan, 189–190

Templewood, Lord: criticizes hasty partition, 61

Tibet: Sino-Indian Agreement concerning, 144; its claim to independence, 147; Chinese invasion of, 147; appeals to United Nations, 147, 160; agreement with China, 147–148; Nehru says wishes of Tibetans should prevail, 147; Lord Curzon on fiction of Chinese suzerainty over, 148; indifference of India and Pakistan toward independence of, 148–149; revolt against Chinese occupation, 159; escape of Dalai Lama to India from, 159; Dalai Lama laments Chinese cruelties in, 160

Times (London): India would prefer to see Pakistan disintegrate, 59; "India's Two Faces," 146–147

Toynbee, Arnold: affinity between Muslims and Christians, 15

Truman, Harry S.: on crises in Iran, Turkey, and Greece, 125; orders aid to France in Indo-China, 125–126;

INDEX

Truman Doctrine, 126; invites Nehru and Liaquat to United States, 127; calls Nehru Communist, 129; reason for not heeding information supplied by Pannikar, 129

Turkey: sympathy of Indian Muslims for, 37–40, 44–45; friendly ties with Pakistan, 137, 138; assists Pakistan in war against India, 190

U-2 incident: effect on Pakistani foreign policy of, 179

Union of Soviet Socialist Republics: Nehru visits, 29, 99–100, 146; Indira Gandhi visits, 29, 99–100, 146; Nehru's admiration for, 99–101; its view on partition of India, 130; poor view of independent India and Pakistan, 130; improvement in relations with India, 131; criticizes Pakistani efforts to forge Muslim unity, 131; schism with China, 151–152; reaction to Sino-Indian border friction, 172–174; improves relations with Pakistan, 180; starts technical assistance to Pakistan, 180; Ayub visits, 180; criticizes India for crossing Pakistani border, 188; attitude during September *1965* Indo-Pakistani war, 189; hosts India and Pakistan at Tashkent, 189–190; supplies arms to Pakistan, 190; proposes regional cooperation between India and Pakistan, Afghanistan, Iran, and herself, 190–191; asks India to settle Farakka and Kashmir disputes with Pakistan, 190; is criticized by Mrs. Gandhi, 190; lowest point in relations with India, 200–201; armed clashes with China at Ussuri River, 201; makes special effort to cultivate Indian friendship, 201, 202; proposes system of collective security in Asia, 201; is criticized by China, 201; stops arms supply to Pakistan, 202; large-scale arms supply to India, 207; Treaty of Peace, Friendship, and Cooperation with India, 209; Treaties of Peace, Friendship, and Cooperation with Egypt and Iraq, 209; failure in invitation to Afghanistan, Indonesia, and Pakistan to join Asian collective security system, 209–210; attitude during East Pakistani crisis and war, 210, 214; rush of arms to India, 210; persuades India to declare cease-fire, 212; fifteen-year economic agreement with India, 226; Mrs. Gandhi's praise for foreign policy of, 226; Mrs. Gandhi's appreciation for economic assistance from, 226; discovery of Soviet-made arms in Iraqi embassy in Pakistan, 229–230; helps Pakistan set up steel mill, 230; clears Bangladesh ports for resumption of navigation, 233

United Arab Republic. *See* Egypt and Nasser

United Kingdom: criticized by Gandhi for creating Hindu-Muslim antagonism, 7; praised by Nehru, 9; exploits Hindu-Muslim differences, 9–10; Maulana Muhammad Ali on its "divide and rule" policy, 10; Muslims resent conquest of India by, 34–36; cultivates Muslim friendship, 36; disenchantment of Muslims with policies of, 36–37, 41–43; warmth toward Muslims during Congress "Quit India" rebellion, 48; natural affinity with Muslims, 49; initial dependence of India and Pakistan on, 121–122; coordination of foreign policy moves with India, 122; joins United States in arming India, 176, 177; mediates Rann of Kutch dispute, 185; praised by Gandhi for benevolence in ruling India, 260n32. *See also* Commonwealth

United Nations: role in *1965* Indo-Pakistani war, 189; role in *1971* Indo-Pakistani war, 212

United States: Nehru notes its "imperialism," 99; bias in favor of India, 123; insufficient understanding of Hindu-Muslim problem, 124; expectations from India, 126–127; Liaquat's visit to, 127; Nehru's visits to, 127, 152, 169; basic differences with India, 129; extends military assistance to Pakistan, 142; improvement in relations with India, 152–153; sharply increases economic aid to India, 153; disappointment with Nehru, 169; attitude toward Sino-Indian border dispute, 175–176; prompt military assistance to India against China, 176; erosion of

INDEX

alliance with Pakistan, 177, 182–183; declares arms aid to India not dependent on Kashmir settlement, 177, 274n2; attitude during September *1965* Indo-Pakistani war, 189; stoppage of arms and economic aid to India and Pakistan in *1965* war, 189; proposes joint economic ventures by India and Pakistan, 190; resumption of economic aid to India and Pakistan, 190; agrees to sell spare parts of weapons to India and Pakistan, 190; annoyance with Indira Gandhi for criticism of bombing of Vietnam, 200, 224; reasons for improvement in relations with China, 202–203; improvement of relations with Pakistan, 202, 229; stoppage of arms and economic aid to India and Pakistan during *1971* crisis, 211–212; attitude during East Pakistani crisis and war, 211–214; why carrier *Enterprise* was sent into Indian Ocean, 212; economic aid to Bangladesh, 214; communiqué marking Nixon's visit to China, 223; blamed for CIA activities in India, 223–224; continuing poor relations with India, 223–226; resumption of economic aid to India and Pakistan, 224–225, 279n122; sale of non-lethal military supplies to India and Pakistan, 224–225; criticized by Indian National Congress president for "vicious designs" on India, 225; rupee agreement with India, 226; Bhutto visits, 229

Vietnam: Truman orders aid to France in war in, 125–126; Mrs. Gandhi criticizes American bombing of, 200, 224

Wavell, Field Marshal Earl: plan for relinquishing British control in India, 63; criticized by Attlee, 63, 64
World War I: effect on India's future, 32
World War II: accelerates India's freedom, 32–33

Yahya Khan. *See* Khan

Zafrulla Khan. *See* Khan